Christological
Dogmatics

Christological Dogmatics

A THEOLOGICAL WITNESS TO THE PERSON AND WORK OF CHRIST

D. Glenn Butner Jr.

Baker Academic
a division of Baker Publishing Group
Grand Rapids, Michigan

Published by Baker Academic
a division of Baker Publishing Group
Grand Rapids, Michigan
BakerAcademic.com

Printed in the United States of America

Library of Congress Cataloging-in-Publication Data
Names: Butner, D. Glenn, 1989– author
Title: Christological dogmatics : a theological witness to the person and work of Christ / D. Glenn Butner Jr.
Description: Grand Rapids, Michigan : Baker Academic, a division of Baker Publishing Group, [2026] | Includes bibliographical references and index.
Identifiers: LCCN 2025022437 | ISBN 9781540967510 paperback | ISBN 9781540969965 casebound | ISBN 9781493453108 ebook | ISBN 9781493453115 pdf
Subjects: LCSH: Jesus Christ—Person and offices | Theology, Doctrinal
Classification: LCC BT203 .B875 2026 | DDC 232—dc23/eng/20250806
LC record available at https://lccn.loc.gov/2025022437

Cover art: *The Deposition* by Giovanni Battista / Bridgeman Images

Baker Publishing Group publications use paper produced from sustainable forestry practices and postconsumer waste whenever possible.

26 27 28 29 30 31 32   7 6 5 4 3 2 1

To Ezra, who can be so full of compassion and love.

I write hoping you see love perfected in Jesus Christ,
through whom guilt and sin are no more.

Contents

Acknowledgments

I have so many people to thank, without whom this project would have been impossible. While writing this book, I moved from Sterling College to Gordon-Conwell Theological Seminary. Faculty and staff at both locations played a tremendous role in refining my thought.

At Sterling, thanks go to Tom Bronleewe, Roy Millhouse, Sheb Varghese, and especially Tim Gabrielson, who tirelessly fielded eight years of questions about trends in biblical studies. As always, Mikki Millhouse, Kristin Robson, and Laurel Watney tracked down hundreds of books for me through interlibrary loan. My writing on the ascension and descent was clarified in dialogue with students at Sterling College in a course on the ascension and descent. I am grateful to Sophia Godfrey, Layla Lope Maldonado, Dakotah Mote, Jared Price, Dawson Urwiller, and Abi Walcher.

At Gordon-Conwell I benefited from a peer review session on my chapter on satisfaction, where Davi Ribeiro Lin, Trey Nation, and especially Adonis Vidu offered extensive and helpful feedback. I previously used some content from the same chapter for my academic presentation in my campus interview, following suggestions from Mateus de Campos. At his invitation, that paper became a dean's forum, where I also received feedback from Sean McDonough, Autumn Ridenour, and Adonis Vidu. Donna Petter also provided invaluable guidance on Old Testament sacrificial practices by email. Clearly, if chapter 8 has problems, it is due to my own failings and not for lack of my new colleagues' efforts at helping me improve my theology. Gordon-Conwell has been an academically rigorous and stimulating faculty community. I am also thankful to my research assistant, Ethan Muller, who helped me compile the dates for historical figures, to Fernando Alejandro, my student and teaching assistant, who read through the first nine chapters testing for readability, and to Joshua Romero, another research assistant, who helped compile part of the Scripture index.

Many people outside of my immediate academic communities strengthened this book. Brandon Smith read a complete chapter, offering helpful feedback, and David Luy helped me correct and nuance my account of Lutheran thoughts on the ascension and eucharist. I confess that time constraints prevented me from fully incorporating his suggestions. Jerome Van Kuiken offered helpful feedback and resources on the impeccability of Christ. Jules Martinez also kindly read selections of the work, offering helpful feedback. I am tremendously grateful for the opportunity to work with Baker Academic's editors, Bob Hosack for the first time in acquisitions and James Korsmo for a second time in editing the manuscript. They are a skilled team, and I am thankful for their guidance. Thanks to James Korsmo's diligent work and with the help of copyeditor Andrew Buss and proofreader Nancy Weatherwax, this work is more polished than when I submitted it. Thanks also to Anna English and the rest of the marketing team for their work to put this book into readers' hands.

Finally, special thanks must go to my family. My wife, Lydia, always supports me and never complained when the need to finally submit the manuscript required me to work some late nights instead of spending time with her. I literally would not have an academic career without her selflessness these past fifteen years. My children, Elias, Ezra, and Sophia, are a great source of joy, providing me motivation to finish this book. This is especially true for Ezra, who kept asking when *his* book would finally come out after his brother's came out in 2022. That question helped me submit this manuscript only two months late despite moving halfway across the country in my final year of writing it. By God's grace, I hope that when he is older, he can be as enthusiastic about the contents of this book as he has been about my promise to dedicate it to him.

Introduction

Christological dogmatics is birthed by the call to evangelism that God places before the church in the Great Commission (Matt. 28:18–20; Mark 16:14–18; Luke 24:44–49; John 20:19–23; Acts 1:7–8).[1] If we are called and sent as witnesses (Luke 24:48; Acts 1:8), then we must know Jesus Christ both as the person who sends us forth in this task empowered by his Spirit (John 20:21–22; Acts 1:8) and as the one whose teachings and works we proclaim (Matt. 28:20; Luke 24:46–48). The challenge to spread the good news of the gospel therefore summons the church to understand the person and work of Christ. The close link between the person of Christ and the evangelistic task even makes it possible to speak of the gospel-as-person, Jesus Christ, in addition to the gospel-as-message, which refers to that information that is shared in Christian proclamation. As Edward Rommen explains, "What we seek to mediate is communion with a personal being upon whose will our existence is contingent. . . . It is only within the framework of such a relationship that the words of the gospel can connote both reality and the knowledge of that reality. Our message, then, is not primarily information about some truth, but is itself a reality—communion with a personal being."[2] Who, then, is this person?

1. Though Christians often label Matt. 28:18–20 as the "Great Commission," missiologist Timothy Tennent does well to recognize that the church's Great Commission actually derives from a wider range of texts. "Each of the Gospels, as well as the book of Acts, records a dramatic pericope of commissioning to a group of gathered disciples." Tennent, *World Missions*, 128. Considering the full range of commissions yields a more thorough understanding of the church's missiological call. See Tennent, *World Missions*, 128–57.
2. Rommen, *Get Real*, 9–10. Rommen uses the terminology of the gospel-as-information and the gospel being a message interchangeably.

John tells us in his Gospel that Jesus did so many things that "if every one of them were written down, . . . not even the world itself could contain the books that would be written" (John 21:25). Deciding what to include in any one book is a difficult task indeed, and to have any hope of success in this task we must proceed with prayer in hopes that the Holy Spirit gives us eyes to see and ears to hear (e.g., Ezek. 12:2; Matt. 13:15). No work of theology can succeed through human effort alone. As such, this is not only a book meant to enable Christian proclamation. It is also a book written primarily to an audience that has accepted that proclamation and therefore received the Holy Spirit, without whom no one can profess "Jesus is Lord" (1 Cor. 12:3). If we acknowledge Christ as Lord, then we are among those who are called to make his name known to the ends of the earth. Though I will not always attend to the evangelistic or missional implications of the dogmatic account I am developing, the reader should know that such implications are often lying beneath the surface of the doctrines discussed.

Dogmatics and Christian Proclamation

Though christological dogmatics is birthed from the Great Commission, the book that you hold in your hands is not an evangelistic work aimed at producing new converts. It is a work of dogmatics. What does this term mean? I understand dogmatics to be a fundamental theology that emerges from three distinct tasks: the church's responsibility to preserve theological truth against heresy, the need for instruction ranging from the initiation of converts to the preparation of church leaders able to teach (1 Tim. 3:2), and the drive to systematize the Bible's teaching.[3] Yet these tasks have a clear significance for the mission of the church. Some have defined "heresy" as teaching that, if true, would undermine the redemption God offers us through Christ.[4] When Christian proclamation bears fruit, converts must then be made disciples by being taught what Jesus taught (Matt. 28:19–20), which raises the need for training teachers. The risen Christ explained himself to the disciples on the road to Emmaus by "interpret[ing] for them the things concerning himself in all the Scriptures" (Luke 24:27). Our evangelism would do well to have such canon-wide roots. Dogmatics therefore serves the Great Commission by ensuring that the church's witness to Christ is rooted in the breadth of Scripture,

---

3. This threefold root of dogmatics is taken from Brunner, *Dogmatics*, 1:93–96. I also elaborate my understanding of this task in Butner, *Trinitarian Dogmatics*, 2–3, 6–9.
4. This is the position of Alister McGrath, drawing on Friedrich Schleiermacher. McGrath, *Christian Theology*, 153.

aligned with the saving work of Christ, and expanded such that converts can move from milk to the solid food of theology (1 Cor. 3:2).

As a work of dogmatics, this book seeks to fulfill the threefold task of navigating theological disputes, training Christians in theology, and synthesizing the teachings of Christ in Scripture. The work explores theological disputes over the person and work of Christ across two millennia. As a dogmatic text exploring fundamental theology, it will at times describe disputes with several possible positions from which the reader can choose without fearing heresy. At other times, in disputes involving more significant matters, I will make an argument for those positions that I deem important for the church's faithful witness to Christ. This book is geared toward the advanced seminary classroom, though I know undergraduate faculty who have successfully used its companion volume. Much here depends on course design. I hope that it will also serve the professional community as well. It includes pedagogical aids such as a glossary, an annotated bibliography with suggested further reading at the end of each chapter, and a list of the birth and death dates of historical figures named in this book. This work of dogmatics is unapologetically rooted in the teachings of the Bible, which will be used in methods ranging from historical-grammatical interpretation to historical criticism to the theological interpretation of Scripture. The details of my dogmatic approach will soon become evident to the reader.

Theologians have been writing works of dogmatics for centuries. Why should another work of dogmatics be written now?[5] In part, the task of dogmatics is continuously ongoing, given its role in addressing challenges to Christian **orthodoxy, orthopraxis,** and **orthopathy.** Since new perspectives continuously emerge, so do new errors. This alone prompts the church to need regularly updated dogmatic works. However, the current moment is particularly apt for a treatment of dogmatics for several additional reasons. First, the rapid growth of Christianity around the world in the last century, combined with the increasing availability of English-language sources from the global church published for a North American audience, means that newer works of dogmatics are better able to represent all parts of the body of Christ.[6] Since no part of the body can say to another, "I don't need you" (1 Cor. 12:21 NIV), the increasing availability of such works for English-speaking theologians like myself is of tremendous value and is an important reason to update many

5. A speaker at the seventy-sixth annual meeting of the Evangelical Theological Society was asked this question by an audience member, prompting me to reflect on the question at some length. I am thankful to this unknown audience member.

6. Though it is now somewhat dated, the classic treatment of this expansion is Jenkins, *Next Christendom.*

currently available works of Christology. Second, the past several decades have seen a tremendous wealth of historical sources newly translated, made available in critical editions, or published for wider consumption for the first time.[7] This allows for a more substantive engagement with historical works of Christology than was possible even a few decades ago, again prompting the need for a new work in christological dogmatics.

A third reason why this work of dogmatics should be published now pertains to the specific structure of this book. Where many christological surveys proceed diachronically, moving from Scripture, through Christian tradition, to modern systematic debates,[8] this book will move from locus to locus, considering christological subdoctrines like Christ's two **natures** or the affirmation of **dyothelitism**, which claims the incarnate Son had two wills. This structure will allow us to simultaneously consider Scripture, tradition, and contemporary systematic debates for each subdoctrine, which I believe is a superior framework for both pedagogical and polemical purposes.[9] Furthermore, many theological series or individual books divide treatment of the person and work of Christ into two separate volumes.[10] On the one hand, such division allows for greater specialization from authors and yields clearer divisions for pedagogical purposes. On the other hand, I find it a precarious task to speak well of the person of the incarnate Christ apart from his work or of the atoning work of Christ unmoored from the metaphysical foundations of the incarnation. This work will therefore seek to explain the person and work of Christ in harmony, with one chapter introducing an aspect of the doctrine of Christ's person followed by a chapter (or at the end of the work, three chapters) that explores the salvific implications of those doctrines just described. For example, chapter 1 will explore the incarnation of Christ

7. Series like Popular Patristics and Victorine Texts in Translation and the efforts of such smaller dedicated publishers as Reformation Heritage Books and Franciscan Institute Publications have made an important contribution.

8. For example, Erickson, *Word Became Flesh*; Macleod, *Person of Christ*; O'Collins, *Christology*; Wellum, *God the Son*. This pattern is not universal. For a recent strong exception to this diachronic pattern, see Treier, *Lord Jesus Christ*.

9. This book will complete some of the synthetic task for students, where diachronic approaches leave students with the need to synthesize distinct sections on Scripture or tradition with later chapters on key dogmatic debates. Since synthesis is a higher level of learning from understanding, many students of theology might not make it to the synthetic task, to the result that their rejection of certain heresies, for example, might be accepted on authority but not recognized as biblically necessary.

10. Consider the example of T. F. Torrance's *Incarnation* and *Atonement*, where a single author's thought is published in two volumes focused on the person and work of Christ, respectively. In a series, see the distinction between Wellum's *God the Son* and Demarest's *Cross and Salvation*, both of which are volumes in the Foundations of Evangelical Theology series.

and related debates of **kenosis** and virginal conception, and chapter 2 will introduce the doctrine of **recapitulation** to consider the salvific implications of the incarnation as the last Adam's reversal of the failings of the first Adam. I hope this approach will better prepare Christians to teach and proclaim the gospel-as-person and the gospel message of that person's work.

Developing a *Christological* Dogmatics

I have briefly described dogmatic theology as I understand it, but it is important to recognize that a *christological* dogmatics will be marked by features specific to the theology of the person and work of Christ. Dogmatics is christological insofar as it speaks about the person of the Son with emphasis on his postincarnate life. This enfleshed Son is the same Son who was eternally the divine Son of his Father. We see this in John 1, for example, where John describes the Word both as the subject of the eternal relationship with God ("In the beginning was the Word, and the Word was with God, and the Word was God" [1:1]) and as the subject of the incarnation ("And the Word became flesh and dwelt among us" [1:14a]). There is a continuity of subject here, but John also draws attention to the connection between the Word's eternal generation within the Trinity and his incarnation: "We observed his glory, the glory as the one and only [*monogenēs*, also translatable as "only begotten"] Son from the Father" (1:14b).[11] As such, there is a sense in which a christological dogmatics oriented toward teaching proceeds under the assumption of the doctrine of the Trinity. My prior volume, *Trinitarian Dogmatics*, may therefore be helpful as background for the reader, though I write under the assumption that the reader has only introductory trinitarian knowledge. In my regular theological connections between the doctrine of the Trinity and Christology, I attempt to explain relevant trinitarian categories to the reader unfamiliar with them.

The task of dogmatics is always delicate insofar as it involves seeking balance and a degree of consensus amid centuries of exegetical and theological dispute. Things are far more tense when it comes to Christ's person and work than in the doctrine of the Trinity. Where most branches of Christianity accept the Nicene position on the doctrine of the Trinity,[12] there are important

11. Irons, "Lexical Defense," 98–116.
12. Exceptions here would include Unitarianism, certain strains of Protestant liberalism, oneness Pentecostalism, Mormonism, and Jehovah's Witnesses. Divergence on such a fundamental issue as the Trinity has led even most casual observers to think of many of these groups as distinct religions. Where Protestant liberalism's hesitancy about the deity of Christ is less likely to result in its being named a different religion, fundamentalist Christian theology has long insisted that liberalism is no longer Christian. See Machen, *Christianity and Liberalism*.

historical divides over ecumenical councils like Ephesus (431) and Chalcedon (451), with the result that groups like the Coptic Orthodox Church, the
Ethiopian Orthodox Tewahedo, and the Church of the East have long rejected
the orthodoxy recognized by Protestants, Catholics, and Eastern Orthodox
Christians. More recently, individual theologians among traditions that accept the ecumenical councils have been prone to challenge the theology of
these councils[13] or to deny that the theology of the Chalcedonian tradition
resolves the necessary dogmatic issues.[14]

My strategy to address these important theological issues is to proceed with
a hermeneutic of charity that seeks to understand the theological rationale
behind the objections raised by such critics of the venerable tradition that
the incarnate Christ was one person or **hypostasis** in two natures. Though
the reader need not yet understand the claim in the prior sentence, what is
important is that this fundamental grammar of one person in two natures
became a significant feature of nearly all Christology developed in the Protestant, Catholic, and Eastern Orthodox branches of Christianity. Attempting
to get behind this grammatical impasse will find certain important theological
concerns even among those groups condemned by the Chalcedonian tradition
as heretical. Yet this book will remain resolutely within the tradition of the
ecumenical councils like Chalcedon.

Another peculiar feature of the theology of the person and work of Christ
is the fact that there was no conciliar consensus regarding how Christ's death
on the cross and subsequent resurrection secured our salvation. This absence
of creedal guidance on the details of the work of Christ is especially surprising given the extensive conciliar debates regarding the theology of his person.
The absence of an official account of the atonement can result in two risks,
labeled by Joshua McNall as "defensive hierarchy" and "disconnected plurality." Where defensive hierarchy "reduced the multifaceted nature of the atonement by elevating a single model as somehow most important," disconnected
plurality tends toward relativism by treating the variety within Scripture as
if it gives us permission to simply pick and choose what aspect of Christ's
work we find personally appealing.[15] My hope is to display the significance

13. For example, evangelicals William Lane Craig and J. P. Moreland are skeptical of dyothelitism from the Third Council of Constantinople (680–81), while attempting to revitalize a
modified version of a heresy condemned at Ephesus (431). Moreland and Craig, *Philosophical
Foundations*, 608–9. I will address this specific example in chapter 7.

14. Among the Eastern Orthodox, consider the controversial example of Sergius Bulgakov,
who writes that the dogmatic formula of Chalcedon did not have an accompanying "theological
achievement," such that by the end of the councils "the cycle of dogmatic development remains
incomplete." Bulgakov, *Lamb of God*, 57, 88.

15. McNall, *Mosaic of Atonement*, 19–21.

of the gospel of salvation by grace as a means of unifying various aspects of Christ's saving work. The Son is graciously sent by the Father to accomplish what we cannot, so that by grace the Spirit may incorporate us into the Son that we may be saved. Different aspects of this atonement are coordinated around a central goal of proclaiming faith in the grace of God manifest in Christ's person and work.

The various doctrines of the Christian faith are connected to one another like strands in a web; move one strand, and the entire web shifts. Doctrines are also like stones in the construction of a cathedral; removing certain stones may risk the entire edifice collapsing. Proclaiming Christ to be the Word made flesh, the one who sends the Spirit, and Savior will require close connections between Christology and the doctrines of the Trinity, pneumatology, and soteriology, respectively. Perhaps surprising to some readers will be the fact that Christology is also one of the doctrines in systematic theology most closely related to moral theology.[16] This close connection exists for several reasons. First, in the incarnation one of three divine persons took on flesh, entering history. Moral formation is shaped by history, embodiment, and involvement in society. Since only the Son enters human historical, embodied, and social life, Christology connects to moral theology more than pneumatology or patrology, as only the Son can truly be our moral example.[17] Second, if the Son is who I describe him to be in this book, then he is worthy of being followed. To put it more forcefully, Christ's entire ministry is a call to discipleship: "Then Jesus said to his disciples, 'If anyone wants to follow after me, let him deny himself, take up his cross, and follow me'" (Matt. 16:24).[18] Third, Christians witness to an incarnate, crucified, risen, and ascended Christ who will come again, which requires at least a rudimentary dogmatic understanding of such stages in Christ's earthly life. But Christ also came as a great teacher whose teaching regularly has moral implications. Making disciples requires elaborating these moral teachings in light of the morally perfect Jesus of Nazareth.[19] For this

16. Moral theology can be distinguished from Christian ethics because the former appeals more overtly to the doctrines of the Christian faith, while the latter is prone to expressing itself in a manner more palatable to a pluralistic society of different faiths and philosophical commitments. See the preface in Long, *Teaching and Learning Christian Ethics*.

17. This is a tendency more than a universal restriction. Sexual ethics, which deals with desire and holiness, is likely better connected with pneumatology, to name only one exception to the centrality of Christology.

18. As William Mattson explains, "Studying who Jesus is should not merely be some theoretical and abstract exercise. It is simultaneously the study of discipleship, or what it means to follow Jesus." Mattison, *Introducing Moral Theology*, 280.

19. "Moral theology . . . belongs, rather inescapably, to the church's mission of making disciples of Christ, teaching them to observe everything he commands (Matt. 28:19–20)." Baugus, *Reformed Moral Theology*, 33.

reason, the reader will find regular connections made between christological dogmatics and Christian moral theology. These connections will primarily be an orientation of the Christian moral life, as specific moral analysis and application would take us too far afield from dogmatics proper. In other words, the virginal conception might reveal the value Christians ought to place on unborn human life, but alone it does not resolve all the complicated debates within moral theology on questions like abortion or stem cell research.

The connection between moral theology and dogmatic theology and between dogmatic theology and the church's ministry of making disciples makes clear a threefold goal of theology. To use classical terminology, theology pursues goodness, truth, and beauty. Using the more recent terminology of systematic theology, we can follow Jon Sobrino in affirming the need for orthodoxy, orthopraxis, and orthopathy. Orthodoxy is likely the most familiar term; it references true teaching about Christ. Orthopraxis indicates right action, which we might understand as conformity to Christ. Here the term "praxis" refers to human action, but especially as considered in its historical and social contexts. Sobrino introduces a novel category of orthopathy to reference "the correct way of letting ourselves be affected by the reality of Christ."[20] False teaching is dealt with severely in Scripture (Ezek. 13:9; Matt. 7:15–20; James 3:1), so this goal is weighty and should humble the theologian (and the student of theology!). Sobrino tends to value orthopraxis over orthodoxy, a judgment I do not share,[21] and he only gradually recognizes the importance of spirituality and orthopathy.[22] Despite this, the general triad provides an important framework for developing a dogmatic account of Christology. Such an account ought to clarify the truth of who Christ is and what he has accomplished (orthodoxy), compel us to moral action in line with his teaching and to follow his example as empowered by the Spirit he sends his church (orthopraxis), while recognizing the necessary spiritual transformation that accompanies our conversion to Christ (orthopathy).

Christological dogmatics is thus marked by several specific challenges, including navigating fragmentation over councils discussing the person of

20. Sobrino, *Christ the Liberator*, 210.

21. See Sobrino, *Crossroads*, 390–91. Sobrino argues that "only in the praxis of following him [Jesus] do we glimpse the mental categories that will enable us to understand the real nature of the kingdom of God and formulate it in a meaningful way." Sobrino, *Crossroads*, 60. While there is some truth to this, it can also be the case that wrong ideas lead to wrong praxis. Furthermore, we are saved by faith, not works. Granting that good works are the fruit of faith, it is still the case that one may pursue good action with all sincerity and yet fail to enter the kingdom of God (Matt. 7:22–23).

22. By 1988, Sobrino can insist, "There must be a spirituality underlying this practice." Sobrino, *Spirituality of Liberation*.

Christ, limited conciliar guidance on the work of Christ, and the need to connect christological dogmatics to moral theology. These typical challenges in christological dogmatics all strengthen the church's witness to Christ. Careful navigation of centuries of debates about the relationship between the incarnate Son's humanity and divinity helps us to ensure that the gospel we proclaim speaks of a Savior capable of saving.[23] Variability in biblical depictions of the atonement yields not only a complicated theological puzzle but the flexibility for the missionary to proclaim the good news in a form that might be best suited for a given recipient culture. Emphasis on orthodoxy, orthopraxis, and orthopathy reminds us that the Savior whom we proclaim is the truth (John 14:6), love itself (1 John 4:8), and the master whose easy yoke (Matt. 11:30) leads to a life of spiritual abundance (John 10:10). To be conformed to Christ, we his followers need to be a people of truth and goodness who are satisfied in the beauty of the Lord Jesus.[24]

The Method and Structure of Christological Dogmatics

I have charted a course for this work of dogmatics, and the time is fast approaching to begin the work of developing a christological dogmatics. Before beginning, it is necessary to briefly explore the method and structure of christological dogmatics. This book will rely on the four sources of theology that are often named the Wesleyan Quadrilateral: Scripture, tradition, reason, and experience. Scripture will be of primary importance, for only Scripture is infallible in its teaching and sufficient in its contents. Sometimes I will assume the authority of Scripture; in other cases I will defend the doctrinal or historical reliability of the Bible. Although the Bible is perfect, Scripture can be read in an incorrect manner, so dogmatics must also be directed by tradition, reason, and experience.[25] Tradition will serve as a test of the truthfulness of a given interpretation, as we rely on the wisdom of generations to read the Bible in a great company of witnesses (Heb. 12:1). Dogmatics is often concerned with truths derived from Scripture indirectly. Direct exegesis might determine what

23. After all, John warns that those who deny that Jesus came in the flesh are of the antichrist (1 John 4:3). While I do not think that salvation requires that every Christian be able to articulate a particular christological metaphysic—what a burden to lay on the faithful!—John's warning surely points to the seriousness of developing a theology that can truly affirm that Jesus is God (and so "came") and also human (and so "came in the flesh").

24. This fact also demands a commitment to holistic mission, on which see Goheen, *Christian Mission Today*, 227–63.

25. A complete theological account of the Bible will need to occur under a pneumatological dogmatics. However, a brief supplemental treatment of my methodology can be found in Butner, *Trinitarian Dogmatics*, 6–10; Butner, *Son Who Learned Obedience*, 6–9.

Matthew and Luke mean in their accounts of the virginal conception, but one will look in vain for an explicit account of how the virginal conception should therefore shape our understanding of Christ's humanity in relation to his deity. Here, reason guides dogmatic theology as we seek to evaluate different theories of the unity of Christ's deity and humanity by exploring the logical implications and assumptions behind various accounts, judging where these implications and assumptions correspond with the virginal conception and other biblical accounts and where they do not. Finally, we will do well to learn from the experiences of Christians from around the world throughout Christian history. Experience itself is of limited value insofar as experience is unreliable as a source of knowledge about God. Yet we must attend to experience for several reasons. First, considering the experiences of others will help us identify our own biases. Second, other cultures might ask important theological questions that we have not thought to ask in our own. Third, attending to experience can help us proclaim the gospel to all nations, a task that will require a good deal of inculturation, so that the gospel proclamation is comprehensible in all contexts.[26]

With these foundations in place, I can begin the task of developing a christological dogmatics. Chapter 1 begins with analysis of the incarnation, including focus on the virginal conception and the idea of kenosis, Jesus's self-emptying. Chapter 2 explores the salvific implications of the incarnation through the idea of recapitulation, where Jesus becomes a new Adam to start the human race anew. This chapter will also include a discussion of original sin. Chapter 3 defends the claim that Jesus has two natures, one fully human and one fully divine. It not only involves discussion of historical heresies that denied two natures but also defends the deity of Christ against modern interpreters who argue that a lower view of Jesus is found in Scripture. Chapter 4 considers Jesus as our moral teacher and example. We can emulate the Son, as the only divine person to become human, in ways that we cannot emulate the Father or Spirit. This chapter provides several models for doing so.

Chapters 5 through 7 pay special attention to the unity of Christ. Chapter 5 introduces the hypostatic union, which claims Jesus's two natures are united in one person. I work to develop an account of what it means to be one hypostasis with reference to historical theological debates and Scripture. The personal unity of a human nature with Christ's deity opens an avenue for other human beings to be in greater union with God, so chapter 6 explores several theological models for thinking about this union. Chapter 7 introduces

---

26. Inculturation is not a primary subject of this book, yet a dogmatic account for the contemporary global church must include elements that point in the direction of fruitful inculturation.

dyothelitism and **dyoenergism**, traditional positions that claim Jesus had two wills and two natures, one proper to each person. This chapter concludes substantive analysis of the person of Christ.

The final three chapters consider the salvific works that were completed by the incarnate Christ, who could act as our human representative and as the God who saves. Chapter 8 therefore addresses **satisfaction**, or the Son paying our debts on the cross. This will require a defense of Anselm of Canterbury, who is often criticized by modern scholarship. Chapter 9 explores the victory of Christ over sin, death, and the devil. This requires an extended theological analysis of what happened to Jesus after he died as well as a detailed treatment of the resurrection. Chapter 10 ends the work by looking at the ascension, session, and second coming of Christ. These final acts draw our gaze to a hoped-for future, rounding out consideration of Christ's past, present, and future work. That future lies ahead of us, but the beginning of this work of theology is found much earlier, with the birth of God's Son to a family in Bethlehem. I turn now to consider the dogmatic implications of this glorious birth.

Recommended for General Reading

Historical Sources

Daley, Brian E. *God Visible: Patristic Christology Reconsidered*. Oxford University Press, 2018.

> Daley is a leading church historian, and this work is one of his most important books. Daley surveys patristic Christology, including a number of later sources that can often be overlooked in some introductory Christologies that end their patristic discussion at Chalcedon.

Davis, Leo Donald. *The First Seven Ecumenical Councils (325–787): Their History and Theology*. Liturgical Press, 1990.

> Davis's classic text is a helpful introduction to the historical context and theological conclusions of the seven ecumenical councils, each of which had at least some connection with Christology. Though it is becoming dated, it remains a necessary read for anyone interested in the history of christological thinking.

Majority World Theology

Chuang Chua, How. *Japanese Perspectives on the Death of Christ: A Study in Contextualized Christology*. Regnum, 2021.

> This helpful text introduces the reader to the theology of Kazoh Kitamori, Shusaku Endo, and Kosuke Koyama. This source enables the English speaker to learn about

the ideas of these figures from texts that are not yet translated into English. Chuang Chua includes helpful contextualization, analysis, and critique.

Escobar, Samuel. *In Search of Christ in Latin America: From Colonial Image to Liberating Savior*. IVP Academic, 2019.

Escobar offers a historical summary of the development of Christology in Latin America, with particular attention to *misión integral*. His work is primarily descriptive, and, to my knowledge, it remains the most thorough account of the development of Latin American Christology in the English language.

Ishak, Shenouda M. *Christology and the Council of Chalcedon*. Outskirts, 2013.

Ishak's is one of the more substantive critiques of Chalcedonian Christology from the non-Chalcedonian branches of the church. This alone makes the text an important one for theologians wanting to understand disputes about the orthodoxy and influence of the Chalcedonian tradition.

Systematic Theology

Duby, Steven J. *Jesus and the God of Classical Theism: Biblical Christology in Light of the Doctrine of God*. Baker Academic, 2022.

Few evangelical theologians are as adept at navigating classical Scholastic categories as Steven Duby, who turns his attention in this work to consider the implications of classical theism for various important christological questions, including, for example, the Son's suffering and his eternal relation to the Father. This is a technical work best read by someone with a solid theological foundation.

McNall, Joshua M. *The Mosaic of Atonement: An Integrated Approach to Christ's Work*. Zondervan, 2019.

McNall advocates for a "mosaic" approach to the atonement that combines elements of Christus Victor, moral exemplar, recapitulation, and penal substitution. McNall is a careful reader of Scripture, and this volume addresses a number of important contemporary challenges to each model.

Rutledge, Fleming. *The Crucifixion: Understanding the Death of Jesus Christ*. Eerdmans, 2015.

Rutledge's important book on the atonement surveys multiple dimensions of Jesus's death, considering the cross in historical and dogmatic context. Often poetic in fashion, this substantive work merits serious consideration. It is also helpful in addressing topics like the descent that are rarely present in works on the atonement.

CHAPTER ONE

Incarnation

A dogmatic account of Christology unfolds from the doctrine of the Trinity, for Christology and its treatment of the coming of God's Son by grace for our salvation assumes prior knowledge of God the Father, Son, and Holy Spirit.[1] It also unfolds from the historical beginning of Jesus of Nazareth, which is his incarnation. The starting point for a dogmatic account of the incarnation must therefore be a treatment of the identity of the One incarnate.[2] When we affirm "the Word became flesh and dwelt among us," we must attend to what follows: "We observed his glory, the glory as the one and only Son from the Father" (John 1:14). The Word made flesh retains his eternal relation as Son of the Father, and he manifests the eternal glory of God, a glory sometimes especially associated with the Holy Spirit.[3]

One of the main aspects of a doctrine of the incarnation is that the one who became incarnate, taking on flesh, was preexistent. **Preexistence** can be understood as ideal preexistence, which refers to preexistence of a thing only in the mind of God, where that thing exists in potency but not in actuality. In the metaphysics of much classical theology, something existing in potency must be acted on (by something external to the self) to become act, actually

---

1. Here there is an important distinction between the order of discovery, where the disciples knew Jesus of Nazareth before they could begin to develop a theology of the Trinity, and the order of teaching, where the metaphysics of the Trinity undergird much of christological dogmatics.

2. I do not intend to use the word "identity" here in a technical sense as is the case, for example, in the theology of Jenson, *Triune Identity*. Identity here merely serves to answer the question, "Who do you say that I am?"

3. Speaking more properly, this glory can be appropriated to the Spirit.

existing or acting in a certain way. For example, when I am standing, I have the potency of jumping, but I must do something to be actively jumping. This sort of preexistence in potency is not what the doctrine of the incarnation traditionally has in mind. Rather, the doctrine of the incarnation affirms real preexistence, where the Son existed as God in act (not just in potency) prior to his assumption of human nature in the incarnation.[4] This preexistence was often expressed by claiming that the Son existed as the *Logos asarkos*, the Word without flesh, a concept that communicates that the Son voluntarily took on human nature and existed as the eternal Son of God in a manner that can be distinguished from the incarnate life lived in the **economy**.[5] The preexistent Son is therefore the one who assumes human nature.

Those familiar with trinitarian theology are aware of the doctrine of **inseparable operations**, which claims that the works of the Trinity *ad extra* (toward creation) are indivisible, meaning that the Father, Son, and Holy Spirit work together yet in a distinctive manner, their intratrinitarian order being preserved in their undivided works.[6] This holds true also for the incarnation. In the words of the Fourth Lateran Council (1215), the Son was "incarnate by the whole Trinity in common."[7] Or, as expressed by Simon of Tournai, "Just as three sisters weave a tunic for only one of them, so also three persons worked the incarnation only for the Son."[8] To clarify, we can distinguish between the act by which the incarnation is caused, which is performed by the Father, Son, and Holy Spirit, and the state of being incarnate that results, which is proper to the person of the Son only as his unique mission.[9]

These dogmatic foundations are rooted in typical biblical language, for it is common to see Scripture speak of the Son being sent by the Father (e.g., Luke 20:13; John 5:37; 6:38; Rom. 8:3). Certainly, in John's Gospel, this language indicates preexistence,[10] but such language is also a means of referencing the act of incarnation as caused by the Father. Similarly, the Synoptic Gospels include the Son using an "I have come" plus a purpose statement formula to

---

4. For a concise summary of preexistence in terms of Christ's humanity and divinity, see Crisp, *God Incarnate*, 56–57.

5. Crisp, *God Incarnate*, 60–61.

6. I have written extensively on this doctrine in Butner, *Trinitarian Dogmatics*, 175–97.

7. Denzinger, "Definition of the Fourth Lateran Council," in *Sources of Catholic Dogma*, §1.

8. Simon of Tournai, *On the Incarnation of Christ* 7.6.

9. The distinction between state and act is helpfully elaborated in Vidu, *Same God*, 159–63. Similar language is found across the tradition. For example, Johannes Wollebius writes, "The incarnation of Christ in its origin is the work of the entire Holy Trinity, but the event is an experience of the Son only." Wollebius, *Compendium Theologiae Christianae* 16.1 para. 1.

10. There is near consensus among biblical scholars on the fact that John's Gospel includes a strong concept of real preexistence, including skeptics of preexistence in many other New Testament texts like James D. G. Dunn. See Dunn, *Christology in the Making*, 239.

speak of his incarnation (e.g., Matt. 5:17; 9:13; 10:34–35; Mark 1:38; 2:17; Luke 5:32; 12:49, 51), language which includes his preexistence as well as the Son's agency in taking on flesh.[11] The Son is the "man . . . from heaven" (1 Cor. 15:47), the one who was "in the form of God" and "emptied himself by assuming the form of a servant, taking on the likeness of humanity" (Phil. 2:6–7). Here again, Paul suggests both preexistence and the Son's agency in the incarnation, for the Son is the subject of the active verbs "emptied" and "assuming" (Phil. 2:7).[12] The Spirit is most clearly seen in Matthew's and Luke's depictions of the virginal conception by which the Son assumed a human nature within Mary (Matt. 1:20; Luke 1:35). These biblical patterns of speech suggest that the incarnation is a joint operation of Father, Son, and Spirit, though only the Son is ever described as having taken on flesh.

Though the doctrine of the incarnation emerges from the foundations of trinitarian theology, it enters into new territory in its consideration of that which is assumed in the incarnation (humanity) and the act of that which assumes (the eternal person of the Son). Both of these dimensions of the incarnation bring with them their unique controversies and exegetical puzzles, and only by seriously engaging these controversies and puzzles can a full doctrine of the incarnation come into view. The remainder of this chapter will seek to clarify the acts of assuming and the humanity assumed. I will begin by exploring Philippians 2:5–11 and the resulting doctrine of kenosis before turning to consider the virginal conception and the related theological disputes concerning the sort of humanity assumed. The chapter will conclude with a dogmatic summary of the incarnation and four implications of the doctrine.

11. This interpretation of the "I have come" statements is defended in Gathercole, *Preexistent Son*.

12. As has been widely discussed, Dunn initially rejected Phil. 2:6–7 as an example of real preexistence, arguing instead that it refers to Christ as a new Adam that did not cling to his Adamic glory. See Dunn, *Christology in the Making*, 114–23. The arguments against Dunn's position are conclusive to the point that he began to see more evidence of preexistence in Philippians 2. There are no verbal correspondences between the Philippians 2 Christ hymn and the Genesis account of Adam in the LXX. It is also unclear how a human being can come to be in the image and likeness of a human being, contrary to Dunn's hypothesis. Fee, "New Testament and Kenosis Christology," 31–32. Further, the overall purpose of Phil. 2:5–11 is presenting Christ as a moral example through his self-emptying, but the full strength of this example depends on Christ having an exalted status prior to his humble human beginnings. Paul clearly accepted preexistence elsewhere (see 1 Cor. 10:4; 2 Cor. 8:9). Bühner, *Messianic High Christology*, 31. Most decisively, however, Christ literally was a human servant of God, so if there is parallelism between the form of God and the form of a servant, why not say he was literally divine? Hurst, "Christ, Adam, and Preexistence Revisited," 85. Dunn later softened his position, allowing for the possibility of Adamic imagery and preexistence. Dunn, "Christ, Adam, and Preexistence," 78–79.

Kenosis

Any treatment of the Son's act of taking on flesh must consider Paul's narrative in Philippians 2:5–11, which has been called "Paul's master story."[13] Here, Paul tells us that Christ existed "in the form of God" (2:6), then "emptied himself by assuming the form of a servant, taking on the likeness of humanity" (2:7) before "he humbled himself by becoming obedient to the point of death—even to death on a cross" (2:8). These three elements give us an exegetical basis for considering the person who was incarnate and the act of being incarnate. The Son was "in the form of God," a phrase that recent commentators have taken to signify the visual characteristics of God,[14] the status of God,[15] being clothed in divine majesty,[16] and the glory of God as a manifestation of the divine nature.[17] Perhaps it is best to admit a "semantic extension" within the word that allows for a range of meanings.[18] In any event, the phrase indicates in some manner the actions of a preexistent divine person. This is evident from three features of the text. First, preexistence is suggested in the fact that Christ is acting prior to his assuming flesh (2:6–7). Second, where Jewish texts treat humans who pursue being equal with God as sinning, Christ is presented in this passage as truly having this equality within his grasp (2:6).[19] Third, when Christ is exalted, he is given the name above all names (2:9), which is widely understood to refer to the divine name.[20]

13. M. J. Gorman, *Inhabiting the Cruciform God*, 12–13.

14. Philo of Alexandria used the term "form" (*morphē*) in this manner, and it would fit the broad tradition of "Jewish traditions of mystical ascent to heaven" evidenced in texts like the *Songs of the Sabbath Sacrifice* from Qumran (4Q403 and 4Q405). "Human beings are never said to be in God's *tabnit* [form]." Bockmuehl, *Epistle to the Philippians*, 127–28.

15. Bühner claims this interpretation "is favored by the immediate context where we find many lexemes that are connected to the notion of a specific status (e.g., 'to humble,' 'to exalt,' or 'the bowing of knees')." Bühner, *Messianic High Christology*, 29.

16. Hellerman, *Philippians*, 109–11. Hellerman notes that the term *morphē* generally refers to appearance, and it can be used in the context of clothing as a sign of status and identity. Notably, a parallel instance of "existing in" is used of clothing in Luke 7:25.

17. Hansen, *Letter to the Philippians*, 133–38. Hansen points to the glory of the Lord as the visible appearance of God in the Old Testament, noting also the link between God's glory and God's name in Exod. 33:18–19, which is significant given that God's name is also referenced in Phil. 2:9. God's glory is said to be displayed in Christ in 2 Cor. 4:6, and a similar theme may be in mind in Heb. 1:3.

18. Silva, *Philippians*, 101–2. Silva centers the meaning of "divine nature" (without a fully specified philosophical meaning being intended) but grants validity to the meanings "status" and "condition" as well as admitting some link with glory and with second-Adam Christology.

19. Hurtado, *Lord Jesus Christ*, 122–23. Hurtado provides the examples of John 5:18, 2 Macc. 9:12, and Philo's *Legum allegoriae* 1.49.

20. See Hansen, *Letter to the Philippians*, 163; Hawthorne, *Philippians*, 91; Martin, *Philippians*, 101.

Our analysis of Philippians 2 requires that we turn attention to the doctrine of kenosis, which draws primarily on the vocabulary of Philippians 2:7, where Christ is said to empty himself (*ekenōsen*), a Greek verb resulting in the English noun "kenosis." The doctrine is not restricted to such texts, however, but can also be seen in 2 Corinthians 8:9: "Though he was rich, for your sake he became poor, so that by his poverty you might become rich."[21] Kenosis is closely linked to the notion of Christ's incarnate humiliation (Phil. 2:8) whereby he served and suffered for our sake.[22] The state of humiliation in Old Testament prophecy (see especially Isa. 52:13–53:12) and in Christ's teaching (e.g., Matt. 20:28) and actions (notably, washing his disciples' feet in John 13:1–15) also hints at the earlier kenosis of the Son. The question of what, precisely, it means to say that the Son "emptied himself" is one to which Christians have given a wide variety of answers, but I begin with a theory of kenosis that has been widely repudiated: **kenoticism.**

Gottfried Thomasius and Kenoticism

At times the varied concept of kenosis can be wrongly reduced to and identified exclusively with the nineteenth-century theory known as kenoticism, which emerged with the writings of Gottfried Thomasius. Several aspects of nineteenth-century German theology and philosophy led to the development of kenoticism. First, in the hands of historical critics like D. F. Strauss and F. C. Baur, traditional claims of Christ's dual humanity and divinity were argued to undermine the true humanity of Christ by presenting the illogical claim that Christ was a unity of two natures, human and divine.[23] Against such critique, Thomasius sought a way to defend the true humanity and divinity of Christ. Second, kenoticism can be interpreted as a reaction against the broad adoptionistic tendencies of much Hegelian German theology of the day, which saw Christ as something of a human being divinized in history.[24] Against this, Thomasius sought to develop the concept of kenosis, which allowed for a preexistent and divine Christ. Third, Thomasius, a Lutheran

21. This passage is frequently interpreted in light of Phil. 2:6. Among contemporary commentators, see Barnett, *Second Epistle to the Corinthians*, 409; Furnish, *II Corinthians*, 405; Martin, *2 Corinthians*, 440–41.

22. Wilhelmus à Brakel explains that Christ's state of humiliation cannot belong to the incarnation itself for two reasons: (1) prior to the incarnation, Christ "was not yet *God-man*" and so could not be humbled to the point of death as described in Phil. 2:8; (2) since the incarnation persists into eternity, but not the humiliation, we cannot treat the incarnation itself as the humiliation. À Brakel, *Christian's Reasonable Service*, 1:576.

23. On this context see Welch, *God and Incarnation*, 26, and especially McCormack, *Humility of the Eternal Son*, 73–78.

24. See Thompson, "Nineteenth-Century Kenotic Christology," 79.

theologian, can be situated within a larger debate between the Reformed and Lutherans (discussed in chapter 10) regarding whether Christ's human nature received divine attributes. Lutherans claimed that Christ's humanity had received such attributes, a belief known as the *genus majestaticum*.[25] The Reformed criticized Lutherans for an imbalance: Would not the *genus majestaticum* logically require an equivalent transfer of human attributes to the divine, which most Lutherans denied? Thomasius's kenoticism sought to introduce balance against these Reformed critiques.

Against this background, Thomasius argued that the incarnation of the preexistent Son involved both the assumption of human nature and a divesting of the divine mode of being.[26] Incarnation is thus also kenosis, which Thomasius defines as "the exchange of the one [divine] form of existence for the other [human one]," or "the renunciation of the divine condition of glory, due him as God, and the assumption of the humanly limited and conditioned pattern of life."[27] Thomasius reasons that the Bible's language of "sending" and "coming" (he cites John 3:13; 6:38; 8:23, 42; 16:27–28) cannot be interpreted spatially, so these terms must refer to a change in the relation between Father and Son as the Son enters a human mode of being.[28] However, Thomasius does not take the Son's new incarnate human mode of being to refer to a loss of the deity of the Son. Through the course of his writings, Thomasius makes this point in several ways. Since God's essence is in his subjective will, a voluntary self-limitation cannot be seen as an abandoning of the essence, especially since the Son retains all divine attributes in potency.[29] Primarily, though, Thomasius appeals to a distinction between the relative and immanent attributes of the Trinity.[30] The relative attributes of the deity of Christ are his omnipotence, omniscience, and omnipresence, terms of relation to creation that exist only because creation does. Because they are nonessential, Thomasius says, they can be set aside.[31] The immanent

25. On which context, see McCormack, *Humility of the Eternal Son*, 67–73; Thompson, "Nineteenth-Century Kenotic Christology," 81.
26. Thomasius, *Christ's Person and Work*, 56. Thomasius found support for this claim in his exegesis of Phil. 2:6–7, where the "form of God" is contrasted with the "form of a servant." Christ did not empty himself of the divine being (*ousia*) or of the divine nature (*physis*), but only of the divine form (*morphē*). Thomasius, *Christ's Person and Work*, 52.
27. Thomasius, *Christ's Person and Work*, 53.
28. Thomasius, *Christ's Person and Work*, 50. Thomasius sees this change as rooted in and an outworking of the eternal generation of the Father. See the discussion in Law, "Gottfried Thomasius," 163, 165.
29. Thompson, "Nineteenth-Century Kenotic Christology," 82–83.
30. For a concise summary, see Law, "Gottfried Thomasius," 153–56.
31. Thomasius will claim that these "are not essential for God, since they deal with God's relation to the world, but the world is not constitutive for God." Schwarz, "Gottfried Thomasius," 111.

attributes of absolute holiness, truth, and love are retained by Christ after the incarnation, argues Thomasius.

The kenoticism advocated by Thomasius pursues three important theological truths against nineteenth-century criticism, but it does so at the expense of other necessary doctrines. Kenoticism rightly insists that Christology affirm the true humanity and true divinity of Christ as well as the unity of both humanity and divinity in the person of Christ.[32] Yet Thomasius does not adequately appreciate the radical difference between God and creation, failing to grasp the full glory of the divinity of the Son who assumed human flesh in the incarnation. This point is well illustrated with attention to the theology of Kathryn Tanner, a contemporary theologian who argues that "God is not simply opposed to the characteristics of human beings but beyond any such contrasts. It is that very radical transcendence that enables incarnation with what is other than God."[33] Tanner advocates a noncontrastive view of transcendence, such that God is not a member of a **kind** or **genus** of things.[34] For example, God and creation are not spatially contrasted as if heaven is literally up and the earth down, for this would put God and creation in a similar genus, "things in space." God, however, is **uncircumscribed**, having no spatial extension or limitation. The incarnation cannot therefore be understood as the Son restricting himself spatially. Of course, Thomasius did not present a theory quite so inelegant, but he does fail to grasp the radical difference between God and creation.

Of central importance to Thomasius's apologetic project is his defense of the unity of Christ, particularly with respect to the divine and human consciousness.[35] Thomasius argues that the Son must lay aside his omniscience, a relative divine property not essential to the Godhead, or else there would be no united person of Christ, for the divine consciousness would exceed the human; "it hovers, as it were, above" the human Jesus.[36] He gives the example of Jesus sleeping (Matt. 8:24). "If the Son did not empty himself of omniscience, while the redeemer slept in the ship he would not only have been awake in his deity but would also himself both have brought about the storm earlier and have stilled it afterward," but then "the miracle dissolve[s]

32. Schwarz, "Gottfried Thomasius," 111. Later kenoticists did develop more radical proposals, but I consider Thomasius to be the main example of the movement.

33. K. Tanner, *Jesus, Humanity, and the Trinity*, 11.

34. On this, see K. Tanner, *God and Creation*; K. Tanner, "Is God in Charge?"

35. Stackpole does well to note the centrality of consciousness for Thomasius, who reduces the consciousness of Christ to a human consciousness. Stackpole, *Incarnation*, 95.

36. Thomasius, *Christ's Person and Work*, 47. Contemporary works often posit a similar contrast between the divine and human consciousness of Christ. See S. Davis, "Is Kenosis Orthodox?," 116–17; C. S. Evans, "Kenotic Christology and the Nature of God," 199.

into mere semblance" and "the unity of subject is again split apart."[37] Yet
note that Thomasius has treated the divine and human consciousness, or even
the divine and human condition of being awake, as if these were basically the
same sort of acts. Thomasius puts God and humanity into the same *genus*,
things that are awake, and thereby creates the very problem that kenoticism
attempts to dissolve. If divine and human consciousness are fundamentally
similar, though different in magnitude, then divine and human consciousness
are contrasted with each other. We are left to choose between a truly human
Christ, divested of omniscience, and an omniscient Christ who lacks human
consciousness as expressed in the Gospels' account of his learning (Luke
2:52), sleeping (Matt. 8:24), or failing to know the hour of his return (24:36).
Kenoticism chooses to embrace the true humanity of Christ at the expense
of full divinity.[38] But is such a choice necessary?

The important medieval Fourth Lateran Council (1215) affirmed a principle whose significance in systematic theology can hardly be overestimated:
the doctrine of **analogy**. According to the definition of the council, "between the Creator and the creature so great a likeness cannot be noted
without the necessity of noting a greater dissimilarity between them."[39] This
principle leads to the conclusion that our language of God is not used in
a straightforward manner, for the sort of uncreated, infinite, self-existent
Being that God is differs radically from the created, finite beings of creatures
who depend on God for their existence. While the doctrine of analogy is
subject to complex philosophical debates regarding both the basis and application of analogy, a subject best reserved for a treatment of the doctrine
of God under patrology, the broad contours of the principle of analogy
must be seen as an outworking of the biblical depiction of God as Creator
and as Redeemer. The Son is creator of all things visible and invisible (Col.
1:15–16), so like God, the Son must exceed even such categories as space,
time, and matter, a fact that has led some philosophers to suspect that we
cannot know God. Yet Christians affirm that God graciously reveals himself
within space, time, and matter, especially in the incarnation. Similarly, the
Holy One set apart from creation is so utterly different that he needs nothing
from creation for his own existence (Ps. 50:12; Acts 17:24–25), nor does he
face any real threat from a creation in rebellion. Redemption *sola gratia* (by
grace alone) implies a radical difference between God and creation, yet one

37. Thomasius, *Christ's Person and Work*, 54.

38. The main critique of kenoticism is that, at the very least during the incarnation, Christ
does not remain fully divine. See Thompson, "Nineteenth-Century Kenotic Christology," 96–98.
Thompson does not find these critiques as compelling as I do.

39. Denzinger, "Definition of the Fourth Lateran Council," in *Sources of Catholic Dogma*, §2.

that God graciously crosses through his covenanting work and its fulfillment in the incarnation, life, death, resurrection, ascension, and second coming of Jesus Christ. The principle of analogy further derives from a biblical tension between affirmations of the ineffability of God with creation (Ps. 145:3; 1 Tim. 1:16) coupled with Scripture's insistence on continuing to speak about this God.[40]

Given the doctrine of analogy, it is not clear that God's consciousness—and here I would note that the word "consciousness" is not used of God in Scripture[41]—is of such a similar sort to human consciousness that divine consciousness would need to be abandoned through kenosis in order for Christ to take on humanity. Given how difficult it is to understand the consciousness of other human beings, it is prudent to expect that understanding what it is for an infinite, eternal, omniscient God to think is beyond our reach, except to affirm through **apophatic theology** that God does not think as we do. Further, there are serious dogmatic reasons for saying that the Son could not give up such properties as omniscience. One aspect of being God is participating in the inseparable operations of the Godhead, "for whatever the Father does, the Son likewise does these things" (John 5:19), including knowing all things omnisciently.[42] To reject this through kenoticism undermines the divinity of the Son, challenging the very logic of salvation, as we shall see in later chapters. Sarah Coakley, drawing on Kathryn Tanner's theology of **noncontrastive transcendence**, explains that "'divinity' and 'humanity' *are* indeed radically distinct and qualitatively different categories, which cannot thus be collapsed into one flat package without seriously deleterious effects for the whole understanding of the salvific process."[43] This qualitative difference between God and humans means that adding a human nature need not require subtracting divine attributes.

Further objections to kenoticism supplement this one. For example, if Christ taking on humanity requires a divestiture of certain divine properties, then the resumption of these properties at the time of the ascension would only delay the purported logical problem that kenoticism seems to avoid.[44] Further, Thomasius seems to ask too much of the texts of Scripture from which he draws his opinion. Though Philippians 2:5–11 certainly expresses

---

40. A. Torrance, *Persons in Communion*, 127–28.
41. Of course, it is permissible to use words of God that are not used in Scripture. The word "Trinity" stands out as an obvious example. However, the absence of a word in Scripture should urge us to caution.
42. I develop the connection between kenosis and inseparable operations by drawing on White, "Divine Perfection and the Kenosis of the Son," 148, 153.
43. Coakley, "Does Kenosis Rest on a Mistake?," 261.
44. Stackpole, *Incarnation*, 99.

metaphysical truths, its emphasis is on the ethical implications of Christ's kenosis (see the context of Phil. 2:5, 12).[45]

We can draw several basic conclusions from this analysis of kenoticism that enable us to begin to craft a theology of kenosis. With Thomasius, we can affirm that an account of kenosis must explain how the divine, preexistent person of the Son took on human nature in a manner that preserves the genuine unity of Christ and his true humanity. However, against Thomasius, we must insist that the one who took on human nature did not by so doing divest himself of his divine nature or actions. A robust doctrine of kenosis must be based on a radical conception of the qualitative difference between the eternal Son in his divinity and the created human nature that the Son assumed. Kenosis is not, therefore, a loss of divine attributes to accommodate a lower yet fundamentally comparable state. Rather, kenosis is the assumption of a lower yet radically different human state of existence by the Son. With this foundation laid, we can turn to consider several historical theories of kenosis beyond that of kenoticism.

Variety in Theories of Kenosis

Though kenoticism is perhaps the best-known interpretation of kenosis among contemporary scholars, Christian history has produced an extensive range of possible interpretations of kenosis. Sarah Coakley helpfully explains several possibilities.[46] Kenosis might mean (1) the temporary relinquishing of power or (2) the pretense of such a relinquishment. The latter view is often linked with **Gnosticism**, which denies the full humanity of Christ,[47] but kenosis could be linked with (3) an epistemological constraint where Christ hides his divinity from us through apparent abandonment. For a more orthodox account, Gregory of Elvira argued that kenosis was not the Son "becoming anything other than what he was" but was like "the sun going behind a

45. Paul's emphasis is on kenosis as a metaphor for moral action, not a metaphysic of what the Son is emptied of. Fee, "New Testament and Kenosis Christology," 34. Yet this is merely emphasis, for it is clear that some judgment about ontology is assumed and that kenosis is not merely ethical but also soteriological. See Barclay, "Kenosis and the Drama of Salvation," 9.

46. I follow Coakley's basic survey here but differ slightly in how I number the accounts, and I supplement her analysis with some examples of my own. I also choose not to weigh in here on feminist concerns about kenosis and its moral implications, since Coakley has done an exceptional job considering such matters and since moral theology is not the focus of this work. I hope to consider these important concerns in a future work on virtue. See Coakley, *Powers and Submissions*, 3–39.

47. Coakley, *Powers and Submissions*, 6. Coakley mentions especially Ralph P. Martin and Martin Hengel as modern commentators who think Paul is following a Gnostic path in Philippians 2.

cloud."[48] Kenosis may also be taken to refer to (4) the Son's choice "never to have certain powers" in his divine/human person[49] or (5) to not have those powers in his human person alone. More ambitiously, kenosis may reveal (6) the humility of the divine nature, perhaps even by revealing some act that occurs within the immanent Trinity.[50] Finally, kenosis may refer to (7) the temporary loss of divine attributes, as in kenoticism, or to (8) the Son's taking on flesh without loss. Though several of these views can acceptably overlap, the seventh interpretation is most problematic and should be rejected, as discussed above, while the eighth is the most accurate understanding of kenosis, though it must be supplemented partially with the third and first views. In kenosis, the Son takes on a human nature, veiling his deity, and voluntarily acting in new, humanly limited ways.

I will illustrate this understanding of kenosis with Augustine of Hippo's theology, confirmed with biblical exegesis. Augustine argues that when Paul says Christ Jesus did not grasp equality with God, it shows a distinction between persons that extends prior to the incarnation, for equality requires at least two persons who are equal.[51] According to Augustine, the kenosis of the Son did not result in the loss of the Son's divinity: "For he did not so take the form of a servant that he should lose the form of God." Drawing on **partitive exegesis** (a subject more extensively explored in chapter 3), Augustine says this interpretation explains why the Son can both speak about himself in ways that make him equal to God (John 5:18) and also teach that the Father is greater than he is (16:28).[52] The latter statement is made with reference to the assumed human nature of the Son. Notably, Philippians 2:6–11 does not include any language of the Father "sending," highlighting instead the agency of the Son as a distinct preexistent agent.[53] As noted above,[54] the term "form of God" (*morphē theou*) probably directly denotes, in its first-century context, the status and/or visual appearance of God.[55] Therefore, we can

48. Gregory of Elvira, *De fide Orthodoxa* §88, as quoted in Hanson, *Christian Doctrine of God*, 525.

49. Coakley, *Powers and Submissions*, 11.

50. Jürgen Moltmann is an example of such a tendency in modern theology when he writes, "The *outward incarnation* presupposes *inward self-humiliation*. That is why the incarnation intervenes in the inner relations of the Trinity." Moltmann, *The Trinity and the Kingdom*, 119.

51. Augustine of Hippo, *Faith and the Creed* §5.

52. Augustine of Hippo, *On the Holy Trinity* 1.7.

53. This is helpfully noted in Fletcher-Louis, *Jesus Monotheism*, 98. I would note, as I have earlier in this chapter, that this distinctive agency does not entail a rejection of inseparable operations. The Son is a distinct agent who indivisibly works with Father and Spirit.

54. See the introductory discussion under the heading "Kenosis" above and the notes there.

55. I am aware that I am emphasizing a different aspect of the "form of God" from many traditional exegetes, who focused on ontology. For example, see the brief survey of medieval Latin exegesis in Dahan, "L'exégèse médiévale," 85–86.

expect, against kenoticism, that the Son's self-emptying of this visual form limits human ability to recognize the divine Son, who is only recognized as God by those who have been enabled to see by the Father (Matt. 16:16–17). Yet regularly, even when the disciples have some vision of who Christ is, this insight is accompanied with continued inability to fully grasp what it is for Christ to be the divine Messiah who must suffer. This is especially evident in Mark's Gospel, where Jesus's teaching about the necessity of the cross— something so central to Paul in Philippians 2—is immediately followed by an attempt by the disciples to reject a messianic state of humility and pursue their own exaltation (Mark 8:27–38; 9:30–37; 10:32–45). Fittingly, Augustine is prone to speak of kenosis as a matter of how the Son *appears*.[56] Here, as elsewhere, the epistemological dimension of kenosis is coupled with an ethical call to follow the cruciform pattern of Christ. Thus, the self-emptying of Christ also has an ethical dimension, pertaining to Christ's laying down of power by assuming the form of a slave.[57]

The epistemological and ethical dimensions of kenosis in Philippians 2:7 do not undermine readings of the passage that conclude that Christ is divine in an ontological sense. Surely, it is reasonable to conclude that what appears to be divine and what has the status of God would, in fact, be God in some ontological sense. However, this would be an indirect inference rather than a direct one from the phrase "form of God" because this concept centers appearance and status. Moreover, other elements of the passage provide stronger and more direct warrant for considering Christ divine in nature. The worship offered to Christ in 2:10–11 and the application of Isaiah 45:23 to Christ more clearly center such claims. If the passage is actually a hymn used in the context of corporate worship, as many suggest, it provides even further evidence of Christ's deity.[58] It is also clear that the passage is not merely ethical and epistemological, for it centers the cross, which is always soteriological for Paul.[59]

In Philippians, kenosis is introduced immediately after the discussion of Christ not clinging to the form of God and the equality this form includes, but its mechanism is stated immediately following the verb: "He emptied

56. See Komline, "Augustine, Kenosis, and the Person of Christ," 119.
57. In 1 Cor. 1:17, "to empty" means "to render it powerless, without effect, and that sense predominates in Paul's use of the adjective *kenos* and the adverbial clause *eis kenon*" (see 1 Cor. 15:10, 14, 58; 2 Cor. 6:1; Gal. 2:2; Phil. 2:16; 1 Thess. 2:1; 3:5). "This gives good grounds for understanding 'he emptied himself' as meaning 'he deprived himself of power.' That would fit the following clause 'taking the form of a slave' (2:7), since, as we have seen, the slave is paradigmatic of the person without social, legal, or personal power." Barclay, "Kenosis and the Drama of Salvation," 16–17.
58. For this argument, see Hurtado, *Lord Jesus Christ*, 112–13.
59. Barclay, "Kenosis and the Drama of Salvation," 9.

himself *by assuming the form of a servant*" (Phil. 2:7). Aware of this, Augustine focuses on kenosis as the taking on of a new human nature, not as a loss of divine attributes.[60] As Han-luen Kantzer Komline says, summarizing Augustine, "Kenosis is a matter of addition."[61] Caution is prudent here. The term "addition" may lead to the false sense of a change from potency to act, something impossible for God, who is pure act. The human nature does not add to the Son's nature, actualizing something latent in him. As God, the Son is perfect, immutable, and thus unable to be actualized or moved from potency to act. Rather, speaking loosely, the Son "adds" the potency of a human nature that finds its actualization, existence, and perfection in him.[62] In kenosis, the relation of the eternally begotten Son to his Father extends through the incarnation into a subordinate, created human nature that newly exists in the Son. Philippians 2:7 uses the verb "taking" the likeness of humanity, which James Dolezal notes "can have the sense of 'to make one's own.' It does not properly mean 'to add to one's self.'"[63]

It is not surprising that we see what Wesley Hill calls "redoublement" throughout Philippians 2:6–11, a "repetition or reduplication" that focuses both on what is common and on what is distinct between Father and Son.[64] Or, as Jamieson and Wittman put it, "Scripture speaks both of what is common to the Father, Son, and Holy Spirit and of what is proper to each person, reflecting the conceptual distinction between the divine nature and the divine persons."[65] There are certain elements in the passage that clearly highlight Christ's oneness with God the Father, such as his bearing God's form (2:6), having equality with him (2:6), bearing the name above all names (2:9), and being worshiped and declared Lord throughout creation (2:10–11), but there are also signs of subordination explained by the assumption of humanity, such as his being obedient to the point of death (2:8) and exalted "to the glory of God the Father" (2:11).[66] The kenosis is an assumption of humanity to the Son, whereby the divine unity of Father, Son, and Spirit is retained but the

60. Komline, "Augustine, Kenosis, and the Person of Christ," 107.

61. Komline, "Augustine, Kenosis, and the Person of Christ," 102.

62. Dolezal, "Neither Subtraction nor Addition," 144–45. Though Augustine uses language of the humanity adding to God, Dolezal argues that Augustine's terminology for kenosis, *accessit*, could mean "joined" instead of "added to." In her translations of Augustine, Komline has Augustine speak of "taking on" and of "addition." Komline, "Augustine, Kenosis, and the Person of Christ," 107–8. However one interprets Augustine, it is clear across the tradition that many theologians in the second millennium rejected any notion of addition. See examples in Dolezal, "Neither Subtraction nor Addition," 147–48.

63. Dolezal, "Neither Subtraction nor Addition," 144.

64. Hill, *Paul and the Trinity*, 99.

65. Jamieson and Wittman, *Biblical Reasoning*, 103; italics omitted.

66. Hill, *Paul and the Trinity*, 88–99.

relational status of the Son is humbled to that of a servant in his humanity.
In Augustine's words, "Some things, then, are so put in the Scriptures concerning the Father and the Son, as to intimate the unity and equality of their
substance." Here, citing Philippians 2:6, he states, "And some, again, are so
put that they show the Son as less on account of the form of a servant."[67]

The Assumption of Humanity

The Son's assumption of humanity can be considered from several angles.
Perhaps most important is a consideration of the role of Mary's humanity in
the assumption, the specific role of the hypostasis of the Son, and the related
work of the Holy Spirit. These considerations are explored in the doctrines
of the virginal conception, enhypostasia, and **Spirit Christology**, respectively.

The Virginal Conception

The doctrine of the virginal conception is the claim that Mary conceived
Jesus without sexual procreation. The virginal conception must be distinguished from the later, more complicated doctrine of Mary's **triple virginity**,
which included the virginal conception, Mary's miraculous continued virginity
even through childbirth, and the perpetual virginity of Mary following the
birth of Christ.[68] Of these three, only the virginal conception has dogmatic
weight, for it establishes a careful balance between Christ's humanity and
divinity and between the work of the persons of the Son and Holy Spirit.[69]
Contrary to the beliefs of some earlier theologians, the virginal conception's
emphasis is not, primarily, the avoidance of sex, which was sometimes centered
for the purpose of ensuring that Christ's flesh was not polluted by original
sin. This understanding of original sin is theologically inadequate (a topic
addressed in chapter 2), and when coupled with modern technologies of in
vitro fertilization it could suggest scientific means of overcoming the pollution of the flesh.

The doctrine of the virginal conception is primarily derived from Matthew
1:18–25 and Luke 1:26–38, though several other texts play a supporting role.
Some interpreters will argue that these passages do not require a virginal
conception, but the weight of the evidence is against such claims. Particularly

67. Augustine of Hippo, *On the Holy Trinity* 2.1.
68. Reynolds, *Gateway to Heaven*, 52–54. In Latin, these three stages are the *virginitas ante partum*, *virginitas in partu*, and *virginitas post partem*.
69. A Catholic theologian would undoubtedly disagree due to our divergent Mariologies, but this debate is best reserved for another context.

controversial is Matthew 1:23's citation of Isaiah 7:14 in the Septuagint (LXX), which uses the Greek *parthenos* to describe Mary. The Hebrew text of Isaiah 7:14 uses *'almâ*, a term meaning "young woman,"[70] while *parthenos* typically, though not always, means "virgin."[71] Conflict over the passage goes back at least to the second century, when Jewish criticism of New Testament usage of Isaiah 7:14 to support a virginal conception was addressed by Justin Martyr.[72] Several points argue in favor of interpreting Matthew to be speaking of a virginal conception. First is Matthew's explanation of the origin of Christ, who is said to be born of Mary (1:16), who was "pregnant from the Holy Spirit" (1:18), rather than being begotten or fathered by Joseph, as is said in other stages of Matthew's genealogy (1:2–16). Some have taken this to mean that Mary was pregnant out of wedlock, perhaps even having been raped, though the Holy Spirit was using the pregnancy.[73] However, there is evidence of an existing expectation in Second Temple Judaism that the Messiah would be miraculously conceived, suggesting that an illegitimate birth need not have prompted the belief in the virginal conception.[74] Second, the broader contexts of the annunciation narratives in Matthew and Luke suggest a miraculous birth. Matthew is citing Isaiah 7:14, the sign offered to Ahaz, a sign "as deep as **Sheol** or as high as heaven" (Isa. 7:11). Surely, Isaiah opens up the possibility of a more miraculous birth than the fairly pedestrian one noted in Isaiah 8:1–3, so Matthew could reasonably expect a miraculous birth even if the specifics of a virginal conception were unclear in the original prophecy.[75] In Luke 1:34, Mary expresses surprise that she will be pregnant, given that she has not "had sexual relations with a man," but the angel replies by promising a conception by the power of the Holy Spirit, concluding "for nothing will be impossible with God" (Luke 1:37). This phrase echoes Genesis 18:14, where

70. Brown notes that *'almâ* would de facto typically refer to virgins too, since most young women would be virgins. R. Brown, *Birth of the Messiah*, 147.

71. See R. Brown, *Virginal Conception*, 64; Schaberg, *Illegitimacy of Jesus*, 70–71. Schaberg argues that Matthew makes a connection with Isa. 7:14's use of *parthenos* because of Deut. 22:23–27, which concerns the rape or seduction of a betrothed virgin (*parthenos*). Schaberg posits rape, rather than a virginal conception, as the explanation for the conception of Jesus.

72. Justin Martyr, *Dialogue with Trypho* §§67–71, 77–78.

73. See Lüdemann, *Virgin Birth?*, 52–60; Schaberg, *Illegitimacy of Jesus*. This option is considered a less likely possibility than a traditional conception within marriage in Roberts, *Complicated Pregnancy*, 143–49.

74. Bühner, *Messianic High Christology*, 105–6, 111–13. Bühner notes examples in Philo, *Questiones et solutions in Genesin* 1.3.18; Philo, *Legum allegoriae* 3.219; *Jubilees*. To a lesser extent, Ps. 110's expectation of a divine begetting of the Messiah may anticipate something similar. Though these births are not virginal conceptions, Bühner is right when he remarks that "the notion of Christ's virginal conception would have been only a minor development within the early Jewish messianic discourse." Bühner, *Messianic High Christology*, 113.

75. Orr, "Virgin Birth," 253.

an angel responds to Sarah's skepticism about her own miraculous (but not virginal) conception by saying, "Is anything impossible for the LORD?"[76] In fact, the Old Testament offers a steady stream of miraculous births overcoming infertility that are typological shadows of the future, more exceptional virginal conception of Christ (see Gen. 21:1–7; Judg. 13:1–25; 1 Sam. 1:1–20). This miraculous context justifies interpreting Matthew and Luke as accounts of a miraculous virginal conception.

Several other biblical motifs and passages offer limited further support of the virginal conception. In Galatians 4:4, Paul writes, "When the time came to completion, God sent his Son, born of a woman, born under the law." While this passage may simply intend to point to the abasement of Christ,[77] or to reference a general human birth,[78] it may also hint at the virginal conception. Interestingly, where Paul typically uses *gennaō* (to beget / give birth to) to speak of human generation (in this context, see Galatians 4:23, 24, 29), he uses the verb *ginomai* in Galatians 4:4 of Jesus's birth from Mary, a term that has a more expansive range of meaning including "to come to be."[79] This expansive meaning allows for (but does not demand) a theological distinction between the eternal begetting of the Son from the Father and the temporal mission of the Son, by which he assumed humanity, coming to be born of Mary and possessing a human nature. Notably, Paul regularly uses *ginomai* to speak of Christ's origin (see Rom. 1:3; Phil. 2:7). Another passage offering limited support for the virginal conception is found in Mark 6:3, where Jesus is called a "son of Mary" rather than "son of Joseph." As Raymond Brown notes, "Generally sons were not called by their mother's name unless paternity was uncertain or unknown."[80] Such evidence further justifies the plain reading of the birth narratives in Matthew and Luke as referencing a virginal conception.

The doctrine of the virginal conception has faced much criticism in recent decades. It has been argued that the doctrine is incompatible with the preexistence of the Son[81] or that it was derived from pagan mythology. However, the doctrine of the virginal conception fits best with a strong conception of

76. Bühner, *Messianic High Christology*, 100.

77. This is the position taken by von Campenhausen, *Virgin Birth*, 17.

78. See Ridderbos, *Epistle of Paul to the Churches in Galatia*, 155–56. Ridderbos argues for this position by noting similar usage in Job 14:1 and Matt. 11:11.

79. T. F. Torrance, *Incarnation*, 93.

80. R. Brown, *Virginal Conception*, 66. T. F. Torrance argues that Mark describes Jesus as "son of Mary" while Matthew and Luke use "Joseph's son" (Luke 4:22) or "carpenter's son" (Matt. 13:55) because they have an account of the virginal conception but Mark does not and so must use "son of Mary" so as not to mislead. T. F. Torrance, *Incarnation*, 93.

81. Pannenberg, *Jesus*, 143.

the preexistent Son as understood within the context of Jewish thought. The virginal conception is distinct from pagan narratives of miraculous conceptions because it happens "without anthropomorphism, sensuality, or suggestions of moral irregularity."[82] In fact, the Greek word for virgin, *parthenos*, is not found in Greco-Roman birth accounts of heroes derived from mingling human and divine origins.[83] The difference between pagan and Christian accounts can also be seen in the traditional Christian emphasis on Mary's consent, given in Luke 1:38.[84] The virginal conception is certainly not rape, as some recent commentators have alleged.[85] As Amy Peeler notes, "Gabriel does not tell Mary of events that have already occurred within her without her knowledge or consent."[86] As Peeler further explains, the virginal conception is far from the sexual interactions of pagan mythology because the Spirit, designated by a neuter noun in Greek (*pneuma*), rather than the Father is the one described as bringing about the birth (Matt. 1:20; Luke 1:35), and no hint of sexual intercourse is present in the narrative.[87] Unlike pagan accounts of the origins of heroes like Hercules, the story of the virginal conception is not an account of the sexual origins of Jesus of Nazareth.[88]

The nonsexual nature of the virginal conception also helps us understand how the virginal conception is compatible with a strong notion of the preexistence of the Son.[89] Since the narratives in Matthew and Luke are not sexual in nature, they need not be taken as the sexual origin of a newly existing Jesus of Nazareth.[90] Rather, the virginal conception can be seen as an explanation

82. Bosloper, *Virgin Birth*, 185. Decades earlier, J. Gresham Machen had argued similarly: The doctrine of God in Christian circles was so different from the anthropomorphic pagan deities with sexual desires that the connection is invalidated. Machen, *Virgin Birth of Christ*, 338. For a more recent point of agreement, see Bühner, *Messianic High Christology*, 104.

83. Machen, *Virgin Birth of Christ*, 335.

84. A short version of a potentially much longer list of historians' affirmation of Mary's consent is found in Reynolds, *Gateway to Heaven*, 66–67.

85. For example, Hereth, "Mary, Did You Consent?"

86. Peeler, *Women and the Gender of God*, 26.

87. Peeler, *Women and the Gender of God*, 20–30. Peeler notes that the story is not sexualized in part because the Holy Spirit does not take on an anthropomorphic or animal form as is the case in many pagan myths. See also Reynolds, *Gateway to Heaven*, 59; Bühner, *Messianic High Christology*, 98.

88. "Because extraordinary birth was a universal theme, the early Christians had a point of contact with the ancient world, and because of the unique content and form of the Christian birth narrative, the Christians had a distinctive message to convey to Jewish and pagan society." Bosloper, *Virgin Birth*, 186.

89. The virginal conception does not necessarily require real preexistence, but neither does it exclude it. See Crisp, *God Incarnate*, 100.

90. It should be admitted, however, that early Ebionites and adoptionists alike could sometimes affirm the virginal conception, suggesting another possible reading of the text. See von Campenhausen, *Virgin Birth*, 23.

of the Son's assumption of a human nature, including the biological process of gestation and the spiritual process of ensoulment. Early heretical groups like the Gnostics and heretical thinkers like Marcion and Apollinaris (sometimes spelled Apollinarius) of Laodicea tended to understand the Son being born "through" Mary, as if she were merely a vessel and Christ's humanity an illusion, but the virginal conception affirms that the Son was born "out of" or "from" (ek) both Mary (Matt. 1:16; Gal. 4:4) and the Holy Spirit (Matt. 1:20).[91] That the child is from Mary shows that he is truly human, having a human body and soul. Jesus is also from the Holy Spirit, but this cannot be seen as the generation of a new person, or else the trinitarian persons would be confused. The Father eternally begets the Son,[92] so if the Spirit is said to beget a Son then it would seem that there are two Fathers in the Trinity, but this cannot be.[93] Therefore, the Holy Spirit's work is both creative, in bringing forth a fully human nature from Mary alone, and unitive, in joining this nature to the person of the Son. The Holy Spirit's work in the virginal conception is not generative, bringing forth a new person. It is noteworthy that Galatians 4:4 can combine a sign of preexistence (the Father sending his Son) with birth from a woman.

Some modern critics dismiss the doctrine of the virginal conception as theologically unnecessary, a trivial piece of mythology.[94] Admittedly, some treatments of the virginal conception do lack a full account of the theological significance. However, the virginal conception actually has considerable dogmatic import. For example, it serves to undermine any notion of **adoptionism**, a heresy which thought that Jesus of Nazareth was a typical human being who was adopted by the Holy Spirit at the baptism of Christ. The adoptionist case is often especially made with reference to Mark, which lacks an account of the virginal conception. Yet it is not obvious that adoption is in the background of the baptismal narratives, which more likely draw on language of the

91. Reynolds, *Gateway to Heaven*, 57; Daley, *God Visible*, 132.

92. For my account of eternal generation, see Butner, *Trinitarian Dogmatics*, chap. 2.

93. For this reason, the Eleventh Council of Toledo (675) teaches, "Yet we must not believe that the Holy Spirit is Father of the Son, because of the fact that Mary conceived by the overshadowing of the same Holy Spirit, lest we seem to assert that there are two Fathers of the Son, which is certainly impious to say." Denzinger, *Sources of Catholic Dogma*, 110.

94. Kyle Roberts explores two "conservative" reasons for the virginal conception—preserving inerrancy and ensuring the divinity of Christ. Roberts dismisses inerrancy and argues that if a virginal conception were required for God to enter the world, then "the irony would be thick. Many conservative Christians resist any suggestion that God is limited," but saying "that God needed a virginal conception to fully enter creation" limits God. Roberts neglects the typical caveat that God is limited by the laws of logic, his covenants, and his character (to name only three constraints on omnipotence). See Roberts, *Complicated Pregnancy*, 162–63.

enthronement of the king (Ps. 2:7) or the anointing of the Isaianic servant (Isa. 42:1).[95] Against adoptionism, the doctrine of the virginal conception affirms that the humanity of the Son was not through typical sexual reproduction. There could be no distinct human person who was Jesus prior to the incarnation of the Son because that humanity did not exist until joined to the person of the Son. However, the fact that Christ was from Mary also rejects early heresies like **docetism**, which would see Christ as merely a phantasm. Closely related, the virginal conception pushes us to recognize that salvation is *sola gratia*. As T. F. Torrance explains, the virginal conception is "an act of God's grace, a coming into man, and as such it carries with it a disqualification of human capabilities and powers as rendering possible an approach of man to God. . . . The birth from the virgin Mary carries with it a real disqualification of human powers as capable of producing Jesus."[96] To affirm the virginal conception is to affirm that the coming of the Savior was an act impossible without the gracious work of God. The gracious advent of Christ further rejects the notion of adoptionism and any pretension that the Messiah was simply a virtuous human being anointed by God. The one who assumes human nature in the incarnation is the one whose origins are from ancient times (Mic. 5:2). Finally, the doctrine of the virginal conception helps to uphold the doctrine of inseparable operations in the incarnation: The joint triune work of creating the human nature is clarified in naming the Spirit as agent in virginal conception to parallel the Son's kenotic coming and the Father's sending.

These central functions of the doctrine of the virginal conception could be supplemented by several other less certain claims. For example, Anselm of Canterbury argued that God had created a human (Adam) from neither man nor woman, a human from man alone (Eve), and many humans from man and woman together. Creating a human from woman alone completed the display of divine omnipotence.[97] While Anselm's argument is elegant and reasonable, it remains speculative. The virginal conception has some apologetic function, pointing to both the miraculous origins of Jesus and the fulfillment of prophecy.[98] This apologetic value is somewhat limited by the recent exegetical debates surrounding key prophecies, as noted with Isaiah 7 above. Recently, Amy Peeler has argued that the virginal conception is important to allow both female humanity (Mary) and male humanity (Jesus) to contribute to the revelation of God in the flesh, so that neither gender is shown to be superior.[99]

95. See Bird, *Jesus the Eternal Son*, 66–76.
96. T. F. Torrance, *Incarnation*, 99.
97. Anselm of Canterbury, *Why God Became Man* 2.8.
98. Von Campenhausen, *Virgin Birth*, 26.
99. Peeler, *Women and the Gender of God*, 141–42.

While this argument counters the complete devaluation of women by men, the imbalance between Mary and Jesus in Protestant circles means that this argument may still do little to combat the most entrenched forms of sexism.

Christ's Enhypostatic Human Nature

Scripture speaks of Christ being born "out of" or "from" (*ek*) Mary (Matt. 1:16; Gal. 4:4), but his conception is atypical since it is virginal. I have already noted that one theological conclusion to be drawn from this fact is that adoptionism ought to be rejected, for Jesus of Nazareth was not a distinct human who became God's Son at a specific point in time. As theological debates about Christology advanced, theologians developed several conceptual frameworks to explain this theological truth. Leontius of Byzantium brought one of the most significant clarifying concepts into christological discussion with his notion of an **enhypostatic** human nature. Here, I can only make initial forays into the important concepts of nature, substance, and hypostasis, a fuller explanation of which will be offered in chapters 3 and 5. For now, suffice it to say that "nature" and "substance" refer to kinds of things, such as humans, horses, oak trees, or angels. "Nature" tends to emphasize the actions or powers proper to a thing, while "substance" emphasizes attributes and allows further philosophical subdivision. "Hypostasis" references what exists as a particular instance of the kind of thing (*this* tree or *that* horse). As will be discussed in chapters 3 and 5, most Christians have accepted the Council of Chalcedon's (451) teaching regarding Christ's one hypostasis in two natures, human and divine.

Writing a century after Chalcedon's declaration, Leontius of Byzantium argued that the human nature of Christ existed enhypostatically in the Word.[100] By this, Leontius intended to reject the idea that the humanity of Christ existed independently of the Word, as if it were a unique adopted hypostasis perhaps merely conjoined with the divine Son. Rather, the human nature existed *in* the hypostasis of the Son. In classical theology, when something existed in something else, it was said to inhere in that thing. Often, when something inhered, it was said to be an **accident**, and the thing in which it inhered was a substance.[101] An accident exists in another in a manner that changes it, giving

---

100. There is some debate about whether Leontius believed that the divine nature of Christ also existed enhypostatically after the incarnation, with many scholars arguing against this position. For a survey of sources and an argument in favor of both natures being enhypostatized, see D. Evans, *Leontius of Byzantium*, 132–38.

101. I simplify to an incredible extent here. For a thorough and technical survey of Greek philosophy, see Gleede, *Development of the Term ἐνυπόστατος*, 69–100.

it a new property. For example, if someone pruned a branch from an oak tree, it would have a new shape, an accidental quality that did not stop it from being an oak tree (ending the substance) and yet which nevertheless changed the tree. If the assumed humanity were in the Son as an accident, it would bring about a change in the divine substance, requiring something like kenoticism. Therefore, the concept of the humanity being enhypostatized claims that the human nature is in the divine hypostasis, not the divine substance.[102] As Benjamin Gleede summarizes, the human nature is "a substantially constituent factor of an individual, i.e., not an accident, but nevertheless does not subsist in itself."[103] An enhypostatized nature has being in a mode of union—that is, in a manner that distinguishes it from the different substance to which it is united in hypostasis.[104] This concept is a complicated one if the philosophical details are pressed to their maximal expression, but in its basic contours, the idea that the humanity is enhypostatized simply rejects adoptionism, ensures the unity of Christ's person, and prevents the doctrine of the incarnation from entailing a change in the divine nature.

Spirit Christology and the Assumption of Humanity

Though the person of the Son is the one who takes on human nature, he is said to do so in the power of the Holy Spirit. The doctrine of the virginal conception establishes the coordinated efforts of Spirit and Son in the incarnation. Recent developments in what is known as Spirit Christology have emphasized the coordinated work of the Son and the Spirit throughout Christ's life. Spirit Christology works to correct a neglect of the Holy Spirit's work in the ministry of Jesus by emphasizing, among other things, Christ being the one anointed with the Spirit (e.g., Acts 4:27; 10:38). Advocates of Spirit Christology argue that this anointing began at the virginal conception.[105] Frank Macchia helpfully explains that we cannot think of Pentecost without a preceding incarnation, nor can we imagine incarnation without the Spirit's role in virginal conception: "The Word seeks *embodiment* by the Spirit so that all things might bring glory to God by becoming the dwelling place of this Spirit in the image of this Word."[106] If salvation involves drawing creation into relationship with the Father, Son, and Spirit, then the virginal conception

---

102. Leontius of Byzantium, *Contra Nestorianos et Eutychianos* §1.

103. Gleede, *Development of the Term ἐνυπόστατος*, 65.

104. D. Evans, *Leontius of Byzantium*, 135.

105. See, e.g., Yong, *Spirit Poured Out on All Flesh*, 87; Habets, "Spirit Christology," 209–12. Habets describes the virginal conception as the first of six "messianic" episodes that reveal Jesus's identity and mission.

106. Macchia, *Jesus the Spirit Baptizer*, 125.

is vital. Through incarnation, human nature belongs personally to the Son, who is eternally beloved by the Father, but without the Spirit's empowerment of that human nature from conception the full Trinity is not related to the humanity of Christ.

Drawing on the Christology of Martin Chemnitz, which he advances in new directions, Leopoldo Sánchez proposes that we interpret the Holy Spirit to have infused supernatural gifts of habitual grace into Christ's humanity.[107] Such gifts can be present only when the Holy Spirit is present, so Sánchez reasons that the Holy Spirit must have indwelled Christ's humanity, explaining that "the Son is filled with the Spirit from conception, and moved or urged by the Spirit throughout his mission."[108] While all Christians have spiritual gifts to differing degrees (Rom. 12:6), Christ has the Spirit without measure (John 3:34).[109] The result is that the human actions of Jesus Christ are the result of genuine human powers proper to the human nature, but this human action is empowered by the Holy Spirit and by the human nature's enhypostatic existence in the person of the Son.[110] More on this subject will be discussed in chapter 7.

Dogmatic Definition of the Doctrine of the Incarnation

A dogmatic summary of the doctrine of the incarnation includes the person who assumes human nature and the nature assumed. In the incarnation, the preexistent Son of God, the Second Person of the Trinity, emptied himself in kenosis by setting aside his status as an ethical example, veiling his divinity that he might not be known, and doing both of these things precisely by adding a human nature. In this act of kenosis, the Son did not lose divine attributes or his deity; rather, kenosis was an additive process. Being sent by his Father, the Son assumed flesh prepared for him by the Holy Spirit in the virginal conception from Mary, a flesh that was only enhypostatic in the

107. Sánchez, *Introduction to Spirit Christology*, 127. Sánchez argues that we should ascribe the supernatural gifts not to the entire Trinity but to the Holy Spirit in order to set the pattern followed by Scripture. I am unclear whether he considers this an appropriation or something proper to the mission of the Holy Spirit. I would personally incline toward the latter interpretation.

108. Sánchez, *Introduction to Spirit Christology*, 128–29.

109. The subject of the verb "to give" in John 3:34 is somewhat unclear and could reference either Jesus as the one who gives the Spirit to his followers or the Father as the one who gives the Spirit to the Son. Since the Father is the giver in John 3:16, 27, and 35, it would make sense to attribute the verb to the Father in 3:34 as well. Further, note that the Father is regularly said to give to the Son in John's Gospel (John 3:35; 5:26; 11:22; 13:3; 17:2). Keener, *Gospel of John*, 1:582–83.

110. Sánchez, *Introduction to Spirit Christology*, 130–32.

person of the Son, not being a distinct **supposit** by having its full existence in and through the Son. Both the kenosis and the virginal conception display God's infinite grace. Kenosis shows the unmerited favor of the Father who "so loved the world, that he gave his only begotten Son" (John 3:16 KJV) and of the Son who emptied himself to death, for "no one has greater love than this: to lay down his life for his friends" (John 15:13; cf. Rom. 5:10). The virginal conception by the power of the Holy Spirit shows our complete lack of ability, for no created capabilities could bring about the birth of the Messiah. Incarnation is thus an act of the triune God, moved by grace alone, whereby the person of the Son was made flesh (John 1:14). As Dong-Kun Kim notes, "The idea that God became a human being is the identity of Christianity. In this sense, the incarnation symbolizes the whole of Christology and is the beginning of our understanding of the Trinity."[111]

Implications of the Doctrine of the Incarnation

I have provided an overview of relevant exegetical and theological disputes related to the incarnation as well as a concise summary of the doctrine of the incarnation. The time has now come to briefly consider its implications. As noted in the introduction, the doctrine of Christology provides not only the foundational principles for systematic loci such as the atonement and the *ordo salutis* but also certain foundational principles in moral theology. Thus, it is no surprise that the doctrine of the incarnation, itself the starting point of Christology, has implications not only for systematic theology but also for moral theology. Such implications are numerous, but here I present only three: The incarnation provides a fundamental ethical emphasis on the value of life, the kenosis reveals a pattern for Christian moral action, and the incarnation raises questions about the permissibility of depicting the incarnate Son in art.

Incarnation and the Value of Life

In the second century, some Christians argued that Christ could not have true flesh. Tertullian of Carthage challenged this position by insisting that if God loves humans, then he must also love the manner in which humans begin to live. More than this, the fleshly incarnation shows that pregnancy and childbirth are not maters of "shame" but rather something to be "honored"

---

111. D.-K. Kim, *Future of Christology*, 22.

and even something "sacred."[112] As Mayra Rivera explains, "In Tertullian's argument, to undermine the necessary link between humanity and flesh is also to undermine the reality of the incarnation."[113] Tertullian recognized that the incarnation establishes the fundamental value of human flesh, pregnancy, and childbirth, an important insight that has remained central to Christian moral theology across the centuries. The fact of the Son's entrance into Mary's womb by virginal conception suggests the value of unborn life, explaining why Christians throughout history have generally been critical of abortion and infanticide.[114] The incarnation only establishes a basic value for unborn life; it does not resolve all ethical questions concerning abortion. For example, throughout the tradition there was some dispute regarding when the unborn child was fully human. Theories of "delayed ensoulment" valued the embryo from conception (though they rarely understood the biology of this process), but they believed that full humanity was attained only at a later stage of development. Abortion before ensoulment was sometimes treated as a moral offense but not as full murder.[115] Others considered ensoulment to be immediate. This debate cannot be resolved by appeal to the incarnation alone. Another ethical dispute not resolved by appeal to the incarnation concerns the permissibility of performing a surgery like a hysterectomy on a pregnant woman if late-stage uterine cancer is discovered. Such surgeries might save a pregnant mother's life but result in the death of her unborn child. Dogmatic theology cannot resolve such issues, and appeal to the incarnation is not sufficient to settle them, so I will leave these questions unanswered here.[116] The point for now is simply to note that the incarnation provides a basic moral value without providing a full ethical framework.

112. Tertullian, *On the Flesh of Christ* §4.

113. Rivera, *Poetics of the Flesh*, 52.

114. For a helpful and concise survey of the history of Christian thought on abortion, see Wedgeworth, "Abortion."

115. For example, see the variety in Christian legal codes. One Irish legal text from ca. AD 800 stated the penalty for the intentional miscarriage of a pre-ensouled body was 3.5 years; post-ensoulment the penalty was 14 years. Both offenses were considered sins in the *Canones Hibernensis*, ca. AD 675. In the twelfth century, Gratian's *Decretum* did not categorize abortion as murder if it was before the soul was in the body. See the discussion in Stensvold, *History of Pregnancy in Christianity*, 43–47.

116. The mistake can run in both directions. Arguing against theologians who claim too much from Chalcedon as a basis for immediate ensoulment, Margaret Kamitsuka draws on a "processive emergent view of the incarnation" to argue that ensoulment must not be immediate in an attempt to carve out space for a pro-choice Chalcedonian Christianity. Her Christology at times seems to conflate the process of deification and recapitulation with a gradual process of hypostatic union, undermining the validity of her argument. The full debate about abortion must be resolved elsewhere (and, admittedly, Kamitsuka provides other arguments for her position). Kamitsuka, *Abortion and the Christian Tradition*, 71–96.

Kenosis and Christian Ethics

The incarnation provides a second important contribution to moral theology by providing a pattern for Christian life. As Paul clearly exhorts the Philippians before discussing Christ's kenosis, "Adopt the same attitude as that of Christ Jesus" (Phil. 2:5). Christ sets this example in two stages: "The *preexistent Christ's* self-emptying, self-lowering incarnation/enslavement finds a parallel action in the *human Jesus'* self-humbling, self-lowering obedience to the point of death by crucifixion."[117] Both examples are treated as paradigmatic for Christian life. When Christ points to the mission by which the preexistent Son enters the world, he teaches that "the Son of Man did not come to be served, but to serve" (Mark 10:45; Matt. 20:28). Here, we see a negative version of the "I have come" plus a purpose statement that was discussed above as a sign of preexistence.[118] Christ's life in the state of humiliation also continues to set an example, perhaps most poignantly seen in his washing his disciples' feet (John 13:1–17). It is no surprise that Paul's treatment of ethical life in the Spirit in Galatians 5:13–26 begins with an appeal to freedom manifested in humble service (Gal. 5:13). As Martin Luther famously taught, "A Christian is a perfectly free lord of all, subject to none. A Christian is a perfectly dutiful servant of all, subject to all."[119] However, the link between the fruit of the Spirit and humble service also reminds us of Spirit Christology, which insists, in the words of Amos Yong, that "Jesus as the man of the Spirit models our lives anointed by the Spirit."[120]

Where the Son in his kenosis and humiliation sets a pattern for individual ethical behavior, Philippians 2 also contains an anti-imperial dimension that is important for the more structural and social aspects of moral theology. Several features of the passage suggest that Paul is also criticizing the Roman Empire. In the first century, language of "equality with God" (Phil. 2:6) had been restricted to use when speaking of the emperor,[121] but this claim and the title "Lord," also rich with political overtones, is applied to Christ (2:11). Furthermore, Philippians 2:10–11 cites Isaiah 45:23, but the broader context of Isaiah 45 includes the defeat of the nations and their humbling before Israel (Isa. 45:14, 24), suggesting another subtle anti-imperial critique.[122] Every knee will one day bow to Christ, and this would include competing authorities such as political rulers. Therefore, the Son's

---

117. M. J. Gorman, *Inhabiting the Cruciform God*, 17.
118. See Gathercole, *Preexistent Son*.
119. Luther, *Freedom of a Christian*, 53.
120. Yong, *Spirit Poured Out on All Flesh*, 110.
121. M. J. Gorman, *Inhabiting the Cruciform God*, 19.
122. Oakes, "Re-Mapping the Universe," 319; cf. Bird, *Jesus Among the Gods*, 345–51.

self-emptying and eventual exaltation are a critique of those self-exalting political authorities that will never be lifted as high as the Son has been in the ascension.

Incarnation and the Visual Representation of the Son

The eighth century brought to a head a long-standing debate in the Christian world regarding whether it was appropriate to depict Christ in art.[123] In 726, the Byzantine emperor Leo III started a campaign against cultic images of Christ, initiating what is known as the **iconoclast controversy**. Iconoclasts appealed to the Old Testament prohibition against the making of idols and their worship (e.g., Exod. 20:4–5; Lev. 19:4; Deut. 27:15), but iconoclasm prompted a flurry of Eastern Orthodox defenses of the use of icons focused on the incarnation and culminating in a vindication of icons at the seventh ecumenical council, the Second Council of Nicaea (787). As John of Damascus explains, it is wrong to make an image of the invisible God or to worship images of created things.[124] God's purpose in prohibiting idols in such passages as Deuteronomy 4:12–19 was preventing the veneration of created things.[125] However, John argues that through the incarnation the humanity of Christ has "become unchangeably equal to God, and the source of anointing."[126] It is therefore permissible to depict Christ's assumed humanity as a true representation of the divine Son.[127] Similarly, Theodore the Studite argues that the second commandment was given in a context before the incarnation.[128] When once it was impossible to have an image of God, now God has provided his own image through his incarnate Son. The image of a thing is in that thing itself. From this it follows that Christ, "the image of the invisible God" (Col. 1:15), is in the Father and the Father is in him, a classic patristic trinitarian argument for what became known as **perichoresis**. Theodore also claims that

---

123. The history of this debate is concisely surveyed in L. Davis, *First Seven Ecumenical Councils*, 291–95.

124. John of Damascus, *On the Divine Images* 2.5.

125. John of Damascus, *On the Divine Images* 1.5–6.

126. John of Damascus, *On the Divine Images* 1.4. A similar argument was made by Germanus of Constantinople at the dawn of the iconoclast controversy when he argued that showing Jesus in human form demonstrated faith that he was truly made human. L. Davis, *First Seven Ecumenical Councils*, 297.

127. Iconoclasts responded to this sort of argument by pointing to the unity of Christ's person, arguing that the human nature could not be depicted in isolation from the divine Son. L. Davis, *First Seven Ecumenical Councils*, 301. Theologians like Theodore the Studite present the counterargument that it must be possible to depict the concrete human nature of the Son because the Son was seen in his incarnate life. Meyendorff, *Byzantine Theology*, 47–48.

128. Theodore the Studite, *On the Holy Icons* 1.24.

this means the image of Christ in an icon is in Christ, and Christ is in the icon, making veneration appropriate.[129] Admittedly, the transformed state of Christ's humanity after the resurrection does prompt questions as to whether Christ can be depicted in his current human state.[130]

Placing modern biblical exegesis in dialogue with Orthodox defenders of icons helps clarify their positions. For decades, modern biblical commentators have agreed that Exodus 21:4–5's prohibition against idols was not a complete rejection of all visual art.[131] As John of Damascus argues, God commands the carving of created cherubim on the ark of the covenant and on the curtain (Exod. 36:8; 37:6–7), so "how can you therefore say that what the law orders to be made is prohibited by the law?"[132] Theodore the Studite adds that God commanded Moses to make a serpent so that whoever sees it can survive being bitten by a snake (Num. 21:8–9), and the apostle John interprets this snake as a type of Christ (John 3:14).[133] Theodore argues that if God allowed the Son to be represented by a snake, surely he would allow representation in human form. While the second commandment does not exclude all art, it does clearly reject worship of any image, whether images of other deities, of created realities, or of God himself.[134] It seems plausible, therefore, that use of artistic depictions of Christ is not contrary to the intention of the second commandment, provided that these images are not worshiped.[135] Here, many Byzantine theologians resorted to a distinction between worship and veneration, with the latter being allowed toward icons.[136] Theodore explains that

129. Theodore the Studite, *On the Holy Icons* 2.18, 21.

130. Eusebius of Caesarea argued that the ascended humanity of Christ is now transformed and no longer able to be depicted. See L. Davis, *First Seven Ecumenical Councils*, 292. Interestingly, Peter Atkins argues that it is precisely the ascension that enables us to depict Christ as human in the style of various cultures and ethnic groups around the world. Atkins, *Ascension Now*, 126. In my estimation, both arguments downplay too much the continuity of Christ's humanity.

131. For example, see Durham, *Exodus*, 285.

132. John of Damascus, *On the Divine Images* 1.15–16; 2.9.

133. Theodore the Studite, *On the Holy Icons* 1.25.

134. Brevard Childs argues that we cannot reduce the prohibition against idols to a prohibition against images of other deities. Historical evidence shows that premonarchial Israelite religion forbade images of the Lord. Further, the first commandment rejected worshiping other gods, so some further prohibition must be intended in the second commandment. It must prohibit worship of all images whatsoever. Childs, *Book of Exodus*, 406.

135. It is not entirely clear why the Old Testament prohibits images, giving the reasoning proposed by the Orthodox some plausibility. The Israelites did not know why they could not have an image because they did not yet understand that God would send his own image, his incarnate Son. On the ambiguity of the reason for the prohibition, see von Rad, *Old Testament Theology*, 1:217–19.

136. For a brief treatment of relevant vocabulary and resulting confusion between Latin West and Greek East, see Meyendorff, *Byzantine Theology*, 46. The distinction between veneration

idol worship occurs when our minds remain focused on the created material, but in veneration as offered by the Orthodox, the mind does not remain with matter but "ascends toward the prototypes."[137] This distinction is unconvincing, given that other religions in the ancient Near East understood their idols to merely represent something more invisible and supernatural to which the idol drew their minds.[138] When applied to an ancient Near Eastern context, the distinction between veneration and worship does not easily work.

The Byzantine theology of the incarnation provides some theological justification for images of the incarnate Christ in art. The veneration of these images, though having the weight of an ecumenical council behind them, seems to rest on a distinction that does not clearly fit biblical evidence. Yet there are two further reasons to critique the use of images in the context of worship. First, one might appeal to the **regulative principle**, which restricts acts taken in worship to those explicitly commanded in Scripture. Those who hold to this principle might argue that God commanded certain images to be present in the temple, but no such images were commanded for use in the context of New Testament worship. Outside of worship, this would seemingly still allow for images to be made of Christ. A second reason would not have occurred to the eighth-century theologians debating icons, but many contemporary Black theologians (among others) raise concerns about the ethnicity in which Christ is depicted.

Historically, American depictions of Jesus as white coincided with slavery, segregation, and white supremacy, such that "calling [or depicting] Christ black explicitly indicates Christ's opposition to white racism," says Kelly Brown Douglas in *The Black Christ*.[139] Douglas surveys three theological treatments from the 1970s that saw Christ as Black. Albert Cleage argued that Christ was literally Black if he had a drop of African blood in him. James Cone argued that Jesus must be understood as Black in 1970s America because Jesus was historically Jewish. The best way to represent Jesus's historical status as an oppressed minority Jewish man was the "ontological symbol" of Jesus

---

and worship was affirmed by the Second Council of Nicaea itself, which anathematizes those who "are not so minded" to venerate images. Denzinger, *Sources of Catholic Dogma*, 123.

137. Theodore the Studite, *On the Holy Icons* 1.34.

138. As Gerhard von Rad notes, "The pagan religions knew as well as Israel that deity is invisible, that it transcends all human ability to comprehend it, and that it cannot be captured or compromised in a material object." Von Rad, *Old Testament Theology*, 1:14. Though he perhaps overstates his case, since Israel does seem to have a more elevated sense of divine transcendence than surrounding cultures, the basic point is well taken. Scholarship has shown that ancient religions did not reduce their deity to a material object but saw the idol as a means to access the deity. See Childs, *Book of Exodus*, 408.

139. Douglas, *Black Christ*, 98.

being Black in the modern United States. J. Deotis Roberts argued that Jesus could be depicted as Black because Jesus was the universal Savior, so he could be presented as the same ethnicity as any human group.[140] Douglas recognizes that seeing the historical Jesus as dark skinned challenges his captivity to white supremacist theology,[141] but she is concerned that depicting Christ as Black might simply affirm everything in the Black community. But "not everything that is black is sustaining or liberating for the black community."[142] Furthermore, not all forms of injustice or oppression are addressed by linking Jesus with Blackness. Given such risks, the strongest argument against depicting Christ may be an ethical one: In a racialized world such depiction will inescapably undermine orthopathy, resulting in some viewers sinfully elevating one race or ethnicity over another due to the depiction.[143]

In practical terms, it is not always easy to avoid depictions of Jesus, given their cultural prevalence. Undoubtedly Baker Academic's marketing team faced a challenge when I requested a cover for *Christological Dogmatics* that matched the color scheme and feel of *Trinitarian Dogmatics*, yet without depicting Jesus on the cover in the way that the prior volume had. Their decision to include a painting of Christ taken down from the cross while covering his body with the title is a profound illustration of how Christian art can function—just as the gaze of the figures in the painting are drawn to Christ who is beyond view, so art (and theological writing) can draw us to seek the one who cannot be exhaustively depicted in art or text. Just as those historical persons depicted in the artwork on the cover were left with the task of witnessing to what they saw, which can hardly be understood, so, too, is the reader of this book challenged to bear witness to what words can only incompletely explain: The infinite God became incarnate for us.

Conclusion

This chapter's discussion of the incarnation, virginal conception, and kenosis has described the Son's taking on flesh as grounding several important aspects of the doctrine and praxis of the church. The impossibility of virginal conception by human effort requires that the salvation attained by Christ be

140. Douglas, *Black Christ*, 158–70.
141. Douglas, *Black Christ*, 91.
142. Douglas, *Black Christ*, 96. Douglas notes that the situation of oppression is characterized by "complexity" such that "racism is not the only barrier to black freedom." Douglas argues that other problems include sexism, classism, and heterosexism, and these are found within the Black community. See Douglas, *Black Christ*, 96–98.
143. Even if such elevation is subconscious, it would be a serious problem.

seen as the provision of grace alone, for no human effort could bring about the needed sacrifice. Yet this affirmation of *sola gratia* must be coupled with the recognition that "faith, if it does not have works, is dead" (James 2:17), and so the kenosis and incarnation begin already to shape the ethical contours of the Christian life according to the pattern of Christ. The incarnation has already raised certain important philosophical questions concerning the immutability of deity, the means of the union of humanity and divinity of Christ, and the causal mechanism behind such unity. These questions must be explored further. Before continuing to develop this account of Christ's person, it is necessary to consider the soteriological implications of the incarnation in greater detail, which takes us to a consideration of recapitulation in chapter 2.

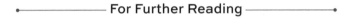

For Further Reading

Clark, John C., and Marcus Peter Johnson. *The Incarnation of God: The Mystery of the Gospel as the Foundation of Evangelical Theology*. Crossway, 2015.

> Clark and Johnson fruitfully explore the significance of the incarnation for a variety of Christian doctrines. Drawing on Scripture and tradition, they offer a robust survey of the implications of the incarnation. Among these is an analysis of the sort of fallen humanity that the Son assumes that I challenge later in this book.

Evans, C. Stephen, ed. *Exploring Kenotic Christology: The Self-Emptying of God*. Regent College Publishing, 2006.

Nimmo, Paul T., and Keith L. Johnson, eds. *Kenosis: The Self-Emptying of Christ in Scripture and Theology*. Eerdmans, 2022.

> These two volumes include an impressive range of essays on the kenosis of Christ, with the Evans volume generally leaning toward the flawed idea of kenoticism and the Nimmo and Johnson edited volume tending toward other understandings of kenosis. Combined, the chapters in these two books provide serious and substantial resources for thinking through the doctrine of kenosis.

Peeler, Amy. *Women and the Gender of God*. Eerdmans, 2022.

> Peeler's text has several major goals. One is to offer a close reading of the annunciation in dialogue with critics who claim that Mary is violated in some way by God. The result of Peeler's work toward this goal is one of the most insightful interpretations of the early chapters of Luke of which I am aware. Peeler also seeks to explain why God is called Father, and her explanation here is more theologically contentious and one with which I have reservations.

CHAPTER TWO

Recapitulation

The person and work of Christ are inseparable. On the one hand, we know who Christ is by what he does; on the other hand, Christ's nature(s) make possible his saving work.[1] Despite this, theologians have often divided the study of the person of Christ from the study of his work. This distinction can lend conceptual clarity, but it can also result in a doctrine of the person and natures of Christ detached from any saving significance. Similarly, a study of the work of Christ lacking a clear understanding of the metaphysics of the incarnation and hypostatic union is sure to fall into error. For these reasons alone, combined analysis of the person and work of Christ is tremendously important. To witness to Christ, one must proclaim his person and work.

It is a well-known fact that no ecumenical council declared an official model of Christ's saving work, and the temptation is to interpret this fact to suggest that there is considerable freedom in explaining the work of Christ. Many modern theological treatments of the work of Christ focus on distinct "models" of the atonement, often pitting different theories of Christ's saving work against one another. Where one author might argue for the central importance of Christ's being punished in our place, another might object that the Son's victory over sin and death is more important. However, much of the best recent writing on Christ's saving work recognizes the limitations of this approach. As Khaled Anatolios explains, the models approach can "contribute

1. See Berkouwer, *Person of Christ*, 101–10. Berkouwer insists that "not to know who he is means not to understand what his work is; and not to see his work in the right perspective is not to understand his person" (105).

significantly to a general uncertainty as to what basic affirmations we can and must make in order to speak the gospel of what God has accomplished in Jesus Christ 'for us and our salvation.' Proponents of the 'models' approach not only fail to achieve clarity and consensus; they often fail even to consider such basic questions as what formally constitutes a 'model,' what materially these specific models are, and how many of them there are."[2] Such doctrinal relativism is a weak point at the heart of Christian proclamation.

Perhaps the fact that no official ruling on the proper "model" of Christ's saving work was embraced is less concerning if the person and work of Christ are closely linked. After all, there were many clear confessional judgments rendered that clarified what and who Jesus was. If Jesus's work follows from his **ontology**, then statements about his person and being would entail certain corresponding affirmations regarding the work of Christ. On this account, detailed theological exposition of Christ's incarnation, his constitution as two natures in one person, and his two operations and **energies** will open up successive aspects of his work. Such an approach will allow us to synthesize many "models" as, in fact, partial explanations of the complete work of Christ. Each new chapter on the metaphysics of the incarnate Christ makes possible further theological analysis on Christ's work in a following chapter or chapters.

This first chapter laid the foundation for the work of Christ by exploring how the incarnation and kenosis of Christ reverse a pattern found in Adam before the fall. As Augustine of Hippo explains, interpreting the Philippians 2 Christ hymn, "There can be no other way for us to return on except the way of humility, because pride was our downfall. . . . Our redeemer, there-fore, deigned to give us in himself the example of humility, the way by which we must return."[3] Christ's humility in kenosis and incarnation reverses the pattern of pride found in Adam, who sought equality with God when he did not deserve it. This simplistic comparison opens into a much larger theology of recapitulation, one aspect of Christ's work that relates to his incarnation, reversing the original sin of Adam.

Recapitulation in Irenaeus of Lyons

Paul speaks of a plan "to bring everything together in Christ, both things in heaven and things on earth in him" (Eph. 1:10). Irenaeus of Lyons develops this Pauline vision of a cosmic unity of all things in Christ into a theology

---

2. Anatolios, *Deification Through the Cross*, 7.
3. Augustine of Hippo, *Faith and the Creed* §6.

of recapitulation. At a basic level, recapitulation is fairly straightforward. As J. T. Nielsen explains, "Irenaeus uses the terms 'recapitulatio' or 'recapitulare' to render that which Christ has done in comparison with Adam."[4] It is therefore no surprise that at various key points of his theology of recapitulation, Irenaeus draws on Paul's contrast between the first and last Adam (Rom. 5:12–21; 1 Cor. 15:45–49).[5] A deeper analysis reveals that recapitulation is a far more complicated concept. Eric Osborn finds eleven ideas present in Irenaeus's theology of recapitulation—"unification, repetition, redemption, perfection, inauguration and consummation, totality, the triumph of Christus Victor, ontology, **epistemology** and ethics (or being, truth, and goodness)"— always "combined in different permutations."[6]

Charting a course somewhat between these two extremes, we can identify the significance of recapitulation in terms of Christ's incarnation, his human life, and his victory through his death, resurrection, and second coming. Irenaeus explains that when the Son became incarnate, "he commenced afresh the long line of human beings, and furnished us, in a brief comprehensive manner, with salvation; so that what we had lost in Adam—namely to be according to the image and likeness of God—that we might recover in Christ Jesus."[7] The incarnation provides a fresh start for humanity at an ontological level, making possible human "incorruptibility and immortality" through the assumption of corruptible and mortal human flesh, which was given a path to perfection through union with Christ.[8] In the context of heresies denying the humanity of Christ,[9] the virginal conception plays a particularly important role. It establishes the full humanity and divinity of Christ—Irenaeus sees in Isaiah 7:14–15's prophecy of the virginal conception the divinity of the child born with the name Immanuel, and he sees humanity in the promise that the child will eat "curds and honey." The virginal conception also brings about the inauguration of a new humanity in a manner similar to the emergence of the first humans. Adam came from the soil, not as if a plant through natural germination, for the soil was virginal, untilled soil (Gen. 2:5), and Adam was formed directly by the hand of God. So, too, Christ came from a virginal conception and assumed in the Spirit a humanity made directly by God in

4. Nielsen, *Adam and Christ*, 15.

5. Irenaeus uses Rom. 5 at key points in book 3 of *Against Heresies* (see especially 3.18.7 and 3.21.10), while 1 Cor. 15 is central to book 5's analysis of the resurrection (in relation to recapitulation, see especially 5.12.2 and 5.13.5).

6. Osborn, *Irenaeus of Lyons*, 97–98. Bold added to indicate glossary term.

7. Irenaeus, *Against Heresies* 3.18.1. The translation "commenced afresh" is based on the Syriac, but the Latin has "recapitulated in himself."

8. Irenaeus, *Against Heresies* 3.19.1.

9. The importance of this context is noted in Nielsen, *Adam and Christ*, 13.

Mary.[10] In the famous Irenaean dictum, "The Word of God, our Lord Jesus Christ, . . . did, through His transcendent love, become what we are, that He might bring us to be even what He is in Himself."[11]

Irenaeus's treatment of the virginal conception hints at the larger trinitarian structure of his theology of recapitulation. The second Adam is the Christ, the anointed one. Irenaeus interprets this in a trinitarian manner, drawing on Isaiah 61:1, "The Spirit of the Lord God is on me, because the Lord has anointed me," a passage that is the text of Christ's first public teaching in Luke 4:16–21. In the able exegetical hands of Irenaeus, this passage speaks of the anointing Father, the Son who is anointed, and the Spirit that is the unction with which the Father anoints.[12] The messianic status of the Son as second Adam is thus based on what Douglas Farrow calls a "perichoretic form of existence" that the Spirit bestows on the human nature of the Son.[13] Similarly, Khaled Anatolios speaks of an "intertwining of human and divine glory" in Irenaeus.[14] More will be said about perichoresis in coming chapters, but for now we can recognize the basic harmony between the triune persons and humans that recapitulation seeks to address.[15] This trinitarian structure is seen in Irenaeus's reference to the two "hands" of the Father, the Son and Spirit, forming the second Adam in Mary, a gesture to what would become the doctrine of inseparable operations.[16] It is also present in Irenaeus's soteriology, where the attachment of humanity and divinity in the incarnation is balanced by the Son's pouring out the Spirit that humans may receive the Father.[17] For this reason, both incarnation and baptism in the Spirit are important to the start of the Son's incarnate ministry in Irenaeus.[18]

While the incarnation and reception of the Spirit are important to recapitulation, so, too, is the fullness of the life and ministry of Christ. As Telford Work puts it, "The Lord's conception and birth *ground* his new alpha [beginning] for humanity, they do not by themselves *constitute* it, even for Mary."[19]

10. Irenaeus, *Against Heresies* 3.21.10.

11. Irenaeus, *Against Heresies*, preface to book 5.

12. Irenaeus, *Against Heresies* 3.18.3.

13. Farrow, *Ascension and Ecclesia*, 60.

14. Anatolios, *Deification Through the Cross*, 271. Anatolios focuses on Irenaeus's teaching that "the glory of God is a living human being" (*Against Heresies* 4.20.7) and that "this is the glory of the human being, to continue and remain permanently in God's service" (*Against Heresies* 4.14.1).

15. On trinitarian perichoresis, see Butner, *Trinitarian Dogmatics*, 133–52.

16. See Irenaeus, *Against Heresies* 5.1.3. On Irenaeus's theology of the Son and Spirit as the two hands of God, see Butner, *Trinitarian Dogmatics*, 153–54.

17. See Irenaeus, *Against Heresies* 5.1.1 and 5.12.2–4.

18. See Sánchez, *Introduction to Spirit Christology*, 62.

19. Work, *Jesus*, 76. Work uses the word "alpha" to describe a new beginning throughout his book.

The second Adam "passed through every stage of life, restoring all to communion with God."[20] Recapitulation is a matter of ontology, correcting the corruption within human nature through incarnation, but it is also a matter of corrective repetition, a historical reversal of the first Adam's sin through the sinless and ethical life of a new Adam. As the preexistent Word, Christ is the beginning of all creation that is made through him (Col. 1:16), but he is also the apex of history (Eph. 1:9–10), and he will be its consummation at his second coming.[21] His life is thus a fulfillment of history but also draws all of creation and every generation into the possibility of a renewed Edenic relationship with the Father in the Spirit.[22] With this emphasis on history, Irenaeus combats claims of Gnostics like Valentinus that history prevented true salvation and knowledge of God. Valentinus saw salvation in terms of an escape from history and from a created world. For Irenaeus, history is part of God's means of recapitulation.[23]

Recapitulation includes the victory of Jesus Christ, the second Adam. Irenaeus explains, "As our species went down to death through a vanquished man, so we may ascend to life again through a victorious one."[24] Jesus took on the weak flesh that seemingly couldn't fulfill the law, but in obedience he did so anyway, reversing the effect Adam had on our humanity.[25] In Irenaeus, we see a comprehensive theory of sin in Adam paired with a comprehensive theory of redemption and victory in Christ.[26] Though I will not follow some details of Irenaeus's theology of redemption, the basic elements are both ontological, curing the corruption and mortality resulting from sin through the resurrection, and positional, defeating Satan and reconciling humanity to the Father through the Son's perfect obedience. If recapitulation involves bringing all things together in Christ (Eph. 1:10), it finds its culmination in Ephesians 1:21–22 in victory through resurrection and ascension over "every ruler and authority, power and dominion," such that all things might be "subjected . . . under his feet" (quoting Ps. 8:6) by being appointed as "head over everything for the church."

Irenaeus provides us with a theology that does not view the incarnation as a mere precursor to the purportedly *real* work of salvation. Rather, the incarnation itself is the important initiation of recapitulation as the union of humanity and divinity begins the reversal of Adam's work in history. Salvation certainly

20. Irenaeus, *Against Heresies* 3.18.7.
21. Nielsen, *Adam and Christ*, 59.
22. See Irenaeus, *Against Heresies* 4.22 and 5.21.1.
23. Daley, *God Visible*, 77.
24. Irenaeus, *Against Heresies* 5.21.1.
25. Rutledge, *Crucifixion*, 550.
26. J. N. D. Kelly calls Irenaeus "the first to work out comprehensive theories both of original sin and of redemption." Kelly, *Early Christian Doctrines*, 170.

cannot be reduced to the incarnation, as if the mere assumption of human nature resolves all sin.[27] Neither, however, can soteriology be cut off from incarnation. Trinitarian in its basic features, and cognizant of the significance of both history and ontology, Irenaeus's theology of recapitulation provides a strong foundation for the balance between the person and work of Christ that a **functionalist Christology** demands. However, more must be said, so I turn now to consider further the Pauline depiction of Jesus as the new Adam as well as the ramifications of this depiction for the doctrine of original sin.

Jesus the New Adam

At times, Scripture depicts the pattern embodied in Adam as recurring later in history. For example, in Ezekiel 28:11–18 the prophet condemns the king of Tyre, depicting him in Adamic terms as one in Eden (28:13), created good but fallen into evil (28:15), and therefore expelled from God's presence (28:16). The pattern of sin repeats itself, but can it be reversed? The hope of reversal finds its fulfillment in Christ, who is depicted in Adamic ways but with the opposite outcomes. Such patterns lead us to a discussion of **second-Adam Christology** and the doctrine of original sin.

Second-Adam Christology

Second-Adam Christology is evident in the title "Son of Man." In the Synoptic Gospels, "Son of Man" is used primarily in three contexts: Christ's authoritative yet humble ministry, his suffering unto death and resurrection, and his second coming.[28] The title "Son of Man" is quite complicated since it can reference an apocalyptic figure, as in Daniel 7:13–14, or serve as a circumlocution for the concept of being a mere human, as is often found in the book of Ezekiel (e.g., Ezek. 2:1, 3, 6, 8).[29] In the second usage, being addressed as "son of man" by God or an angel would be something roughly like being called a mere mortal. However, I am convinced that central to our understanding of the phrase is the way that it points to a second-Adam Christology. Attention to the actual Greek reveals the peculiar fact that articles are used before both nouns. The phrase is literally *"the Son of the Man"* (*ho huios tou anthrōpou*),

27. J. N. D. Kelly calls it a "dangerous half truth" to reduce recapitulation to a physicalist account that does not see the need of the cross. Kelly, *Early Christian Doctrines*, 173.
28. O'Collins, *Christology*, 63. A slightly different schema is offered in Marcus, "Son of Man as Son of Adam," 47–48.
29. These are often treated as the two main relevant contexts—mistakenly, as I will show. For example, see the treatment in Porter and Dyer, *Origins of New Testament Christology*, 50–54.

a peculiar construction not found in the Septuagint or in classical Greek literature but used in all New Testament instances with one possible exception, John 5:27.[30] As Joel Marcus notes, the articles immediately prompt the question, "The son of *which* man?"[31] Since Adam is called "*the* man" (*ho anthrōpos*) in the Septuagint of Genesis 1–3, Adam would be the logical answer to this question.[32] Juan Cortés and Florence Gatti put the argument slightly differently: An article may signify a representative of a class par excellence, like when "the prophet" (*ho prophētēs*) is used of John the Baptist (John 1:21; 7:40). Adam was unique, and he was the human par excellence due to "his solidarity with the human race," so this would be further reason to take the **articular** reference as pointing to him.[33] Even if the apocalyptic connotations of the title "Son of Man" are most central to its understanding, the apocalyptic imagery of Daniel 7:13–14 likely has Adamic influences as well, suggesting an indirect reference to a second-Adam Christology.[34] Oscar Cullmann even argues that second-Adam Christology emerges from a unique tension within Jewish theology. While an original perfect man was expected to return eschatologically for salvific purposes in many ancient Near Eastern religions, the fact of Adam's sin made this impossible in Judaism. Nevertheless, such apocalyptic images as that of Daniel 7:13–14 seemed to demand a human eschatological figure, which led to the idea of a "second Adam."[35] Linking the title "Son of Man" to a second-Adam theology can make sense of the Gospels' use of the term in eschatological contexts, while focus on the dominion given to Adam at creation makes sense of the term's use in reference to the authority and ministry of Christ, and the fall of Adam makes sense of the need for the second Adam to die.[36]

The Adamic sense of the title "Son of Man" suits and clarifies a theology of recapitulation. Irenaeus links "Son of Man" to a second Adam,[37] and this

30. Cortés and Gatti, "Son of Adam," 466; Marcus, "Son of Man as Son of Adam," 40. Cortés and Gatti note that Colwell's rule might provide a grammatical basis for the single exception, though it must be admitted that Colwell's rule is itself debated. See Cortés and Gatti, "Son of Adam," 468.

31. Marcus, "Son of Man as Son of Adam," 41.

32. Marcus, "Son of Man as Son of Adam," 45. This is especially true since there was already occasional conceptual overlap between the concept of the Son of Man and Adam. Marcus notes two chief examples: 1 En. 62:7 links "the Son of Man" with being the offspring of Eve, and the Syriac of 4 Ezra 8:44 says the Son of Man was fashioned directly by God and bore his image, traits typically linked with Adam. Marcus, "Son of Man as Son of Adam," 46.

33. Cortés and Gatti, "Son of Adam," 469–70.

34. As Brandon Crowe puts it, "The son of man in Daniel is the fulfiller of the Adamic task of ruling in God's image." See the discussion in Crowe, *Last Adam*, 39.

35. Cullmann, *Christology of the New Testament*, 140–45.

36. Marcus, "Son of Man as Son of Adam," 48–49.

37. Irenaeus, *Against Heresies* 5.21.1.

interpretation was widespread in the patristic and medieval eras.[38] Here we find exegetical support for the broad contours of Irenaeus's theology. Yet it must be recognized that patristic treatments of recapitulation were not always sufficiently eschatological. The recapitulation begun through the Son's assumption of humanity in the incarnation is the dawn of the new age, and so Christ's preaching was characterized by the basic message, "The time is fulfilled, and the kingdom of God has come near. Repent and believe the good news!" (Mark 1:15). Recapitulation is not only a restoration of humanity but the firstfruits of the redemption of a creation that groans in anticipation of its full eschatological renewal (Rom. 8:19–25).

Second-Adam Christology is not restricted to the title "Son of Man" but is found throughout the New Testament, sometimes subtly and sometimes with vivid clarity. When Luke 3:38 calls Adam "son of God," it may be making a connection between Christ and Adam.[39] While Adam had breath/spirit (the Hebrew could reference either) put into him by God (Gen. 2:7), Christ receives a special outpouring of the Spirit at his baptism. The transfiguration may intend to reflect the deity of Christ, but it may also reflect "Jewish and Christian traditions, in which Adam in his prelapsarian state was clothed in divine glory," explains Brandon Crowe.[40] In John 19:5, Pilate presents Jesus to the crowds, saying, "Behold, the Man!" (NASB). This may also intend a comparison to Adam, alluding to the Hebrew of Genesis 3:22, "Behold, the man has become like one of Us" (NASB). The statement is ironic in Genesis, for Adam is about to be cast out of Eden. It is ironic in John 19:5 as well, for the crucifixion reveals Christ is not a mere man but is divine, truly like his Father (see John 12:23; 13:31; 17:11 and their reference to the Son being glorified through the cross).[41] Second-Adam Christology is most clear, however, in Paul's antitheses between Christ and Adam (Rom. 5:12–21; 1 Cor. 15:22, 45–49). This example of second-Adam Christology brings us to the doctrine of original sin.

The Doctrine of Original Sin

In brief, the doctrine of original sin explains that the universal sinful state of humanity is a result of the free actions of Adam in disobeying the divine command to not eat of the tree of the knowledge of good and evil. The dogmatic function of this claim is threefold. First, it protects the goodness

38. Burkett, *Son of Man Debate*, 7–11.
39. Crowe, *Last Adam*, 29.
40. Crowe, *Last Adam*, 49. Crowe notes Sir. 49:16; Apoc. Mos. 20:1–2; 21:2, 6; 2 En. 30:11–14; Apoc. Adam 1:2. Like me, Crowe thinks the transfiguration may more clearly reference divine glory.
41. See Litwa, "Behold Adam."

of God by insisting that creation was originally very good (Gen. 1:31) while also taking seriously the problem of evil.[42] Second, the doctrine of original sin describes the contemporary situation as one of fundamental estrangement from God, such that all human beings are in some sense trapped in sin (see Rom. 3:9–19). I use the word "describes" advisedly, for as Ian McFarland notes, the doctrine of original sin does not necessarily *explain* the universal and fundamental condition of human depravity in a detailed metaphysical manner, a fact that explains the variety in theories of the transmission of original sin that will be addressed later in this chapter.[43] Instead, the doctrine of original sin locates the problem of sin after the fall within human agency itself as that agency's precondition, not merely as a subsequent effect of an individual's misuse of their agency.[44] Third, and perhaps most importantly, by insisting on the universality of sin, the doctrine of original sin also demonstrates the universal need for grace, without which salvation is impossible. This third dimension of universal sin was of decisive importance in the rejection of **Pelagianism** by Augustine, who was widely seen as the first theologian to develop a full doctrine of original sin. In Augustine's words, "Whoever maintains that human nature at any period required not the second Adam for its physician, because it was not corrupted in the first Adam, is convicted as an enemy of the grace of God."[45] The doctrine of original sin finds a degree of scriptural support in the Bible's emphasis on the universality of sin and on passages that suggest the existence of sins in individuals before actual sins are committed.[46] It also finds some limited support in passages that speak of the creaturely impossibility of bringing something good out of something evil (e.g., Job 14:4; Matt. 7:16–19; John 3:6). Nevertheless, the central passages in any doctrine of original sin must be Genesis 3 and Romans 5:12–21.

The third chapter of Genesis narrates what is commonly called "the fall," providing more support for the doctrine of original sin than is often recognized. Though Genesis 3 does not depict the tempting serpent as Satan, nor does it ascribe an ontological deterioration of human nature as a result of the fall, a proper reading of Genesis 3 in canonical context reinforces both

---

42. In the words of Dumitru Stăniloae, "Only the Christian explanation that evil has its origin in freedom avoids linking evil to the essence of reality—whether reality as eternal or understood as that created by God—while at the same time taking it seriously." Stăniloae, *Experience of God*, 2:148.

43. McFarland, *In Adam's Fall*, 47.

44. McFarland, *In Adam's Fall*, 9–10.

45. Augustine of Hippo, *On the Grace of Christ* 2.34. Augustine is not alone in this position. See also Aquinas, *On Evil* Q. 4, A. 1; Wiley, *Original Sin*, 4; J. Smith, "What Stands on the Fall?"

46. See the discussion in Blocher, *Original Sin*, 20–25.

claims.[47] God had warned that eating the fruit of the tree of the knowledge of good and evil would result in death (2:17), and the question of whether death would truly occur is central to the serpent's line of questioning (3:4).[48] Though God, by grace, delays any biological death after their disobedience, Genesis is certainly clear that Adam and Eve will die, by the recurring reference to "all the days of your life" (3:14, 17), by the promise that Adam will "return to the ground" (3:19), and by the confirmation in the genealogies that Adam did, in fact, die (5:5). The transition from a creation that is "very good" (1:31) to one marked by death can rightly be said to include an ontological change from incorruption to corruption. By corruption, I refer at the least to mortality,[49] but there is also good reason to interpret Genesis as depicting a new proclivity toward sin and evil. In the Genesis narrative, sin expands to Adam's offspring—it is with good reason that many interpreters across Christian history have understood Adam's begetting Seth in his own image (5:3) to suggest transmission of a corrupted nature. Adam's descendants are mired in sin, to the point that God declares them "corrupt" (6:3) and having evil inclination of the mind (6:5), both concepts suggesting a moral decay of human nature.[50] Subsequent biblical interpretation of the event sees Adam and Eve's sin as a matter of culpability[51] but also as the fruit of Satan's work, who is the liar and bringer of death from the beginning (John 8:44) depicted as a great serpent in Revelation 12:9 and 20:2.

The doctrine of original sin rests especially on Romans 5:12–21, a passage complexified by the fact that Paul's initial comparison in 5:12, "Therefore, just as sin entered the world through one man, and death through sin, in this way death spread to all people, because all sinned," lacks any completing clause

47. John Toews objects that there is no "fall" in Gen. 3, arguing that "there is no hint that Adam's moral condition is fundamentally changed by his act of disobedience or that his essential human or genetic nature was essentially altered." Further, Toews argues that the Gen. 3 account defines sin in "relational, not ontological terms." I grant to Toews, however, two points. First, there is no sexual dimension to the fall, contrary to some later Christian developments. Second, the term "the fall" was not used until Methodius of Olympus in the late third century, though the absence of the word does not entail the absence of the concept. Toews, *Story of Original Sin*, 12–14.

48. Interpreters like Herbert Haag who see this merely as a warning of the death penalty and not of the introduction of death as a principle miss the fact that death is not easily reconciled with the goodness of creation. See Haag, *Is Original Sin in Scripture?*, 88.

49. Here I reject conditional immortality that treats death as the default and eternal life as a contingent gift of God.

50. In later theology, corruption was taken to suggest an ontological deterioration of the nature, while inclinations may suggest a new orientation away from God toward human desires.

51. In the Old Testament, there are hints of Adam's culpability, perhaps most clearly (yet still contestably) in Ps. 82:7 and Job 31:33. See Blocher, *Original Sin*, 45–46. Rom. 5, as we will see, is even clearer on this point.

with the expected introduction "so also." This is one of several factors leading to considerable variety in the doctrine of original sin. Nevertheless, a clear sense of Paul's basic meaning is discernible, even if many details are up for debate. Some interpret Paul to be saying in 5:12 that all die because of their own sins, as if Adam were merely a pattern repeated in history.[52] This was the interpretation of Pelagius in the fifth century.[53] This interpretation would deny any doctrine of original sin at all. However, such an interpretation is not tenable given Paul's later regular emphasis on *one sin* from *one man*: "By the one man's trespass the many died" (5:15), "From one sin came the judgment, resulting in condemnation" (5:16), "By the one man's trespass, death reigned through that one man" (5:17), "Through one trespass there is condemnation for everyone" (5:18), and "Through one man's disobedience the many were made sinners" (5:19). Clearly, the emphasis of the passage is a contrast between Christ and his antitype, Adam, whose singular sin brought about death, condemnation, a condition that is rectified by Christ's "grace" (5:15, 17) and singular "righteous act" (5:18) leading to our "**justification**" unto life (*dikaiōsin zōēs*—5:18) and our being "made righteous" (*dikaioi katastathēsontai*—5:19). It is simply untenable to interpret Adam as the mere historical originator of sin with no connection to future generations' sin, condemnation, and death.[54] Rather, many interpreters affirm a "paradoxical" view where both Adam and individual humans are responsible for the sinful condition of the world.[55] To speak in the terms of systematic theology, Adam is responsible for **originating original sin** (*peccatum originale originans*)—he is the one man with the one trespass. We are all under the influence of **original sin as originated** (*peccatum originale originatum*), being condemned and sinning, but as a result also committing actual sins for which we are culpable—"all sinned" (5:12).

If we cannot minimize our connection with Adam, so, too, we must be careful to not overstate the connection. Some have taken the Greek phrase *eph hō* (rendered "because" in the CSB translation of 5:12: "because all sinned") to mean "in whom all sinned," referencing Adam.[56] There is good reason to

---

52. For example, Haag, *Is Original Sin in Scripture?*, 95–100.

53. For a brief summary of Pelagius, see Wiley, *Original Sin*, 67–71.

54. There is considerable agreement on this point. See, for example, Blocher, *Original Sin*, 67; Moo, *Romans*, 323; Dunn, *Romans 1–8*, 273–74; Murray, *Imputation of Adam's Sin*, 19.

55. The word "paradoxical" is explicit in Jewett, *Romans*, 376; Käsemann, *Commentary on Romans*, 140–41. See also Dunn, *Romans 1–8*, 274. Dunn speaks of a need to "balance" individual responsibility with hereditary factors.

56. Richard Longenecker breaks down possible translations of *eph hō* into four categories: (1) "in whom" (meaning Adam), (2) "under which circumstances," (3) "because" or "since," and (4) "for this reason." Longenecker, *Romans*, 587–89. As is well known, Augustine worked with the Latin Vulgate, which had translated *eph hō* into the Latin *in quo* (in whom).

doubt this translation[57] and the belief that Christians sinned in Adam semi-
nally as if they were present in him when he sinned. This typical theory takes
our presence in Adam quite literally. Anselm of Canterbury, for example,
writes that "everything that comes from a seed exists in seeds" such that
"infants were in Adam when he sinned."[58] Admittedly, Paul is willing to say
elsewhere that "in Adam all die" (1 Cor. 15:22), but this can be taken in less
literal ways. Furthermore, the author of Hebrews seems to rely on a theory of
seminal presence in ancestors to argue for the superiority of the priesthood of
Melchizedek over the Aaronic priesthood, stating that Levi gave an offering to
Melchizedek through Abraham's offering, since Levi was "still within his ancestor when Melchizedek met him" (Heb. 7:9–10). Modern scholarship tends
to read this phrase as an oblique reference to ancestry or collective identity
and not to the complete biological presence of Abraham's descendants within
him.[59] Something of the theological position of our seminal presence in Adam
could remain. However, such seminal presence is not explicit in the text or
demanded by it, leaving us with the puzzling question of how Adam's sin
results in our current state of sinfulness. The tradition has offered abundant
explanations, some noteworthy examples of which I turn to consider now.

THEORIES OF ADAMIC HEADSHIP IN CHRISTIAN TRADITION

I will categorize versions of the doctrine of original sin based on how they
explain the relationship between Adam's sin as something foreign to us and
our own actual sins that are proper to us.[60] To put the matter another way, the
largest puzzle is how originating original sin is related to original sin as originated. This relationship can be further subdivided into two questions. First,
what is the effect of Adam's sin on all human beings? Against Pelagianism,
all versions of original sin hold that Adam's sin has some lasting impact,
but the specific nature of this lasting effect is up for debate. Second, what
is the mechanism by which all human beings are connected to Adam's sin?
Granting that there is some lasting effect, theologians are regularly concerned
with the question of *why* this is so. While there is general consensus, at least
in the Catholic and Protestant traditions, that there is some effect, there has
never been consensus on the mechanism by which Adam's sin is passed to all

57. Fitzmyer argues that "Adam" as an antecedent would be too far away from the phrase.
Plus, a more natural prepositional phrase would be *en hō* to express the meaning "in Adam."
Fitzmyer, *Romans*, 414. On this point, he has persuaded many, such as Longenecker, *Romans*,
587; Jewett, *Romans*, 375–76.
58. Anselm of Canterbury, *Virgin Conception and Original Sin* §23.
59. See Peeler, *Hebrews*, 190; Grindheim, *Letter to the Hebrews*, 348, 350.
60. I draw the centrality of this question from the helpful insights of Berkouwer, *Sin*, 432.

humanity, except in the most general details. I should note that these questions, which are already marked by complex exegetical and doctrinal issues, are further complicated in recent discussion by their entanglement with scientific questions about human origins and descent.[61] Given the speculative nature of solutions given to the scientific dimension of the problem of original sin and noting the rapid development of science, which demands ever-changing dialogue between science and theology (not to mention my own limits in scientific knowledge), these questions must lie beyond a dogmatic treatment like the one I am attempting to present.[62] Nevertheless, many resources are available to the interested reader for further consideration.[63]

Typically, three possible effects of Adam's sin on his posterity are considered. **Original corruption**, sometimes called "**original pollution**," treats the fall as the sufficient reason for all humans to have a corrupted nature prone to sin.[64] Often, such corruption is linked with a broken will. As Ian McFarland explains, "To have a fallen will is to *be* a sinner, because, unlike Jesus, who is divine as well as human, we have no pre-existing ontological leverage that allows us to turn our fallen wills to the good."[65] Original corruption is evident in Old Testament metaphors about sin being written on the heart (Jer. 17:1), or our hearts being uncircumcised (6:10; 9:25), or in references to the heart being of stone (Ezek. 11:19).[66] Each metaphor suggests that sins emerge from a prior condition of sinfulness. **Original guilt** may be suggested by Ephesians 2:3: "We were by nature children under wrath." Some argue that a better translation is "wrathful children,"[67] which would negate any idea of original guilt. However, a better interpretation sees the phrase as a

61. For example, evolutionary theories posit an original community rather than an original pair, and they assume that biological death was an important component of evolutionary development long before the original human community.

62. Dogmatic theology cannot remain blind to scientific questions, but neither can it be bound by the dictates of modern science. Were this a chapter focused on an in-depth study of original sin and not a chapter focused on original sin as it reveals second-Adam Christology, there would be need to dig into these important scientific questions. However, the christological angle of this chapter will aim merely to provide certain dogmatic parameters that must be maintained in any analysis of the doctrine's compatibility (or lack thereof) with scientific theories.

63. For example, see Cavanaugh and Smith, *Evolution and the Fall*; Houck, *Aquinas, Original Sin*; Madueme and Reeves, *Adam, the Fall, and Original Sin*.

64. In modern theology, see Berkhof, *Systematic Theology*, 246; McCall, *Against God and Nature*, 159. Berkhof uses "original pollution" and McCall "original corruption."

65. McFarland, *In Adam's Fall*, 145.

66. Blocher, *Original Sin*, 20–21.

67. See Grenz, *Theology for the Community of God*, 203–4. Grenz argues that "children" (*teknon*) plus an "abstract noun" is a Hebraism, such as "children of light" (Eph. 5:8) and children of wisdom (Matt. 11:19), meaning "persons characterized by" light, wisdom, or, in this case, wrath.

genitive of destination: "The coming wrath is the inevitable destination of those living in fleshly desires."[68] The context of Ephesians 2:4–5, "But God, who is rich in mercy . . . made us alive with Christ even though we were dead in trespasses," also suggests a mercy (the nonapplication of punishment) that stands in contrast to the wrath we would be under by nature. Condemnation is clearly in mind, but what is less clear is that the phrase "children of wrath" intends literal children, given that the audience of the epistle would be adults.[69] The doctrine of original guilt will require a more sturdy foundation than this verse alone. Finally, original sin may have resulted in a loss of **original righteousness**, a grace-given empowerment of Adam and Eve's human nature to goodness. As Anselm of Canterbury explains, Adam's nature "lost the grace given to it which it was always able to keep for those to be propagated from it."[70] This grace gave humans the ability to act according to God's will, so any removal of this grace results in guaranteed sinfulness.[71]

The concept of original guilt seems plausible in the larger canonical, historical, and dogmatic context. Many worry that original guilt is unjust because it is wrong to condemn someone for an act they have not committed. Ian McFarland points out that the Old Testament treatment of unintentional sins (e.g., Lev. 4:2, 13, 22, 27) is evidence that "sin cannot simply be equated with conscious choice."[72] More broadly speaking, Walther Eichrodt notes that the regular prophetic corporate condemnation of the entire nation of Israel

> strips each individual action of all contingent circumstances, and allows it to be seen in the full import of its guilt as a reinforcement of the corporate anti-God attitude of the nation, thus convicting men of a *common involvement of all its members* in the transgression of the divine will. What is more, there is also a vision of *all mankind as associated in sin*, inasmuch as the prophetic proclamation of judgment reproaches the Gentile world as well with thoroughgoing rebellion against God's will, and so calls it to account, together with Israel, before his universal assize.[73]

Such collective guilt fits with the notion that all are guilty from birth, linking our condemnation in Romans 5:16 directly to Adam's sin and not indirectly, as

68. Campbell, *Ephesians*, 87.

69. See M. Barth, *Ephesians*, 231. Though Barth goes too far in denying original sin altogether, his interpretation does suggest the limited weight that Eph. 2:3 can bear on this question.

70. Anselm of Canterbury, *Virgin Conception and Original Sin* §10.

71. A helpful brief summary can be found in Wiley, *Original Sin*, 79–82.

72. McFarland, *In Adam's Fall*, 7. A similar point is made with respect to Num. 15:27 and following in Blocher, *Original Sin*, 25.

73. Eichrodt, *Theology of the Old Testament*, 397.

if we are condemned because Adam's sin leads to original corruption, which leads to our actual sins and through those sins to guilt.[74] Paul is certainly not the first Jewish interpreter to see in Genesis 3 an explanation for the current and universal human predicament, as Second Temple texts like 4 Ezra, 2 Baruch, and Life of Adam and Eve treat Adam as the source of all death and/or all future human corruption.[75] However, Paul's theology apparently leads to a decisive shift. In 4 Ezra, for example, Adam is clearly seen as having a lasting effect on his descendants: "O Adam, what have you done? For though it was you who sinned, the fall was not yours alone, but ours also who are your descendants" (4 Ezra 7:48[118]). However, in 4 Ezra this wretched inheritance is offset by the hope of being "victorious" (7:59[129]) in the "contest which every man who is born on earth shall wage" (7:57–58[127–28]). The victory itself is achieved by choosing life (7:59–60[129–30]), with a clear recognition that God shows mercy and grace "to those who turn in repentance to his law" (7:63[133]). In 4 Ezra, Adam bestows corruption and sinful acts on his progeny because we break the law, but the same law offers grace through righteous acts and devout sacrifice. Though Paul would agree with 4 Ezra that God is gracious and merciful, he argues that the law itself cannot justify (Rom. 3:20–21). In Romans 5:13, we read that "sin is not charged to a person's account when there is no law," meaning that the law itself illuminates sin and increases condemnation (7:7–11). For Paul, grace is accessible through the second Adam who gifts "justification" (5:16, 18) and "life" (5:17, 21). Since Adam is a "type of the Coming One" (5:14), the benefit of imputed righteousness through Christ suggests an imputed guilt as the best explanation of our "condemnation" arising from Adam (5:16, 18).[76]

Imputed guilt immediately raises an important question, expressed simply in the words of Oliver Crisp: "How is it moral for me to suffer for the sin of a long dead ancestor?"[77] To make the issue a bit more pointed, we might ask, How is it moral for infants who die to be viewed as guilty? It is ironic that a doctrine intended to preserve the goodness of God by insisting that humans created sin is often thought to jeopardize that very goodness. While there is dogmatic consensus among theologians that God is good and biblical attestations of divine goodness are manifold, we are far from any consensus on the

---

74. This is called mediate **imputation**.

75. A helpful brief summary of these texts can be found in Green, "Adam, What Have You Done?," 100–104. There are many relevant briefer references throughout Second Temple literature. Tim Gabrielson helpfully explains, "Many times the primeval history is present with other symbols: Eve, the tree of life, a conniving serpent, a fruit—usually the fig or grape was specified—that imparts sin." Gabrielson, *Primeval History According to Paul*, 95–96.

76. This perspective is argued in Murray, *Imputation of Adam's Sin*, 40–41.

77. Crisp, "Sin," 201.

resolution to this particular puzzle. Where some are content to reject original guilt or even original sin itself, many strategies for defending God's goodness are available. At the time of the Pelagian debates, the doctrine of original sin was seen to be a necessary correlate of infant baptism, which was understood to wash away guilt inherited from Adam.[78] Though infant baptism and its connection to regeneration are far more contested today, this may be a divine provision for infants to protect them from guilt. However, this just pushes questions of God's justice back to the doctrine of providence by forcing the question, Why are some born in non-Christian contexts where baptism is not available? Another solution to this dilemma could be to embrace **universalism** or else to accept the possibility of postmortem conversion, options for which I see no biblical warrant. Others have argued that infants are not held accountable for their guilt until they reach an age of accountability, a position that results in something of a paradoxical view of original guilt. Our current focus prevents us from fully resolving this theological puzzle, except to affirm that there are good theological reasons to affirm the goodness of God and the doctrine of original sin, including original guilt. Perhaps we are merely left, like Job, with questions that will receive an answer only at the Father's final appearance, and that answer itself may be only partial. Without denying the importance of further exploring this issue for apologetic and pastoral ends, a dogmatic account of original sin can go no further down this path but must instead consider theories of the transmission of original sin.

Perhaps the most straightforward account of the transmission of original sin relies on biological descent. John Calvin puts the matter simply: "All of us, therefore, descending from an impure seed, come into the world tainted with the contagion of sin." For scriptural warrant, he cites Job 14:4: "Who can produce something pure from what is impure? No one!"[79] Descent can easily explain original corruption, if we imagine it to be something akin to genetic traits. If the problem resides in biological matter, something like epigenetics, the situation is straightforward. However, the transmission of original corruption by descent is complexified to the extent that sin is typically thought to inhere in the soul and the manner of the reception of the soul in the fetus is questioned. **Traducianism** holds that sexual reproduction produces a new human body and soul, but other theologians contend that reproduction only produces a new body and God creates a new soul in this body.[80] If God directly

78. See, for example, Augustine of Hippo, *On Forgiveness of Sins* 1.24, 1.35, 1.55.

79. Calvin, *Institutes* 2.1.5. Though Calvin's language of Adam as "root" and of how Adam's sin "plunged our nature into like destruction" may imply realism (discussed below), it is not clear to me from the text that this is what Calvin intends. See Calvin, *Institutes* 2.1.6.

80. Wiley, *Original Sin*, 47.

creates each soul, corruption of the soul must arise from the body's influence on it, a need that can spawn complicated explanations. Nevertheless, if we adopt what Thomas McCall has called the "corruption-only" version of original sin,[81] transmission by descent is straightforward at a basic level. Original guilt could be included if we adopt a theory of seminal presence, discussed above. However, it is difficult to adopt this perspective to scientific understandings of human reproduction, leaving an explanation of original guilt wanting if mere descent is our causal explanation.

Because natural descent may not be enough to explain original guilt, other theologians have developed different theories to account for the connection between Adam and all humanity that might explain the rationale behind original guilt. **Realism** is the theory that there is a real connection between the particular natures of individual humans such that what one does, all can be said to do. Thomas Aquinas, for example, argues that biological descent is the **instrumental cause** for the transmission of original sin[82] but that descent alone cannot explain original guilt because we are not guilty of what we inherit but have not done.[83] Further, Aquinas does not understand a loss of original righteousness to be original sin; rather, such a loss is the *effect* of Adam's "turning away from the mutable good" (the formal element of originating original sin) and "turning toward a transient good" (the material element of originating original sin), which resulted in a distortion of Adam's nature.[84] Certainly without original righteousness controlling reason, the moral will, and the body, we wind up with each component infected with ignorance, malice, and concupiscence, respectively.[85] But again, having inherited such a nature, it would not be obvious that we are born with original guilt. Aquinas resolves this puzzle by arguing that "all men born of Adam may be considered as one man, inasmuch as they have one common nature, which they receive from their first parents."[86] Thus, he argues that original guilt is due not to the acts of persons but rather to the nature that sinned in Adam.[87] In defense of this he cites Ephesians 2:3, taking the passage to teach that the problem is human nature. Some realists also appeal to Hebrews 7:9–10, interpreting the passage to speak not of seminal presence but of presence in nature, but this reading depends more on realism as a presupposition than it demands

81. McCall, *Against God and Nature*, 156. McCall lists Zwingli and Arminius as examples of this perspective.

82. Aquinas, *On Evil* Q. 4, A. 3.

83. Aquinas, *Summa Theologica* I-II, Q. 81, A. 1.

84. Aquinas, *On Evil* Q. 4, A. 2.

85. See the helpful and brief summary of Aquinas's views in Wiley, *Original Sin*, 85–86.

86. Aquinas, *Summa Theologica* I-II, Q. 81, A. 1.

87. Aquinas, *On Evil* Q. 4, A. 1, R. 4.

realism as a conclusion.[88] There is a lively debate regarding whether one can truly be guilty by nature and not through personal actions,[89] the results of which may put the viability of realism in question. Further, though realism could fit with Scripture, it is not clear to me that the Bible demands it, and the philosophy of realism is much debated today.[90]

Where realism posits an ontological connection as the basis of original guilt, the theory of **federal headship** posits a legal connection as an explanation. It is clear that "Jesus has also become the guarantee of a better covenant" (Heb. 7:22). Given that Adam is a type of Christ (Rom. 5:14) and that Christ's work reverses Adam's work, many Protestants have suspected that original guilt is rooted in the imputed guilt of Adam much like our justification depends on the imputed righteousness of Christ.[91] Christ is thus our head in terms of a covenant (Latin *foedus*), a federal headship. John Wesley explains the rationale behind this theory: "Christ was the representative of mankind, when God 'laid on him the iniquities of us all, and he was wounded for our transgressions' [Isa. 53:5–6 paraphrased], but Adam was a type or figure of Christ; therefore, he was also, in some sense, our representative; in consequence of which, 'all died' in him, as 'in Christ all shall be made alive.'"[92] One might object that there is no clear covenant in Genesis 1–2, but certainly the basic features are present, including clear responsibilities (reproducing and exercising dominion in 1:28), prohibitions (not eating from the tree of the knowledge of good and evil in 2:16–17), and the punishment for violation. More substantively, Oliver Crisp raises the "authorization objection," which points out that typically representatives are authorized by those whom they represent. Noting that the Father was the authority here who appointed Christ, Crisp notes that such a solution raises the concern that God's appointment and justice are arbitrary, as there was no authorization.[93] I am not convinced that the objection fully holds. Within political theory, few actually actively consent to every detail of the existence of the state, yet political theory will regularly accept a sort of tacit or implied consent as the basis for authorization. In this case, if humans want to live in a sinful world because of their

88. Berkouwer, *Sin*, 443.

89. In the recent Reformed tradition, for example, Berkouwer admits that realism allows us to die for our own sins, but Murray argues that individuals can bear guilt for sins they did not personally commit but which were only committed in nature. See Berkouwer, *Sin*, 438–39; Murray, *Imputation of Adam's Sin*, 32–33.

90. For an interesting survey of realism and original sin in debates in contemporary analytic theology, see McCall, *Against God and Nature*, 192–96.

91. For example, Murray, *Imputation of Adam's Sin*, 16.

92. Wesley, *Doctrine of Original Sin*, 332.

93. Crisp, "Sin," 203.

love for sin, then we might affirm a sort of tacit authorization. Sinners did not choose Adam as representative, but they apparently are willing to choose daily the world that Adam our representative selected. If Adam chose what all humans *would* choose, then the authorization problem is not so devastating to the federal view of original sin.

We now turn to consider a final theory. Modern theologians often analyze original sin in the context of the social dimensions of human nature. According to Karl Rahner, for example, a person "actualizes himself [*sic*] as a free subject in a situation which itself is always determined by history and by other persons."[94] Because human history and other persons are marked by sin, human beings will inevitably sin. Taken in isolation, theories of social transmission suggest a political solution—namely, that some humans simply be removed from society to escape the malformation society brings about. The idea that social engineering can lead to perfection is Pelagian; pursuit of salvation through social engineering is not compatible with Christianity and the universal need for the grace of Christ. However, it is possible to consider the social transmission of sin to be one of several dimensions of the mechanism of transmission of original sin.[95] When this is done, it opens the door for theologians to consider original sin not only in terms of its effects on individuals but also and more accurately in terms of its influence on societies, cultures, and even the entirety of creation. The social transmission of original sin thus cannot stand on its own, but it can contribute to our understanding of recapitulation. We will have occasion to return to these theories of the transmission of original sin throughout the remainder of the book, but for now it is important to address substantive concerns about the doctrine.

Eastern Orthodox and Feminist Hesitations

Despite the general consensus regarding broad contours of the doctrine of original sin among Protestants and Roman Catholics, there are several concerns that must be addressed that will help us to name more precisely what evils we face. Eastern Orthodox theologians often raise concerns about the doctrine of original sin, generally offering a more optimistic view of human capacities against ideas like total depravity while also raising objections to satisfaction as an aspect of atonement, which is often seen as a logical

---

94. Rahner, *Foundations of Christian Faith*, 107.

95. For example, when Roger Haight argues that "sin is the condition prior to the exercise of personal freedom, constituted by the native structure of each individual and by a socially inherited second nature," he links original sin to original corruption while allowing for a second, social dimension of original sin as originated. See Haight, "Sin and Grace," 106.

consequence of original guilt.[96] A defense of satisfaction is found in chapter 8. For now, I will dwell on what I consider to be a more insightful critique. John Romanides raises concerns that original sin and the theology of the curse lead to viewing death as a punishment while missing the fact that death is an "instrument of Satan"[97] that God permits to allow an end to evil and to provide the possibility of recreating humanity through resurrection.[98] In some Orthodox accounts of the first sin, special care is made to name Satan and the personal dimensions of sin.[99] While Orthodox explanations of sin generally retain space for what the West has called original corruption, this emphasis on the demonic and personal dimensions of the fall prevents an account of original sin that is either too materialist, narrowly focusing on corruption of human nature, or too forensic, overly emphasizing the covenantal dimensions of original guilt. One might add a concept along the lines of original captivity to reference the human race's ongoing voluntary self-subjugation to Satan to maintain a more balanced position. While it must be admitted that any simple dichotomy between East and West is sure to be far too simplistic, in this case a reductionist heuristic of this nature can be illuminating for doctrinal purposes.[100]

Finally, it must be acknowledged that the transmission of original sin has been too often linked with sexual activity itself, and especially with women insofar as women prompted sexual desire from male theologians. In Augustine, for example, Adam was thought to represent rationality gone awry, but Eve was seen to represent unrestrained passions.[101] Feminists raise several concerns: "By linking the transmission of sin with sexual relations," many theories of original sin "devalued human sexuality."[102] By linking women with sexuality and desire, those same theories of original sin devalued women. Feminist theology has also tended to pay more attention to the social implications of the fall, developing theologies of **social sin** and considering the fall's implications in terms of systemic violence against those weaker in society, a category that generally includes women.[103] Feminist theology thus challenges

96. For example, see Pomazansky, *Orthodox Dogmatic Theology*, 165–68.

97. Romanides, *Ancestral Sin*, 103.

98. Romanides, *Ancestral Sin*, 158.

99. Consider Lossky, *Dogmatic Theology*, 95–99.

100. For example, see Anatolios, *Deification Through the Cross*, 50–52. Anatolios provides evidence of legal dimensions of sin in the Byzantine liturgy, a fact that serves as a counterweight to some modern Orthodox concerns about the covenantal and legal understanding of original guilt.

101. See the discussion in Komline, *Augustine on the Will*, 59–60.

102. Wiley, *Original Sin*, 207.

103. For example, see Gebara, *Out of the Depths*; Suchocki, *Fall to Violence*.

a complete christological dogmatics to attend to the social implications of sin and to the ways that theology has oppressed women.

Dogmatic Summary

The doctrine of recapitulation, in its basic dogmatic structure, links the fundamental problem facing humanity and all of creation to a reversal provided through Jesus Christ, the Son of God incarnate. The salvific recapitulation found in Christ begins in the incarnation and is the soteriological dimension of the christological affirmation of the Son's kenosis and assumption of humanity. It is no surprise that the discussion of kenosis in Philippians 2 likely includes allusions to Adam, who grasped at what was not his, in contrast to the eternal Son's refusal to "exploit," "grasp," or "cling to" the equality he shared with God from eternity (Phil. 2:6).[104] The reversal that is recapitulation finds its efficient cause in the mission of the Son as it extends from kenosis through the state of humiliation of Christ's ministry and the cross into the glories of the resurrection. Its formal cause is the assumption of a restored human nature, which becomes available to the believer through the working of the Holy Spirit. The doctrine of original sin is best seen as a subset of recapitulation since Christ's work in establishing himself as a new head of his church (Eph. 5:23; Col. 1:18) and of all things (Eph. 1:22; Col. 2:10) suggests that there was an old head of humanity that is being replaced. The doctrine of original sin functions to ensure that all stand in need of the grace offered by this new head and second Adam, Jesus Christ. While the exact means of transmission of original sin and of explaining its effects remain open to disagreement, there are good dogmatic reasons for all Christians to reject the Pelagian position and any theory that reduces the transmission of original sin to a result of intercourse construed as evil. It is also clear that the mechanism of transmission is more than (but not exclusive of) the negative influences of society. I find good reasons to accept original guilt as an important component of original sin, with some caution, even as the mechanism of God's gracious provision for infants remains open to debate. Ultimately, it is certain that Christ's incarnation initiates the eschatological reversal of whatever effect Adam's originating original sin has on humanity. If we bear corruption from Adam, Christ's incarnation opens a path to incorruptibility. If we bear Adam's guilt, Christ offers his righteousness. Where Adam is seen as our representative in an old covenant or as polluter of our natures, Christ must be seen as our representative in a new covenant and as purifier

---

104. These translations are from the CSB, ESV/NASB, and NLT, respectively.

of our humanity. While the full details of the fruits of recapitulation remain to be explored in subsequent chapters, as does the mechanism of atonement by which we can participate in these fruits, it is clear that the second Adam opens for us the possibility of a future beatific state in a new creation that exceeds the Edenic conditions of the first creation.

Recapitulation in Modern Contexts

The theology of recapitulation has faced challenges in modern theology, two of which must be addressed at the end of this chapter.

Modern Criticism of Recapitulation

James Cone, the patriarch of Black liberation theology, worries that the Irenaean dictum that Christ "was made man that we might be made god" neglects the "concrete history of Jesus of Nazareth." An allegedly other-worldly soteriology that determines Christology results from this theology of **divinization**, and Cone finds it no surprise that this theology was so popular in the early church that was long the "favored religion" of the Roman and Byzantine state. Cone believes this theology of recapitulation explains why "the Nicene Fathers showed little interest in the Christological significance of Jesus' deeds for the humiliated."[105] In Cone's mind, recapitulation is the theology of oppressive empire. We could certainly contest the argument at the level of historical analysis, pointing to the theologies of justice found in the pro-Nicenes,[106] or exploring how the roots of the theology of recapitulation and divinization begin in an era when Christians were a victimized minority more prone to martyrdom by the Roman Empire than leadership in it. However, it is often the case that a narrative of decline of this sort is more concerned to illustrate the contemporary situation than to detail history accurately.[107] Perhaps we should charitably read Cone first and foremost as diagnosing a potential problem with any theology of recapitulation today: It can neglect the social dimensions of sin.

105. Cone, *God of the Oppressed*, 106.
106. On which, see Avila, *Ownership*.
107. "The paradox to be fully accepted is that when a certain historical moment is (mis)perceived as the moment of loss of some quality, upon closer inspection it becomes clear that the lost quality emerged only at this very moment of its alleged loss." Žižek, *Plague of Fantasies*, 12–13. It may be the case that the lack of historical and social transformation purportedly found in the patristic era is evident partly due to the emergence of more sophisticated critiques of the Roman Empire, moving beyond a simple ethic of pacifism into a metaphysical system that challenged the dominant social order and yet was still unable to fully overcome that same empire.

Similarly, Jon Sobrino argues that Irenaeus's theology of recapitulation "makes no impact in Latin America" for several reasons. Most significantly, while he acknowledges that Irenaeus had some vision of a recapitulation of all of history in an eschatological kingdom, Sobrino argues that patristic accounts of recapitulation theology quickly became detached from creation and oriented toward transformation of an abstract metaphysical nature.[108] The solution, Sobrino explains, would require a theology more attuned to salvation in history, to the plural as well as the individual, and to concrete actions of solidarity with the poor.[109] To put it another way, since the early theology of recapitulation has allegedly been abstracted from historical significance, Sobrino concludes that "the patristic age offers no help." What is needed is a new starting point for Christology and soteriology.

Recapitulation in Robert Clarence Lawson

Robert Clarence Lawson, a first-generation Pentecostal theologian, develops a particularly interesting theology of recapitulation in the context of white supremacy in the United States. To understand his theology, we must understand one trend in white-supremacist exegesis. One of the most important texts used to justify practices of colonialism, slavery, and Jim Crow segregation was what is known as the **Hamaitic curse**.[110] In Genesis 9:18–28, Noah plants a vineyard, gets drunk, and passes out naked. "Ham, the father of Canaan" (9:22) sees this and does nothing, but Shem and Japheth, Noah's other two sons, cover their father. When he wakes, Noah curses Canaan, saying, "He will be the lowest of slaves to his brothers" (9:25), blessing both Shem and Japheth but repeating twice "Let Canaan be Shem's slave" (9:26, 27). The passage was a favorite among white supremacists, slaveholders, and architects of colonization, who connected the passage to the table of nations (Gen. 10:6–14; 1 Chron. 1:8–16) to link Ham to Africa and argue that the African descendants of Ham are cursed, justifying their enslavement by white Europeans allegedly descended from Japheth.[111] Given that the sin committed by Ham was somewhat unclear, wild speculative theories were developed

---

108. Sobrino, *Christ the Liberator*, 234–35. Sobrino denies that patristic Christology can truly be popular in Latin America, at least in the sense of the "life, hope, praxis, and mission of the community," helping it "grow, work, struggle, and even produce life" (231).

109. Sobrino, *Christ the Liberator*, 236.

110. This curse is strangely named given that Canaan is actually cursed. This name reflects the fact that Ham is the one who acted wrongly and to show that the curse was used to justify the oppression and enslavement of all of Ham's descendants.

111. For an extensive but not exhaustive list of sources drawing on the curse of Ham in American society, see Goldenberg, *Black and Slave*, 218–37.

suggesting that Ham had committed some kind of sexual sin. Such speculation was then used to further denigrate African Americans as promiscuous or
otherwise sexually immoral.[112] As Cain Hope Felder explains, use of the curse
of Ham is an example of sacralization, "the transposing of an ideological
concept into a tenet of religious faith (or a theological justification) in order
to serve the vested interest of a particular ethnic/racial group."[113]

The curse of Ham was not restricted in its use to a North American context. Consider the example of the 1994 Rwandan genocide, in which the
Hutu ethnic group killed an estimated 750,000 Tutsis. The Hamaitic curse
was introduced to Africa during the colonial period as a legitimizing basis for
exploiting Africans.[114] However, it took a peculiar twist when the ruling Tutsis
were said to have originated in the Caucasus, having later moved into Rwanda.
To some interpreters, this suggested that the Tutsi were descended from Ham,
while the Hutu and Twa (a numerically smaller group) were subhuman and
not related to Noah.[115] Josias Semujanga has called Tutsi supremacists' appeal to the curse the "myth of Ham upside down," and it was reinforced
by religious leaders and local churches and used to justify Tutsi oppression
of the Hutu.[116] When socialism began to influence the Hutu, revolutionary
movements incorporated the theme of resisting Hamite invaders, becoming a
factor in the genocide.[117] After the genocide, some Tutsi wrote defenses of their
peoples' origination in Rwanda, rejecting or downplaying the idea that they
were Hamaitic outsiders.[118] Semujanga summarizes: "The birth and evolution
of the Hamite stereotype is one of the essential elements of the progressive
transformation of African societies by the process of colonization."[119]

There are many good reasons to reject the idea of the curse of Ham, including
but not limited to the violence and injustice it was prone to produce. The idea of
the curse of Ham was also widely critiqued on exegetical grounds. It was given
by a "newly awakened drunken man," not by God.[120] The fact that Canaan is
cursed, not Ham, argues against the possibility of the curse being valid, given

112. Felder, "Race, Racism, and the Biblical Narratives," 131–32.
113. Felder, "Race, Racism, and the Biblical Narratives," 128–29.
114. Semujanga, *Origins of Rwandan Genocide*, 112–14.
115. Mayerson, *On the Path to Genocide*, 105–6.
116. Mayerson, *On the Path to Genocide*, 108; Semujanga, *Origins of Rwandan Genocide*,
117–18.
117. Linden and Linden note that the Hamaitic explanation of the Tutsi was accomplished
initially through Belgian and Tutsi historiography, but eventually the theme of resistance to
Hamite invaders was the fruit of more socialist influence among the Hutu. Linden and Linden,
Church and Revolution in Rwanda, 2–8.
118. See, for example, efforts in Mujawiyera, *Rwandan Tutsis*, 17–22.
119. Semujanga, *Origins of Rwandan Genocide*, 128.
120. Ward, *Autobiography*, quoted in Goldenberg, *Black and Slave*, 149.

its apparent injustice. In any event, Genesis names the descendants of Canaan as peoples in the Levant (Gen. 10:15–19), not African peoples who would be more easily associated with Put (Libya) and Cush (Ethiopia).[121] If the curse is, in fact, valid, the purpose of Genesis was likely targeted to Canaanites, not Africans, given the political context in which the book was written.[122] It is against this background that Robert Clarence Lawson develops a theological response to racist uses of the curse of Ham that drew on a theology of recapitulation.

Lawson provides a forceful challenge to the segregationist theology of the Hamaitic curse in his pamphlet "The Anthropology of Jesus Christ Our Kinsman," which argues that in Christ the three Noahic lines of the human race are reunited to establish the possibility of redemption.[123] Lawson offers a close reading of the Old Testament to show that Ham, Shem, and Japheth were all ancestors of Christ. In some cases, we know of broad patterns of intermarriage between Canaanites and Israelites (e.g., Judg. 3:5–6). In other cases, we know of specific intermarriage, as when Miriam and Aaron objected to Moses marrying a Cushite (Num. 12:1).[124] Such cases dispel the myth of a racially pure Jewish bloodline. More tellingly, within the Matthean genealogy of Christ itself Lawson identifies three examples of wives of the line of Ham: Tamar the Canaanite (Matt. 1:3), Rahab the Canaanite (Matt. 1:5; Josh. 2), and Bathsheba, presumed to be Hittite (Matt. 1:6).[125] Lawson identifies Ruth the Moabite as Japhethic.[126] As a Jew, Jesus would clearly be descended from Shem. Therefore, God accomplished his plan "to mingle and inter-mingle the blood of the three branches to produce the best and most perfect man."[127]

Lawson emphasizes two major implications of the Son's birth into all three Noahic lines. First, Lawson challenges white supremacy by arguing, "If our

121. For these identifications, see Wenham, *Genesis 1–15*, 221.

122. S. Johnson, *Myth of Ham*, 28.

123. Lawson, "Anthropology of Jesus Christ Our Kinsman."

124. Lawson, "Anthropology of Jesus Christ Our Kinsman," 22.

125. Lawson, "Anthropology of Jesus Christ Our Kinsman," 29–31. Lawson notes that Judah found wives for himself and his family among the Canaanites (see Gen. 38:2, 6), such that Tamar is Canaanite. Lawson appears to assume that Bathsheba was also Hittite like her husband Uriah. In 1 Chron. 3:5 she is named Bathshua, a name that could be of Canaanite provenance (see 1 Chron. 2:3) or linked with a Mesopotamian people (see Ezek. 23:23). This is largely speculative. On the other hand, when Bathshua is identified as the daughter of Eliam as well as the wife of Uriah the Hittite, it might be with the intent to identify her as an Israelite and not a Hittite. Uriah (Yong-Hwan) Kim, "Uriah the Hittite," 77. Alternately, it has been suggested that the variant spelling of Bathsheba (Bathshua) was an attempt by the Chronicler to link David with Judah's family, including his wife Bathshua in 1 Chron. 2:3, not relevant to determining her lineage. See Sparks, *Chronicler's Genealogies*, 242.

126. Lawson, "Anthropology of Jesus Christ Our Kinsman," 31.

127. Lawson, "Anthropology of Jesus Christ Our Kinsman," 27. In certain respects, Lawson's treatment of the genealogies mirrors that of Irenaeus in *Against Heresies* 3.22.3.

Lord would return to the earth again in the flesh, and would go down South incognito, he would be jim-crowed and segregated."[128] (Note that he wrote this in 1925.) Prejudice against any ethnicity is prejudice against Christ.[129] Second, Christ's recapitulation of all branches of humanity in himself is a necessary precondition for redemption. Where Irenaeus shows that Christ recapitulates "all Adam's progeny,"[130] Lawson situates this within the context of a racialized society by arguing that Christ recapitulates all races descended from Adam. Where the Hamaitic curse had been used to "encode 'others' as illegitimate," to use the words of Sylvester Johnson,[131] Lawson develops a theology that denies any peoples are illegitimate and cut off from the family of Christ. He then expands his theology by appeal to the biblical concept of the kinsman-redeemer as seen in the book of Ruth, making the recapitulation of all peoples fundamental to salvation. Here, a kinsman-redeemer is one who as close kin can marry a widow so that she can be provided for and saved from a life of destitution. Lawson should be quoted at length here:

> Christ, in order to be a redeemer of man from sin, became a near kinsman when he looked and saw that there was none to help, and that no eye pitied, and there was no arm to save. God disrobed himself of his glory and overshadowed the Virgin Mary, a prepared vessel in whose veins flowed the blood of Japheth, and of Shem, and of Ham. For so had been the purpose and work of God in mixing the bloods of all three branches of the human race, that upon the basis of kinship, He might have the right to redeem all men.[132]

Kinsmen who cannot redeem take off their shoes (see Ruth 4:6–8), notes Lawson, and so we see major figures like Moses (Exod. 3:5) and Joshua (Josh. 5:15) being told to take off their shoes when on holy ground—they cannot redeem. John the Baptist, however, says that he is not worthy to untie the sandal of the Lord (John 1:19–27).[133] Only Christ is the true kinsman-redeemer. With this bit of typological interpretation, Lawson insists that the recapitulation of all Noahic lines in Christ is fundamental to his work of redemption. Yes, Jesus is Jewish, and thus the fulfillment of the promises to Abraham and David, but in his ancestry one also finds all lines coming from Noah, suggesting his ability to redeem universally.

128. Lawson, "Anthropology of Jesus Christ Our Kinsman," 32.
129. "Whatever race one chooses to hate, remember, our Lord is of that race—whether Semitic, Hamitic or Japhethic." Lawson, "Anthropology of Jesus Christ Our Kinsman," 47.
130. The summarizing phrase is from Minns, *Irenaeus*, 110.
131. S. Johnson, *Myth of Ham*, 18.
132. Lawson, "Anthropology of Jesus Christ Our Kinsman," 40.
133. Lawson, "Anthropology of Jesus Christ Our Kinsman," 39–40.

In Lawson we have a clear deployment of a theology of recapitulation to undermine white supremacist exegesis, to insist on equal access to Christ by all races,[134] and to denounce bigotry. More broadly, Lawson's soteriology is quite traditionally Protestant—this is not radical revisionism. His overall theology is very problematic—as a Oneness Pentecostal, Lawson rejects the doctrine of the Trinity. Yet, as a whole, Lawson's particular account of the recapitulation is insightful and biblical, except for one concern. In particular, I am concerned that Lawson adopts a race essentialism invalidated by modern genetics and that this essentialism may perpetuate the social divisions it seeks to dismember.[135] Yet Lawson's theology shows that the concerns of otherworldliness put forward by Cone and Sobrino are unwarranted. It is not just an abstract birth of Christ that matters for a proper understanding of recapitulation and incarnation but rather birth under particular historical circumstances into a particular historical life.

African Brother Ancestor Christology

While critics consider Irenaeus's theology of recapitulation to be overly Hellenized, contemporary African Brother Ancestor Christology shows that a theology of humanity's interconnectedness need not depend on a Platonic realism but can be recognized as a valid theological insight that can be contextualized in many contexts. Brother Ancestor Christology has been thoroughly developed in the theology of Charles Nyamiti. In many African cultures, Nyamiti explains, brother ancestors are those who (1) have a natural relationship with the living, (2) possess a supernatural status due to having died, (3) serve a mediatorial role, (4) regularly communicate with the living, and (5) serve as moral exemplars for the living.[136] Nyamiti argues that the concept of the brother ancestor is "grounded on the social constitution of man"[137] and "founded on human spirituality, bodily and societal structures."[138] In other words, various African cultures have valid insights into the natural and spiritual interconnectedness of humanity that is rooted in the reality of creation and can be considered an example of natural revelation. Nyamiti says that Jesus Christ fulfills all five roles of the brother ancestor, though with many important differences. Most obvious is the fact that Christ is the God-man whereas deceased brother ancestors are merely exalted humans. Also, kinship

---

134. Lawson, "Anthropology of Jesus Christ Our Kinsman," 47.
135. So, Johnson argues that transformation of biblical genealogical myths can "recapitulate the liminality and perduring alterity to which they were responding." S. Johnson, *Myth of Ham*, 61.
136. Nyamiti, *Christ as Our Ancestor*, 16.
137. Nyamiti, *Christ as Our Ancestor*, 17.
138. Nyamiti, *Ancestor of Humankind*, 69.

ties with a brother ancestor are not voluntary, but union with Christ requires conversion and faith.[139] Nyamiti skillfully shows the concept of the brother ancestor to be analogous to the role of Christ.

Kwame Bediako has also developed a Brother Ancestor Christology, which he sees as a functional Christology: "Jesus is who he is (Saviour) because of what he has done and can do (save), and . . . he was able to do what he did on the Cross because of who he is (God the Son)."[140] Bediako says that a member of the Akan people group, for example, would wonder why they should "relate to Jesus of Nazareth who does not belong to his clan, family, tribe, and nation."[141] The answer must be that Jesus is related to the Akan people through a familial link established by the incarnation and by fulfilling the promises to Israel, which have been extended in the new covenant to the church.[142] Though Bediako sees the concept of a brother ancestor as a myth meant to project the community ideal and establish community identity, he finds in the concept of brother ancestor a helpful tool for understanding Christ's connection to humanity. Yet brother ancestors need saving, and Christ alone has gone into the realm of the ancestors through death to save them by resurrection since they had no power over death.[143] Christ's brotherhood also extends beyond tribe and clan, being rooted in the Melchizedekian priesthood rather than the tribal Aaronic priesthood (Heb. 7:14–15).[144]

Brother Ancestor Christology functions quite similarly to Irenaeus's theology of recapitulation. It involves repetition: To count as an ancestor, "one must have passed through the critical stages of life to attain adulthood."[145] It is grounded in the ontology of consanguinity (shared blood),[146] but it extends this ontological connection into the totality of humankind, challenging African concepts to expand beyond tribe or clan.[147] This emphasis on unification is possible because Christ is a universal ancestor like Adam but also because, as Son of the Father, he offers us adoption as his siblings.[148] Christ can do what he does because of what and who he is. Christ the brother ancestor

---

139. For a complete list of differences, see Nyamiti, *Christ as Our Ancestor*, 19–24.
140. Bediako, *Jesus and the Gospel in Africa*, 22.
141. Bediako, *Jesus and the Gospel in Africa*, 23.
142. Bediako, *Jesus and the Gospel in Africa*, 24.
143. Bediako, *Jesus and the Gospel in Africa*, 26–27, 30–31.
144. Bediako, *Jesus and the Gospel in Africa*, 27–33.
145. Stinton, "Africa, East and West," 127.
146. Nyamiti, *Ancestor of Humankind*, 66.
147. Nyamiti says, "Christ's brotherhood transcends all family, clanic, tribal or racial limitations. In this regard its closest parallel is that of Adam himself, the father and ancestor of all men, without regard to their family, tribal, or racial qualifications." Nyamiti, *Christ as Our Ancestor*, 20–21. See also Bediako, *Jesus and the Gospel in Africa*, 28.
148. Nyamiti, *Christ as Our Ancestor*, 29–30.

initiates an eschatological new era, but he also restores us to a protological "paradisical innocence," consummating the first creation.[149] While Brother Ancestor Christology is sometimes criticized for treating the ancestors as genuinely present mediators in this world in a manner that concerns some African Christians,[150] it seems to this cultural outsider that when carefully qualified, Brother Ancestor Christology is a helpful inculturated theology of recapitulation that also demonstrates that the concept is in no way a mere by-product of overzealous Hellenization but rather reflects an insight from natural revelation that can be developed in any culture once its truth is revealed in the special revelation of Jesus Christ.

I conclude this chapter having explored a theology of recapitulation as a reversal of original sin through the second Adam. Recapitulation begins with the incarnation and reveals that the person and work of Christ cannot be separated. Besides showing this doctrine's roots in Scripture and tradition, I have shown that it is not detrimental to moral theology or overly Hellenistic. Rather, recapitulation is the important first dimension of a dogmatic synthesis of the person and work of Christ. Yet much more remains to be said, so I turn now from a treatment of the ontological and soteriological consequences of the Son's assumption of humanity to consider the metaphysics of the ongoing union of two natures in one hypostasis, the subject of chapters 3 and 5.

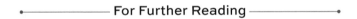

For Further Reading

Crowe, Brandon D. *The Last Adam: A Theology of the Obedient Life of Jesus in the Gospels*. Baker Academic, 2017.

> Crowe's work is the most thorough treatment of last-Adam Christology in biblical theology of which I am aware. It helpfully connects the idea of the last Adam to concepts like glorification and the related title of the Son of Man.

Murray, John. *The Imputation of Adam's Sin*. Presbyterian and Reformed, 1959.

> *The Imputation of Adam's Sin* defends federal headship and the idea of immediate imputation, offering a close reading of Romans 5 and discussing other possible theories along the way. The text is brief and a relatively easy read.

149. Nyamiti, *Christ as Our Ancestor*, 32, 40, 42.
150. For example, see Ezigbo, "Jesus," 51; Mburu, *African Hermeneutics*. Ezigbo notes that some accuse it of accepting necromancy, contrary to Lev. 19:31–32. Mburu raises concerns about Africans who read the "cloud of witnesses" in Heb. 12:1 to refer to ancestors.

Nyamiti, Charles. *Christ as Our Ancestor: Christology from an African Perspective.* Mambo Press, 1984.

> Nyamiti's treatment of Brother Ancestor Christology is the most precise of which I am aware. He offers a detailed analysis of aspects of the concept that apply to Christ and aspects that would be improper if applied to Christ, resulting in a clear delineation of the concept's applicability in Christian theology.

Wiley, Tatha. *Original Sin: Origins, Developments, Contemporary Meanings.* Paulist Press, 2002.

> Wiley's book on original sin offers a theological summary of millennia of historical thought on original sin, including analysis not only of patristic and medieval reflections on the doctrine but also of more recent critiques. This expansive study is beginning to be out of date, but it still serves as an accessible reference work whose emphasis is something of a foil to my own conclusions.

CHAPTER THREE

Two Natures

T he first two chapters argued that the eternal Son of God assumed humanity through the incarnation as a result of the virginal conception and that this assumption of humanity is a self-emptying not through a kenotic loss of divine attributes by the Son but through the addition of a human nature in its frailty. This theology raises a number of subsequent questions: Is the Son equal in divinity to the Father and Spirit, or was his incarnation the result of being inferior in deity? What sort of humanity did Christ take on in the incarnation? How does Christ's humanity relate to his divinity after the incarnation? In the history of Christian doctrine, the dogmatic basis for these questions emerges out of the Council of Chalcedon (451), which established the foundational parameters of orthodox Christology,[1] while requiring much further development and elaboration. After affirming the trinitarianism of the Councils of Nicaea (325) and Constantinople (381), Chalcedon offers the following christological definition:

1. Not all Christians accept the Chalcedonian definition, most notably including the Coptic Orthodox, the Oriental Orthodox, and the Ethiopian Orthodox. For some in these groups, much of the debate is procedural, with the concern that the council did not adequately address debates regarding the interpretation of the Council of Ephesus, the language of Christ being "from two natures," and the validity of the formula "one incarnate nature of God the Word." These concerns are expressed in Samuel, *Chalcedon Re-Examined*, 126–27, 226–32. Throughout the next two chapters, I will also occasionally address the concerns of various non-Chalcedonian orthodox Christian groups. However, I also take many of my constructive arguments in defense of Chalcedonian language to be a response to these concerns, and since my audience is less likely to encounter these groups than others, I have opted not to center this discussion but rather to treat the Chalcedonian definition as the dogmatic starting point for an account of the union of humanity and divinity in Christ.

We then, following the holy fathers, all with one consent, teach men to confess one and the same Son, our Lord Jesus Christ, the same perfect in Godhead and also perfect in humanity; truly God and truly man, of a rational soul and body; consubstantial with the Father according to the Godhead, and consubstantial with us according to humanity; in all things like unto us, without sin; begotten before all ages of the Father according to the Godhead, and in these latter days, for us and for our salvation, born of the Virgin Mary, the Mother of God, according to the Manhood; one and the same Christ, Son, Lord, Only-Begotten, to be acknowledged in two natures, inconfusedly, unchangeably, indivisibly, inseparably; the distinction in natures being by no means taken away by the union, but rather the property of each being preserved, and concurring in one Person and one Hypostasis, not parted or divided into two persons, but one and the same Son, and only begotten, God the Word, the Lord Jesus Christ, as the prophets from the beginning said concerning him, and the Lord Jesus Christ himself has taught us, and the Creed of the holy Fathers has handed down to us.

This definition gives us the basic grammar of Christology: Christ is two natures in one person or hypostasis. This chapter will explain what it means to say that Christ is two natures, while chapter 5 will explore what it means to say that Christ is one person or hypostasis.

The definition uses several terms that must be defined moving forward. First, Christ is two natures. A "nature" refers to the fundamental character of a thing, with a special emphasis on that thing's distinctive powers and operations. It is in the nature of a duck to quack, fly, and swim. To claim that Christ is two natures is to affirm that he is properly human and divine, being able to do all actions proper to humanity and divinity. Chalcedon also teaches that Christ is **consubstantial** to the Father in the Godhead and consubstantial to us in humanity. The term "consubstantial" focuses more on the whatness or quiddity of a thing. Chalcedon here affirms that the Son has all attributes necessary to be God and to be human, though the term leaves some ambiguity about what it means to be both human and divine in this way.[2] Are the properties of humanity mixed together? How are they joined? Such questions are important but must be resolved later in this work. For now, we must consider the bare fact that Christ has two natures.

Significant for the purposes of this chapter, Chalcedon also affirms that Christ exists "in two natures." This language is a response to a monk named Eutyches, who was condemned as a heretic at the Council of Chalcedon; Eutyches affirmed Christ as perfect God and perfect human but, when deposed by

---

2. For an elaborate treatment of consubstantiality, see Stead, *Divine Substance*. See also my treatment in Butner, *Trinitarian Dogmatics*, 15–46.

the council and asked to elaborate his position, put forward the formula "*from* two natures before the union, but after the union one in nature."[3] Language of being "from" two natures could suggest a human nature that existed prior to and independently of the incarnation.[4] If the humanity of Christ does not remain distinct from the divinity, it could suggest that salvation "must basically destroy who we are"[5] because a humanity mixed with deity would remain unrecognizably human. While it is certainly true that Christ is from two natures in the sense that he is eternally begotten of the Father and born of the human Mary through the Spirit's work in the virginal conception, both facts that the Chalcedonian definition affirms, it is better to emphasize language of existing in two natures to demonstrate the ongoing existence of both.

The majority of this chapter explores the two full natures, leaving to subsequent chapters the work of developing a full explanation of the unity and ongoing distinction of the natures. I begin by exploring the deity of Christ in light of debates in modern biblical studies, much of which would challenge Chalcedon's assertion that Jesus is "perfect in Godhead," instead suggesting that he might be lesser in deity than the Father or not divine at all. Here, I mount the argument that there are good biblical reasons for affirming Chalcedon. In the second half of this chapter, I focus more attention on the question of what it means for Christ to be consubstantial with us. What sort of human nature did Christ assume? Here, I will consider how a theological rule expressed by Gregory of Nazianzus against **Apollinarianism** guides us to affirm that the Son took on all basic human powers and abilities in the fall. This claim requires clarification, so I will also consider arguments against the Byzantine-era aphthartodocetists, who denied that Christ could suffer, and modern theological debates surrounding the question of whether the Son took on a fallen human nature in the incarnation. At the end of the chapter, I hope to have greatly clarified what it means to say that Jesus is fully human and fully divine.

Fully Divine

The Chalcedonian definition also affirms that Jesus is fully divine, a subject that can be explored in various ways. For example, we might explore the

---

3. Samuel, *Chalcedon Re-Examined*, 48–51; L. Davis, *First Seven Ecumenical Councils*, 171. Samuel depicts Eutyches as a victim of conciliar politics, who was forced to use philosophical terminology he would have rather avoided. There seems to be some truth to this. Davis depicts Eutyches as a "confused and muddled thinker." In neither case can we consider Eutyches a heretic of the caliber or danger of someone like Eunomius of Cyzicus or even Arius of Alexandria.
4. This is the interpretation of Leo the Great, *Tome*, 369.
5. B. Jones, *Practicing Christian Doctrine*, 129.

trinitarian debates regarding whether Jesus is semidivine as the homoiousians argued, an exalted created mediator as Arius of Alexandria argued, or fully divine and consubstantial with the Father, as the Nicene Creed affirms.[6] I consider these debates to be most proper to the doctrine of the Trinity, and I have discussed them in considerable detail elsewhere.[7] Instead, in this chapter, I want to focus on an important series of modern debates concerning whether Jesus is actually depicted as fully divine in the New Testament.[8] In particular, we must consider whether claims of divinity in the New Testament intend to suggest that the Son has equal deity to the Father. Further, the **quest for the historical Jesus** often results in historical reconstructions of a Jesus of Nazareth who never claimed to be divine, so we must briefly consider the methods and conclusions of that quest. Finally, even if the New Testament and the **historical Jesus** both can be plausibly said to affirm the full deity of the Son, we can question whether this deity is properly expressed in onto-logical categories from Nicaea and Chalcedon or whether other categories would be preferable.

Though the New Testament describes Jesus as *theos* (a god or God, de-pending on the circumstances, hence early Christian debates on the Trinity), in recent biblical studies there is considerable debate regarding how the New Testament authors understood Jesus to be divine.[9] In part, this debate exists because divinity was often understood along a hierarchy in first-century Greek and Roman thought.[10] As Paula Fredriksen wittily notes, "God is not the only god, not even in his own book."[11] In the context of Second Temple Judaism, a wide range of semidivine mediatorial figures could be present even within Jewish monotheism, including exalted humans, personified divine attributes, living charismatic human figures, and angelic figures that were not always easy to distinguish from God himself.[12] Chalcedon treats the Son as coequal in deity to the Father, treating Jesus as divine to the same extent, in the same way, excepting a difference between the Son being generated God and the

6. For a historical overview of these debates, see Ayres, *Nicaea and Its Legacy*; Hanson, *Christian Doctrine of God*.

7. See Butner, *Trinitarian Dogmatics*, 25–33, 82–85, 177–80; Butner, "Exegetical Founda-tions of Consubstantiality."

8. I have also addressed this question briefly in Butner, *Trinitarian Dogmatics*, 18–25. How-ever, the treatment and methods presented there can be updated in this context.

9. Further, there is the question of *which* New Testament authors thought Jesus was divine, with some scholars claiming that texts like the Synoptics have no such conception of a divine messiah. See Kirk, *Man Attested by God*.

10. See the brief discussion in Fredriksen, "How High?," 297–98.

11. Fredriksen, "How High?," 300.

12. See Davila, "Of Methodology, Monotheism and Metatron," 6–7.

Father being God who generates.[13] We must consider now whether this sense of the Son's deity is found in Scripture. Recent debates in New Testament studies explore this question from many different angles, only some of which will be considered here. I will explore the Son's enthronement, worship of Christ, and the New Testament's citation of Scripture with respect to Christ.

Divinity and the Meaning of the New Testament

Though I could focus on many arguments, I intend to focus here on three main ways in which some modern biblical scholars have argued that the Son is coequal in divinity to the Father. First, much attention has been paid to **christological monotheism** and the manner in which the Son is incorporated into the cultic worship of the Father, suggesting equal divinity.[14] Second, much debate has focused on the ways in which the Son shares the throne of the Father. Third, the New Testament's use of the Old Testament with respect to Jesus points toward a close unity of Father and Son. Combined, these dimensions of recent debates in biblical studies provide warrant for affirming the full deity of Christ in line with Chalcedon and other ecumenical councils and against those who would place Christ at a lower position in a hierarchy of divinity.

One of the most important arguments for the full deity of Christ is found in his incorporation into worship in ways typically reserved for God. Most famously, Larry Hurtado has argued that the sort of cultic worship offered to Christ in the New Testament is a "distinctive and variant form of exclusivist monotheism" that incorporates Jesus into the worship typically reserved for God.[15] Here, we might think of the Son's incorporation in benedictions and doxologies (e.g., 2 Cor. 13:13; Eph. 6:23), in the Matthean baptismal formula (Matt. 28:19), and in songs and hymns (e.g., Eph. 5:18–20).[16] This argument has received some pushback since there is some evidence of angel veneration and prayer to angels in return for their care,[17] and Jewish literature includes examples of prostration before nondivine figures (1 Chron. 29:20; Rev. 3:9; 1 En. 62:9). Notably, James McGrath argues that the important dividing line in Judaism is that of sacrifice—veneration and worship of other kinds may be offered to that which is not God, but sacrifices are for God alone.[18] I am

---

13. This distinction was affirmed through Chalcedon's continued affirmation of the Niceano-Constantinopolitan Creed.

14. See the helpful introductory survey in B. Smith, "What Christ Does, God Does."

15. Hurtado, *Lord Jesus Christ*, 52.

16. On hymns, see Hengel, *Between Jesus and Paul*, 80–81.

17. See Stuckenbruck, *Angel Veneration and Christology*, 161–63.

18. McGrath, *Only True God*, 7, 35.

not convinced that this is an acceptable dividing line in the context of the New Testament for two reasons. First, early Christian theology decenters sacrifice by typologically treating sacrifice as prefiguring Christ's "once and for all" sacrifice (Heb. 9:12; 10:10). I take it no one is required to sacrifice going forward, so we cannot identify deity by seeking who received sacrifices. Second, many early Christian texts are written after the destruction of the temple, which ends the sacrificial cult even in Judaism. In light of this, the doxological and cultic reverence to Jesus must be considered an important sign of his elevated status.

Turning from debates about the worship of Christ, another important debate focuses on the enthronement of Christ, which is prominently featured in Revelation 4–5 but is also a central theme of Psalm 110, the Old Testament passage most cited by the New Testament. I will consider the second passage momentarily. In Revelation 4–5, the Son appears to have always shared his Father's throne,[19] a status that seems to suggest the Son eternally sharing the authority and rule of the Father. While enthroned angelic beings are found in Jewish literature (e.g., Ezek. 1:2–28; Dan. 7:10; 11Q17 5.8; Apoc. Zeph. A; 3 En. 16), several features make Revelation's treatment of the Son different.[20] First, many Jewish texts work to distinguish God from the enthroned angelic being. For example, in 3 Enoch 10:1, Metatron is enthroned on the throne of glory, but in 3 Enoch 16:5 Metatron is lashed to show his inferiority to God.[21] Similarly, enthroned angels in the ascension of Isaiah refuse worship.[22] John situates this throne room scene in an apocalypse that shares the divine title of "the Alpha and the Omega" and "the First and the Last" between God and Christ (Rev. 1:8, 17; 21:6; 22:13),[23] and in which Jesus welcomes worship (e.g., 1:17), even receiving the same words of praise offered to the Father (4:11; 5:13).[24] Where angels are unworthy to open the scroll (5:2), the Lamb is worthy (5:7).[25] Third, Revelation 5:5 draws on Isaiah 11:1–10, yet instead

19. Note B. Smith's analysis: In Rev. 5, there is no symbol of new status, no taking of the throne, nothing to suggest that this is new and not an eternal role. B. Smith, *Trinity in the Book of Revelation*, 115–16.

20. See Bühner, *Messianic High Christology*, 139–42. Bühner suggests that the parables of Enoch are the unique exception to this common rule, though even here the Enochic image does not suggest that the Son of Man and God share the throne simultaneously in the way that Revelation does.

21. Bird, *Jesus Among the Gods*, 267–68.

22. See the discussion in Bauckham, *Climax of Prophecy*, 120–21. This is a common theme across Second Temple Jewish literature. For example, see also 2 En. 1:4–8; 3 En. 1:7; 16:1–5; Apoc. Zeph. 6:11–14; Tobit 12:16–22.

23. B. Smith, *Trinity in the Book of Revelation*, 114–15.

24. Bühner, *Messianic High Christology*, 128.

25. B. Smith, *Trinity in the Book of Revelation*, 119.

of calling Jesus the shoot of Jesse (Isa. 11:1), Revelation speaks of the "root of David," suggesting the Son's preexistence.[26] In context, then, Jesus's enthronement is fundamentally different from other enthronements in Second Temple literature.

The New Testament's use of Old Testament passages also reveals a high Christology through applying passages that speak of Yahweh in the Old Testament to Christ in the New Testament. At least seventy-six times, the New Testament applies Old Testament passages about Yahweh to Jesus.[27] For example, in Romans 9:33, Paul takes two Old Testament citations, Isaiah 28:16 and 8:14, and uses them to point to Christ as the stone of stumbling. However, in Isaiah 8:13–15, Yahweh is the stone of stumbling.[28] While Second Temple Jewish literature did have a tendency to attribute such Old Testament passages about Yahweh to "Wisdom, the Word, the angel of the LORD and the glory of the LORD," Carl Judson Davis notes that such figures are ambiguous in that they are already linked with the deity of God in various ways.[29] In other words, the phenomenon of such redeployment of Old Testament texts to apply to a new figure like Christ does not require something like trinitarianism, but it does likely suggest a high Christology of some sort.[30] A closer examination of several texts, though, suggests that a very high Christology may be in mind, even up to the full deity of Christ. For example, in 1 Corinthians 1:31, Paul cites Jeremiah 9:24 or 1 Samuel 2:10 LXX and applies "boasting in the Lord" to Christ instead of the Father. Noting that the original context of 1 Samuel 2 is Hannah's song with its emphasis on the uniqueness of God, Capes argues that this citation is all the more evidence of an exalted view of Christ as God.[31] More persuasive to my mind is analysis of New Testament use of Joel 2:32a—"Then everyone who calls on the name of the LORD will be saved"—where the phrase "calls on the name of the LORD" speaks of liturgical worship in the Old Testament (see Ps. 105:1; Isa. 41:25; Jer. 10:25).[32] This passage is cited throughout the New Testament to speak of the saving effects of trusting in Jesus (Acts 2:21, 38; 9:14, 21; 22:16; Rom. 10:13; 1 Cor. 1:2). Coupled with the widespread New Testament use of "Lord" (*kyrios*) as a title for both Jesus and

26. Bühner, *Messianic High Christology*, 124–25.
27. C. Davis, *Name and Way of the Lord*, 182.
28. See discussion in Capes, *Divine Christ*, 112.
29. C. Davis, *Name and Way of the Lord*, 59–60. Davis explains that such precedent does not require us to view Jesus as divine or early Christians as nascent trinitarians, but neither can such passages preclude a conclusion of this sort.
30. The uniqueness of applying such passages to a historical person and not merely to an ideal and abstract trope like the great priest or messiah should also not be ignored.
31. Capes, *Divine Christ*, 124–27.
32. C. Davis, *Name and Way of the Lord*, 105–6.

his Father,[33] and coupled with a lack of evidence that this phrase is applied to nondivine figures in a pre-Christian context, this passage suggests that Christ is being incorporated into the soteriological and liturgical aspects of Israel's understanding of God in a way pointing to his deity.[34]

The Quest for the Historical Jesus and Full Deity

If, as I have argued, the texts of the New Testament depict Jesus as God, a final challenge to the deity of Christ remains: It may be the case that Jesus did not consider himself to be divine. While Jesus's full self-understanding is a complicated topic that is difficult for us to discern,[35] Jesus's teachings are more accessible to the historian. Since the late eighteenth century, some biblical scholars have adopted a hermeneutic of suspicion to argue that we cannot trust the Gospel accounts or take them at face value but must instead use the tools of history to discover what can be shown to be historically plausible, thereby finding the historical Jesus in contrast to the so-called Jesus of faith. In other words, if we set aside (for theoretical, critical, or apologetic purposes) the reliability of Scripture, or if we were to deny the reliability and authority of Scripture, we could then doubt the picture of Jesus that the Bible provides. Were we to do so, would there be any evidence persuasive to a historian that Jesus thought he was divine? Some have argued that there is no such evidence. While I take the canon in its entirely as a reliable source for theology, it is necessary to utilize the methods of historical Jesus studies to explore whether an answer can be given to such criticism.

Bart Ehrman offers one typical contemporary treatment of the historical Jesus. Explaining the range of varieties of divinity found in the first century, including exalted humans, semidivine figures, and supernatural intermediaries,[36] Ehrman uses the tools of historical Jesus research to consider whether the historical Jesus would have thought he was divine. Skeptical of the historical reliability of the canonical Gospels,[37] Ehrman centers three criteria for detect-

---

33. Hurtado, *Lord Jesus Christ*, 111–12.
34. C. Davis, *Name and Way of the Lord*, 139–40. Davis admits "there is always the possibility that a New Testament example is the first [example of applying Joel 2:23 to a nondivine figure]." However, given other evidences of the deity of Christ across the New Testament, there is reason to think instead that the passage is applied to a fully divine person.
35. Three complications are obvious to me: (1) There is always some difficulty to truly understand what another human being is thinking and feeling; (2) since Jesus is fully divine, he also knows and thinks in an analogous manner as God, and human knowledge of God's means and mode of knowing is certainly limited; and (3) since Jesus is fully human and divine, we face the puzzle of how Jesus can have both minds.
36. Ehrman, *How Jesus Became God*, 11–84.
37. Ehrman, *How Jesus Became God*, 88–94.

ing historically reliable material. The criterion of independent attestation is rooted in the fact that independently corroborated sources are more likely to point to authentic historical data. The criterion of dissimilarity suggests that "if a tradition about Jesus is dissimilar to what the early Christians would have wanted to say about him, then it more likely is historically accurate."[38] Finally, the criterion of contextual credibility says that the historical Jesus's teachings and beliefs must fit his cultural context and not be anachronistic. With these criteria in hand, Ehrman argues that there is independent attestation of Jesus preaching an apocalyptic message, and instances of Jesus speaking of the Son of Man in third person instead of first person (e.g., Mark 8:38) would pass the criterion of dissimilarity since they may suggest that Jesus did not see himself as the key apocalyptic agent.[39] Did Jesus consider himself divine? Ehrman says no, arguing that the statements of high Christology found in John[40] are not multiply attested, do not pass the criterion of dissimilarity, and "are not at all contextually credible."[41] Thus, Ehrman says, the historical Jesus did not claim to be divine.

Two possible strategies exist for responding to such quests for the historical Jesus. One is to question their basic methodology. As Albert Schweitzer argued over a century ago, the quest for the historical Jesus often uncovers a Jesus surprisingly similar to the convictions of the scholar(s) seeking Jesus.[42] In part, this is because of the limitations of trying to understand the development of the inner thought life of any human person, which is surely amplified if that person is also divine[43]—here I recognize that the latter claim is often not one shared by those seeking to understand the historical Jesus. In part, the tendency toward projection in the quest for the historical Jesus is undoubtedly also a result of divergent views on the historical reliability of the Gospel texts.[44] Christians are more likely to view the texts as reliable and so likely to accept a historical reconstruction of Jesus as claiming divinity, whereas agnostics, atheists, and members of other religions are less likely to view the texts as

---

38. Ehrman, *How Jesus Became God*, 96.
39. Ehrman, *How Jesus Became God*, 103–9.
40. He mentions John 10:30; 14:9; 17:24.
41. Ehrman, *How Jesus Became God*, 125.
42. See the summary of the first quest in Schweitzer, *Quest of the Historical Jesus*, 397–99. The brief reconstruction of the historical Jesus I will offer certainly follows this pattern, as does Ehrman's own reconstruction.
43. "In the depths of our being we are different from [the Son], so different in fact that we could become like him only through a new birth, a new creation. How then can we hope to analyze and explain Jesus' development, its stages and changes, in analogy with the common experience of humanity?" Kähler, *So-Called Historical Jesus*, 53.
44. Hence Ehrman's extensive treatment on why the Synoptics are unreliable historical sources.

reliable (for if they were, why not follow Christ?), leading them to accept a historical reconstruction different from the canonical depiction of Christ.

Methodological problems are further complicated by the fact that there is no consensus on the most reliable criteria to use in reconstructing the historical Jesus. Ehrman's preferred criteria of independent attestation, dissimilarity, and contextual credibility are all subject to critique. The criterion of dissimilarity, for example, can find idiosyncratic dimensions of Jesus's life and teachings that may or may not have been central to his ministry, but it can needlessly silence aspects of his teaching and life that might be in continuity with his context or that would continue to be held by his followers.[45] Further, nothing contained in the New Testament was so dissimilar as to be excluded from these early Christian texts by early Christian authors, so in one sense, nothing would pass the criterion of dissimilarity.[46] Similarly, focus on contextual credibility requires a prior judgment be made about which contexts to consider: Is Christ primarily interpreted against a Jewish background or a Hellenistic gentile one? Such prior judgments greatly shape the outcome of any pursuit of the historical Jesus, perhaps suggesting that the entire project should be abandoned. Even the criterion of multiple attestation is complicated by the debates surrounding the relationship between the Synoptic Gospels and their textual interrelatedness. While some argue that modifications in the criteria could improve the accuracy of the quest,[47] there is reason for great skepticism about the project as a whole. At the very least, there must be some agreement that what can be verified using a set of historical criteria is different from full historical reality, for not all historical events are verifiable, and certainly not with the limited criteria of historical Jesus research.

A second response to reconstructions of the historical Jesus that deny that he claimed deity for himself is to offer counternarratives arguing that there may be good historical reasons to believe that Jesus claimed a divine status for himself. This approach can accept, for the sake of argument, the methods of the historical Jesus movement while attempting to show that those methods can validate a high Christology.[48] For example, Denis Farkasfalvy claims that there is a "block of independently formulated testimonies" about the mutual revelation of the Father and Son.[49] Here he especially focuses on what

45. See Meier, *Marginal Jew*, 1:172–73.
46. Rodríguez, "Embarrassing Truth About Jesus," 146–48. I take there to be considerable overlap between the criterion of embarrassment and the criterion of dissimilarity.
47. For a defense of the quest and the ability to improve criteria, see Theissen and Merz, *Historical Jesus*, 93–118, especially 115–18.
48. For my own part, I have concerns about most of the criteria used for historical Jesus research.
49. Farkasfalvy, *Triune God*, 13.

he calls the Synoptic logion in Matthew 11:25–27 and Luke 10:21–22, which both include the affirmation that "no one knows the Son except the Father, and no one knows the Father except the Son and anyone to whom the Son desires to reveal him" (Matt. 11:27; see also Luke 10:22). Farkasfalvy notes that this saying would be early because (1) it is shared verbatim by Matthew and Luke but likely taken from an earlier source, and (2) it likely reflects Aramaic features, since Aramaic lacks capability of expressing "each other" concisely, explaining the verbosity.[50] Its unique structure makes it easily memorable, which some have considered a criterion increasing historical plausibility of a saying.[51] Galatians 1:15–16 and Matthew 16:16–18 include parallel concepts, the first from an early Pauline source reflecting the spirituality of early Christians and the second again attributed to Jesus himself, reflecting the Aramaism "flesh and blood," both suggesting that the revelation of the Son is from the Father.[52] These early verses together suggest "four aspects of essential knowledge between Father and Son: (1) a subject-object distinction between Father and Son, (2) mutuality, (3) reciprocity, and (4) exclusivity, implying that nobody can share in this relationship unless it is granted by the Father's sovereign will."[53] Many other features of the Gospel narratives reinforce this basic picture of Christ, resulting in its general historical plausibility.[54]

Aramaisms and a pattern of common, memorable sayings about the Son revealing the Father are not sufficient to build the claim that Jesus saw himself as a divine Son. Supplementing Farkasfalvy, further evidence may be found in the most cited psalm in the New Testament: Psalm 110.[55] In the Septuagint, Psalm 110:1–3 attributes bestowal of divine sonship to the Davidic king in the context of enthronement. Jesus quotes this in reference to himself in Mark 12:35, using **prosopological exegesis** to identify the Messiah as David's Lord and hence older than and superior to David.[56] Mark also depicts Jesus

---

50. Farkasfalvy, *Triune God*, 6–8.

51. For a brief summary of this criterion, see Powell, *Jesus as a Figure in History*, 48.

52. Farkasfalvy, *Triune God*, 14.

53. Farkasfalvy, *Triune God*, 16.

54. Joseph Ratzinger, who became Pope Benedict XVI, notes quite a few examples: Jesus's prayer to God as "Abba," his closeness to the Father in his prayer life in general, his use of "my Father" as a singular relationship, and the sense of mission expressed in such statements as the "I have come" statements in the Gospels all suggest Christ had a sense of a unique connection with God the Father. Ratzinger, *Behold the Pierced One*, 18–22.

55. Farkasfalvy does engage this passage (see *Triune God*, 30–31), but I will draw largely on other sources to augment his argument.

56. See the analysis in Bates, *Birth of the Trinity*, 47–54. Bates is convinced that "it is at least plausible that the historical Jesus had determined that he was the *messias designatus*, the chosen Christ awaiting his enthronement." Further, he thinks it "indubitably clear" that the Synoptic authors think of Jesus in this way. Bates, *Birth of the Trinity*, 48.

appealing to the psalm at his trial (Mark 14:61–62).[57] Use of Psalm 110 as speaking of a messianic or apocalyptic figure was common in texts around Jesus's time, including 11Q13, 1 Enoch, Acts, Clement of Rome, and Epistle of Barnabas.[58] The possibility of a messianic claimant identifying Psalm 110 as speaking about himself is contextually plausible and would explain why later followers of Jesus would be so prone to using this psalm (see Acts 2:34–35; 1 Cor. 15:25; Eph. 1:20; Col. 3:1; Heb. 1:3, 13; 8:1; 10:12–13; 1 Pet. 3:22). The widespread prevalence of exalted mediatorial theologies in the first-century context adds further plausibility to Christ adopting such a theology of himself. Combine this enthronement Christology with the Synoptic logion speaking of the Son revealing the Father, and you wind up with a historical reconstruction of Jesus of Nazareth who claimed a unique messianic role in revealing his Father to the people of Israel and who understood messianic status to involve coenthronement with God. While this treatment has been brief and will likely not be compelling to many critical scholars, I hope it demonstrates the limitations of historical Jesus research for questions of the deity of Christ while showing that affirming the Son's consubstantiality with the Father need not require abandonment of modern scholarly methods entirely.

Ontological Categories and New Testament Christology

If the New Testament teaches that Jesus is divine, and if there is some historical evidence that Jesus believed this as well, it could still be the case that the expression of Jesus's deity in terms of consubstantiality may be a mistake. Here, the debate tends to focus on whether Nicaea's introduction of concepts of being or substance to speak of the Son is fair given the New Testament content, with some scholars being quite critical of Nicaea's ontological assumptions. For example, Michael Peppard argues that asking whether Jesus is eternal begotten deity or created is "anachronistic when asked of the New Testament era (with the possible exceptions of John and Hebrews)."[59] Peppard instead argues that language of adoptive and begotten sonship is used of both Christ and Christians (e.g., Luke 1:35; Acts 2:36;

57. For an argument that use of this Scripture at the trial is "completely possible linguistically and conceptually in Jewish tradition before Easter," see Stuhlmacher, "Messianic Son of Man," 336.

58. Matthew Bates argues that we can consider later texts as helpful in interpreting earlier texts in a limited way. We need not seek an intended meaning that must be entirely removed from "later taint." "Why? Because the correct identification of the alleged later taint *as later taint* and its removal is highly conjectural." Bates, *Birth of the Trinity*, 57.

59. Peppard, *Son of God in the Roman World*, 11.

13:32–33; Rom. 8:23), blurring any strong creator/creature distinction until much later when Nicene Christians emphasized creation *ex nihilo* and began to draw more heavily on Platonic ontology.[60] Where Peppard suggests that Nicaea misinterprets the title "Son of God" by shifting from the cultural context of imperialism to a Platonic ontology, even biblical scholars like Raymond Brown who are friendly to Nicaea suggest that "by the time of Nicaea there had been a definite progression from a more functional approach to Jesus to an ontological approach."[61] Here, one might wonder whether it would be better to abandon such ontological categories when speaking of Christ to return to an allegedly purer functional Christology along the lines of the New Testament.

Several recent scholars have argued that Greco-Roman religious views included a fundamental distinction between eternal, immortal gods and exalted or created deities.[62] Michael Bird, for example, argues persuasively that Greco-Roman philosophy, religion, and culture understood a distinction between absolute/ontological deity and **euergetic**/relative deity. For example, Herodotus, Plato, Chrysippus, Diodorus Siculus, Cicero, Quintillian, and Plutarch all speak of a distinction between God by nature (ungenerate) and exalted figures.[63] Early Christian apologists like Aristides, Athenagoras, Justin, Minucius Felix, and Tertullian all critiqued the idea of exalted or euergetic deities,[64] a trend we find continued among pro-Nicene theologians like Gregory of Nazianzus, who writes, "If any assert that he was made perfect by works, or that after his baptism, or after his resurrection from the dead, he was counted worthy of an adoptive sonship, like those whom the Greeks interpolate as added to the ranks of the gods, let him be anathema. For that which has a beginning or a progress or is made perfect is not God, although the expressions may be used of his gradual manifestation."[65]

At the very least, such early arguments push the date for the entrance of ontological distinction earlier than the Council of Nicaea, suggesting that second-century Christians rejected the idea of euergetic deity. However, granting Peppard's point about the ambiguity of "begetting" language, which itself was a major contributor to the confusion of the trinitarian debates of

---

60. Peppard, *Son of God in the Roman World*, 132–35, 160–71. Peppard suggests that the adoptive/begotten distinction is blurred at least in part due to Ps. 2:7 speaking of the king being begotten "today," with the latter word suggesting adoption.

61. R. Brown, *New Testament Christology*, 171.

62. For example, see Talbert, *Christology During the First Hundred Years*, 7–8.

63. Bird, *Jesus Among the Gods*, 2, 44–45, 49.

64. Bird, *Jesus Among the Gods*, 58.

65. Gregory of Nazianzus, *To Cledonius*, 218.

the fourth century, it seems that a basic distinction between euergetic and ontological deity is present in portions of the New Testament.[66] Here, Bird points to how Jesus is said to be an uncreated figure involved in creation, which sets him apart from both subordinate demiurgic figures, who were created, and polytheistic deities like Zeus, who did not create.[67] He concludes that the combined ways in which Christ is exalted in cultic worship, through participation in divine actions, through sharing in divine attributes, and in an incipient trinitarianism "are simply unprecedented when collated together," clearly setting Jesus in the category of ontological deity.[68]

Further, ontology is found within the texts of Scripture, so there is no reason to entirely deny some biblical basis for the later ontological language of Nicaea. For example, Christopher Seitz has recently argued that the Old Testament cannot be reduced to narrative, for narrative neglects large blocks of the Old Testament, many prophetic texts are neither chronological nor overly concerned with narrative or temporal location, and the final form seems unconcerned with missing information and gaps in the story.[69] Some dimensions of the Old Testament demand an ontology: The "flexibility" of the term "Lord" raises certain ontological questions, as do various texts suggesting God being involved in some sort of colloquy.[70] Seitz concludes that the Old Testament tends to consider ontology in ways that prompted the early church to develop "a sustained interest in ontology."[71] Similarly, some ontological concepts common in first-century philosophy are evident in the New Testament's language of the Son having the "form of God [*morphē theou*]" (Phil. 2:6) and being "the exact expression of his nature [*hypostaseōs*]" (Heb. 1:3), while Christians were formerly "enslaved to things that by nature [*physei*] are not gods" (Gal. 4:8). Here, Jesus appears to be folded into divine ontology where other categories of being are excluded.[72] The apostle Paul, among other authors, seems to have been aware of and at times consciously

---

66. Leander Keck critiques an alleged distinction between "functional" Christology in the New Testament and later Nicene "metaphysical" Christology, arguing instead that there are metaphysical elements across the New Testament corpus, especially in terms of Christ's preexistence. Here euergetic Christology nearly corresponds to functional Christology—Christ is divine because of what he does—while the metaphysical dimensions Keck points to are closer to Bird's ontological category. See Keck, *Why Christ Matters*, 134–42. Keck concludes that the New Testament offers a metaphysic closer to Arius, but I have argued against this elsewhere, in Butner, "Exegetical Foundations of Consubstantiality."

67. See Bird, *Jesus Among the Gods*, 167–68, 385–86.

68. Bird, *Jesus Among the Gods*, 384.

69. Seitz, *Elder Testament*, 72–74, 80–82.

70. Seitz, *Elder Testament*, 199, 252.

71. Seitz, *Elder Testament*, 261.

72. See Bird, *Jesus Among the Gods*, 59–64.

drawing on the philosophy of his day.[73] This philosophical influence appears in his Christology, for example, when in 1 Corinthians 8:6 he incorporates Jesus not only into the Shema (Deut. 6:4) but also into Stoic conceptions of deity as that from which, through which, and to which are all things.[74] Such philosophical influence within the canon suggests that it is permissible to use philosophical concepts to describe the deity of Christ.

Despite critics ancient and modern who denied a biblical foundation for affirming that Christ has a fully divine nature, consubstantial with his Father, I have argued in this section that there are good reasons to affirm the full deity of Christ. Beside passages that support the claim of Jesus's full deity, there are some reasons to accept the claim that Jesus himself believed in his deity. Furthermore, there are good reasons to understand the divinity of Christ in ontological terms. Undoubtedly, skeptical readers may not be persuaded by these arguments, but dogmatic theology proceeds from a position of faith. Those who believe can find sufficient evidence in Scripture to boldly witness to the divinity of Christ.

Fully Human

The Chalcedonian definition affirms that Jesus is fully human, but the full humanity of Christ was the subject of heated debate from the earliest days of Christianity. From the time of the Johannine epistles some Christians apparently denied Christ's coming in the flesh (see 1 John 4:2–3; 2 John 7), apparently affirming a form of docetism that claimed Jesus only appeared to be human.[75] A full dogmatic account of Christ's flesh involves centuries of debates regarding the particularities of what it means that he became human. A dogmatic understanding of Christ's consubstantiality with us in his human nature requires that we consider what type of human nature Christ actually assumed. To address this question, I will survey three important historical debates related to this question: the rejection of Apollinarianism at the First Council of Constantinople (381), Byzantine critique of **aphthartodocetism**, and modern debates around **impeccability** and the effect of sin

---

73. See Malherbe, *Light from the Gentiles*, 197–208; Strom, *Reframing Paul*, 103–14. Malherbe notes Paul's familiarity with philosophical ethics, and Strom notes his broad links to his philosophical milieu.

74. See Dunn, *Christology in the Making*, 180; Keck, *Why Christ Matters*, 139.

75. Rejection of those who deny Christ coming in the flesh likely points to a docetist movement to which the Johannine community was exposed.

(or lack thereof) on Christ's humanity. Chapter 7 will introduce dyothelitism, a fourth important aspect of Christ's full humanity.

Apollinarianism and Nazianzus's Rule

One of the most important heresies prompting doctrinal clarification on Christ's full humanity was Apollinarianism. In order to focus on the development of orthodox doctrine, I will not elaborate the beliefs of Apollinaris in great detail, but it is important to know the basics of his theological position. Apollinaris rightly seeks to affirm the full deity of Christ against Arianism, and he is rightly conscious that the virginal conception required a rejection of any autonomous, adopted human being.[76] In other words, Apollinaris argued that Jesus was God and that his humanity was never a distinct human being but was always the Son of God. For Apollinaris, Christ was one substance because human flesh was united with the divine mind to make a complete human being who was also consubstantial with the Father and Holy Spirit. This christological proposal also included a clear soteriological dimension. As Frances Young notes, it may be that Apollinaris's idea of the mind of God enfleshed "arose from a sense that what Christianity had to offer was truth— direct and genuine knowledge of God."[77] The absence of a human mind could be the basis for the unity of Christ's natures, where unity is necessary for Christ's second salvific work of raising flesh from the dead.[78] In other words, Apollinaris seems to have thought that the divine mind took on flesh but not a human mind in order to be able to convey theological truth in human form and to defeat death in his flesh.

Apollinarianism can be rejected for many reasons. For one, Christ is described in Scripture as having emotions and thoughts that are proper to a human mind but not a divine mind. Thus, Christ is said to grow in wisdom (Luke 2:52), to learn (Isa. 7:15), and to lack knowledge of certain things (Matt. 24:36), while the divine mind shared by Father, Son, and Holy Spirit is omniscient.[79] A more famous argument against Apollinarianism comes from the Cappadocian theologian Gregory of Nazianzus, whose dogmatic rule against the Apollinarians became widely influential across the church. Gregory writes, "If anyone has put his trust in him as a man without a human mind, he is

76. Daley, *God Visible*, 129–30; Kelly, *Early Christian Doctrines*, 290. Kelly too sharply distinguishes between an Alexandrian and Antiochene approach to Christology in his analysis of Apollinarianism.

77. Young, *Nicaea to Chalcedon*, 248.

78. Kelly, *Early Christian Doctrines*, 291; Daley, *God Visible*, 133.

79. For a good historical treatment of such verses, see Chemnitz, *Two Natures in Christ*, 58–59.

really bereft of mind, and quite unworthy of salvation. *For that which he has not assumed, he has not healed; but that which is united to his Godhead is also saved.* If only half Adam fell, then that which Christ assumes and saves may be half also; but if the whole of his nature fell, it must be united to the whole nature of Him that was begotten, and so be saved as a whole."[80] I have italicized the important rule. The rhetorical flair of the sentence preceding this rule and the ambiguity of the concept of healing both require further investigative work to fully discern the dogmatic content of the rule and its metaphysical basis.[81]

In order to understand **Nazianzus's rule**, we must consider Nazianzus's vague metaphor of "healing." What might he mean by this term? As Maurice Wiles notes, the healing analogy is limited as proof of the validity of the principle: Different ailments are healed in different ways. It does not obviously follow that healing requires assumption.[82] Here, two of Nazianzus's concepts are illuminating: **theosis** and mixture. We will begin with mixture. As Aloys Grillmeier explains, Gregory only "dimly grasped" the metaphysics of the incarnation.[83] This is evident in the fact that one of Gregory's preferred ways of speaking of the incarnation was in terms of "mixture," a term eventually rejected by Chalcedonian and neo-Chalcedonian theology.[84] Yet beneath this underdeveloped theological and philosophical language is an important insight: Because the divine and human natures in Christ are "mixed"—here, it is better to say "joined hypostatically in the incarnation"—it is possible for us to be united with Christ. In fact, Nazianzus had just spoken of the mingling or mixing of natures right before he introduces his rule.[85] The hypostatic union clearly is the basis for Nazianzus's rule. This brings us to the terminology that Gregory uses to describe this union between Christ and the Christian.

Gregory is famous for his development of the term "theosis," the process whereby qualities naturally proper to God are bestowed on the Christian

---

80. Gregory of Nazianzus, *To Cledonius*, 218–19; italics added.

81. See Hofer, *Gregory of Nazianzus*, 131. The claim that the Apollinarian is bereft of mind follows a pattern Nazianzus has taken against other heresies earlier in the letter. Thus, the one who says the humanity is not the same Son as the divinity loses their own sonship, and the one who does not worship the crucified one is guilty of deicide. See Gregory of Nazianzus, *To Cledonius*, 217.

82. Wiles, *Working Papers in Doctrine*, 113–14.

83. Grillmeier, *Christ in Christian Tradition*, 368.

84. I think much of what Gregory intends is later preserved under the language of "perichoresis," which also finds some roots in Gregory. Further, mixture has a complicated range of meaning in Greek philosophy. In Aristotelianism, mixture entails mutual adaptation, change, and the continuation of all mixed elements. In Stoicism, it involves mutual extension and ongoing distinction. The latter is closer to the eventual Chalcedonian model. Hofer, *Gregory of Nazianzus*, 99–101.

85. Gregory of Nazianzus, *To Cledonius*, 218.

by the work of the Holy Spirit as a result of the incarnation of the Son. In many respects, the concept of theosis is similar to that of sanctification. A full discussion of theosis appears in chapter 6, along with other related theological concepts, but a brief discussion of its basic features now will help us understand Nazianzus's rule. For Gregory, theosis is particularly linked with the mind (*nous*),[86] though broadly Gregory is also committed to a bodily component of theosis—this is required by the resurrection.[87] For example, in his second letter to Cledonius against the Apollinarians, Gregory exegetes 1 Corinthians 2:16—"We have the mind of Christ"—in the following way: "Those who have purified their mind by the imitation of the mind which the Saviour took of us, and, as far as may be, have attained conformity with it, are said to have the mind of Christ."[88] The term "theosis," in Gregory's usage, implies an important ethical component, and here we must note that ethical acts require mind and will.[89] However, where the emphasis in some Platonism and Aristotelianism is on being divinized through intellectual contemplation alone, Gregory tends to speak of the theosis of the entire human being, mind, body, and will.[90] In other words, by theosis, the Holy Spirit imparts divine qualities to the basic powers of human nature, whereby Christians can engage these basic human faculties of mind, body, and will to perform transformed operations or acts.[91] This theological interpretation of Nazianzus's rule reveals how Apollinarianism is flawed. By denying that Jesus has a human mind, Apollinaris undermines theosis by denying a complete union of humanity and divinity in Christ. If Christ has no human mind to which we can be conformed through the work of the Spirit, we do not have a healed human power of thinking, and as a result we cannot perform those ethical acts that are foundational for Christian life.[92]

86. Russell, *Doctrine of Deification*, 220.

87. Maslov, "Limits of Platonism," 448–49.

88. Gregory of Nazianzus, *Second Letter to Cledonius*, 226.

89. Maslov, "Limits of Platonism," 452. Maslov argues that this is the main difference between Gregory of Nazianzus's "theosis" and the earlier term found in theologians like Athanasius: *theopoiesis*. The latter can more easily be taken to denote a mechanistic exchange, while the former suggests a place for human ethical action.

90. Russell, *Doctrine of Deification*, 223; Maslov, "Limits of Platonism," 459. Gregory also avoids the Platonic dichotomy between the material and spiritual, acknowledging the goodness of creation.

91. I am here developing the inchoate distinction between essence and energies that is latent in Gregory of Nazianzus and fully developed later in Gregory Palamas, though I do not use the essence/energies distinction here, waiting to discuss it in chapter 6. See Alexis Torrance, "Precedents." I also here draw on the patristic insight that all natures have distinctive powers by which a thing is known to be what it is. On power in patristic theology, see M. Barnes, *Power*.

92. Something like this interpretation of Nazianzus is briefly offered in Miles, *Word Made Flesh*, 108.

Perhaps it will be helpful to explain this concept by stepping away from Gregory's theology and turning to Scripture. Consider Paul's theology in 1 Corinthians 2. We can know God because the Spirit who searches "the deep things of God" (2:10 NIV) has given us the "mind of Christ" (2:16), two key phrases from 1 Corinthians 2. In this same chapter, Paul discusses such sanctified intellective operations as wisdom, understanding of God's gifts (2:12), speaking of and interpreting spiritual things of God (2:13), and using spiritual discernment (2:15). Such are among the noetic dimensions of sanctification, and they are not available to us if our human minds cannot be conformed to Christ. But if the divine Son has taken on a complete human nature, including those powers that are capable of knowing, understanding, interpreting, and discerning, then the Spirit can sanctify our minds to have similar powers to Christ. In 1 Corinthians sanctification as a whole is said to be "in Christ Jesus" (1:2) who is himself "our . . . sanctification" (1:30). Paul teaches not only that we have the "mind of Christ" (2:16) but also that we will one day have the spiritual resurrected body of Christ, the second Adam (15:39–49). If we assume the ontological distinction between divine nature and human, as discussed above, then we must conclude that if Christ did not have a human body, mind, or will, we could not become like Christ in these areas.

In modern theology, Nazianzus's rule has raised a number of questions about what, precisely, must have been assumed. For example, some feminist theology has wrestled with the question of whether women can be healed if the Son was not incarnate as female, assuming the life of a woman.[93] Some medieval theology dealt with this concern through an appeal to Aristotelian biology, where women were considered to have defective or incomplete versions of the male human nature.[94] Were this account true, then Jesus assuming a male nature would also redeem women, since the entirety of female nature would also be assumed. Of course, Aristotelian biology's solution comes at far too great a cost: the sacrifice of a realistic scientific understanding of gender and sex and, worse, the sexist elimination of the equal dignity of women made in the image of God. We must be attentive to ensure that our Christology does not result in an unbiblical theology of women being incomplete or defective human beings. More recent responses frame Nazianzus's rule and gender in terms of the need for Christ to assume all properties of the human essence. As a result, they either jettison gender as an essential property, making it accidental and ultimately unimportant for human identity, or else attempt to resolve

93. For a brief example and response, see E. Johnson, "Redeeming the Name of Christ," 120.
94. See the discussion in Ruether, *Sexism and God-Talk*, 125–26. For the most famous example of medieval adoption of Aristotle's theory, see Aquinas, *Summa Theologica* I, Q. 92, A. 1, Obj. 1.

the issue through appeal to formal logical solutions.[95] In my articulation of Nazianzus's rule, this entire debate is off target, except insofar as it remains necessary to affirm the value of women. Since men and women equally have minds, bodies, and souls capable of basic human powers like thinking, communicating, desiring, and so forth, Christ's assumption and transformation of these powers and resulting operations makes such transformation possible for all men and women.

I have argued this interpretation of Nazianzus's rule based on one interpretation of the concept of healing, but two further points warrant this conclusion. First, a precedent version of this dogmatic rule is found in Origen of Alexandria, who argues that "the whole man would not be saved unless he had taken on himself the whole man." For Origen, the whole man consists of body, soul, and spirit—he is concerned about fundamental components of humanity, with corresponding powers, not with every aspect of human existence.[96] The second feature here is the fact that the main target of Gregory's *To Cledonius Against Apollinaris (Epistle 101)* is not the Apollinarians but the theology of Diodore of Tarsus, who tends to divide the natures too sharply. In other words, Gregory's main concern in the letter is about the "mixing" of humanity and divinity to establish genuine unity (again, "mixing" is an unfortunate term) and not about Jesus assuming an exhaustive list of properties necessary to become human.[97] In other words, Gregory's theology demands that Christ assume all fundamental powers of humanity, but it does not require that the Son assumed every aspect of humanity, or else the particularity of Jesus's human life as a first-century Jewish man would exclude countless other human beings who had a different gender, ethnicity, or even different physiological characteristics. It was sufficient for Christ to assume a body, spirit, mind, and will for our complete healing.

Leontius of Byzantium and Aphthartodocetism

In the early sixth century, the Byzantine theologian Julian of Halicarnassus taught that Christ assumed an incorruptible flesh, which has often been

---

95. Richards, "Can a Male Savior Save Women?" Richards frames the entire debate in this manner, offering the solution that human nature essentially has the inclusive disjunction "either male or female."

96. Origen of Alexandria, *Dialogue with Heraclides*, 442. Origen has just cited 1 Thess. 5:23 to show that our body, soul, and spirit will all be sanctified. It is these basic capacities that he has in mind.

97. Interestingly, the first eight of the ten anathemas in *To Cledonius Against Apollinaris (Epistle 101)* are actually against Diodore of Tarsus. See Beeley, "Early Christological Controversy," 399–400.

interpreted as a functional denial of Christ's full and true humanity.[98] His perspective became known as aphthartodocetism, from the combination of *aphthartos* (incorruptible) and the heresy of docetism, where Christ was believed to have only human appearance, not full humanity. Julian's position was criticized by both neo-Chalcedonians and miaphysites like Severus of Antioch,[99] but it was subject to great debate and often adopted by the Armenian church, including at the Second Council of Dvin (555) and at the Council of Shirakavan (862).[100]

Using phrasing reminiscent of Nazianzus's against the Apollinarians, Leontius of Byzantium argued against the aphthartodocetists that if the soul assumed was not like ours in every respect, "then surely what was saved was something other than my soul." Further, if the flesh assumed was not subject to death, suffering, and decay, like ours, then it was a different type of flesh, not ours, that was saved.[101] Where the aphthartodocetists interpreted passages like Acts 2:27 to teach that Christ did not see corruption because his humanity was incapable of corruption, Leontius argued that the verse is instead pointing to an act whose very supernatural dimensions depend on Christ having a nature capable of corruption. In fact, passages like Isaiah 53:3–4 suggest that Christ bore our suffering, sickness, and pain, all marks of a corruptible nature subject to decay.[102] For Leontius, a main concern was that Christ assume the sort of corruptible humanity that we have, so that by passing through death and being raised, we might share in the same process of resurrection.[103] Yet an important caveat should be added here from later theologians: That Christ was capable of dying need not imply that he would necessarily die, for the gratuity of his death is an important component of the theology of the cross as Christians witness to the grace of God.[104]

Careful explanation of the errors inherent to aphthartodocetism helps us clarify the sort of humanity that Christ assumed. To an extent, the debates over whether Christ was corruptible depended on what was meant by "corruption." Julian of Halicarnassus linked corruption to two conditions that he was concerned did not apply to Christ: sinfulness, which certainly is not true of Christ (see Heb. 4:15; 7:26; 1 John 3:5), and subjection to a condition that one did not willingly assume for themself. If Christ willingly accepted

---

98. For example, see Dowling, "Incarnation and Salvation," 102.
99. Louth, "Christology," 105.
100. Thomson, "Armenian List of Heresies," 360–61.
101. Leontius of Byzantium, *Contra Aphthartodocetists*, 349.
102. Leontius of Byzantium, *Contra Aphthartodocetists*, 371.
103. See the helpful discussion in Daley, *God Visible*, 205–10.
104. A full analysis of how his death was not necessary must be reserved for chapter 8.

death, then perhaps it was not proper to speak of corruption, which might imply something inflicted on him.[105] Against Julian, a conceptual distinction can be made between corruptibility and sinfulness—as we shall see, further clarification is needed regarding sin and the assumed human nature. This distinction allows us to affirm that Christ's mortality is distinct from any condition of guilt—if Jesus were guilty, then his death would be a punishment for his own guilt and not a satisfaction of our guilt.[106] This is the most important dimension of Christ's corruptibility: He was capable of dying. A close second is the affirmation that Jesus suffered, which is widely affirmed in Scripture (e.g., Matt. 16:21; Luke 24:26; 1 Pet. 3:18). The suffering of our Lord is one important dimension of a pastoral response to the existential problem of evil. As Emmanuel Katongole argues, the genuineness of the Son's laments not only confirms that God "stands with his people in their cry" but also leads to a clear social ethic as we seek those who currently lament.[107] Returning to Julian's concern that language of corruption implies that Christ suffered against his will, I grant that Christ willingly suffered, both through kenosis and the addition of a corruptible human nature and by voluntarily accepting his fate of death on the cross (Matt. 26:39, 42, 44; John 10:18). Yet it seems easier to safeguard against error by saying that Christ voluntarily took on a corruptible human nature than to deny use of the word altogether when speaking of Christ's humanity. Here, Christ was corruptible in an ontological sense, being capable of death, and in an existential sense, being able to suffer physically and emotionally,[108] but not corruptible in a moral sense, because Christ was unable to sin.

Impeccability, Fallen Humanity, and the Sinlessness of Christ

We turn now to one of the most challenging puzzles regarding the kind of humanity that Christ assumed: To what extent, if any, was it affected by sin? Contemporary and historical theologians offer a range of possibilities, only four of which I will consider here. As Marilyn McCord Adams explains, the assumed flesh can be the prefall humanity of Adam, postfall humanity before grace, graced postfall humanity, or glorified humanity.[109] It is possible to find all options present across the tradition. For example, in the seventh century Pope

---

105. Draguet, *Julien d'Halicarnasse*, 100–105.

106. I draw this important distinction from John Meyendorff, who would likely bristle at its connection to satisfaction. Here, we simply disagree. Meyendorff, *Byzantine Theology*, 158.

107. Katongole, *Born from Lament*, 119–20. Much more must be said on this topic when we reach the cross, but without a humanity capable of suffering, nothing further can be said.

108. This is emphasized in Lombard, *Sentences* 3.15.1.

109. Adams, *What Sort of Human Nature?*, 9.

Honorius I explained to the patriarch of Constantinople that the Son assumed "our nature, not our guilt" and that this nature was "that certainly, which was created before sin, not that which was vitiated after the transgression."[110] Much later, the Puritan William Ames wrote that "in the human nature [the incarnation] effects a change whereby that nature is elevated to highest perfection."[111] In the nineteenth century, Edward Irving famously argued that there was no humanity in existence for Christ to take except fallen humanity. If we affirm that Christ was born from Mary, and deny that he just passed through her, he must have assumed the humanity which she had. Therefore, unless we accept the Catholic doctrine of the immaculate conception that claims Mary was sinless, the Son assumed a fallen nature.[112] I find it unhelpful to structure the argument in this manner. This structure assumes that it is clear what the pre-fall, ungraced postfall, graced postfall, and glorified conditions are, but such distinctions have to be established outside of Christology if they are intended to define what humanity Christ assumed. Further, even if Irving is correct and the Son had to assume a fallen nature, it would remain unclear whether that fallen nature was immediately purified at the virginal conception or whether it was gradually purified throughout the life of Christ. Technically, Ames and Irving could both be correct, at least in terms of the limited dimensions of their theology discussed here. It seems best to me to frame the discussion differently.

In modern theology, Nazianzus's rule is sometimes cited to argue that the Son must have assumed fallen humanity in the incarnation.[113] I have already noted above the need for caution in deploying Gregory's argument—we cannot, for example, say that women are not saved because Jesus did not assume a second X chromosome or a female body. Similarly, it would be wrong to say that if Christ did not assume a fallen nature, he would be different in essence, for sin is not an essential property of humanity, but an accidental one.[114] In any case, I have argued that Nazianzus's rule is not about an exhaustive list of essential properties but refers instead to the need for Christ to assume certain fundamental powers and their associated operations or acts, such that Christ must have assumed those operations necessary for our theosis or sanctification.[115] The question now is to what extent these powers were stained by Adam's sin. I offer here some cautious reflections on this question.

110. Denzinger, *Sources of Catholic Dogma*, 99.
111. Ames, *Marrow of Theology*, 18:17.
112. Irving, *Incarnation Opened*, 115–16.
113. For example, see T. F. Torrance, *Incarnation*, 62; Clark and Johnson, *Incarnation of God*, 114; Dawson, "Far as the Curse Is Found," 68.
114. The point is well made in Duby, *Jesus*, 304.
115. To my knowledge, Jerome Van Kuiken has offered the most extensive interpretation of Nazianzus's rule that differs from my own. He interprets the rule in light of Nazianzus's

The effects of sin that are seen in the body, will, and mind only partially affect Christ's humanity such that we must be precise when saying that Christ assumed a fallen humanity. On the one hand, we must affirm that Christ is sinless, both in the sense that he committed no sinful acts (Heb. 4:15) and in the sense that sin as an evil power did not dwell in him (1 John 3:5b). On the other hand, Romans 8:3 teaches clearly that Christ came "in the likeness of sinful flesh," and, as Thomas Weinandy reminds us, "Paul consistently used 'likeness' to denote appropriate correspondence or congruity (cf. Rom. 1:23; 5:14; 6:5; Phil. 2:7)."[116] But what does it mean to be in the likeness of sinful flesh? At least two possibilities are available.

Jerome Van Kuiken helpfully distinguishes "assumption from" and "assumption to."[117] Assumption from refers to the humanity as he received it. The Son did not take on a preexisting human being, but he did receive human nature from Mary, which Protestants agree would have been fallen.[118] It may be that this nature was purified at the moment of hypostatic union, or the nature might have continued as stained by original pollution, which would be assumption to or into a fallen nature. Edward Irving was notorious for arguing the latter, teaching that the Holy Spirit's ongoing role in the life of Christ was the restraint of this sin nature that persisted in Christ after the virginal conception and until his risen humanity was glorified.[119] This view was rightly condemned, for it

---

insistence, in *Theological Orations* 30.6, that Christ was subject to our human experiences, being held captive by sin. Van Kuiken, "Fallen Flesh," 333. Highlighting Gregory's teaching that Christ assumes our experiences (*pathos* and cognates) in our redemption, he argues that Christ "unites to himself not only the various constituents of humanity (mind and body) but also the various experiences (*pathē*) of humanity (e.g., birth, temptation, suffering, death), sanctifying them by contact with his divinity." Van Kuiken, *Christ's Humanity*, 113–17. While I agree with Van Kuiken that Nazianzus sees Christ taking on our human experiences, and I agree with Nazianzus that this was necessary in some sense, I do not see how interpreting Nazianzus's rule as applying to human experiences works at a dogmatic level except in the most generic of senses. Christ apparently never experienced the death of a spouse, terminal cancer, victimization from sexual assault, or physically abusive parents. Similarly, Christ never experienced the guilt and shame that arise from having committed a sin, though I will have to argue this case more fully when I discuss the cross. Yet humans are redeemed by Christ from such experiences, which will be overcome in the general resurrection that he makes possible. We cannot say that since he did not take on these experiences, these aspects of *pathē*, that he did not redeem them. Nazianzus's rule can apply to experiences only indirectly, insofar as human experience (as a broad category) requires a human mind, will, and body. Thus, Nazianzus's rule does little, to my mind, to clarify the kind of humanity that Christ assumed nor the sort of fallen experiences that he may or may not have had during his life and ministry.

116. Weinandy, *Likeness of Sinful Flesh*, 79–80. See also Van Kuiken, "Fallen Flesh," 337.

117. Van Kuiken, "Fallen Flesh," 329.

118. Karl Barth claims that the assumption of a fallen human nature for its redemption is the main difference between "incarnations" in other religions (e.g., Isis or Osiris) and the incarnation of the Son in Christianity. Barth, *Church Dogmatics* I/2, 152–53.

119. See Irving, *Incarnation Opened*, 124, 129–31, 143.

does not fit with the biblical teaching that Christ was "an unblemished and spotless lamb" (1 Pet. 1:19) who was "holy, innocent, undefiled, separated from sinners" (Heb. 7:26). Since perfect beings are necessarily good, we must also affirm Christ's impeccability—the doctrine that Christ could not have sinned. Thus, it is necessary to reject assumption to an ongoing fallen humanity stained by original sin, but assumption from Mary's fallen humanity seems entailed by a Protestant view of the virginal conception. Whether we should attribute the purification of the fallen humanity to the Son's hypostatic assumption of that nature or to the work of the Holy Spirit in the virginal conception is a speculative matter not to be resolved here.[120] It is clear, though, that assuming fallen nature from Mary is the first step of recapitulation.

Turning to the individual faculties of Christ's humanity, we can ask how they were affected by Adam's fall. Clearly, Christ's human body could suffer and die, which requires that his body be capable of corruption.[121] Turning to the mind of Christ, it is clear that, like Adam and Eve after the fall, Christ had firsthand knowledge of the effects of good and evil such as experiencing human grief (Luke 19:41; John 11:35), emotional conditions that will be eliminated in the new creation for glorified human beings (Isa. 25:8; Rev. 21:4). It does not seem that Christ experienced the full noetic dimensions of sin, because the Gospels consistently depict Jesus as one able to authoritatively interpret the law because of his understanding of it, constantly in communion with his Father and the Spirit, and clearly aware of his Father's will. Whether his human spirit experienced the beatific vision to the degree that the glorified saints one day will seems speculative in my estimation.

Christ's human will is a matter of more complexity. It is clear that Jesus was tempted (e.g., Matt. 4:1–11 and parr.), but what does it mean for an impeccable being to be tempted? Certainly, we must reject in Christ the condition of total inability that affects other human beings, all of whom unavoidably sin (e.g., Eccles. 7:20; Jer. 13:23; 1 Cor. 2:14). Christ could and did avoid sin; indeed, impeccability insists that he must avoid sin necessarily. As Augustine of Hippo clarifies, in the garden, Adam and Eve could avoid sin, but after the fall they could not avoid sin. After conversion, they had the freedom to possibly not sin, but only in humanity's glorified state are they freed from the power to sin. In this respect, at least, the incarnate Christ was in the condition of glorified

---

120. Rafael Bello worries that attributing to the incarnation a certain sanctification of the fallen humanity seems to disturb the taxis of trinitarian action, attributing to the Son what is more clearly proper to the mission of the Spirit. Bello, *Sinless Flesh*, 72–90.

121. Interestingly, the medieval *Summa fratris Alexandri* claims that Christ's suffering could be voluntarily accepted or rejected. I suspect this is true only by virtue of Christ's divine omnipotence and not by virtue of some special feature of Christ's humanity. C. Barnes, *Christ's Two Wills*, 65.

humanity. But how can an impeccable being be tempted? Several theories offer possibilities, enough to show that our faith in an impeccable, tempted Savior is not illogical, but nothing certain enough to definitively answer the question. It may be, as Maximus the Confessor taught, that demonic influences were amplifying Christ's "natural appetites in ways that make them violent and strong," to use the words of Benjamin Heidgerken.[122] As Steven Duby explains, the temptations are properly so called because they "are an occasion of painful, costly submission to the Father's will because they involve Christ denying his natural desires and forgoing things that often would be, in ordinary circumstances, legitimate human pursuits."[123] Christ still suffers the pain of forgoing these goods, even if he could not do otherwise. What is clear, though, is that Christ could not be tempted in a sinful way.[124] More will be said on temptation when chapter 7 considers the temptation in the garden of Gethsemane.

———————

Here is a dogmatic summary of my reflections on the full humanity of Christ. God the Son, Second Person of the Trinity, assumed a full human nature, not by a kenotic leaving behind of the divine nature but by the addition of a complete human nature, possessing the fundamental human capacities and powers of the will, mind, body, and soul. This nature came from Mary through the virginal conception in a fallen state but was purified of all of original sin's guilt and pollution at the moment of the hypostatic union. The Son's assumed humanity was truly capable of suffering, corruption, and death, and it bore the effects of the fall in this frailty as well as in being susceptible to temptation from the devil and experiencing the possibility of emotions like grief. However, Christ's sinless person ensured that the humanity was not only sinless but entirely impeccable, and in this respect he partially foreshadowed our future glorified state.

Partitive Exegesis and the Two Natures

This chapter has unfolded exegetical reasons for affirming the full deity of Christ as well as dogmatic reasons derived from Scripture for affirming the full

———

122. Heidgerken, *Salvation Through Temptation*, 119. Maximus is clear that this need not entail that Christ lacked virtue. Heidgerken, *Salvation Through Temptation*, 107.

123. Duby, *Jesus*, 310.

124. Oliver Crisp argues that we can distinguish between innocent and sinful temptation, where the latter requires a state of sin prior to temptation, perhaps in willingly seeking out that which tempts. Similarly, internal temptation is self-caused, but external temptation comes from Satan, demonic forces, or other human beings. Perhaps Christ is only capable of innocent, external temptation. Crisp, *God Incarnate*, 130.

humanity of Christ. The Chalcedonian definition balances these theological demands by affirming that Christ exists in two natures, human and divine. This Scripture-derived metaphysical framework then provides the hermeneutic rule of partitive exegesis to resolve some remaining theological puzzles. For example, how should we interpret the two teachings of Jesus in the Gospel of John that "I and the Father are one" (10:30) and "the Father is greater than I" (14:28)? In the words of Gregory of Nazianzus, "What is lofty you are to apply to the Godhead, and to that nature in him which is superior to sufferings and incorporeal; but all that is lowly to the composite condition of him who for your sakes . . . was made man."[125] Or, to use the wording of contemporary North American theologians Bobby Jamieson and Tyler Wittman, "Biblical reasoning discerns that Scripture speaks of the one Christ in two registers in order to contemplate the whole Christ. Therefore read Scripture in such a way that you discern different registers in which Scripture speaks of Christ, yet without dividing him."[126] Partitive exegesis is a practice warranted by Scripture. Jamieson and Wittman provide several examples to make this case. Romans 1:3 and 9:3 both qualify the human birth and genealogy of Christ as "according to the flesh." Taken in line with the doctrine of the hypostatic union, this clarification protects the eternal, uncreated divine nature. First Peter similarly links Christ's suffering with the flesh (3:18; 4:1), using partitive exegesis because the divine nature does not suffer or die.[127]

Certain metaphysical assumptions lie beneath partitive exegesis. As Augustine of Hippo explains, some scriptural statements reference the divine substance of the Son, while others reference the human substance. For example, in the divine substance the Father and Son (and Spirit) do all things together (John 5:17, 19), but the human substance or nature is that which performs the embodied acts of Christ[128] Other statements, Augustine admits, could have two senses, one referencing each nature. For example, Jesus's teaching in John 7:16 that "my teaching isn't mine but is from the one who sent me" could reference the divine nature, including the divine mind and knowledge, which the Son has from the Father through eternal generation. Or it could reference the Son's knowledge and teaching from his humanity, which is the "form of a servant" (Phil. 2:7) and not equal to God.[129] If statements about Christ reference, pick out, and specify either the human or divine nature and substance, it seems to me that these natures must be concrete natures,

125. Gregory of Nazianzus, *Theological Orations* 30.18.
126. Jamieson and Wittman, *Biblical Reasoning*, 154–55; italics omitted.
127. Jamieson and Wittman, *Biblical Reasoning*, 156–59.
128. Augustine of Hippo, *On the Holy Trinity* 2.1.3.
129. Augustine of Hippo, *On the Holy Trinity* 2.2.4.

meaning that they are discrete things and not merely abstract natures that are mental lists of properties.

If the Son is one person with two natures, the dogmatic affirmation of two concrete natures raises the puzzle of explaining how he is a composite person. Such language, which is found across the tradition, is not meant to imply that the hypostasis is a unity of two hypostases. Rather, it is intended "to express that, after subsisting only in the divine nature prior to the incarnation, the Son now subsists in two natures."[130] Explaining how such a composite of two natures can be one person and hypostasis is the subject of chapter 5. Before turning to this question, we can summarize the basic dogmatic conclusions of this chapter. Christ exists in two concrete natures, each continuing in its distinct existence, one fully divine and the other fully human. The incarnate Son's human nature is consubstantial with our humanity in that it possesses all the same basic powers, including a real human body, soul, mind, and will, such that the Son can be said to have two minds and two wills as well as two natures. The human nature is also like ours in its corruptibility, being able to suffer and die. The Son's human nature is also like ours in the sense that it can be tempted, but not in the sense that it wills sin, and while aspects of original corruption are evident, including corruptibility but also perhaps noetic limitations, it seems unlikely to me that Christ's humanity is born with original guilt and certain that the Son is not peccable as a result of the incarnation. With this dogmatic account of the two natures in hand, we can turn to consider the implications for salvation of claiming that Jesus was fully human and fully divine. While the duration of this book discusses implications of the two natures, I will begin the next chapter by exploring ethical implications of the two natures for the Christian life.

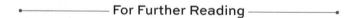

For Further Reading

Adams, Marilyn McCord. *What Sort of Human Nature? Medieval Philosophy and the Systematics of Christology*. Marquette University Press, 1999.

> Adams's brief survey is condensed from a series of lectures explaining theories about the sort of human nature assumed by Christ in the incarnation. Adams focuses on different aspects of this question than I do, making this a helpful supplementary text.

Bird, Michael F. *Jesus Among the Gods: Early Christology in the Greco-Roman World*. Baylor University Press, 2022.

130. Duby, *Jesus*, 366. Duby notes Aquinas, Polanus, and Turretin adopt this language.

Michael Bird offers an extensive analysis of the relationship between canonical depictions of Jesus and depictions of other intermediary figures in Jewish and Greco-Roman literature. Importantly, he argues that there was a distinction in Greco-Roman literature between beings that are made God and beings that are true deity by nature. Jesus, Bird shows, fits the second sort of description.

Hurtado, Larry W. *Lord Jesus Christ: Devotion to Jesus in Earliest Christianity*. Eerdmans, 2003.

Hurtado is perhaps the most discussed recent scholar who argues that Christ is depicted in the New Testament as equally God with the Father. Hurtado makes his case by focusing on the way that the New Testament directs cultic worship to Christ. Besides making an important, much discussed argument, Hurtado exegetes many major texts in the christological monotheism debates.

Van Kuiken, E. Jerome. *Christ's Humanity in Current and Ancient Controversy: Fallen or Not?* Bloomsbury, 2017.

This book surveys multiple perspectives on the question of Christ's fallenness. A detailed and technical survey, Van Kuiken's work is a necessary read for all interested in the debates about the kind of humanity that Christ assumed.

CHAPTER FOUR

Moral Exemplar

The Son's assumption of a full and perfect humanity has considerable implications for systematic and moral theology. While Scripture
can exhort the Christian to "be perfect, therefore, as your heavenly
Father is perfect" (Matt. 5:48), one can have some empathy for the Christian
who does not know how to follow the pattern of an omnipotent deity who
creates and governs the universe. When the Son assumes a complete human
nature, including a human mind, will, and body, he takes on a form that more
easily serves as a guide for Christian life. As a result, it is common to speak
of Christ as our moral exemplar or even to discuss moral exemplar atonement, though including this as atonement would be a misnomer.[1] Certainly,
Scripture describes Jesus as an example to the Christian (1 Pet. 2:21; 1 John
2:6), but the work of the cross extends much further than this in atonement.
Yet, other explanations of atonement also depend on the full humanity and
moral perfection of Christ, for the fulfillment of the law is a precondition
to any satisfaction offered on the cross (more on this in chapter 8). Christ's
sinlessness is also an important component of recapitulation, such that the
sin introduced by Adam is reversed by the sinless Christ. The moral perfection of the human Christ is thus at an important junction between systematic
and moral theology.

This chapter will explore the moral perfection of Christ in terms of both its
example for the Christian and its contribution toward the reversal of Adam's

---

1. One can distinguish between moral exemplar approaches, where Jesus shows us an example, and moral influence approaches, where Jesus's death on the cross demonstrates God's
love. See, for example, Erickson, *Christian Theology*, 801–6.

sin, leaving for later chapters a full exposition of atonement. Moral theology is not a monolithic discipline, so I will draw on Samuel Wells's distinction between universal, subversive, and ecclesial moral theological systems.[2] Universal ethics, which understands Christian ethics to apply in the same manner to everyone, tends to focus on moral laws, so I will begin the chapter by briefly considering Jesus's prophetic role as interpreter and fulfiller of the law. Subversive ethics considers Christian moral theology to particularly speak on behalf of the oppressed, a perspective that draws heavily on Jesus's teaching of the kingdom. Ecclesial ethics considers Christian ethics to be especially for the church, a perspective that fits well with virtue ethics, which will conclude the chapter. As I explore these ethical perspectives, I will demonstrate Christ's significance for all moral theologies by examining Christ's ministry holistically and in terms of a particular concrete example of his teaching or work. I will also show how Christ the second Adam fulfills the aspirations of each moral perspective.

Jesus as Prophetic Interpreter of the Law

Universal ethics is, as Samuel Wells admits, "seldom a name any strand of ethics would give itself."[3] Yet it is appropriate insofar as it identifies perspectives that consider an ethical system to be universally applicable and to favor no particular perspective. Wells includes within universal ethics both divine command theory, which prioritizes God's commands as the basis of moral obligation, and natural law ethics, an approach that analyzes right and wrong in terms of the intrinsic nature of a thing, often considering whether actions are in line with God's purposes inscribed in nature. Christ plays an important role in each of these perspectives. As the definitive prophet (a less emphasized christological title, but see Matt. 13:57; Mark 6:4; Luke 4:24; John 4:44), Jesus is the most important interpreter of the moral law, whether we restrict that law to the special revelation of the covenant or include natural revelation manifest in natural law.[4] The Gospel of Matthew especially highlights Jesus's role as interpreter of the law through the Moses **typology** found in its early chapters.[5] The Sermon on the Mount can be interpreted both as the definitive

---

2. See Wells, *Introducing Christian Ethics*, 123–25.
3. Wells, *Introducing Christian Ethics*, 127.
4. Prophets could play a variety of roles but generally were understood to be intermediaries between God and humans. Often, this intermediary role focused on declaring God's judgment, especially with the context of covenant violation, though prophets could also bring novel insights into God's will. Petersen, *Prophetic Literature*, 5–8; Childs, *Biblical Theology*, 174–75.
5. Hays, *Moral Vision*, 94–95.

interpretation of the law and as a rejection of certain moral teachings in the first century by some religious leaders.[6] As an itinerant prophet, Jesus would have traveled and repeated similar teachings in various communities, often of covenantal import.[7] The earliest generations of Christians often understood Jesus to be, among other things, a moral teacher, whose teachings opened up the "way of life" in opposition to the "way of death," to use the terminology of the Didache.[8]

Jesus is not only the interpreter of the law but the one who fulfills the law. Here, he stands in stark contrast with the first Adam, who in Genesis 3 violated the entire law. As Edward Fisher explains, Adam violated all ten commandments (see Exod. 20:1–17). He followed the devil, as if Satan were a god, while idolizing his stomach. He bore God's name in vain by not believing God, and he did not rest in his assigned estate, violating the spiritual significance of Sabbath. Adam also dishonored his heavenly Father, was murderously responsible for his own death and the death of all his progeny, and he "committed spiritual fornication." He stole the fruit that was not his, while bearing false testimony against God by treating him as a liar. In doing so, he coveted the knowledge of good and evil.[9] In contrast, Jesus came to fulfill the law (Matt. 5:17), being the one without sin (Heb. 4:15). While Christ's atoning death did establish a new covenant (Heb. 8:7–13), this covenant does not abolish the law but by the power of the Holy Spirit inscribes the law that Christ fulfilled in the heart of every Christian (Heb. 8:10 quoting Jer. 31:33). In order to understand both Jesus's interpretation of the law and his fulfillment of it, we must now turn to Jesus's teaching on the two greatest commandments.

The Two Greatest Commandments

Across the Gospels (Matt. 22:34–40; Mark 12:28–34; Luke 10:25–28), Jesus teaches that the two greatest commandments are to love God with all our heart, mind, soul, and strength (Deut. 6:4–5) and to love our neighbor as ourselves (Lev. 19:18). "All of the Law and the Prophets depend on these two

6. Turretin notes four reasons for this conclusion. First, Jesus exhorts his audience to have a better righteousness than the Pharisees and scribes (Matt. 5:20). Second, the emphasis on "you have heard it said" suggests a new interpretation and not a rejection or improvement of the law. Third, the teaching of loving our neighbor but hating our enemies (Matt. 5:43) is not canonical but likely comes from contemporary religious leaders. Fourth, from the fact that the teachings of Jesus are contained implicitly in the law. See Turretin, *Institutes* 11.3.9.

7. N. T. Wright, *Jesus and the Victory of God*, 170. Wright notes that this plethora of repeated oral tradition may explain the variability of some content in the Synoptic Gospels.

8. Teaching of the Twelve Apostles, 171.

9. Fisher, *Marrow of Divinity*, 36.

commands" (Matt. 22:40). This teaching of Christ therefore authoritatively summarizes Old Testament ethics. Admittedly, a full New Testament ethic may require further discussion. Richard Hays, for example, has worked to develop "focal images" that effectively summarize the full New Testament canon while allowing tensions in the texts to stand.[10] For example, one might read the moral rigorism of the Sermon on the Mount in such a way that it silences Paul's teaching on justification by faith, or emphasize faith and freedom from the law's commands to such an extent that the Sermon on the Mount is ignored. Hays argues that the three images of community, cross, and new creation adequately summarize New Testament ethics.[11] Interestingly, Hays argues that love cannot summarize New Testament ethics because love is only marginally important in books like Mark, Hebrews, Revelation, and Acts. The word "love" does not even appear in the latter work. Were we to center love as a summary of New Testament ethics, we might exclude Acts altogether.[12] The risk is well noted, so it is important to distinguish between a summary of the law, which can be done in terms of love, and a summary of all ethics in the canon, which may be more diverse. This diversity requires that we also consider other moral theories and biblical emphases, including Jesus's teaching on the kingdom. Before turning to this teaching, I must further clarify the connections between Jesus's teachings on love and his role as second Adam.

Jesus fulfills the two greatest commandments to love God and love your neighbor in a maximal way. As the eternal Son of God, Jesus eternally loves the Father and Spirit through the perfect perichoretic sharing of the divine being. In fact, we can think of the Son as one of the three unique eternal modes of existence of the God who is perfect love (1 John 4:16).[13] When the Son assumed full humanity, a human nature was drawn into the perfect loving relationship that already existed between Father, Son, and Spirit. As Donald Fairbairn explains, "The life of Jesus shows us both what it looks like for God to share in the love of the Trinity—since Jesus is the second person of the Trinity—and what it looks like for a human being to share in that same love, since this second person of the Trinity has taken humanity upon himself."[14] Christ thus loves God more than any other human, but he also shows an unsurpassed love for his human neighbor. The greatest love is to

10. Hays, *Moral Vision*, 189–90.
11. Hays, *Moral Vision*, 196–200.
12. Hays, *Moral Vision*, 200–201.
13. One here thinks of Richard of St. Victor's trinitarianism, which describes the three divine persons as perfectly existing in three different modes of loving: gratuitous, owed, and mixed. See *On the Trinity* 3.14, 19–20; 5.16–19.
14. Fairbairn, *Life in the Trinity*, 149.

die for another (John 15:13). While some human beings have died for others, no one has ever died for someone else with a death that was fully gratuitous. Since death comes from sin (Rom. 5:12; 6:23), the sinless Christ was not under the curse of death except insofar as he accepted this death himself.[15] Christ's death is itself an act of perfect love of neighbor, just as his very incarnation is brought about through love (John 3:16). Christ, the second Adam, the perfect Son of God, perfectly lives out the universal moral law as summarized in love of God and neighbor.

Jesus's Proclamation of the Kingdom

One major focus of Jesus's ministry was on proclaiming the arrival of the *basileia tou theo*, which is alternately translated as "kingdom of God," "dominion of God," "reign of God," or even "kin-dom of God." The latter usage, advocated by Ada María Isasi-Díaz, draws on Jesus's naming of God as Father and on his teachings relativizing family or extending family into new domains (Matt. 8:21–22; 10:37; Mark 3:31–34),[16] though it is less a translation of the term than an attempt to contextualize Jesus's teaching in a new sociocultural context. I will continue to use the traditional English phrasing of "kingdom of God," in part because it reveals Scripture's language of a historical and eschatological reality that can be entered (e.g., Matt. 7:21; Mark 10:23).[17] While much Jewish apocalyptic and eschatological thinking places deliverance in a cosmic future, the preaching of Christ, which includes this future element, also insists that the kingdom is being made present in the ministry of Jesus.[18] Christ is the one who fully manifests the kingdom in all its subversive reversals on behalf of the oppressed. I will consider the kingdom in terms of Latin American liberation theology, *misión integral*, and Jesus's table fellowship.

Latin American liberation theology is a subversive theology that focuses on theology through the lens of liberative action on behalf of the poor, drawing much of their theology from Jesus's proclamation of the kingdom of

15. Chapter 8 will discuss this important theological point more.

16. Isasi-Díaz, "Kin-dom of God," 183–85. Another motive driving Isasi-Díaz's usage is that language of "kingdom" may result in social consequences that "counter the values that can be ascertained from the Gospels" (172, 175–78). While I grant the risk and historical actuality of misusing the terminology of kingdom, in the end I judge the risk to be less than she deems it.

17. I also find too much emphasis on the power of ideas in much theological critique of the ethical implications of specific terms. Certainly, such terms can have harmful consequences. Ideas, too, have considerable importance for spiritual formation and right teaching. I am, after all, writing a work of dogmatics. Yet, more liberative outcomes are possible from specific economic, social, or political changes than through the change of a term like "kingdom."

18. Cahill, *Global Justice*, 96–97.

God, which is definitively mediated by and through Jesus Christ.[19] Though many liberation theologians have written on Christology and on the kingdom of God, Jon Sobrino is likely the most famous for his engagement with both of these subjects. Sobrino calls for a **re-messianization** of Jesus, which would draw clearer sustained attention to Jesus as the Messiah, the anointed one.[20] Noting modern Christianity's tendency to make salvation a transcendent matter without historical import,[21] Sobrino reminds us of the political dimension of anointing, which was often linked with Old Testament kings (e.g., 1 Sam. 9:19; 24:7). While Latin American Christians, including Sobrino, have consistently rejected the idea that Jesus was Messiah through political victories or violent means,[22] Sobrino is also part of a growing Latin American consensus that the kingdom is at least partly manifest in history.[23] Jesus certainly focused his proclamation on the kingdom—his preaching is frequently summarized as focusing on the arrival of this kingdom (Matt. 3:17; 9:35; Mark 1:15; Luke 4:43; 16:16)—so it is unsurprising that Sobrino considers the concept of the kingdom to be "systematically organizing the whole of theology."[24]

Sobrino explains that there are three possible ways of knowing what Jesus means by speaking of the kingdom of God. The first approach is the notional way, which asks what Jesus thinks about the kingdom. Much scholarship on the significance of Jesus's proclamation draws attention to Luke 4:17–21, where he unrolls a scroll and reads Isaiah 61:1–2:

> The Spirit of the Lord is on me,
> because he anointed me
> to preach good news to the poor.
> He has sent me
> to proclaim release to the captives
> and recovery of sight to the blind,
> to set free the oppressed,
> to proclaim the year of the Lord's favor.

19. See the discussion in Martinez-Olivieri, *Visible Witness*, 56, 59–62.

20. Sobrino, *Christ the Liberator*, 138–48.

21. He identifies this process with de-messianization. In these moves, salvation becomes about saving individual souls to heaven, and the connection with the Messiah as an expected political figure is completely lost. Sobrino, *Christ the Liberator*, 145.

22. For example, see Sobrino, *Christ the Liberator*, 147; Escobar, *Christ in Latin America*, 252; Boff, *Jesus Christ Liberator*, 281. Gustavo Gutiérrez, putting it in terms of the kingdom, makes a helpful distinction: historical, political liberation "is a salvific event," but "it is not *the* coming of the Kingdom, not *all* of salvation." Gutiérrez, *Theology of Liberation*, 177.

23. See, e.g., Escobar, *Christ in Latin America*, 203; Martinez-Olivieri, *Visible Witness*, 76.

24. Sobrino, "Reign of God," 42.

Hak Joon Lee links this text with the broader practice of Sabbath days and years, which relativizes ownership, work, and economic hierarchy, setting the stage for the larger redistributions of the year of Jubilee.[25] Christian Collins Winn argues that the proclamation of the kingdom is closely tied to two other "conceptual fields," Jubilee and apocalyptic.[26] Focusing on enthronement psalms that describe God's reign as an immanent reign of justice (e.g., Pss. 89:10, 14; 94:16), Collins Winn argues that the commandment for a year of Jubilee that redistributes and restores property, frees indentured labor, and leaves land fallow (Lev. 25:8–55) is a command that extends God's liberative justice evident in the exodus into further stages of history.[27] Similarly, apocalyptic texts anticipate "judgment and new life" but manifest in a new earthly reality that reveals God.[28] As Sobrino remarks, "God is inseparable from his reign," so such notions of the kingdom reveal the character of God and of his Son.[29] Yet Sobrino can fairly critique this approach to the kingdom because it remains abstract, unable to guide the concrete ethical action of the church.[30]

Sobrino therefore points to a second way of understanding the kingdom: the way of the praxis of Jesus, a method that uses Jesus's actions to interpret the meaning of the kingdom and the best ways for the church to embody the kingdom today.[31] Sobrino considers several examples of Jesus's actions in terms of their implications for praxis. For example, Jesus's miracles are "beneficent realities, liberative realities in the presence of oppression."[32] Sobrino makes this claim because Jesus regularly acts compassionately toward the weak in terms of both physical weakness and social weakness (see Matt. 7:11–16; 9:36; 15:32; 20:29–34). Similarly, we cannot ignore the fact that many of the people whom Jesus forgives, offers mercy, or heals are also in social situations where they have "no possibilities left to them."[33] Consider, for example, the woman caught in adultery (John 8:1–11), the paralytic lowered

25. H. Lee, *Christian Ethics*, 307–12.
26. Collins Winn, *God's Reign*, 8.
27. Collins Winn, *God's Reign*, 28.
28. Collins Winn, *God's Reign*, 89.
29. Sobrino, *Crossroads*, 45.
30. Sobrino, "Reign of God," 46–47.
31. There is some debate regarding the extent to which the kingdom can be identified with the church. See Padilla, *Between the Times*, 9; Martinez-Olivieri, *Visible Witness*, 71. These perspectives consider the kingdom as the basis for the church's mission and the church as the location of the kingdom's presence. Yet Escobar wisely cautions that ideologies identifying the church with the kingdom as the goal of history were quick to resort to political violence during the colonial period, which prompts us to caution when fully identifying church and kingdom. Escobar, *Christ in Latin America*, 196.
32. Sobrino, "Reign of God," 49.
33. Sobrino, *Crossroads*, 49.

through the roof (Mark 2:1–12; Luke 5:17–26), and the woman who had been bleeding for twelve years (Matt. 9:20–22; Mark 5:25–34; Luke 8:43–48). The woman caught in adultery faced execution, the paralytic had no real means of earning income through work, and the woman bleeding would have been set apart from others in the Jewish community for being unclean (Lev. 15:17–23) and had already spent all her money trying to be healed and restored to society (Luke 8:43). Jesus's healings of such persons are not only miraculous interventions but "signs of liberation,"[34] and he tells his followers to proclaim the kingdom while adopting similar practice of liberative ministry (Matt. 10:7–8; Mark 5:12–13; Luke 9:2; 10:9). We must not fail to recognize the link between Jesus's kingdom acts toward liberation and his personhood. As Lisa Sowle Cahill remarks, "Not only is the kingdom real and effective for Jesus, it is present in and through Jesus."[35]

Sobrino further elaborates the way of the praxis of Jesus by pointing to Jesus's denunciations. He argues, "We can deduce something of what the Reign itself signified as a totality" from Jesus's "view of the anti-Reign as a totality." Denunciations tend to be toward groups, though Sobrino admits that Jesus does not have a theory of social class.[36] For example, in the Gospel of Luke the Beatitudes are followed by the pronouncement of a series of woes directed at plural groups: the rich, those who are full, those laughing, and those spoken highly of (Luke 6:24–26). Similarly, denunciations of the scribes and Pharisees in the seven woes in Matthew 23 target the religious leaders as groups, chastising them for, among other things, tithing herbs but neglecting "the more important matters of the law—justice, mercy, and faithfulness" (v. 23). Consistently, then, Jesus denounces those who use the law in an imbalanced way to lay unnecessary religious burdens on the people while ignoring real sociopolitical burdens of oppression that the law and the prophets would challenge (Matt. 23:4). In so doing, the religious leaders misunderstand what it means to love God and fail to love their neighbors. The way of the praxis thus provides a fundamental orientation for Christian action, which, like Christ's action, should act in solidarity with those in need and should challenge and critique those who contribute to injustice. Like earlier lessons in ethics drawn from Christology, this basic orientation, though pointing to broad categories of actions, requires careful work to contextualize what it means to act in solidarity in a given context or what it means to challenge those in power who work injustice. Here, a basic moral

34. Sobrino, *Crossroads*, 48.
35. Cahill, *Global Justice*, 114.
36. Sobrino, "Reign of God," 51.

orientation and a point of contact between dogmatics and moral theology are found, not a complete social ethic.[37]

It is necessary to digress here momentarily to connect this discussion of the kingdom with the doctrine of sin. While I have already introduced the doctrine of original sin in distinction from actual sin, it is important to note that within the category of actual sins are found both individual and social dimensions.[38] The social dimensions of sin are drawn from several aspects of Scripture. Biblical language of "the world" as a source of evil points to a social dimension of sin. As Stephen Mott explains, *kosmos*, which is often translated as "the world," often means "order, that which is assembled together well." Mott argues that the term *kosmos* includes "the system of property and wealth" (in 1 John 3:17), the "stratification of class and status" (1 Cor. 1:27–28; James 2:5), and "political rule" (Matt. 4:8; Rev. 11:15).[39] Similarly, the Old Testament includes examples of entire communities being held responsible for the sins

37. This fundamental orientation is perhaps the most important aspect of biblical ethics. Certainly, when turning to individual moral teachings in the Bible, there is broad consensus among ethicists that the purpose behind a law is more important than the particular details of how that purpose is fulfilled. For example, many take the teaching to "turn the other cheek" (Exod. 21:24; Lev. 24:20; Deut. 19:21) to intend mercy, such that Jesus's claim to not resist the evildoer merely expands on that purpose (Matt. 5:38–39). For a detailed discussion, see Cosgrove, *Scripture in Moral Debate*, 12–50. When understanding the significance of the kingdom, one can identify the cumulative purposes behind Jesus's frequent teaching. Yet Sobrino's emphasis on praxis reminds us that we cannot leave social ethics at the level of a basic orientation, nor can we merely affirm broad intended purposes, however frequently these occur. Such purposes must be contextualized in the form of particularized actions, and this process must extend beyond even the way of the praxis of the kingdom to the development of particular social programs. Ivan Petrella is right to criticize even Sobrino for a lack of specificity. See Petrella, *Liberation Theology*. Yet the task of developing a specific social program is one beyond the scope of dogmatics proper, though I hope, as this book, and especially this chapter, shows, that social task is not separable from dogmatic insights.

38. I have explored this question in far greater detail in Butner, *Work Out Your Salvation*, 106–14.

39. Mott, *Biblical Ethics and Social Change*, 4–6. Mott's conclusion is not universally shared. Sasse agrees that *cosmos* in Hellenistic usage is "the order whereby the sum of individual things is gathered into a totality," but he concludes that the term is "never used in the sense 'order'" in the New Testament. Sasse, "κοσμός," 870, 883. A similar position is found in the definition of *kosmos* in Silva, *New International Dictionary*, 730–36, which concludes that *kosmos* "always has the spatial meaning 'world'" (733). Najeeb Haddad argues that *cosmos* frequently has both the positive sense of created order and the negative sense of an order dominated by sin, death, and spiritual powers. Haddad also helpfully shows how various social concepts like the "fellowship of the Spirit" (Phil. 2:1), customs (1 Cor. 11:6), imitation of the Lord (1 Thess. 1:6), vice lists (Mark 7:21–22), and the unity of the one body of Christ (1 Cor. 12:12) establish a "translocal standard" for churches against the patterns of the world. His account offers clearer support of Mott's thesis, though some difference remains. Notably, Haddad downplays anti-imperial dimensions of Paul's theology compared to some scholars, though he does admit Paul sees Rome as fundamentally opposed to God. Haddad, *Paul, Politics, and New Creation*, 140–46, 154–61, 163.

of individuals (e.g., Josh. 7:1, 11) or of Israelites praying in repentance for prior generations' sins (Exod. 20:5; Num. 14:18; Deut. 9:5; Neh. 9:2; Dan. 9:16).[40] As the promised new covenant approaches, the corporate dimensions of sin are deflated (Ezek. 18), but corporate elements certainly remain, most notably in the corporate and covenantal original guilt, which is reversed by the second Adam, who represents a group, his people (Rom. 5:12–21), though the corporate woes named by Sobrino also contribute to a doctrine of social sin. The doctrine of social sin is relatively new, and terminology varies. I prefer a threefold distinction between the sins of social groups, which refer to collective actions, social sin, which refers to the ways that sins are culturally and socially conditioned, and **structures of sin**. The latter term, which is idiosyncratic compared to the more common language of "structural sin," is meant to indicate those impersonal dimensions of societies, such as laws, policies, customs, or economic distributions of resources that prompt sin. Strictly speaking, structures of sin are not examples of actual sin, since the latter category refers to human acts. However, the Bible is clear that human customs (Col. 2:8), imbalanced or false weights and measures (Prov. 11:1), and unjust laws and decrees (Isa. 10:1–4) can contribute to sin and injustice. Social sin, on the other hand, refers to the direct social influence of sinners on one another, as humans drag one another further into sin. Combined, these three aspects of the doctrine of sin reveal the need to attend to the corporate dimensions of evil and hence to the corporate dimensions of moral theology derived from the life of Christ. In his teachings about the kingdom, Christ proclaims a corporate and social reality against the corporate and social reality of this world.[41]

Returning to Sobrino's threefold analysis of the kingdom, besides the notional way of understanding the kingdom and the way of the praxis of Jesus, Sobrino also advocates considering "the way of the addressee of the reign," which argues that we can understand the kingdom when we understand to whom Jesus was proclaiming the kingdom.[42] The right conclusion to this analysis seems to me to be that Jesus especially proclaims the kingdom to those who are poor, spiritually or materially (e.g., Matt. 5:3; Luke 6:20), with the expectation that few who are rich will be able to accept the kingdom (Matt. 19:23; Luke 18:25). Included among the addressees are those who are poor, captive, blind, and oppressed (Luke 4:18), though the blind can be literally

40. A detailed version of this account that mildly overstates the evidence is found in Everhart, "Communal Reconciliation," 7–11.

41. We must be careful to explain social sin so that it is not inescapable, for Christ was a member of human society and yet free from sin. See Hill and Kieser, "Social Sin."

42. Sobrino, "Reign of God," 54–55.

blind (Matt. 20:29–34) or spiritually unable to see (Matt. 13:10–13; John 9:39). Regarding the latter, it is more common for Jesus's preaching to reveal the blindness of the religious leaders and other cultural elites than to remove it (Matt. 15:12–14), though by God's grace some do come to be his disciples (Matt. 27:57; John 19:39). Similarly, while Jesus proclaims deliverance to the oppressed, he also praises the faith of a centurion, a military leader in the occupying and oppressing Roman army (Matt. 8:5–13). The social dynamics of the kingdom are complicated, and emphasis on preaching to the downtrodden does not result in full exclusion of social elites. Fundamentally, Jesus's self-understanding is that "the Son of Man has come to seek and to save the lost" (Luke 19:10),[43] and while many who are lost are social outcasts, poor, sick, or otherwise in dire straits, some are in more complicated situations. Zacchaeus, for example, is powerful, rich, and likely socially ostracized, yet "salvation has come to [his] house" (Luke 19:9) in the context of his giving half his possessions to the poor and restoring fourfold what he had earned by defrauding people (Luke 19:8). The way of the addressee of the reign helps us to understand how Jesus's message would have been heard in historical context, so that we can seek to have preaching today resound with similar effect.

While there is much to agree with in the theology of the kingdom presented so far, there is also a clear risk of doctrinal imbalance. This is evident in the recurring insistence of liberation theologians that, to use Leonardo Boff's wording, "the historical Jesus did not preach about himself or the church or God but rather about the kingdom of God."[44] In chapter 3 I raised concerns about the methodology of much historical Jesus research, and here we see the fruit of selective rejection of large components of the Gospels. To argue that Jesus does not preach himself, one must reject the historicity of the "I have come" statements in which Jesus centers his divine purpose (e.g., Matt. 5:17–18; 10:34–35), the parables that focus on the Son (e.g., Mark 12:1–12 and parr.), and the three passion predictions (Mark 8:31; 9:30–32; 10:32–34 and parr.). One must deny the various symbolic actions that point to the unique authority of Jesus, ranging from his calling twelve disciples to the signs and miracles he works that center his person. All of this rejection is done under the guidance of historical criteria of dubious validity. Some theological corrective is needed for liberation theology in light of its reliance on such methods.

Though liberation theology is most famous among recent Latin American theologies, a parallel yet independent movement among evangelicals known as *misión integral* offers a more balanced synthesis of the kingdom into a

---

43. See also Matt. 18:11; Mark 2:17; Luke 5:31–32; 1 Tim. 1:15.
44. Boff, *Jesus Christ Liberator*, 280. For another example, see Sobrino, *Crossroads*, 41, 47.

traditional, conciliar Christology.[45] René Padilla is an exemplary representative of this movement. He insists that salvation is both individual and cosmic and that witness to Christ requires an evangelistic and a social dimension.[46] Padilla notes how Jesus describes Zacchaeus's response to the gospel (Luke 19:8) as "salvation" (19:9).[47] He also explains that Jesus's proclamation of the gospel must be set in the context of Isaiah 52:7, in which a messenger brings good news (gospel) that God the King reigns.[48] This juxtaposition of gospel and kingdom is found in a portion of Isaiah that also includes the prophecy of John the Baptist as a messenger in the wilderness (Isa. 40:3; Matt. 3:3; Mark 1:2–3; Luke 3:4–6; John 1:23) and the passage that Jesus reads in his early sermon to declare the Jubilee (Isa. 61:1–2; Luke 4:17–20). Proclamation of good news is inseparable from the theology of the kingdom. Here, we might add to Padilla's insights the fact that the year of Jubilee begins on the Day of Atonement (Lev. 25:9), which indicates that "entering into Jubilee necessitates cleansing and conversion."[49] Jubilee includes the need for atonement, and the kingdom includes the proclamation of good news. Padilla rightfully insists that the proclamation of the "call to repentance . . . comes to people enslaved by sin in a specific social situation, not to a 'sinner' in the abstract. It is a change of attitude that becomes concrete in history."[50] The ethical dimension of Christian calling is thus to embody the kingdom in history in response to the forgiveness of sins received in Christ as they await his second coming in glory. One means of embodying the kingdom in this way is by continuing Jesus's table fellowship.

Table Fellowship

One of the more contentious dimensions of Jesus's ministry was his open table fellowship with individuals who would have been social outcasts in socially esteemed Jewish circles in first-century society. He was accused of being a glutton and drunkard (Matt. 11:18), and religious leaders regularly asked why he ate with tax collectors and sinners (Mark 2:15–17; Matt. 9:10–11; Luke 7:33–34). In fact, Jesus being asked about eating with sinners (Luke 15:1) prompts his famous parable of the prodigal son (Luke 15:11–32). Coupled

---

45. For the argument that *misión integral* was independent and earlier, see Escobar, *Christ in Latin America*, 171–81.

46. Padilla, *Between the Times*, 11, 16, 25.

47. Padilla, *Between the Times*, 41.

48. Padilla, *Between the Times*, 81–83.

49. Collins Winn, *God's Reign*, 29.

50. Padilla, *Between the Times*, 40.

with his proclamation of the kingdom, this table fellowship would be seen by Jesus's contemporaries as a significant eschatological sign.[51] As George Soares-Prabhu explains, such table fellowship would be an anticipatory "partaking in the eschatological banquet God has prepared for them (Isa. 25:6; Matt. 8:1; Luke 22:30)."[52] But here we must remember that Jesus is himself the Son of Man, the awaited eschatological figure with whom we will feast (Luke 22:16). If a subversive social ethic must center Christ, that centering cannot be at the expense of Christ's saving work but must be a historical dimension of a more expansive salvation.

Soares-Prabhu offers a robust analysis of Jesus's table fellowship while exploring its ethical implications. As he explains, "The table fellowship of Jesus is . . . the expression of a radically new (and therefore thoroughly disturbing) theological vision, rooted in a new experience of God and calling for a new kind of society."[53] While the Gospels depict the Pharisees as being concerned about ritual purity at meals, they depict Jesus's primary concern as mercy (Luke 6:36), for it is not what goes into a person's mouth but what comes out of it that makes them clean (Mark 7:15).[54] In an Indian context, Soares-Prabhu points to how Jesus's table fellowship challenges the caste system still prevalent in the church. He insists that a community focused on meals emphasizing the universal brotherhood and sisterhood of humanity cannot accept caste distinctions.[55] The point is well made in the context of caste in India, but it certainly extends to other social contexts. A general thrust of Jesus's eating is a symbolic enactment of the eschatological reversal, and he exhorted others to practice this reversal in table fellowship as well (Luke 14:1–14). Jesus's table fellowship is a practice that clearly establishes intentional solidarity in a subversive manner.

Jesus and Virtue Ethics

A third typical approach to ethics focuses on the church, hence Wells's label "ecclesial ethics." One important strand of ecclesial ethics focuses on **virtue**, which must be formed in community. In particular, certain virtues may best be formed in the community of the church as a result of the church's shared

51. N. T. Wright, *Jesus and the Victory of God*, 431.
52. Soares-Prabhu, *Dharma of Jesus*, 120.
53. Soares-Prabhu, *Dharma of Jesus*, 120.
54. Soares-Prabhu, *Dharma of Jesus*, 122, 125. Soares-Prabhu notes connections with Jesus's response to laws about contact with lepers (Mark 1:41), eating with unwashed hands (Mark 7:2), and being touched by an "unclean" woman (Mark 5:25–34).
55. Soares-Prabhu, *Dharma of Jesus*, 127–30.

narrative of salvation history, its common identity in Christ, and the important communal practices that build habits. This virtue ethics approach has a long Christian history, and lists of virtues and **vices** are common in Scripture (e.g., Prov. 6:16–19; Matt. 15:19–20; Gal. 5:19–23; Col. 3:12–15). In tradition, perhaps the most famous account of virtue is found in Thomas Aquinas, who defines "virtue" as "a good habit of the mind, by which we live righteously, of which no one can make bad use, which God works in us, without us."[56] As Étienne Gilson summarizes Aquinas, "Since habit measures the greater or lesser distance of the individual from his proper goal and causes him to conform more or less to his proper type, a careful distinction must be made between a habit disposing him to perform an act conforming to his nature, and one disposing him to act in disagreement with his nature. The former are good habits, and these are virtues."[57]

Virtue can be said to be fulfilled in Christ in three ways. First, the proper goal of human life is communion with God, so the eternal Son is the goal of human virtue. Second, by embodying the virtues we are conformed to our proper type, but the perfect human to whom we ought to conform is Christ. Third, Jesus can be said to perfectly embody the virtues. Aquinas especially focuses on the four cardinal virtues, which are prudence, temperance (which is approximately self-control), fortitude (better known as courage), and justice.[58] To these he adds three theological virtues of faith, hope, and love (see 1 Cor. 13:13).[59]

Vices are those evil habits that are contrary to the proper goal of our prefall nature and prevent our fulfilling our ideal type.[60] Since the time of Evagrius of Pontus, Christian theologians have spoken of eight deadly vices.[61] These vices were first systematically explained by John Cassian, Evagrius's disciple, and then more popularly reproduced as the seven deadly sins.[62] The eight

56. Aquinas, *Summa Theologica* I-II, Q. 55, A. 4. Initially, Aquinas uses "quality" but admits that "habit" is more appropriate in the definition.

57. Gilson, *Philosophy of St. Thomas Aquinas*, 316.

58. Aquinas, *Summa Theologica* I-II, Q. 61. The four cardinal virtues are named in the apocryphal Wis. 8:7 but not directly as a list of four in the Protestant canon. However, emphasis is found in Scripture on justice, self-control, courage, and wisdom, so the cardinal virtues are certainly present if not singled out.

59. Aquinas, *Summa Theologica* I–II, Q. 62.

60. Gilson, *Philosophy of St. Thomas Aquinas*, 316.

61. See Evagrius of Pontus, *On the Eight Thoughts*. Evagrius speaks of the eight thoughts, while later discussion tends to focus on vices. The latter terminology better reflects the dispositional and habitual aspects of these struggles.

62. The eight vices were reduced to seven under Gregory the Great, likely to reflect the number of completeness. Sloth was subsumed under sadness. For a brief history, see DeYoung, *Glittering Vices*, 27–29.

vices are gluttony, fornication or lust, avarice (better known as greed), anger, sadness, acedia (which is "anxiety or weariness of heart," a concept later described as sloth), vainglory (which pursues the esteem of others), and pride.[63] Detailed analysis of the vices can be found across monastic literature and in much contemporary literature on virtue ethics. To illustrate the nuance necessary to understand vice, consider, for example, the vice of gluttony. Cassian explains that gluttony includes not only eating too much but also partaking of excessively "costly and choice dishes" or eating at improper times.[64] Recently, J. Nicole Morgan has argued that gluttony might also include eating expansively when others have too little or being too scrupulous about food.[65] The vices are clearly linked, with each vice contributing to the development of others. Both Evagrius and Cassian believed that gluttony, which involved the inability to control bodily desires, led to increased fornication.[66]

As with the virtues and with the law, we find in Christian tradition clear depictions of Jesus reversing the vicious actions of Adam in his recapitulation of humankind. John Cassian eloquently explains this reversal as follows— Adam shows three vices before the fall: gluttony, vainglory, and pride.[67] "For it was by gluttony that he took the food from the forbidden tree; by vainglory that it was said: 'Your eyes shall be opened' (Gen. 3:5); and by pride that it was said: 'You shall be as God, knowing good and evil' (Gen. 3:5)."[68] Here, gluttony indicates Adam's succumbing to the temptation of eating inordinately, desiring food more than submission to the will of God. Pride is manifest in Adam thinking he could be like God. Vainglory is not as clear to me in Cassian's interpretation, but I suspect Cassian interprets the verse to indicate an increase in awareness by Adam of others thinking him good, for he now can see his own goodness. Cassian is clear that where the first Adam fell and is cast from the garden into the wilderness, the second Adam is victorious over these same temptations in the wilderness and then in the garden of Gethsemane. When tempted to break his fast by Satan, Jesus values the Word of God over food (Matt. 4:4), overcoming gluttony. The devil then takes Jesus to the pinnacle of the temple, saying, "If you are the Son of God, throw yourself down" (4:6), tempting Jesus to vainglory by the doubt conveyed in the conditional

---

63. Cassian, *Conferences* 5.2.
64. Cassian, *Conferences* 5.11.2.
65. Morgan, *Fat and Faithful.*
66. Evagrius of Pontus, *On the Eight Thoughts* 2.1; Cassian, *Conferences* 5.10.1.
67. Like many in the Christian tradition, Cassian shifts the focus to Adam and away from Eve, though both were surely guilty of sin. Whether this shift is to clarify the typology of Adam prefiguring the recapitulation of Christ or whether it indicates something about which ancestral parent had central responsibility is a matter up for debate but beyond the scope of this work.
68. Cassian, *Conferences* 5.6.1.

"if . . . ," but Jesus, rather than seeking to be recognized as God, resists. Finally, the devil tempts Jesus to pride by offering him all the splendor of the world (4:9), but Jesus remains humble and committed to serving God (4:10).[69] The second Adam is the embodiment of virtue, while the first Adam is full of vice.

Jesus Christ thus reveals in himself a virtuous life, but more explanation is needed in order to connect his example to the life of contemporary Christians hoping to develop virtue. Here, the work of recent ethicists pursuing a biblical foundation for Christian ethics is particularly helpful, given their tendency to appeal to virtue ethics. For example, James Keenan and Daniel Harrington explain that Jesus's proclamation of the kingdom of God provides a basic horizon and *telos* for our moral action, seen in parables such as the treasure in the field, the pearl of great price, and the net (Matt. 13:44–50), which suggests the kingdom leads to a "total commitment" and taking "every means toward that goal."[70] One's development in virtue is certainly shaped by their intentionality in acting habitually toward the good,[71] and the kingdom provides an orientation and committed intentionality. Development of virtue also depends on our understanding of who we are—namely, disciples called to "go and do likewise" (Luke 10:37 NIV) and seeking to become members of the kingdom in union with Christ.[72] Jesus thus serves as an exemplar of Christian action.

We must be careful when attempting to pattern our behavior after the Messiah. As Alan Verhey notes, the plurality of the Gospels suggests "four faithful (but different) ways to envision a life that is worthy of one gospel."[73] The fact that four truthful depictions can highlight different aspects of Christ's ministry for us to emulate reminds us of the variability of virtue ethics— living out the virtues occurs within a narrative understanding of a life, but a faithful Christian life can be narrated in different ways, especially given the wide range of contexts in which Christians find themselves. Furthermore, it is important to remember that identifying Christ as an ideal or exemplar may lead to a striving after perfection by willpower alone. If we view Jesus only as an example and do not also trust him as Savior, then we will lack the power wrought through sanctification to follow him.[74] Virtue ethics cannot displace the centrality of grace in sanctification.

69. Cassian, *Conferences* 5.6.1. Cassian also notes the close parallels between the two passages: "Your eyes shall be opened" // "He showed him all the kingdoms of the world and their glory"; "You shall be as gods" // "If you are the Son of God . . ." Cassian, *Conferences* 5.6.6.

70. Harrington and Keenan, *Jesus and Virtue Ethics*, 37. Harrington and Keenan add that the kingdom includes a promise of rewards (e.g., Mark 10:29–31) that are meant to motivate (p. 39).

71. Mattison, *Introducing Moral Theology*, 59–60.

72. Harrington and Keenan, *Jesus and Virtue Ethics*, 49, 58.

73. Verhey, "Gospels and Christian Ethics," 45.

74. Gustafson, *Christ and the Moral Life*, 160, 182.

The development of virtue requires the encouragement of community, a fact embodied in Jesus's calling of the Twelve and other followers and assumed in his teaching. This assumption is evident in the Sermon on the Mount, when Jesus speaks to a community exhorting them to be the salt of the earth, the light of the world, and a city on a hill (Matt. 5:13–14).[75] As Richard Hays explains, "Matthew is not interested merely in soliciting converts; the gospel, according to Matthew, summons people to join a disciplined community of Jesus' followers who put his teachings into practice."[76] Scripture is addressed to the community of the church, establishes practices for this community, narrates the story of redemption that is central to the church's self-understanding, and provides the community the basis for understanding its identity in Christ.[77] With this focus on the development of ethics in the church, we see the full emphasis of what Wells has labeled "ecclesial ethics."

Christ is clearly at the center of Christian ethics, whether one adopts the universal, subversive, or ecclesial perspective. In each perspective, it is also clear that he is not only central to ethics but also the only good human being who fulfills that paradigm. Jesus embodies the perfect fulfillment of the law, loving God and neighbor perfectly. He is the person through whom and in whom the kingdom of God is manifest in all its liberative potential. Jesus is also the exemplar we must follow to build virtue and the only one who has perfectly resisted temptation and vice. Christ's full humanity as one who wills, thinks, and acts in a perfectly moral human way is therefore central to our understanding of ethics but also a necessary prerequisite for his atoning work, which depends on his perfect fulfillment of human moral obligations. Before concluding the chapter and continuing toward a Christology culminating in the cross, resurrection, ascension, and second coming, I once more need to consider in detail a specific example from Jesus's life to illustrate with greater specificity Christ's role as moral exemplar.

Virtue Ethics and the Lord's Supper

So far, I have considered table fellowship, a pattern of behavior that Jesus's disciples continued, and Jesus's definitive interpretation of the law in terms of love of God and neighbor. I turn now to Communion, a practice that

75. Harrington and Keenan, *Jesus and Virtue Ethics*, 66.
76. Hays, *Moral Vision*, 97.
77. L. Chan, *Biblical Ethics*, 111–12.

was formally instituted by Jesus himself for the church. In the last century especially, Christians have emphasized the moral implications of this meal. Without downplaying the theological significance or spiritual transformation made possible in the Eucharist, it must be recognized that repeated practice of the Eucharist contributes to the development of virtue when accompanied with a proper understanding of the ritual and a sincere spiritual response. The ethical implications of Communion are found in a proper understanding of the words of institution and the preparatory actions required for proper reception of the bread and wine.

The words of institution are the words used by Christ when celebrating the Passover in the upper room that are also often used in congregations when partaking of the Lord's Supper. As the Gospel of Luke recounts the event,

> He took a cup, and after giving thanks, he said, "Take this and share it among yourselves. For I tell you, from now on I will not drink of the fruit of the vine until the kingdom of God comes." And he took bread, gave thanks, broke it, gave it to them, and said, "This is my body, which is given for you. Do this in remembrance of me." In the same way he also took the cup after supper and said, "This cup is the new covenant in my blood, which is poured out for you." (Luke 22:17–20)

The words of institution prompt moral formation in several ways. The anamnesis—"Do this in remembrance of me" (Luke 22:19; cf. 1 Cor. 11:24–25)—certainly centers remembrance of the sacrificial death of Christ, since the words of institution point to the sacrifice of Christ's body and to his blood. However, given the larger New Testament emphasis on following the example of Christ (e.g., Phil. 2:5), it is reasonable to think that anamnesis also involves remembering Christ's past way of life in order to repeat it now.[78] Christ speaking of sharing the cup (Luke 22:17) and of the bread being his body (Luke 22:19) also leads to recognition of the need for a unity among Christians that transcends class, ethnicity, gender, and other possible social statuses, for there is one body, the church, just as there is one body of Christ (1 Cor. 10:17).[79] For this reason, it is unsurprising that New Testament writings focusing on Eucharist, on community meals, or more broadly on worship gatherings show a consistent concern for unity across such divides (1 Cor. 10:16–17; 11:17–22; Gal. 2:11–21; James 2:1–13). It is also significant that Jesus's teachings use the imagery of a banquet to explain the kingdom (Matt. 22:1–14; Luke 14:15–24), a connection Jesus directly makes with the meal in the upper room (Luke 22:16, 18 and parr.).

78. M. Scott, *Eucharist and Social Justice*, 69.
79. This emphasis is found in a variety of analyses, including J. Evans, *We Have Been Believers*, 163.

Finally, the words of institution provide a general eschatological orientation to the ritual because it is practiced "until the kingdom of God comes" (Luke 22:18), and this orientation prompts hope, a fundamental theological virtue.[80]

While it is possible for Christians to grow complacent with the regular practice of Communion, such that it becomes a dead ritual, careful spiritual preparation before partaking of the bread and wine can help maintain a spiritual vibrancy to the practice while also further contributing to our moral formation. We would do well to remember that practices play a central role in virtue ethics. As Lúcás Chan remarks, "Practices both develop the characters of the moral agent and, in turn, express them."[81] Paul advocates self-examination prior to taking the bread and the cup (1 Cor. 11:27–28), a practice I suspect finds its origins at least partly in Jesus's earlier admonition to be reconciled with one's brother before offering a sacrifice (Matt. 5:23–24).[82] Repeated self-examination that prompts reconciliation with others not only develops virtues such as honesty and humility that are necessary for reconciliation but also becomes an occasion to express our Christian character as ministers of reconciliation (2 Cor. 5:18–19). In the Lord's Supper, then, Christ's call to love God and neighbor is manifest in our commemoration of God's love for us, which prompts our act of worshipful love, but also in our commitment to love our neighbors as a constitutive element of the practice of the Lord's Supper. When analyzing practices, I do not intend to suggest that Communion alone can produce beneficial moral formation. As Lauren Winner has well documented, many practices also include an intrinsic risk of malformation. Winner notes, "Judas received the Eucharist and then he immediately betrayed the Lord; written into the rite from its Dominican inception, then, was the certainty of its going wrong."[83] In Christian history, this is particularly manifest in the history of host desecration stories that were the basis for much anti-Judaism and many atrocities. Practices like the Lord's Supper can shape our character when practiced rightly, but these practices must occur in communities rightly exercising moral discernment while relying on the gracious work of the Spirit in ensuring our moral development.

80. McClendon, *Systematic Theology*, 401.

81. L. Chan, *Biblical Ethics*, 87–88. Chan identifies practices/habits as one of the four main dimensions of virtue ethics.

82. Certainly such self-examination regards consideration of whether one believes in Christ, such that Communion serves as a gospel proclamation. However, the context of Paul's exhortation to self-examination is the presence of factions among the body (1 Cor. 11:19), especially in the form of an offense against those who have nothing (1 Cor. 11:21–22), and those who act inappropriately in this way do not come together "to eat the Lord's Supper" (1 Cor. 11:20). The ethical dimension of self-examination is also clear.

83. Winner, *Dangers of Christian Practice*, 20.

Conclusion

I have argued in this chapter that the Son's assumption of a complete human nature allows him to both teach and model a virtuous and moral life in ways that his human followers can emulate. The life and ministry of the incarnate Word provide a clear picture of what it means to fulfill the law, loving God and neighbor perfectly. Jesus's life also provides a pattern for virtue formation, while his teaching about the kingdom orients Christian moral reasoning on many subjects. Here, as is so often the case when deploying Christology toward the needs of moral theology, our dogmatic conclusions drawn from Christology provide a broad orientation, while full moral reasoning requires deeper analysis. Yet closer attention both to Jesus's teachings and to the wider moral teachings of the Bible would result in a significantly clearer understanding of important moral issues. Such work is beyond the scope of a book on dogmatic theology. Here, I hope only to show that Christology is indispensable to a properly robust and sufficiently expansive Christian ethic. However, we must also be cautious to not overextend this truth in two senses. First, a balanced trinitarian ethic must also account for the work of revelation, which is appropriated to the Father. This work directly guides the Christian in moral reasoning through the teachings of Scripture and through natural law, insofar as that can be discerned. A balanced ethic must also attend to the sanctifying work of the Spirit, which makes moral action possible. The need to incorporate the sanctifying work of the Spirit also points to a second sense in which Christology ought to not be overextended into Christian ethics: a Christian understanding of ethics cannot be mere emulation of Jesus's human actions, for such a theory would neglect the necessary supernatural work of grace needed to overcome sin in the lives of Christians. Neglect of this work of grace leads down a Pelagian road. Moral theology that draws from Christology must be conscious of this risk, which can partly be overcome by attending to the unity of divine and human in Christ. The virtue of the human Christ is also shaped by the divine life of the Son in which Christ's human nature exists; so, too, our human virtue is shaped by the grace of the Spirit who indwells us. With this in mind, we turn now to consider the doctrine of the hypostatic union.

For Further Reading

DeYoung, Rebecca Konyndyk. *Glittering Vices: A New Look at the Seven Deadly Sin and Their Remedies*. Brazos, 2009.

While most of this chapter considered the positive example provided by Christ, with a concluding emphasis on virtue, the malformation of the sinner is also an important theological topic. Here, the concept of the capital vices serves as a helpful supplement to this chapter's treatment of the virtues, and DeYoung's work is widely recognized as one of the best surveys of the vices in recent history.

Harrington, Daniel, and James Keenan. *Jesus and Virtue Ethics: Building Bridges Between New Testament Studies and Moral Theology.* Rowman & Littlefield, 2002.

In this volume Daniel Harrington, a Bible scholar, and James Keenan, an ethicist, contribute portions of each chapter to explore connections between biblical studies and virtue ethics. Their joint effort produces a helpful introduction to Jesus's role in virtue theory.

Padilla, C. René. *Mission Between the Times: Essays on the Kingdom.* Langham, 2010.

Padilla's theology presents many insights into the kingdom that are shared by liberation theologians, but with more attentiveness to evangelism and with greater appreciation for traditional Christology. His insights have great implications for missions, but their importance for dogmatic theology is often neglected.

CHAPTER FIVE

One Hypostasis

In the fifth century, a series of christological disputes resulted in the two ecumenical councils of Ephesus (431) and Chalcedon (451), each of which dealt with the unity of Christ's humanity and divinity. The result of these councils is the doctrine of the hypostatic union, a doctrine that attempts to explain the unity of Christ's human and divine natures in a manner that preserves the singularity of his person while maintaining the distinction between God and creation through a continued distinction between the Son's divinity and his assumed humanity. Yet the debates surrounding Chalcedon and Ephesus certainly did not fully explain the unity of natures in Christ. As Sergius Bulgakov remarks, "One should not deceive oneself by thinking that, at the time of its formulation, the Chalcedonian dogma was theologically justified or even fully understood."[1] For this reason, our analysis of the unity of Christ must span further theological development, though we must begin at earlier stages.

To best understand the hypostatic union, it is helpful to begin with the debate between Cyril of Alexandria, who largely introduced the language of union of hypostasis into fourth-century debates, and Nestorius, the archbishop of Constantinople who was condemned at the Council of Ephesus. The impetus for the council was Nestorius's rejection of the language of Mary as *Theotokos*, the "God bearer," or, more loosely, the mother of God. Nestorius's immediate concern appears to be preserving the distinction between God and creation, for God could neither have a mother nor be born

---

1. Bulgakov, *Lamb of God*, 62.

since the divine nature was impassible, immutable, and eternal.[2] This concern was typical among Antiochene theologians like Nestorius, who worried, for example, that teaching that the Word was born or suffered in the flesh would either reject the great divide between God and creation, a major emphasis of Antiochene theology, or else deny the full and impassible divinity of Christ, paving the way for Arianism.[3] It was customary among Antiochene theologians to draw on John 2:19–21 to describe Christ's humanity as a temple in which divinity dwelt,[4] but the concept as deployed by Antiochenes suggested that the humanity was fully distinct from the divinity as Solomon's temple was from God, for the temple itself was not God. Thus, Nestorius can insist "obviously God the Word was not the Son of David."[5] Diodore of Tarsus, an Antiochene theologian from a generation prior, taught in a similar manner that the Son of David and Son of God could only be identified with one another inexactly (*katakrēstikōs*).[6] Rather than speaking of unity, Nestorius preferred to speak of the conjunction of natures into one *prosōpon*, by which he meant something like one object of perception. While affirming this **prosoponic union**, Nestorius could also speak of two *hypostases*, by which he meant something like two ongoing concrete realities, humanity and divinity. Occasionally he also spoke of two *prosōpoi*, again to denote the ongoing plurality of the natures.[7] In other words, Nestorius's concept of unity, though unclear, could be taken to refer to the human and divine appearing to be one due only to close proximity. Nestorius's emphasis on the genuine distinction between humanity and divinity in Christ struggled to explain how Christ was a single subject, a fact that resulted in his condemnation.

Cyril of Alexandria was Nestorius's main critic, arguing that the concept of a mere "conjunction" of natures is inadequate because it seems to suggest that the Son assumed a discrete, independently existing human being in the incarnation.[8] Recall from chapter 1's discussion of the incarnation that assumption of a complete human being might suggest some potency in humanity itself that could undercut the radical need for God's grace, expressed by Protestants through the dictum *sola gratia*. Cyril's arguments reveal that the assumption of a discrete human being also jeopardizes what Protestants call *solus Christus*, since Christians are linked to the Son through "virtue and

2. This concern is evident in Nestorius, *Reply to Cyril's Second Letter* §§2, 4, 7.
3. On these emphases in Nestorius and Antiochene theology and the different emphases of Cyril, see Young, *Nicaea to Chalcedon*, 286; Daley, *God Visible*, 195–98.
4. See Daley, *God Visible*, 174, 181, 186; Young, *Nicaea to Chalcedon*, 281.
5. Nestorius, *Reply to Cyril's Second Letter* §7.
6. Young, *Nicaea to Chalcedon*, 258.
7. See Grillmeier, *Christ in Christian Tradition*, 458–61; Daley, *God Visible*, 146.
8. Cyril of Alexandria, *Scholia on the Incarnation* §13.

holiness" bestowed through union and since we, too, have an acquired relation with Christ.[9] Christ is truly unique only if in him alone we find a more
significant union between humanity and divinity. Cyril also argues that conjunction is inadequate because it jeopardizes salvation and invalidates much
Christian worship. Without genuine unity between humanity and divinity, it
would be unclear whether the Son of God was our Savior through his death
on the cross or whether we are indebted to some distinct human being.[10] If
the humanity of the Son is only conjoined to the divinity, it is unclear that it
should be worshiped, yet when Christ is worshiped in Scripture, notably it can
be a response to the embodiedness of Christ's resurrection (John 20:27–28)
or directed to Christ the lamb because of being slaughtered, a state possible
only due to Christ's human nature (Rev. 5:8–14).[11] Therefore, where Nestorius
might insist that Mary is merely **Christotokos**, the "bearer of Christ" understood as the human nature, Cyril insists that the Word "assumed flesh from a
woman and was made one with it in the womb, and in this way the selfsame
came forth God and Man."[12] Where Nestorius claimed that the distinction
preserved the deity of Christ, Cyril feared it undermined the unity of Christ.

Cyril describes the oneness of the Son's humanity and divinity as "the Word
united hypostatically to flesh,"[13] likely drawing on the distinction between
being (*ousia*) and hypostasis that had been central to Cappadocian thought,
though there is some debate regarding how technical of a definition Cyril applied to the term.[14] Whereas Nestorius's use of "conjunction" and the idea of
a prosoponic union seems to suggest the incarnation is united in our perception only, language of a hypostatic union implies an ontological reality to the
unity.[15] Cyril leaves considerable ambiguity here. Partly, this is because Cyril
has a humble view of human capacities to understand an infinite God. He
insists that the union of humanity and divinity in Jesus is "greater than human
understanding,"[16] "mysterious and incomprehensible."[17] Yet his thought is
also characterized by a degree of ambiguity, insofar as he can speak of the
ongoing existence of two natures after the incarnation,[18] while also affirming

9. Cyril of Alexandria, *On the Unity of Christ*, 74; Cyril of Alexandria, *Third Letter*, 351.
10. Cyril of Alexandria, *On the Unity of Christ*, 70.
11. Cyril of Alexandria, *On the Unity of Christ*, 73.
12. Cyril of Alexandria, *Scholia on the Incarnation* §25.
13. Cyril of Alexandria, *Third Letter*, 350.
14. See Beeley, *Unity of Christ*, 259–60; McGuckin, *St. Cyril of Alexandria*, 141–42, 212–16.
Beeley argues that the concept is "ambiguous" since Cyril can also speak of a union of nature.
McGuckin argues that the concept does signify the idea of a "single individual subject."
15. McGuckin, *St. Cyril of Alexandria*, 212.
16. Cyril of Alexandria, *Scholia on the Incarnation* §8.
17. Cyril of Alexandria, *On the Unity of Christ*, 77.
18. See Daley, *God Visible*, 193; Beeley, *Unity of Christ*, 263.

"one incarnate nature of the Son."[19] Cyril argues, for example, that when Jesus says in John 9:35–38 that the man born blind has seen the Son of God, this requires a unity of natures because divinity is invisible.[20] However, Cyril also recognizes that the divine nature is impassible, immutable, and eternal, so he regularly insists that the divine and human natures are not joined by synthesis, composition, mixture, or any other process that would change or violate the divinity of the Son.[21] How these concepts fit together is not always clear.[22]

The Council of Chalcedon's definition emerges in large part from Cyril's theology, maintaining his language of one hypostasis and rejecting confusion, change, division, and separation between the natures. Yet it also maintained some of the ambiguity in Cyril's thought, and it is not surprising that the language of two natures endorsed by the council was contested, especially given the politicized context as the major centers of Christian thought like Antioch, Alexandria, and Rome vied for power. As a result, there is much work to do to elaborate on what it means for Christ's humanity and divinity to be united in one hypostasis. In this chapter, I endeavor to work out this question, starting with a brief account of the basic philosophical and creedal parameters at Chalcedon and moving to consider five dimensions of what it means for Jesus Christ to be one person or one hypostasis in two natures. The goal is to be as ecumenical as possible, pursuing the biblical call for unity, while also recognizing that certain theological foundations of Christology cannot be compromised.

One Person or Hypostasis

The Council of Chalcedon built on Cyril of Alexandria's language of "one hypostasis" while adding that Christ was two natures, the topic of the previous chapter. The language of Christ being "one hypostasis" is quite helpful, though initially quite ambiguous. This is partly due to the wide range of meaning that the term could have in antiquity; I will note nine meanings drawn from the analysis of G. L. Prestige.[23] Most problematically, "hypostasis" could be a

19. For example, Cyril of Alexandria, *Letter to Eulogius*, 349.
20. Cyril of Alexandria, *To Theodosius* §34.
21. This theme is found across Cyril's corpus. See, e.g., Cyril of Alexandria, *Letter to Acacius* §7; Cyril of Alexandria, *Scholia on the Incarnation* §8; Cyril of Alexandria, *On the Unity of Christ*, 77.
22. In part, this may be because Cyril is more open to paradox than some of his contemporaries and less prone to drawing on philosophical categories. See the discussion in Daley, *God Visible*, 195–98.
23. See Prestige, *God in Patristic Thought*, 163–73.

synonym for "nature" or "substance," a usage likely found in Hebrews 1:3.[24] This fact led Severus of Antioch, a later opponent of Chalcedon, to argue, "The person who speaks of 'one hypostasis' necessarily affirms one nature as well."[25] Clearly Chalcedon's insistence on affirming Christ's two natures entails another intended meaning, one that could meaningfully affirm one hypostasis while maintaining that there are two substantial natures in Christ. Chalcedon does not provide a complete metaphysical resolution for this problem. As Aloys Grillmeier remarks, "It is not the task of councils to produce metaphysics, but to serve the church's proclamation of revelation."[26] Though the point is well taken, it still is the case that some metaphysical exposition of the single hypostasis of the incarnate Son is worthwhile. A thorough analysis of the lexical meanings of hypostasis in antiquity reveals many senses in which Christ can meaningfully be one hypostasis in two natures.

Chalcedon combined the language of Cyril with that of Leo the Great, who affirmed two natures that "meet in one person."[27] Chalcedon interprets unity in person to be the same as unity in hypostasis, so to speak of one hypostasis is also to speak of one person. In order to explain how the incarnate Christ is one person, I will draw on the various historical dimensions of the term "hypostasis" in dialogue with the dogmatic definition of "person" that I developed in my *Trinitarian Dogmatics*. There, I claimed that some flexibility exists when considering the definition of "person" in the Trinity, but viable definitions must meet several criteria: Divine persons are rational, dissimilar to human persons, relational, in unity with one another, and unique.[28] Further trinitarian concepts of personhood must fit with Christology, so we will see in this christological analysis that any concept of person or hypostasis must fit with trinitarian theology. Placing these criteria in dialogue with the term "hypostasis," we see significant overlap. "Hypostasis" can mean the "basis or foundation" of a thing, often in a material sense, or the "source or ground" of a thing.[29] Though divine persons are not material, we can say the incarnate Christ is one hypostasis because the person of the Son is the one basis or grounding of Christ's humanity. To use Herman Bavinck's words, the Son's person is "sustaining and determining the existence of" one human nature.[30]

24. Prestige, *God in Patristic Thought*, 166–67.
25. Severus of Antioch, *Ad Nephalium*, 63. Note that Severus did not accept language of "one essence" in Christ but maintained rather "one composite nature," intending to still accept a distinction between humanity and divinity. See L. Davis, *First Seven Ecumenical Councils*, 213.
26. Grillmeier, *Christ in Christian Tradition*, 549.
27. Leo the Great, *Tome*, 363.
28. See Butner, *Trinitarian Dogmatics*, 105–27.
29. Prestige, *God in Patristic Thought*, 165, 171.
30. Bavinck, *Reformed Dogmatics*, 3:306.

Explaining this will require a defense of what I am calling the singularity criterion, an additional criterion of any theory of the personhood of the Son. Hypostasis can refer to a presentation of a discrete reality, perhaps indicating something like the perceptibility of a real, discrete thing.[31] This, too, relates to the singularity criterion because the divine Son is presented to us as the human Jesus of Nazareth; Jesus of Nazareth is the Son as a single subject and single agent of divine-human acts. Hypostasis can refer to "firmness, obduracy, or persistence." Though it is often used quite literally to speak of a stubborn person, we can apply this meaning more metaphorically to understand hypostasis to reference that which persists across time, giving continuity to a thing.[32] That Jesus Christ is one hypostasis is evident in the relationality criterion, for in the mission of the incarnation the Son extends his eternal relation to the Father into human nature. Hypostasis can refer to the "inherent law by which objects in their creation were designed to function."[33] Though uncreated, the Son's operations and existence extend to his humanity, ensuring that there is one hypostasis with the same operative functions and existence. This fact will require further elaboration of the unity criterion as well as what I will call the trinitarian compatibility criterion for speaking of the hypostasis of the Son. To summarize, a hypostasis is a unique, singular, relational existence of a rational nature (or, in the case of Christ, of rational natures), though Christ's hypostasis is dissimilar from ours in certain ways. Much more remains to be said, but with this brief survey in place I can turn to the task of explaining the singular personhood of the incarnate Son.

Explaining the One Hypostasis of the Incarnate Son

In order to explain how the two distinct natures of Christ are one hypostasis and person, it is necessary to elaborate and expand on the understanding of personhood evident in trinitarian theology. I will therefore begin by exploring dimensions of personhood newly important in Christology, the singularity criterion and trinitarian compatibility criterion, which must be met for any adequate account of the incarnate Christ. I will conclude by connecting the relationality, unity, and dissimilarity necessary for any account of the divine persons in the Trinity to the doctrine of Christology. The rationality criterion, which insists that persons are rational, requires no further elaboration here.

31. Prestige, *God in Patristic Thought*, 169.
32. Prestige, *God in Patristic Thought*, 170.
33. Prestige, *God in Patristic Thought*, 172.

The Singularity Criterion

The doctrine of the hypostatic union must be able to account meaningfully for the unity of humanity and divinity in a singular reality, the Son of God. The singularity criterion therefore requires that any account of the one hypostasis of Christ explains how Christ is one subject and one person while still two natures. In other words, our understanding of hypostasis and person must be able to account for biblical language like 1 Corinthians 8:6's naming of "one Lord, Jesus Christ." On what account is the human Messiah Jesus one and the same as the Lord God?[34] Though this requirement can be met in different ways, I find three concepts from Christian tradition to be particularly illuminating: the enhypostatic and **anhypostatic** qualifiers for the human nature, the **communication of idioms**, and the rejection of *homo assumptus* and *habitus* **theories of the incarnation**.

Christ's human nature exists enhypostatically in the person of the Son. I have already discussed this concept in chapter 1 in terms of its role in rejecting adoptionism and preserving immutability, but here the focus must be on the way in which this concept preserves the singularity of Christ's natures. To claim that Christ's humanity exists enhypostatically is to claim that it has no existence independent of the Son or prior to its assumption by the Son.[35] Apart from the Son, the human nature is anhypostatic, meaning it has no existence apart from the Son.[36] Ancient philosophical interpretation of Aristotle understood accidents to be anhypostatic, having their existence in the substance in which they inhere, but in early Christian usage of this concept, for example, in Leontius of Byzantium, this possibility is ruled out.[37] An accident in philosophy refers to a property that could be otherwise and which does not make something what it is. For example, I might have brown hair, but I could dye my hair blue without ceasing to be human. Both accidents and the humanity of Christ exist enhypostatically, meaning they exist in something else, but they do so in different ways. Accidents require some substance or nature as necessary determinants of their existence. For example, if I speak of "a brown," my language immediately prompts the question, A brown *what*?

34. I draw this framing from Riches, *Ecce Homo*, 3.

35. Much modern scholarship has debated the extent to which the concept of enhypostasia as being in-hypostatized is found in the patristic era, where the concept frequently just meant "real." I am convinced that there is patristic warrant for the term being used as I do, though the validity of usage in this manner does not depend on patristic precedent. See Riches, *Ecce Homo*, 110–12.

36. For a concise treatment, see T. F. Torrance, *Incarnation*, 84.

37. Gleede, *Development of the Term ἐνυπόστατος*, 56, 65. Gleede gives the example of Sextus Empiricus as one such commentator on Aristotle.

For a particular brown to exist, there must be an answer to this question: a brown horse, a brown sofa, or my brown hair. For accidents to be what they are, they require a substance or nature—that is, a what by which they are what they are. On the other hand, natures exist enhypostatically "as wholes fully determined in themselves."[38] The necessary properties for the determination of a nature are in the nature itself. For example, if I speak of "a human," no further information is needed. I do not need to answer the question, A human what? The characteristics of the human nature determine what we are naming. However, the category of nature speaks of what is common, so it does not answer the question, Who? This question is answered by the category hypostasis. Christ's humanity could exist as a hypostasis and person distinct from the divine Son, which is clearly Nestorianism. Or, the humanity of Christ could exist in the person of the Son as a whole nature, not as something inhering in and determined by the divinity of Christ. In the words of Robert of Melun, "The statement, 'a person is composed of man and Word' does not mean that that person has being (*esse*) from those parts."[39] The Son has being and exists as the second divine person of the Trinity, and Christ's humanity exists because it is in the Son as one nature of a singular hypostasis.

It is necessary to address several misinterpretations of the concepts of anhypostasis and enhypostasis that can lead to theological problems. First, the concept of anhypostasis should not be taken to deny any human personality to Christ because it denies an independent personal and hypostatic existence of the Son. Christ has everything that moderns would attribute to personality, such as mind, will, emotions, body, life history, and so forth. But these things are not independent of the life of the Word but proper to him.[40] Second, Leontius of Byzantium, who is often discussed as one of the originators of speaking of the enhypostatic human nature of Christ, actually had reservations about using the concept because it could reduce the union of Christ to a speculative question about origin, ignoring the historical biography of Christ.[41] For this reason, it is helpful to follow T. F. Torrance's explanation of enhypostasia. Torrance insists that the concept refers to an active and ongoing personal union, a "dynamic personal event" that is essential to Christ's ongoing mediatorial role.[42] Though we say that the hypostasis of the Son answers the question, Who?, it is not merely a matter of identification but also a means of naming the event of the human life of a discrete individual. To put the

---

38. Gleede, *Development of the Term ἐνυπόστατος*, 67.
39. Robert of Melun, *Sentences* §116.
40. Barth, *Church Dogmatics* I/2, 164.
41. Gleede, *Development of the Term ἐνυπόστατος*, 68.
42. T. F. Torrance, *Incarnation*, 84, 105, 212.

matter another way, assumption refers to the punctiliar act of the Son taking on flesh, but hypostatic union refers to the ongoing mutual subsistence of the two natures.[43] Like the human nature of Christ, this second-Adamic life is not independent of the Son, a fact that requires us to recognize that Jesus the second Adam and the Son of God are the same subject, which leads to the doctrine of the communication of idioms.

When Nestorius rejected the title *Theotokos* for Mary, he was also indirectly rejecting what theologians call the communication of idioms (*communicatio idiomatum*) or the communication of attributes. This doctrine claims that properties and actions proper to either nature can be applied to the concrete person of the Son, even using titles that are proper to the Son because of the other nature. The great Lutheran systematician Martin Chemnitz gives many examples of this phenomenon in Scripture. Phrases like "You killed the source of life" (Acts 3:15), challenges to "shepherd the church of God which He purchased with His own blood" (Acts 20:28 NASB),[44] claims that they "crucified the Lord of glory" (1 Cor. 2:8),[45] and the Lord's prophetic word that "they will look at me whom they pierced" (Zech. 12:10) all involve the attribution of an act proper to Christ's human nature and body (dying, bleeding, being pierced and crucified) to a title properly his because of his divinity (source of life, Lord of glory, God, and Lord).[46] Parallel to this "descending" communication of idioms, as it has been recently called, in "ascending" communication of idioms divine acts and properties can also be attributed to titles proper to the Son by virtue of his humanity (e.g., 1 Cor. 15:47).[47] Mary can be called *Theotokos* and the Son can be said to be born of her because the act of being born, which is proper to the human nature, must be ascribed in the concrete to the person of the Son as the single subject of everything that happens to the human and divine natures that exist in him.

43. See Owen, *Person of Christ*, 226.

44. This example of the communication of idioms is probably least clear of those I provide. With textual variants and translation disputes, the phrase could be translated to speak of God (the Father) buying the church with the blood of his own Son. This is the view of M. Harris, *Jesus as God*, 131–41.

45. Regarding "Lord of Glory," Wittman and Jamieson argue that we can "triangulate the phrase's meaning" by comparing this title with three other titles typically used of God: "the LORD's glory" and "the glory of the Lord" (e.g., Exod. 16:7; Num. 14:10), "God of glory" (Ps. 29:3), and "King of glory" (Ps. 24:7–10). Jamieson and Wittman, *Biblical Reasoning*, 135.

46. Chemnitz, *Two Natures in Christ*, 176. Chemnitz will see the communication of idioms in the *genus idiomaticum*, discussed here, but also in the *genus majestaticum* addressed in chapter 10 and in a *genus apotelesmaticum*, which references theandric actions. See Chemnitz, *Two Natures in Christ*, 215–31, 241–46; Duby, *Jesus*, 167.

47. On "ascending" and "descending" communication of idioms, see Jamieson and Wittman, *Biblical Reasoning*, 134.

At times, such ascription can be clarified by identifying the nature that makes a statement true, as in "descendant of David *according to the flesh*" (Rom. 1:3; see also, e.g., 1 Pet. 3:18; 4:1) or by using a **reduplicative**, such as "Christ as God existed before Mary."[48]

Scripture also describes the God-man as a single subject in its narration of the incarnation. Nestorius would read Philippians 2:6–7's distinction between the "form of God" and the "form of a servant" to require two distinct hypostases perceived as a single *prosōpon*.[49] Reading more carefully, Cyril of Alexandria saw a continuity of subject in naming both of these forms, for the subject of the action is the same for "existing in the form of God" (2:6), "assuming the form of a servant," and "had come as a man" (2:7).[50] Many other texts show a continuity of subject when speaking of the incarnation (e.g., John 1:14; Gal. 4:3–4; 1 John 4:2–3). Recognizing the unity of subject in Christ must balance the partitive exegesis discussed in chapter 3.[51] Ultimately, this unity is necessary for salvific purposes—if the Son did not become human, then humanity could not be transformed and saved.[52]

A brief summary of a typical medieval Scholastic debate can further clarify what the singularity criterion requires of any adequate understanding of the person of the incarnate Christ. At the dawn of the medieval Scholastic era, four theories examined how the natures of Christ were united. The *partes* theory understood the divine and human natures to be two parts of a whole (Christ). This theory was largely rejected, sometimes for violating divine **simplicity** and sometimes because a "part" signifies that which is incomplete, and neither nature is incomplete.[53] Peter Lombard's *habitus* theory[54] argues that the body and soul do not constitute something when in the Word but are rather put on like a habit or garment.[55] Just like clothing takes on a form when worn that it lacks when taken off, so the human nature is externally fitted to the person of Christ.[56] Formally condemned by Pope Alexander III in 1177 in the letter *Cum Christus*, this theory of the incarnation faces many

48. For an account of reduplicatives, see T. Morris, *Logic of God Incarnate*, 48–55, where Morris explores the limitations of the reduplicative strategy. I hold it to bear more weight for precise description than for metaphysical explanation.

49. Daley, *God Visible*, 186–87.

50. Cyril of Alexandria, *On the Unity of Christ*, 85.

51. This is seen in Cyril of Alexandria. See Beeley, *Unity of Christ*, 263–65.

52. See Weinandy, "Mystery of the Incarnation," 27.

53. See C. P. Evans, "Introduction," 37–38. Aquinas rejects this view because the natures are not incomplete. See M. Gorman, *Hypostatic Union*, 43.

54. The theory itself is older, being traceable to at least William of Champeaux. However, Lombard is the most famous advocate of this view. See Riches, *Ecce Homo*, 159.

55. Lombard, *Sentences* 3.6.4.1.

56. Lombard, *Sentences* 3.6.6.1–2.

problems. By making the human body and soul only accidents of the person of Christ, this view was seen to be "implicitly Nestorian"[57] because the natures were not linked at the level of existence but only by happenstance. The later fourteenth-century Christologies of John Duns Scotus and William of Ockham were able to revive a theory of the humanity of Christ inhering in the deity like an accidental property, but in such a way that the humanity did not seem merely Nestorian as in Lombard's account.[58] Genuine singularity is required of any christological account, and the humanity cannot be merely extrinsic to the hypostasis like clothing to a body.

The third Scholastic theory explaining the unity of natures is the *homo assumptus* theory, which claims that the Son took on a complete man, a theory with a solid patristic pedigree.[59] The *homo assumptus* theory claims there are two natures and two supposits but only one person.[60] In this context, the word "supposit" refers to a specific self-existing reality. In other words, the humanity already had self-existence as a distinct human thing, but it grew into personhood in the Son. As Joseph Wawrykow summarizes this theory,

> The human nature is concretized by a human subject or supposit, which then is united in assumption to a divine supposit, the second divine Person. Thus, there are two natures and two supposits. However, there will be only one person. Normally, a supposit of a rational nature finds its perfection in coming to person, achieving its own personhood. But in the case of Christ this has not occurred for the human supposit. Rather, in his case the *homo* that is assumed receives its person from the divine Person, who is both supposit and Person.[61]

Two primary problems require rejection of this theory. First, if the humanity of Christ were a full man that was assumed, the result would seem to be Nestorianism. Positing two supposits must therefore be joined by something

---

57. White, *Incarnate Lord*, 85.

58. As Marilyn McCord Adams explains, Scotus and Ockham accepted three ways one could explain an accident inhering in a substance *per accidens*. Inherence might imply colocation, but since the divine substance is uncircumscribed, this would not apply to the hypostatic union. An accident may inhere through "potency actualization," but as God, the Son is both simple and pure act, so this is not what inherence would mean. The third option is "ontological dependence," by which the humanity "essentially depends" on the hypostasis of the Son "for its existence in a non-efficient-causal way." This sort of inherence would be analogous to the Word's assumption of humanity. Adams, *Christ and Horrors*, 125.

59. Theories with similar features are found in Eustathius of Antioch, Theodore of Mopsuestia, and Diodore of Tarsus. See Riches, *Ecce Homo*, 17, 19; Young, *Nicaea to Chalcedon*, 244.

60. Wawrykow, "Hypostatic Union," 237.

61. Wawrykow, "Hypostatic Union," 235.

less ontologically fundamental than a supposit, to the result that the duality of natures is far stronger than their unity, a christological imbalance to be sure.[62]

Second, as discussed in chapter 1, any Christology that grants too much autonomy to the humanity of Christ can seem to suggest a Pelagian tendency where human capabilities might attain or merit salvation apart from the grace available through the person and work of Christ. This risk is certainly present here.[63] It is also a concerning aspect of later theories of a conjunction of humanity and divinity that seek to describe the conjunction as voluntary, as in the theology of Babai the Great from the Church of the East, a Syriac non-Chalcedonian church.[64] Babai described the union of humanity and divinity as "voluntary," not passive or compulsory, implying, perhaps unintentionally, that the human will autonomously consented to, caused, and acted toward the union.[65] This Pelagian risk found in *homo assumptus* theories of the union of natures is often merely implied. Babai explicitly rejected the notion of one hypostasis out of concern that any human hypostasis might become divine by nature,[66] and though he did teach that the perfection attained through Jesus the high priest was through his human hypostasis, he admitted that this nature was empowered by divinity.[67] Babai is thus not purely Pelagian, but he is certainly not entirely free from Pelagian elements either. Babai's theology shows that when a contrast is set up between human and divine natures or operations in an attempt to limit human abilities by denying that humans can independently attain full divinity, the result can actually increase human autonomous agency through a theology of conjunction.

The fourth medieval theory was known as the subsistence theory, which claims that the very existence or subsistence of the human nature exists only in the person of the Son. On this theory, the person of the Son is composite, but only a single supposit, or particular individual thing.[68] How, then, is discussion of a composite person different from the *partes* theory discussed above? Where the *partes* theory might be seen to say that the person of the

62. Aquinas, *Summa Theologica* III, Q. 2, A. 3 and A. 6.

63. Riches notes that John Cassian had criticized Nestorius for promoting a Pelagian Christology, seeing both as having a sort of *homo assumptus* Christology. Further, the Council of Ephesus condemned not only Nestorius but Pelagius. For a complete discussion of connections between Pelagianism, Nestorianism, and the *homo assumptus*, see Riches, *Ecce Homo*, 46–49.

64. Babai affirmed two natures (*kyana*) and two *qnômê*, which are concretizations of natures, but not quite the same thing as hypostases. These were united in one *parsopa*, or person, which named the unique mode of filiation proper to the Son and shared by the humanity of Christ. See Kitchen, "Babai the Great," 241.

65. Metselaar, *Defining Christ*, 152.

66. Metselaar, *Defining Christ*, 129–30, 137.

67. Metselaar, *Defining Christ*, 162.

68. Riches, *Ecce Homo*, 158.

Son is made up of two parts, humanity and deity, it can be taken to refer to two parts of a single hypostasis. This would violate the logic of the incarnation as it would result in a change in the divine person through the addition of a new part. Medieval theology struggled with the idea of a composite or compound person, but safeguards were put in place. Part of the problem with the *partes* theory is that it is too simplistic without such safeguards. Eventually these safeguards were developed as a component of a different explanation of the incarnation. Alexander of Hales, for example, makes a distinction between the ways that something can be composite. As Walter Principe summarizes, "A composite can either be constituted from (*ex*) others or it can result from something being united to another that existed before it."[69] The human nature does not compose the divine hypostasis of the Son in the sense of making it; rather, there are two natures that exist in the Son. The human nature is united to the divine hypostasis, existing in it but not in a way that the Son's hypostasis is changed. In other words, the eternal relations between the Son and the Father and between the Son and the Spirit remain unchanged, with humanity drawn into these relationships. Similarly, the Son's display of the attributes of the divine nature is unchanged.[70] Yet the two natures exist as a singular hypostasis. What we have seen, then, is that medievals tried to preserve the singularity of the divine person by denying that the person was two divisible parts (the *partes* theory) and by rejecting the claim that the humanity previously had existence independently of the Son (the *homo assumptus* theory) or existed only externally to the Son like clothing (the *habitus* theory). Rather, in the subsistence theory, both natures exist fully in the Son, with the humanity becoming a composite that exists in the Son, being dependent on the hypostasis of the Son, while the hypostasis of the Son did not depend on the humanity for its existence.

A final component of the singularity criterion for divine personhood must explain the unity of the actions of Christ's human and divine natures. It should be noted that this synthesis was affirmed at the Council of Chalcedon, which endorsed Pope Leo's *Tomus*, in which he teaches that each nature

69. Principe, *Alexander of Hales' Theology*, 129. On the wider use of compound person, see Duby, *Jesus*, 366.
70. Notice that the significance of the doctrine of simplicity is that it seeks to preserve the aseity of God and to ensure that he is the uncaused cause that explains all of existence. By saying that the human nature does not compose the divine person, we avoid having to find an explanation for the Son's personal existence by seeking an external efficient cause by which these natures came to compose the Son. Rather, the Son already existed and then assumed a human nature, being the efficient cause of this assumption of humanity. Further, since the deity was unchanged in hypostasis or nature, one need not affirm parts of the divine hypostasis or nature.

"does the acts which belong to it, in communion with the other."[71] A lingering concern regarding the council is whether these two operations implied two distinct agents and two discrete existing things, contrary to the singularity demanded by the communication of idioms and, a century after Chalcedon, by the concept of enhypostasia. This subject in various dimensions will be addressed in chapter 7. For now, suffice it to say that the two powers and two operations that belong distinctively to the two natures eventually were understood to be joined into a singular **theandric action**. Thus, John of Damascus can say that the operations of the human and divine natures are not "separated" but "act conjointly," such that each operation is found in the other—the human operation as an instrument of divine agency and the divine operation in volitional harmony with the human operation, together as one theandric operation.[72]

The Trinitarian Compatibility Criterion

What is said of the one hypostasis and person of the incarnate Son must be compatible with what is said about the Son in his eternal trinitarian relations with the Father and Spirit, which leads to a trinitarian compatibility criterion for any attempted explanation of the way that the humanity and divinity of Christ are a single hypostasis.[73] This compatibility must occur in at least three ways. First, there must be compatibility between how key concepts like "person," "hypostasis," and "nature" are used in trinitarian theology. As Leontius of Byzantium argues, if nature refers to what is common to a class of things and if hypostasis refers to what is proper to a single subject in trinitarian theology, why would the terms be fundamentally different in the incarnation?[74] At a deeper level, the trinitarian compatibility criterion requires metaphysical compatibility between trinitarian and christological dogma. For example, Western medieval theologians wrestled with a puzzle clearly presented by Roscelin of Compiègne: If the Son took on flesh and is consubstantial with the Father and Spirit, then it appears that either we need to affirm that all three took on flesh, which is contrary to Scripture and the ecumenical creeds, or else we have to say that there are three distinct things in God. Anselm of Canterbury, among others, developed a metaphysical

---

71. Leo the Great, *Tome* §4.

72. John of Damascus, *Orthodox Faith* §19.

73. The inverse is also true, which I have explored in Butner, *Trinitarian Dogmatics*, 111–18. The trinitarian compatibility criterion can be seen as the correlate of the christological compatibility criterion for the doctrine of the Trinity, or both together could be seen as a larger compatibility criterion for any account of divine personhood.

74. Leontius of Byzantium, *Epilyseis* §3.

response to this puzzle by developing a clear distinction between person and nature.[75] At an even deeper level, however, the Trinity can be seen as a dogmatic precondition for the doctrine of the incarnation. Thus, Herman Bavinck writes, "Only the theistic and trinitarian confession of God's characteristic essence opens the possibility for the fact of the incarnation. For here God remains who he is and can yet communicate himself to others."[76] Because God is an eternally self-giving God, with the Father eternally generating the Son and spirating the Spirit, we can understand God as capable of full self-communication such that a divine self-communication through incarnation is not surprising but fitting. Returning to the basic definitional continuity necessary between the doctrine of the Trinity and Christology, it is apparent that both Eutychianism and Nestorianism "share a common premise," notes Thomas Joseph White—namely, that "a hypostatic union presupposes a union of natures."[77] The doctrine of the Trinity, however, requires us to recognize that there is not always a one-to-one correlation between nature and hypostasis.

Analysis of the hypostatic union in a more metaphysical register is often concerned to explain how properties of the shared divine nature are compatible with claims about the incarnation. For example, immutability and eternality are important for a robust understanding of eternal generation and spiration, which are said to happen eternally and without change in the Father.[78] How can the incarnation account for such attributes? To address this concern, the Chalcedonian definition insists that the natures are joined "inconfusedly, unchangeably, indivisibly, inseparably." This formula has a long pedigree. When participants of the Council of Chalcedon itself were deliberating as to whether to accept the *Tome* of Leo, a group of thirty bishops represented by Bishop Sozon of Philippi signed a document in which they accepted the *Tome* and anathematized whoever denied that Christ "possesses both the divine and human attributes without confusion, change or division."[79] Nestorius and Cyril both were driven by the concern that the incarnation could be taken to signify a change in the divine nature, but where Nestorius responded by downplaying the genuine hypostatic singularity of the incarnate Christ, Cyril affirmed that the Son could take on human nature without "synthesis, . . . composition, or mixture, or fusion" while retaining

75. Anselm of Canterbury, *On the Incarnation of the Word*.

76. Bavinck, *Reformed Dogmatics*, 3:275.

77. White, *Incarnate Lord*, 82.

78. For my explanation of this, see Butner, *Trinitarian Dogmatics*, 52–60; Butner, *Son Who Learned Obedience*, 136–46.

79. *Acts of the Council of Chalcedon* 2.4.98.

divine immutability.[80] Like Roscelin of Compiègne, Nestorius was also alleged to claim that if divinity became human, all three divine persons would have become human, a subject to which I will return.[81] More recently, ecumenical dialogue between Roman Catholic and Armenian Apostolic theologians has found a point of agreement in the claim that humanity and divinity are one in Christ "without commixtion, without confusion, without division, without separation."[82] A joint statement signed by Shenouda III and Pope Paul VI in 1973 agreed but added "without mingling."[83]

One specific challenge that the trinitarian compatibility criterion must face is the question of how one of the divine persons, with an immutable, simple, eternal divine nature, could assume a human nature that is mutable, compound, and time-bound. Divine simplicity, immutability, and eternality are important divine attributes for the doctrine of the Trinity, notably for qualifying eternal generation and spiration such that they do not produce inferior, temporally subsequent persons external to the essence of the Father.[84] Though such attributes are important for trinitarianism, it must be admitted that they raise intellectual puzzles in the context of Christology. For example, how can the immutable divine person of the Son assume a new nature? Often, analysis of such questions hinges on the precise definitions. We might argue with Aquinas that mutability requires the activation of a potency, in which case the assumption of humanity is not a change in the divine nature since this assumption does not activate a potency in the divine nature.[85] Alternatively and more recently, Timothy Pawl has argued for a truth condition for immutability that can be met with the hypostatic union: "S is immutable just in case S has a concrete nature such that it is not the case that the nature is able to change."[86] When the person of the Son assumes a discrete, concrete human nature capable of change, then the Son is both immutable, having a concrete divine nature that cannot change, and mutable, having a concrete human nature capable of change.[87] Pawl argues—rightly, I think—that a similar view of immutability and impassibility must have been assumed by the

80. See Cyril of Alexandria, *To Theodosius* §§10–11; Cyril of Alexandria, *Scholia on the Incarnation* §8; Cyril of Alexandria, *On the Unity of Christ*, 77. On Nestorius, see Daley, *God Visible*, 188.
81. See "The Session of 22 June," 53.
82. Krikorian, *Christology*, 148. Interestingly, the extent to which dogmatic disagreement centers on whether nature and hypostasis are synonyms is evident in the fact that the ecumenical statement reached consensus partly by avoiding using either term altogether!
83. Krikorian, *Christology*, 154.
84. See Butner, *Trinitarian Dogmatics*, 52–60; Butner, *Son Who Learned Obedience*, 136–46.
85. See the extended discussion of Aquinas's views in M. Gorman, *Hypostatic Union*, 57–67.
86. Pawl, *Conciliar Christology*, 191.
87. Pawl, *Conciliar Christology*, 194.

Second Council of Constantinople (553) when it anathematized those who do "not confess his belief that our lord Jesus Christ, who was crucified in his human flesh, is truly God and the Lord of glory and one of the members of the holy Trinity."[88]

The attempt to preserve divine attributes important to the doctrine of the Trinity by appeal to two concrete natures results in a typical concern often raised by critics of Chalcedon, ancient and modern. Does the existence of two concrete natures imply two hypostases, thus undermining the genuine unity of the incarnate Son? Two subsistences is declared a heresy at the Second Council of Constantinople.[89] In my estimation, we can understand the singular hypostasis of the two concrete natures of the Son most clearly when we remember that God is not part of a kind or genus and that the doctrine of analogy qualifies all words used to describe God.[90] Such rules would extend even to concepts like existence, for the divine nature does not exist in the same manner that other natures exist. Therefore, when the Son takes on a concrete human nature that is made concrete enhypostatically in the Son, the act of existence by which that human nature is concrete is the Son's act, but it is a different sort of existence than the existence of the divine nature, for the human existence is not necessary existence, to name only one difference. Perhaps something of this sort is what Thomas Aquinas means when he occasionally posits a secondary act of existence (*secondarium esse*) of the human nature of the Word—namely, that the human nature is concrete, but at the deepest ontological level, this concrete existence is entirely in, through, and because of the eternal act of existence of the Son. Yet the existing human and divine natures remain distinct, unmixed natures.[91] With this clarification in hand, we can turn to consider the relationality, unity, and uniqueness criteria for any definition of divine personhood, which will further elucidate the manner in which the incarnate Son is one hypostasis.

The Relationality Criterion

It is a standard claim of contemporary trinitarian theology to explain the mission of the Son in the incarnation as an extension of the Father's eternal generation of the Son. Thus, Fred Sanders writes, "The missions are temporal fromness, for us and our salvation, which manifest eternal fromness."[92] In the

88. N. Tanner, *Decrees of the Ecumenical Councils*, 118.
89. See canon 5. N. Tanner, *Decrees of the Ecumenical Councils*, 116.
90. K. Tanner, "Is God in Charge?"
91. On the *esse secondarium*, see Riches, *Ecce Homo*, 168–76.
92. Sanders, *Triune God*, 124.

words of Kathryn Tanner, "The life of the Word is constituted by its dynamic relationships with the other members of the Trinity from which it is insepa-rable, the Word has no life apart from the other two. In becoming incarnate the Word therefore extends this same pattern of trinitarian relationships into its own human life so as to give it shape according to that pattern."[93] Jesus of Nazareth is the Son of God because he continues to live out the relation-ship of eternal sonship in the new context of a historical human life. It is in this historical life that the Father or his angelic representative repeatedly can declare that Jesus is the beloved Son, first at the annunciation (Luke 1:32, 35), then at the baptism of Christ (Matt. 3:17; Mark 1:11; Luke 3:22) and at the transfiguration (Matt. 17:5; Mark 9:7; Luke 9:35). Notably, the first two of these moments also reveal the relation between Jesus and the Holy Spirit who brings about the virginal conception (Luke 1:35) and descends as a dove at the baptism (Matt. 3:16; Mark 1:10; Luke 3:22). Each of these moments also centers the embodiedness of the incarnate Son. The Holy Spirit creates the human nature of the Son at the virginal conception; the Son is bodily submerged in water at the baptism; and, as John of Damascus notes, Christ as God is "light from light," to use the words of Nicaea, but the light of the transfiguration extended from "the holy body," which was "**circumscribed**" and "stood on Thabor, it did not extend beyond the mountain." To summa-rize: "The shining forth of light originated within his body."[94]

Summarizing in more Thomistic language, the missions are the eternal processions with a created term.[95] The Word's sonship is rooted in his eternal generation by the Father, and when human nature is assumed by the Son, that human nature is incorporated into the Father-Son relationship and serves as a created term for generation. The humanity of Christ therefore exists in relationships to the Father and Spirit that are constitutive of that human existence as sonship, a mode of existence comparable to the mode by which the divine nature exists in the Son. This is important for the claim that the two natures are united hypostatically in the Son. Recall that "hypostasis" can refer to that which has "obduracy" or "persistence."[96] Personhood is constituted by relations, so the personhood of the Son is constituted by the Father-Son and Son-Spirit relationships. If the humanity of Christ is drawn through the incarnation into these same relationships, it exists as the same hypostasis of

---

93. Tanner, *Christ the Key*, 140.
94. John of Damascus, "Oration on the Transfiguration," 222.
95. Doran, *Trinity in History*, 40.
96. Prestige, *God in Patristic Thought*, 170. In the sense I am exploring here, "obduracy" would apply more metaphorically, while "persistence" would apply in a literal ontological manner.

the Son, the same persistence. The Chalcedonian definition expresses this persistence by regularly highlighting how the Lord Jesus Christ is "one and the same" as the one born of Mary and begotten of the Father. The natures are one hypostasis because the same constitutive relations endure before and after the incarnation.

The Unity Criterion

An adequate theological account of the divine persons must insist that though the Father, Son, and Holy Spirit are distinct persons, they are still united to one another. This unity persists through the Son's incarnation, a fact that requires us to consider how the human nature assumed by the Son is related to the Father and the Spirit with whom the Son also shares a divine nature. As John Clark and Marcus Peter Johnson explain, "By becoming incarnate, the Son of God extended his relationship with his Father and the Spirit into our human existence so that we come to know and experience God as he really is."[97] Any explanation of the unity of two natures in Christ must continue to be able to account for the ongoing trinitarian unity of the persons of the Father, Son, and Holy Spirit.

The divine persons are partly united through inseparable operations, a doctrine that teaches that all divine acts *ad extra*, or toward the created world, are undertaken inseparably by all three divine persons. A superficial reading of this doctrine might lead an observer to the conclusion that it is impossible for just the Son to be incarnate without the Father and Spirit being incarnate too.[98] Theologians have long been aware of this possible misinterpretation and have often explained this puzzle in different ways. Medieval theologians argued that assuming a human nature was a state or condition of a hypostasis, not an act, and so the assumption of human nature does not require the Son to have causal powers or to perform an operation apart from the Father and Spirit in a manner that might jeopardize the ultimate unity of the Trinity.[99] There is a tradition of talking about divine actions as terminating on a divine Person. Adonis Vidu explains that this can mean two things. First, it might signify the Son being both an agent of the shared divine action and also the passive recipient of that action—the three persons act inseparably on the Son, bringing about the assumption of humanity. Second, the operation terminates on a person according to the ordering of divine operations from the Father,

---

97. Clark and Johnson, *Incarnation of God*, 164.

98. Some in the Church of the East have made this claim, including Mar Babai the Great. See Kuhn, *God Is One*, 143.

99. See the discussion in Cross, *Metaphysics of the Incarnation*, 151–53.

through the Son, to the Spirit. In this sense, incarnation terminates on the Spirit as the one most clearly seen in the virginal conception.[100] Similarly, we cannot view the human nature as a mere instrument of the divine causality of the Word with no agency proper to itself, because in this case the human nature seemingly would be reduced to the inseparable operations of all three persons, but then how would we say the Son was uniquely incarnate? Despite divergences in important details, both Scotist and Thomist resolutions of this problem insist on a genuine operation proper to the human nature of Christ.[101]

What are we to make of the ongoing unity of the divine persons after the virginal conception and the assumption of the human nature by the Son? An interesting theological debate among the Ethiopian Orthodox in the nineteenth century raises important questions on the subject. The Ethiopian Orthodox Tewahedo Church has traditionally been miaphysite, affirming Christ out of two natures, following the Coptic Orthodox Church that typically sends a bishop to Ethiopia.[102] The introduction of Chalcedonian Christology in the 1600s by Jesuit missionaries sparked controversy and two new christological views. One, called *qeb'at* (in English they are known as **unctionists**), appealed to Acts 10:38's teaching that "God anointed Jesus of Nazareth with the Holy Spirit and with power," arguing that the anointing was the basis for the full unity of natures.[103] These unctionists were condemned by Yohannes IV if they did not affirm "the Son [himself as] the unction," an effort to argue that the hypostasis was the basis for the full unity of the two natures.[104] Both sides of the debate are attempting to affirm something important. The traditional view advocated by Yohannes IV is attempting to preserve the idea that the hypostasis of the Son is the source or ground of the human nature, being that without which the humanity would not exist. However, the theology of *qeb'at* is concerned to preserve the inseparable work of the Trinity in incarnation. Citing Luke 4:18/Isaiah 61:1 and Acts 10:38, one unctionist text argues, "We say about the Father, 'He generated his Son for us'; we say about the Son, 'He is born for us.' What would we say about what the Holy Spirit did for us if he had not, having created the flesh, made (the Son) incarnate? Our faith as well as our love would not have been steadfast in the Holy Trinity."[105] The point is well taken, and so we must have a role for the Holy Spirit in the

---

100. Vidu, *Same God*, 167–68.
101. Vidu, *Same God*, 195–99.
102. See Tibebe and Giorgis, "Ethiopian Orthodox Church."
103. Crummey, "Imperial Reconstruction in Ethiopia," 430.
104. Crummey, "Imperial Reconstruction in Ethiopia," 438.
105. Haile, "Materials on the Theology" §45. The cited text is the *Treatise on the Theology of Qebat*.

incarnation. Further, unctionists traced this role of the Holy Spirit back to the inner life of the Trinity. The movement believed that the Father eternally gives the Spirit to the Son, and so argued that the humanity of Christ also becomes the Son through the reception of the Holy Spirit.[106] Here again, *qeb'at* offers a helpful insight by insisting that the eternal relation between the Son and Spirit now includes the humanity of Christ due to the incarnation, much as the Son's eternal generation by the Father extends through the incarnation to include the human nature in Jesus's sonship. However, *qeb'at* was probably still rightfully condemned insofar as the union of natures was said to be through the work of the Spirit and *not through the hypostatic assumption of the Son*, since this makes the doctrine seem adoptionistic.[107] We must affirm that Father, Son, and Spirit jointly cause the incarnation in a manner that draws the humanity of Christ into the eternal relations of Father, Son, and Spirit, but it is important to also preserve the uniqueness of the Son as the only incarnate person.

The triune persons are also one in perichoresis, a concept that signifies unity amid distinction, or "union without absorption."[108] Trinitarian perichoresis can be understood in spatial terms such that where one person is present, all are, or it can be explained in terms of motion so that what one does, all do, or it can be explained in terms of unity of consciousness, love, and will.[109] The perichoresis between the Father, Son, and Holy Spirit persists even after the incarnation, but it is important to be careful in delineating how the human nature relates to this trinitarian perichoresis. Successive generations of theologians developed clearer terminology for considering how the presence of the human nature and shared divine nature related. For example, Gregory of Nazianzus tended to speak of a mixing of natures (Greek, *krasis* or *mixis*), intending to signify the transformation of the human nature as it is penetrated by the more powerful divine nature.[110] This concept of mixing was deployed in an attempt to reject a complete separation of humanity and divinity in

---

106. Haile, "Materials on the Theology" §55. Here, the Ethiopian Orthodox follow the pattern of many Orthodox theologies in rejecting a Western Scholastic tendency to reduce the processions and relations between the trinitarian persons to a matter of causation alone. For similar tendencies in other Orthodox theologies, see Gregory of Cyprus, *Tomus*; Bulgakov, *Comforter*, 95–97.

107. Crummey, "Imperial Reconstruction in Ethiopia," 430. I must here admit that the limited texts available in English, combined with secondhand accounts of the dispute, lead me to some degree of uncertainty about both the full views of the unctionists and the validity of their condemnation. However, assuming the accounts available to me are accurate, then the apparent adoptionistic tendencies are worth condemning.

108. Twombly, *Perichoresis and Personhood*, 47.

109. See Butner, *Trinitarian Dogmatics*, 134–38.

110. Daley, *God Visible*, 135.

Christ as distinct hypostases or prosopa by attempting to posit Christ as a single subject, though the terminology was eventually rejected for fear that it suggested change in the divine nature and a combination of two natures into a third thing that is neither human nor divine.[111] Instead, terminology of perichoresis began to be used to describe the mutual interpenetration and coinherence of natures in Christ.[112]

The concept of christological perichoresis plays an important though subsidiary role in explaining the singularity of Christ. It has a clear benefit over the preferred Nestorian terminology of conjunction of natures because the coinherence of perichoresis suggests a unity of subject that can serve as the basis for a robust doctrine of the communication of idioms.[113] Where conjunction and prosoponic union is empirical or phenomenological, pertaining to our ability to perceive Christ as one object, perichoresis also is superior in that it suggests a unity that reaches down to ontology, what the Son fundamentally is.[114] Note, however, that perichoresis is best understood not as a basis of that union—in Christology the hypostasis of the Son is the basis for the unity of natures—but rather as a consequence of the hypostatic unity of natures. Perichoresis is a superior concept to Gregory's concept of "mixing" as well since the concept includes within it a union of elements that remain distinct.[115] In this way, perichoresis signifies something similar to Chalcedon's language of a hypostatic union that occurs without confusion, change, division, or separation.

Despite the strengths of the concept of perichoresis, when the concept is applied to Christology it cannot have as extensive a meaning as it does in trinitarian application. Most significantly, christological perichoresis cannot include a unity of consciousness and will of the sort seen between the trinitarian persons. More will be said in chapter 7, but for now it must be noted that such a unity could not make sense of phenomena like the Son's growth in wisdom and stature (Luke 2:40, 52) through the natural progress of a human

111. Riches, *Ecce Homo*, 92–93. On Cyril of Alexandria's rejection of Nazianzus's concept of mixture, see Beeley, *Unity of Christ*, 271.

112. The most important theologian to make early use of this concept was Maximus the Confessor. For example, see his *Dispute at Bizya* §6.

113. On the use of "conjunction," see the discussion at the start of this chapter or see L. Davis, *First Seven Ecumenical Councils*, 144–46. The term is occasionally still used after the condemnation of Nestorius, though with other important qualifiers included. For example, Maximus the Confessor, *Ambigua to Thomas* 1.5.14.

114. On the empirical dimensions of conjunction and a singular *prosōpon*, see Riches, *Ecce Homo*, 31.

115. Twombly, *Perichoresis and Personhood*, 54.

life.[116] Perichoresis can also be understood as spatial coinherence, referring to the mutual presence of two distinct realities, and as mutual interpenetration, indicating the mutual action or operation of distinct realities. These senses can apply christologically, though in a more restricted manner than in trinitarian theology.[117] In John's Gospel, a pattern of mutual indwelling explicitly takes on trinitarian and ecclesial dimensions, with a christological sense being implied throughout.[118] Certainly, when Jesus says, "The one who has seen me has seen the Father" (John 14:9), it suggests that the divine nature shared by Father, Son, and Spirit is somehow manifest in the visible human nature of the Son. At the level of dogmatics, the concept of the human nature being enhypostatically in the Son also suggests a perichoretic coinherence. There is imbalance here: The human nature is in the divine such that it visibly reflects the divine glory in moments like the transfiguration (Matt. 17:2; Mark 9:3; Luke 9:29), and the human nature depends on the efficient causality of creative acts possible through the power of the divine nature, but the **aseity** of the divine nature requires us to affirm that the human nature does not change the divine, and the infinite, uncircumscribed divine nature is present in places where Christ's human nature is not.[119] In a similar manner, perichoresis as mutual interpenetration is evident in the theandric actions of Christ, where Christ is the single subject of both the human and divine actions he performs.[120] This also entails that acts of the human nature are in unity with divine acts that Father, Son, and Spirit also work inseparably (John 5:17, 19). Yet where trinitarian perichoresis requires us to affirm that all divine acts *ad extra* are indivisibly performed by Father, Son, and Spirit, certain acts of Christ, such as dying on the cross, are properly only acts of the Son by virtue of his human nature and are not performed by the divine nature.

116. Stephen Wellum offers insightful analysis in making this point and raises the real risk that a concept of perichoresis applied to consciousness could result in eliminating the genuine humanity of Christ. However, I believe he goes too far in dismissing the concept in Christology altogether, especially in his suggestion that the communication of idioms serves "in its place." As I have just argued, perichoresis serves as a healthy complement to and, perhaps, foundation for the doctrine of communication of idioms. See Wellum, *God the Son*, 324–25.

117. Twombly, *Perichoresis and Personhood*, 54–55.

118. For a brief survey of relevant texts, see Swain, "John," 202–5.

119. Chapter 10 will discuss this important topic in greater detail.

120. Though I agree with Oliver Crisp that the perichoresis of the two natures of Christ is asymmetric, I still speak of interpenetration because of the doctrine of enhypostasia, for the humanity of Christ exists in the Son who is the divine nature. Crisp prefers to speak only of the divine penetrating the human nature. Without this reciprocity, perichoresis becomes different only in degree from the presence of the omnipotent Son in all of creation, and Jesus's claim that he is one with his Father (John 10:30) becomes merely a fact of which Christ is aware that could also apply to us, were we aware of the same. This undercuts the uniqueness of Christ. Crisp, *Divinity and Humanity*, 22–25.

At the end of our survey of the unity of the Son's humanity with the Father and the Spirit, basic points are clear. First, the humanity of Christ is united to the Father and the Spirit perichoretically and operationally (i.e., in terms of actions) in a manner analogous to the Son's perichoretic unity with the Father and Spirit with whom he acts inseparably. This shared unity further clarifies how the humanity of the Son is one hypostasis with the divine nature: The unity that Father, Son, and Spirit had apart from the incarnation endures through the Son's assumption of flesh. If saying the Son is one hypostasis points to the ongoing persistence of the Son as a discrete person, the persistence of such unity is vital to demonstrating a hypostatic unity. Second, christological perichoresis allows for the affirmation of Christ having two natures in one hypostasis in terms of both natures being presented as a single, discrete reality. Third, though the unity of the Son incorporates the humanity of Christ into a singular hypostasis, it does so in such a way that the humanity remains a distinct nature. Therefore, christological perichoresis is both asymmetrical and incomplete in comparison with trinitarian perichoresis. The theandric action of the Son is also different from trinitarian inseparable operations. Yet christological perichoresis and the theandric action of the God-man must be seen as the perfect analogues of their trinitarian counterparts. Fourth and finally, there must be a clear role for the Father and Spirit in the incarnation since the Son is united to both in the Trinity. However, the doctrine of the hypostatic union helps us to see that the humanity is unique to the Son in whom it enhypostatically exists. Against the unctionists, we cannot reduce the union of natures to a work of the Spirit, nor can we make Christ's human actions instrumental to the three persons inseparably. Rather, the one incarnate hypostasis of the Son must be seen to retain his eternal relations to and unity with the Father and Spirit.

The Dissimilarity Criterion

As this discussion nears a close, I have argued for several important senses in which the two natures of Christ are one hypostasis by exploring the criteria of an adequate account of divine personhood. A hypostasis refers to the ontological foundation of a thing, or that which renders something an object. The doctrine of enhypostasia and the rejection of *homo assumptus* theories of the incarnation demonstrate that the person of the Son is the ontological foundation for the existence of the human nature. A hypostasis can refer to a productive agency, and so in theandric action we see the hypostasis of the Son is the agent of both human and divine acts of Christ. Much more remains to be said about this in chapter 7. Hypostasis refers to a singular presentation of an object, and so the doctrine of the communication of idioms and of christological perichoresis explains that Jesus Christ is the one subject bearing the human and divine natures with a unified presence and agency. Finally, to speak of a hypostasis is to speak of what endures, and the same Son who is one with the Father and Spirit and eternally in relationship with them draws a human nature into these relations and into this union, though without mixture or change. In all these ways, we see a hypostatic unity that avoids the errors of Nestorius and that provides greater clarity than Cyril of Alexandria was yet able to describe.

Despite this theological clarification, I must admit that not all questions about the hypostatic union have been resolved. In part, this is because I am offering a dogmatic account that I hope is acceptable to a wide range of Christians, so some theological questions have remained unexplored. Beyond this, we must remember that trinitarian persons are persons in a dissimilar sense from human persons. Since only one divine person has been incarnate, the hypostatic union is a unique phenomenon beyond exhaustive human comprehension. Yes, some Christians have put forward analogies to try to explain the union of two natures in the person of the Son. For example, Cyril of Alexandria's analogy of a scent permeating and perfuming a flower is a particularly eloquent way of describing the hypostatic union, particularly in terms of christological perichoresis.[121] The two natures are in each other and in the hypostasis something like the way that perfume is in a flower. Yet this analogy is quite limited. Perhaps the most used analogy is that of the unity of body and soul in a single person.[122] Even here, the analogy is limited in several ways. Christ has the unity of human body and soul into a singular person plus an additional divine nature. The body and soul technically are not complete natures either, since both combined are a nature, so they imperfectly image the union of two natures. The most significant limitation, though, is that the qualitative difference between body and soul is infinitely smaller than that between divinity and creation, and we do not even fully understand the unity of body and soul. All analogies fall short of perfect explanation.[123]

Moving beyond metaphors for the hypostatic union, the closest theological analogue to the hypostatic union is our union with Christ by the work of the

---

121. Cyril of Alexandria, *Scholia on the Incarnation* §10.

122. Among other places, we see this also in Cyril of Alexandria, *Scholia on the Incarnation* §8.

123. Bulgakov, *Lamb of God*, 16, 25–26, 50. I am not quite as critical of the metaphor as Bulgakov, though I grant the weight of his concerns. The metaphor must also be handled cautiously since it originated with Apollinaris, who took it more literally to compare the soul with the Word and the body with his assumed human nature.

Holy Spirit. Yet John Owen helpfully chastens any major comparison between union and hypostatic union: "How ineffably distinct the relation between the Son of God and the man Christ Jesus is from all that relation and union which may be between God and believers."[124] In the end, despite considerable theological advances, the dissimilarity criterion requires that any account of the hypostasis of the Son must admit such radical dissimilarity with creation to include a strong apophatic element. Yet the minimal similarity here does reveal a few theological truths to close out the chapter. First, the unity of divinity and humanity into a single hypostasis allows us to worship Jesus Christ without being idolators, for the human Christ is a divine person.[125] The fact that the natures are joined without mixture or confusion is encouraging to us because it reminds us that our union with the person of the Son does not require us to lose our humanity. This is especially the case since believers' union with Christ is far more limited than the Son's hypostatic assumption of a human nature. Beth Felker Jones summarizes well: "The rejection of Eutychianism is also the rejection of mistaken ideas that our salvation must basically destroy who we are."[126] The practical implications of the hypostatic unity of Christ's natures include the moral example of the God-man and the union with Christ that hypostatic union makes possible. We turn now to engage substantively with these questions.

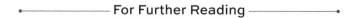

For Further Reading

Beeley, Christopher A. *The Unity of Christ: Continuity and Conflict in Patristic Tradition*. Yale University Press, 2012.

> Beeley offers an extensive historical analysis of patristic christological debates that synthesizes the views of various groups into a single coherent narrative extending from Origen to the post-Chalcedonian patristic thinkers. This thorough source serves as a helpful and detailed resource for the debate.

Pawl, Timothy. *In Defense of Conciliar Christology: A Philosophical Essay*. Oxford University Press, 2016.

> I have avoided focusing on analytic theology, partly due to my limited training in this area. But this theological methodology is growing in importance and influence, and one of the larger areas of debate is in Christology. Timothy Pawl's work is quite important in its defense of conciliar Christology, which would include the concepts

---

124. Owen, *Person of Christ*, 223–24.
125. Cyril of Alexandria, *To Theodosius* §31.
126. B. Jones, *Practicing Christian Doctrine*, 129.

of two natures and one person. His project resists tendencies toward kenoticism and monophysitism in some analytic circles, making this book an important read.

Riches, Aaron. *Ecce Homo: On the Divine Unity of Christ*. Eerdmans, 2016.

Riches's text is a more expansive historical survey, including not only patristic debates but also Byzantine, medieval, and modern treatments. Though largely a text on historical theology, *Ecce Homo* regularly incorporates the concerns and arguments of systematicians, with particular emphasis on the *homo assumptus* view of the incarnation.

CHAPTER SIX

Union with Christ

The union of humanity and divinity in the person of the Son, pre-serving the distinction between natures, is a fundamental precondi-tion for much of the salvific work of Christ. Without the hypostatic union, Christ's atoning work on the cross would not benefit us. As John Mur-ray puts it, "The precise nature of Christ's priestly offering and the efficacy of his sacrifice are bound up with the constitution of his person."[1] We have not completed our discussion of the constitution of Christ, for the means by which the natures will and work together must be explained before a full theology of the cross and resurrection is possible. However, the basic gram-mar of the hypostatic union is sufficient to lay the theological foundations for the transformation that Christ makes possible for the Christian to whom the benefits of the cross and resurrection are applied.

Across denominations and eras, theologians have developed various means of speaking of our transformation in Christ, each highlighting different aspects of the Christian's connection with Christ. This chapter will focus on three such ways of description, beginning with an account of Jesus's role in giving the Spirit, moving to discuss Eastern Orthodox accounts of theosis, and then summarizing Protestant theologies of union with Christ, language I prefer to use for both theological and cultural reasons.[2] Each survey will start with a brief discussion of a passage of particular importance to that theological

---

1. Murray, *Redemption Accomplished and Applied*, 15.
2. My theological reasons should be clear by the end of the chapter, but culturally I point to two factors. First, as someone of a Reformed theological camp, I find language of union with Christ is far more familiar than other means of describing our transformation. Second, as an English speaker, I find language of union carries less ambiguity than does language of theosis.

perspective on Christ's connection to the Christian and conclude with a brief summary of one exemplary theologian for the given approach. Combined with a general theological explanation, this threefold perspective should clarify the variety and commonality found in each perspective. At the end of the chapter, I will offer a dogmatic synthesis that draws on strengths from each theological tradition represented in these models of our participation in Christ.

Jesus and the Gift of the Spirit

Those with a basic understanding of how God transforms the Christian see the Holy Spirit playing an important role in this process, so it is fitting to begin by considering a model of this transformation that focuses especially on the Spirit. Yet the prevalent emphasis on the Spirit in the Christian life should not lead us to imagine that there is no wisdom to retrieve from theological history to better understand the Scriptures. Therefore, I begin with a brief survey of the baptism of Christ before offering a theological analysis of Christ's role in sending the Spirit.

The Baptism of Christ

The Gospel accounts of the baptism of Christ (Matt. 3:13–17; Mark 1:9–11; Luke 3:21–22; John 1:29–34) play an important role in the doctrine of the Trinity, revealing the three persons interacting simultaneously, but we ought not to ignore the important christological implications of the event. Some early Christians interpreted the Spirit's descent on Jesus at his baptism to indicate his adoption as divine Son at that moment, having previously been a mere human being.[3] This position is known as adoptionism or dynamic monarchianism. Their perspective has a small degree of plausibility when one considers the question of why a divine person would need to be baptized, though the cumulative weight of Scripture stands firmly against adoptionism. Indeed, even the Gospel writers anticipated the question, offering brief answers. So, in Matthew Jesus says that his baptism "fulfill[s] all righteousness" (Matt. 3:15), while John the Baptist explains in John's Gospel that baptism was "so [the Messiah] might be revealed to Israel" (John 1:31). Yet such brief answers have led theologians across the centuries to seek further details about how Jesus's baptism fulfills righteousness. For example, Augustine of Hippo explains that the righteousness Jesus fulfilled (Matt. 3:15) was that of being an example of humility.[4] Augustine

---

3. For a brief overview, see Kelly, *Early Christian Doctrines*, 114–17.
4. Augustine of Hippo, "Words of St. Matthew's Gospel" §1.

explains the baptism of Christ within the context of the inseparable operations of the Trinity. Yes, all three divine persons work together in all things, Augustine argues, but they can jointly cause something to happen to one of the divine persons, as when only the Son is baptized.[5] Augustine's interpretation of the passage shows an early trinitarian emphasis, but an exemplary interpretation of baptism was later replaced by other understandings of how baptism ful-filled righteousness. In terms of the law, Peter Lombard suggests that Christ's extent of humility and righteousness allowed him to be a sufficient and perfect sacrifice.[6] John Owen links Christ's righteousness at baptism with his being unstained by original corruption, such that he could fulfill the law entirely.[7] For Athanasius of Alexandria, "the very descent of the Spirit on [Jesus] in the Jordan was a descent on us because of his bearing our body."[8]

Another notable feature of the baptismal narrative is the prophecy that Jesus will baptize "with the Holy Spirit" (John 1:33) or "with the Holy Spirit and fire" (Matt. 3:11; Luke 3:16). Often, this promise is linked with Jesus's own teaching that he will send a new Counselor, the Holy Spirit, from the Father (John 15:26). Jesus's role as the Spirit Baptizer is important in a twofold sense in the narrative of the Gospels. As one of the earlier functions applied to Jesus in three of the Gospels, Jesus baptizing with the Spirit raises an immediate christological question: Who is this One who can baptize in this manner? Moreover, in Luke-Acts especially, this role is one of the places in the early chapters where Luke foreshadows what is to come. John's baptism for repentance and Jesus's promised baptism in the Holy Spirit are both evident in dramatic ways when Jesus promises that repentance preached to the nations will be done in his name (Luke 24:47), and the risen Jesus reminds the disciples in Acts 1:5 that they "will be baptized with the Holy Spirit in a few days."[9] Much of the remainder of Acts chronicles the conversion of the nations and their reception of the Holy Spirit. The significance of Jesus's role as Spirit Baptizer in the narratives of the Gospels demands further theological analysis.

Jesus as the Spirit Baptizer

The hypostatic union draws human nature into the Father-Son relationship insofar as the incarnation is the ground or basis of the Christian's connection with Christ, the second Adam. Thus, the hypostatic union is the basis for the

---

5. Augustine of Hippo, "Words of St. Matthew's Gospel" §§2–4.
6. Lombard, *Sentences* 3.16.5.2.
7. Owen, *Communion with God*, 166–67, 275.
8. Athanasius, *Contra Arianos* 1.47.
9. Kurz, *Reading Luke-Acts*, 19–20.

adoption of Christians as sons and daughters of the Father and as brothers and sisters of Christ (Heb. 2:14–17). The category of relation is, after all, proper to hypostasis or person, not nature, so any natures that subsist enhypostatically share in the same relations, though perhaps in different ways. Thus, the same hypostatic union draws human nature into the Son-Spirit relationship, and that consequence of the hypostatic unity of humanity and deity is one that has tended to be explored less frequently in the tradition. However, the insights that are found in the tradition are quite illuminating. We can begin by recognizing the association of the perfecting of God's work with the Holy Spirit. In some more speculative trinitarian theology, the love of the Father and Son is incomplete unless perfected by the love that is the Holy Spirit.[10] Such theories are likely overconfident in their ability to discern the inner workings of the Trinity. Yet there is some basis for thinking that the economic taxis of the triune persons is reflective of the immanent life of the triune God. Therefore, theologians have sometimes also associated perfective causation with the Holy Spirit.[11] This association has some basis in Scripture, especially given the Spirit's regular link with eschatology. However, it may also be suggestive of the Spirit's role in Christ's perfect offering of himself to his Father in the Spirit (Heb. 9:14). Appropriating the perfecting of God's work to the Spirit also fits the fact that the Son had to ascend to the Father in order to send his Holy Spirit to the church—work remained to be done in the application of the benefits of the cross. More will be said of the relationship between the ascension and the Holy Spirit in chapter 10.

At the dawn of his ministry, Jesus was first identified as one who would baptize in the Spirit,[12] meaning Jesus was always publicly known as one advocate who would send another, though this wasn't fully clarified until near the end of his ministry (John 14:15–17, 26; 15:26; 16:7–15). The New Testament Epistles also clearly testify to the Spirit's role in regeneration (John 3:5–8), sanctification (2 Thess. 2:13), and glorification (2 Cor. 3:18). It is no surprise that early Christians therefore connected the baptism of Christ with

---

10. For example, Richard of St. Victor argues that there is benefit to reciprocal love. If there are only two eternal persons, then the love offered between them might be selfish, since it is given in hopes of receiving reciprocal love. However, if a third person exists and is included in the love, this selfish motive is not necessarily the case, for reciprocated love could be received if one person only loved another person. Including a third is truly gratuitous. Further, extending mutual love to a third is a unique form of love. See Richard of St. Victor, *On the Trinity* 3.18–19.

11. Notable here is Bonaventure, *Disputed Questions* Q. 4, A. 2, Arg. 8.

12. In two of the Gospels, Jesus is identified by John the Baptist as one who would baptize in the Spirit and fire (Matt. 3:11; Luke 3:16). There are various theories explaining how these baptisms relate. Perhaps they refer to the same baptism in different ways, to two baptisms (one saving, one eschatological judgment), to one baptism experienced in two ways, or to a saving and purgative dimension of the same baptism. See the discussion in Cole, *He Who Gives Life*, 181–82.

the transformation of Christians. Cyril of Alexandria, for example, argued that the Spirit withdrew from human beings after the fall, but when the Spirit anointed Jesus at the baptism, "the nature of man was made radiant so that it now became worthy to participate in the Holy Spirit."[13] Soon, theologians developed theologies of the multiple births of Christ and of human beings. Commenting on Gregory of Nazianzus, Maximus the Confessor pointed to three births in Christ. As the second Adam, the Son had a human birth. In the baptism, he had a spiritual birth and adoption, making him "firstborn among many brothers and sisters" (Rom. 8:29).[14] In resurrection, Christ had a third birth, being "firstborn from the dead" (Col. 1:18).[15] Somewhat earlier, the monophysite Philoxenus of Mabbug developed a similar theology of the three births and two baptisms of the Christian. The first birth is normal, bodily birth. In the sacrament of baptism—Philoxenus and his community would have primarily practiced infant baptism—a Christian starts a spiritual life as a spiritual fetus, a second birth, but growth in the womb of the world is limited. But a second baptism happens in the ascetic life, as the sacramental baptismal possibility of sensing God is actualized, and this is a third birth into the fullness of spiritual life.[16]

In more recent times, the possibility of multiple births and baptisms has led to theologies that affirm a second reception of the Holy Spirit, often linked with a view of sanctification known as **perfectionism**, where the Christian could reach a state of not sinning.[17] There was a clear growth in this theology of the second blessing of the Spirit in the nineteenth century in the United States, often in a manner that gave women an uncommonly prominent theological voice. For example, Phoebe Palmer appealed to such scriptural language as being sanctified "completely" (1 Thess. 5:23) and redeemed "from all lawlessness" (Titus 2:14), and she taught that the Christian willing to place themselves on the altar of Christ might, due to the "Spirit's operations on the heart," be cleansed "from all unrighteousness" (1 John 1:9) thanks to the "faithfulness and justice of God."[18] In some respects, such emphasis on sancti-

---

13. Cyril of Alexandria, *Scholia on the Incarnation* §1.

14. The Son's status as firstborn follows Paul's teaching that the predestined would be conformed to the image of the Son. The title "image" could be taken as something proper to the divine person of the Son, who is eternal image of his Father (Col. 1:15), or it could be taken as a reference to the image of God given to humans (Gen. 1:26–27) and thus proper to Christ by virtue of the incarnation. The latter interpretation fits better with Maximus's theology.

15. Maximus the Confessor, *Ambiguum* 42, 94.

16. See the discussion in McDonnell and Montague, *Baptism in the Holy Spirit*, 271–80.

17. What it means to be free from sin is something of a debate among perfectionists; it might reference freedom from intentional sins or complete freedom from all sins.

18. Palmer, *Way of Holiness*, 177.

fication was a welcome relief from popular neglect of an important doctrine. Speaking of her experience of sanctification, Jarena Lee explains that she felt led in prayer to pray for sanctification, which she realized she had not even thought of in her entire life of prayer.[19] However, the suddenness with which Lee, Palmer, and others would claim that sanctification came upon them and the claimed total extent of this sanctification were quite controversial. Analyzing and resolving such a controversy is proper to pneumatological dogmatics, so I will not address the issue here.[20] For present purposes, I should note that, though talk of such baptism in the Spirit often contains trinitarian elements, as we see in Palmer above, the tendency in such theology is to focus relatively more on pneumatology and relatively less on the significance of the hypostatic union for such transformation. We turn to consider now an early twentieth-century example of such a pneumatological emphasis, though of a slightly different variety than nineteenth-century second blessing Wesleyanism.

Aimee Semple McPherson

In the early twentieth century, Aimee Semple McPherson was an influential American Pentecostal evangelist and author. Many of her works are collections of sermons or occasional writings, but combined they yield a trinitarian theology of Jesus as the Spirit Baptizer who gives the Spirit to the church. The centrality of Jesus's role as Spirit Baptizer is evident in the fact that the forerunner, John the Baptist, highlights this role of Christ over all others (Matt. 3:11; Mark 1:8; Luke 3:16; John 1:33).[21] Jesus also regularly taught of the promised gift of the Spirit (Luke 11:9, 10–13; 12:11–12; John 7:38–39; 14:26).[22] Not only does Jesus's work include giving the Spirit, but all his other works are empowered by the Spirit. In fact, his ministry begins only after his baptism in the Spirit at the Jordan River.[23] Curiously, McPherson interprets John 14:10's claim that "the Father who lives in [Christ] does his works" to refer to the indwelling of the Spirit in the Son, which perhaps shows an overemphasis on the Holy Spirit.[24] Despite this imbalance, McPherson's

---

19. J. Lee, "Prayer for Sanctification," 15.

20. For a basic overview of positions on spirit baptism, see Brand, *Perspectives on Spirit Baptism*.

21. McPherson, *This Is That*, 527.

22. McPherson, *Fire from on High*, 27–28.

23. McPherson, *Fire from on High*, 16.

24. "Yet, though he was very God, and though all power was in his hand, he humbly but emphatically declared that the works which he wrought and the words which he spoke were not of his own power or strength. He clearly stated that he who dwelt within him did the works." McPherson, *Fire from on High*, 14.

theology is overall quite trinitarian. She explains the plan of redemption in line with the taxis of inseparable operations, which proceed from the Father, through the Son, to the Spirit when God acts toward creation, but in the Spirit, through the Son, to the Father when creation is divinely empowered to act toward God.[25] In McPherson's wording, in a descending pattern, the Father's gift to the believer is the Son, the Son's gift is the Spirit, and the Spirit directly gives charismatic gifts.[26] At this point, she sees a juncture between the "former rain" at Pentecost and a modern "latter rain" (Joel 2:23 KJV)[27] divided by the "loss of gifts and power." The latter rain initiates an ascending trinitarian pattern, where the return of the Spirit's charismatic gifts precedes the imminent return of the Son, who will return the kingdom to the Father after a millennial reign on earth (1 Cor. 15:24, 28).[28] Now is not the time to debate eschatological theories. Instead, I intend to note the trinitarian shape of the entirety of redemption history in McPherson's telling of it.

Jesus's role as Spirit Baptizer is an important component of McPherson's understanding of the gospel, known as the **foursquare gospel**. Jesus is the savior, baptizer, healer, and returning Son of Man. Obviously these four aspects of Jesus's ministry are clear in Scripture, but few accounts of salvation cover all four in equal measure.[29] McPherson appeals to an allegorical reading of the paralytic carried by four friends who is lowered through the roof to find salvation in Christ (Mark 2:1–12).[30] Mark's literal account displays salvation as forgiveness of sins (2:5) and results in the healing of the paralytic (2:10–12) by the Son of Man (2:10), an eschatological title—notably the baptism of the Spirit begun at Pentecost had not yet occurred. Allegorically, McPherson suggests that each of the four friends represents one of the four aspects of the foursquare gospel. Overemphasizing one of these four aspects would have results similar to one of the four letting down the paralytic pulling harder than the others—the entire bed would be upset, and the man needing salvation dropped.[31] In McPherson's understanding, Christ receives the Spirit in baptism

25. See Butner, *Trinitarian Dogmatics*, 190–91.

26. McPherson, *This Is That*, 384, 404, 528.

27. The promise of a former and latter rain precedes the promise of the Spirit poured out in Joel 2:28, which is central to Peter's preaching at Pentecost in Acts 2:17.

28. McPherson, *This Is That*, 529–31.

29. This is especially the case of "healing," though note the surprising Reichenbach, "Healing View."

30. McPherson, *Fire from on High*, 154.

31. McPherson, *Fire from on High*, 154–55. Similar allegorical readings are found in later advocates of the foursquare movement. For example, the term "foursquare" (an antiquated term for square) is used in the King James Version to describe the altar at the entrance to the tabernacle (Exod. 27:1), the priest's breastplate (Exod. 28:16), and the tabernacle incense altar (Exod. 30:1–2). It is then used to describe Solomon's temple (1 Kings 7:31) and the eschatological

partly to give the Spirit to Christians, empowering them for "union, fellowship, praise, worship, prayer, love and service."[32] Ultimately, this empowering is also missional and evangelistic—the disciples must wait to fulfill the Great Commission until they are "empowered from on high" (Luke 24:49; see also Acts 1:8).

McPherson's treatment of Jesus the Spirit Baptizer and the foursquare gospel clarifies basic necessary components of a salvific account of the hypostatic union while leaving need for further dogmatic clarification. Helpfully, McPherson reminds us that the arc of redemption history must be trinitarian, and so, too, must any account of the benefits of the union of humanity and divinity in the person of the Son. She also reminds us to leave a clear role for the Holy Spirit, whose giving was important for the Messiah, resulting in a wider range of benefits than is sometimes recognized in accounts of the benefits of salvation. Furthermore, McPherson's theology assumes a strong doctrine of the hypostatic union. After all, the divine Son eternally shares the same substance of and lives in perichoretic harmony with the Spirit, making it difficult to see how divine nature could be baptized in the Spirit. It is easier to conceive of how a human nature joined to deity without mixture or confusion could receive empowerment from the Spirit. Despite this, further theological work must be done. Setting aside the obvious contentious debates surrounding whether the supernatural charismatic gifts are operative today, a subject that must be reserved for pneumatology proper, at least two major concerns remain. First, McPherson's corrective against the neglect of the Spirit seems to overcompensate, de-emphasizing the Son's role in our transformation by limiting the significance of the incarnation itself.[33] Second, this account of Christian empowerment by the Spirit leaves unanswered any metaphysical explanation of how human nature is transformed—indeed, McPherson at times associates transformation itself with the Son's work, undermining her trinitarian integration of the Spirit.[34] For this reason I now turn to a second theological framework that offers a more robust account of how the metaphysics of our transformation in Christ are linked to the hypostatic union.

---

temple's courtyard (Ezek. 40:47). The new Jerusalem is also described by this term (Rev. 21:16). Cox argues that this central imagery in the sacrificial, priestly, and atonement system reveals the centrality of a foursquare salvation. Cox, "What Is the Foursquare Gospel?," 6–8.

32. McPherson, "Jesus Christ the Baptizer," 121.

33. This is only relative, as McPherson clearly values the atoning work of the Son and defends traditional Protestant concepts like justification by faith alone. For only one example of this, see McPherson, *This Is That*, 395–96.

34. "Salvation is not the baptism of the Holy Spirit. Sanctification is not the baptism of the Holy Spirit. Salvation and sanctification . . . all must agree, are wrought through Jesus and His precious atoning blood." McPherson, *This Is That*, 407.

Theosis

A second theological framework used to understand the salvific implications of the hypostatic union is called divinization, deification, or theosis, the latter being the preferred term of this book. This vocabulary is somewhat unfortunate and sometimes meets resistance from Protestants because divinization, for example, can imply that the human becomes divine, suggesting an absorption of creatures into the Creator. This is not the intent of the doctrine. The terminology intends a biblical origin, drawing especially on 2 Peter 1:3–4: "His divine power has given us everything required for life and godliness through the knowledge of him who called us by his own glory and goodness. By these he has given us very great and precious promises, so that through them you may share in the divine nature, escaping the corruption that is in the world because of evil desire." Note that Peter promises participation in the divine nature, and this participation is associated with (1) God's power and (2) glory, resulting in (3) knowledge of God, (4) freedom from corruption, and (5) transformation of desire. The theology that links participation in God with these concepts is called theosis. The doctrine is also derived in important ways from the transfiguration, an event to which we now turn.

The Transfiguration

At several points in Scripture (Matt. 17:1–13; Mark 9:2–13; Luke 9:28–36; 2 Pet. 1:16–18), we read about the transfiguration of Christ. Synthesizing these stories, we learn that Christ's "clothes became dazzling white" (Luke 9:29), "white as the light" (Matt. 17:2), such that "no launderer on earth could whiten them" (Mark 9:3), while "his face shone like the sun" (Matt. 17:2),[35] and he was accompanied by Moses and Elijah (Matt. 17:3; Mark 9:4; Luke 9:30). This transfiguration is a clear account of the Son receiving glory (2 Pet. 1:17), but we must remember that it is the *incarnate* Son who receives glory, such that the person of the Son is glorified in both his divine nature, as he eternally has been (John 17:5), and in his human nature, as is now evident on the holy mountain. As a way to introduce theosis, I want to highlight three dimensions of the transfiguration: its trinitarian elements, its revelatory function, and its relation to salvation.

Two divine persons are clearly evident in the transfiguration, as the Father speaks to the Son, but some commentators have argued that the cloud that rests on the mountain represents the Holy Spirit. For example, Patrick Schreiner defends this connection by pointing to a common biblical link between

---

35. Luke 9:29 is somewhat more vague when it states that "his face changed."

the Spirit and the cloud of the Lord's presence. Isaiah 63:10–14 interprets the cloud from Exodus 19:9, 33:9, and 40:34–38 as the Spirit, and Haggai 2:4–5 may do the same.[36] Taking a slightly different perspective, Gregory Palamas explains that the light of the Son is always present but is visible only when the Holy Spirit enables a human being to see it. Here he cites 1 Corinthians 2:9.[37] The transfiguration thus reveals the possibility of humanity being drawn into the life of the Trinity, being one with the beloved Son and sharing in his glory.

The transfiguration is generally thought to be a display of the status of the God-man but also an anticipatory revelation of the Christian's future state. Schreiner notes that the transfiguration reveals Jesus's double sonship: "In the transfiguration, both the future glory of the earthy and suffering messianic Son and the preexistent glory of the heavenly and eternally begotten Son are revealed."[38] Keep in mind that the transfiguration follows Peter's confession of Jesus as the Messiah (Matt. 16:13–20; Mark 8:27–30; Luke 9:28–36), revealing his messianic status as soon-to-be-exalted second Adam.[39] Imagery of light may also evoke God who is light (1 John 1:5),[40] while the Father's language of being well pleased in his Son might allude to Psalm 2:7, which includes language of eternal generation in the Septuagint.[41] While there are similarities between Christ's glowing presence on the mountain and Moses's (Exod. 34:29–35), Christ's glory at the transfiguration is due to the perichoresis of the divine and human natures, a direct revelation of deity rather than the reflection of deity present in Moses.[42] The transfiguration thus hints at what was already discussed in the previous chapter—Jesus is both fully God and the fully human Messiah. The transfiguration also reveals the future state of human beings. Theologians have long noted that the transfiguration occurs immediately after Jesus promises that some "will not taste death until they see the Son of Man coming in his kingdom" (Matt. 16:28; see also Mark 9:1; Luke 9:27).[43] The power of the kingdom is thus already manifest in the person of Christ, who reveals what the saints will one day be.[44] Again, much of the tradition has understood the transfiguration to reveal the future state

36. P. Schreiner, *Transfiguration*, 73–74.
37. Palamas, *Homily 34* §8.
38. P. Schreiner, *Transfiguration*, 4.
39. P. Schreiner, *Transfiguration*, 9.
40. P. Schreiner, *Transfiguration*, 61. Schreiner also points to Gen. 15:17; Exod. 3:2; 13:21; 19:18; Isa. 6:3, 6; Hab. 3:3–4. Schreiner adds that this is especially clear against a background of pagan theophanic transfiguration accounts (66–67).
41. Bates, *Birth of the Trinity*, 64–67.
42. Chemnitz, *Two Natures in Christ*, 95.
43. For example, Cyril of Alexandria begins a homily on the transfiguration by interpreting it in the context of Matt. 16:28. Cyril of Alexandria, *Homily 51 on Luke*, 100.
44. See the discussion in D. Lee, *Transfiguration*, 122–25.

of the saved. Thus Alexander of Hales, one of the earliest Western medieval Scholastics to treat the transfiguration, understands it as an appearance of the glory of the resurrection available to all resurrected Christians.[45] It is no surprise that the Father therefore tells Peter, John, and James to listen to Jesus (Matt. 17:5), for the one revealed as eternal Son and Messiah is the only mediator with the final ability to reveal truth to the disciples.

Finally, the transfiguration has salvific implications. When the Father speaks about the Son out of the cloud, he calls him "my beloved Son, with whom I am well-pleased" (Matt. 17:5; 2 Pet. 1:17). The fact that the Son is pleasing to the Father is a necessary prerequisite to his death on the cross paying a satisfaction to the Father, for if he were not pleasing, then the offering would be in vain. It is possible that this language of being pleased points back to Abraham's near-sacrifice of the "only son Isaac, whom [Abraham] love[d]" (Gen. 22:2), an event on a mountain that resulted in a promise of future blessing for the nations.[46] The transfiguration more clearly reveals that future blessing, anticipating the eschatological transformation of the faithful who will shine like stars forever (Dan. 12:3) once they have been transformed into the likeness of Christ's glorious body (Phil. 3:21). As Gregory of Sinai summarizes, in the transfiguration, the Word made flesh is revealed in glory, a glory that those who believe will share (Matt. 13:43; 2 Cor. 3:18), being freed from corruptibility (1 Cor. 15:53) and coming to be "united completely with the Word who exists before the ages, the only God, and made divine in a way beyond understanding."[47] The transfiguration is an important biblical starting point for discussing the doctrine of theosis, which links God's glory and power with the transformation in Christ by the Spirit of human knowledge, desire, and, ultimately, nature. Yet further clarification is required to explain how it is that Christians participate in God.

Jesus and Theosis

Theosis centers on Christology and the hypostatic union. In part, this is seen in the frequently used and ancient *admirabile commercium* formula, evident in Athanasius of Alexandria: "For He was made man that we might be made God."[48] Unsurprisingly, statements like Athanasius's needed clarification, even if they are rooted in biblical language calling us "gods" (Ps. 82:6; John 10:34).

45. Canty, *Light and Glory*, 53–57.
46. P. Schreiner, *Transfiguration*, 103–5.
47. Gregory of Sinai, "Discourse" §23.
48. Athanasius of Alexandria, *On the Incarnation* §54.3. Asproulis calls this "an almost universal pattern in the early patristic literature." Asproulis, "Eucharistic Personhood," 32.

Similarly, 2 Peter 1:4's claim that we participate in the divine nature raises many questions. How do we "become divine" or "participate in the divine nature" without becoming additional persons in the Trinity? Does this process eliminate the distinction between Creator and creature? In the Eastern Orthodox tradition, dogmatic clarification comes in two ways, first by emphasizing the hypostatic union in relation to theosis and second by clarifying the nature of human participation in the divine by distinguishing between God's essence and energies.

When robustly explained, theosis clearly is linked with the doctrine of the hypostatic union.[49] Theosis is not possible through a mixing of natures—remember that the Chalcedonian definition explicitly ruled out such a mixture.[50] Theosis happens because human nature and divine nature have been united in the hypostasis of the Son.[51] As Georgios Mantzaridis explains, theosis is "an ontological regeneration of human nature in the hypostasis of the incarnate Logos of God, accessible to every man who participates personally and freely in the life of Christ."[52] This regeneration of humanity is by grace in two ways. First, we have the grace of the incarnation. Christ is the image of God (Col. 1:15; cf. Heb. 1:3), and as such, he is able to restore the image of God in us by imprinting it again in the incarnation. Athanasius of Alexandria uses the following parable to illustrate the process. If an artist paints an image of a person, but something happens to damage the painting, the only thing to be done is for the subject of the painting to return so that the artist can paint him again.[53] Yet the incarnation was itself an act of grace, so that all theosis made possible through the incarnation is grace. Second, participation in the life of Christ is given by grace, such that the restoration of the image is itself a second gift of God made possible by God's gift of the incarnation.[54] This,

---

49. Some recent analysis of theosis distinguishes between "ousianic" accounts that focus on participating in the divine nature and "hypostatic" accounts that focus on participation through the hypostasis of the Son. See Asproulis, "Eucharistic Personhood"; Ciraulo, "Divinization as Christification." Though there is certainly a range in emphases in the doctrine of theosis, this distinction might be too sharp. For example, Ciraulo describes Palamas's model as ousianic because the energies "are about God's nature and not about what is particular to the Persons" (481). Yet Palamas is quite clear that the energies are never anhypostatic, so the distinction breaks down. See Palamas, *Dialogue* §32.

50. Pomazansky explains, "In itself humanity in general, and likewise man individually, remains in that nature in which and for which it was created: for, in the person of Christ also, the human body and soul did not pass over into the Divine nature, but were only united with it, united 'without confusion or change.'" Pomazansky, *Orthodox Dogmatic Theology*, 222.

51. Asproulis, "Eucharistic Personhood," 36.

52. Mantzaridis, *Deification of Man*, 31.

53. Athanasius of Alexandria, *On the Incarnation* §14.

54. As Frances Young writes, "God's image in humankind is a divine gift rather than inherent property, and communion with one another, with Christ, and ultimately with the Triune God, is found in reciprocal mirroring of the glory of the divine image." Young, *God's Presence*, 175.

then, is one helpful dogmatic clarification—Christians participate in God by grace, but Father, Son, and Spirit are God by nature.

Another important dogmatic clarification developed most clearly beginning in the fourteenth-century debates between Gregory Palamas and his opponents, Barlaam the Calabrian, Gregory Akindynos, and Nikephoros Gregoras. Palamas, as we shall see in the next section, developed the most expansive explanation up to that time of the divine energies as distinct from the nature and essence. As summarized by the Synodal *Tomos* of 1351, "Even the saints, who have been deified by union with God, participate not in the divine essence, but in his divine energy."[55] Tikhon Pino explains that in Palamas, we see theosis linked to the energies such that "the gift by which human beings are saved" is "divine grace itself," which is also "the eternal radiance of the Deity."[56] It will be helpful to understand how some see this distinction arising from Scripture, reserving a more exhaustive account for our treatment of Palamas.

Advocates of theosis sometimes point to precedent found in the Old Testament, especially the account of Moses on Mount Sinai in Exodus 33.[57] Here, Moses asks for knowledge of God (33:13), for God's presence to accompany him (33:15), and to see God's glory (33:18). God answers that his glory and goodness will pass by Moses, who can see God's back but not his face (33:19–23). Stephen Thomas interprets this passage to teach that "on the one hand 'face' *panim* is like the incomprehensible essence, on the other hand the Goodness of God which passes Moses by in the cleft of the rock has affinities with the Orthodox idea of the uncreated energies."[58] The essence/energies distinction is an attempt to express in a metaphysical register what Exodus describes anthropomorphically as God's face and back. After forty days of this encounter between Moses and God, Moses descends the mountain and his face is glowing (Exod. 34:29), as if the glory of God has somehow been imparted to him. Paul draws on this event in 2 Corinthians 3:18, which offers a trinitarian picture of how the glory radiating from Moses is offered to all Christians. Christians view the Father directly without a veil and are transformed into the image of the dying and rising Son,[59] a work completed by

---

55. Synodal *Tomos* of 1351, §40.

56. Pino, *Essence and Energies*, 58. Pino notes that though grace is the primary energy discussed by Palamas, there are others.

57. Khaled Anatolios writes, "In its narrative context, [the story] stands as a paradigmatic scriptural presentation of salvation as access to divine glory." Anatolios, *Deification Through the Cross*, 111.

58. Thomas, *Deification in the Eastern Orthodox Tradition*, 119.

59. The "image" likely refers to the Son, given the explicit naming of the Son as the image in 2 Cor. 4:4.

the Spirit who is the Lord.[60] The paradigmatic New Testament locus classicus for theosis is the Gospels' accounts of the transfiguration, which has already been discussed, but transfiguration is also alluded to in 2 Corinthians 3:18's use of the word *metamorphoō*, which can be translated as "transfigure," in this case "we all . . . are being transfigured" (2 Cor. 3:18).[61]

Based on these passages and a growing body of patristic literature, Byzantine theology increasingly emphasized participation in the divine energies as the main, though not exclusive, understanding of the transformation made possible in salvation. This is the first of several distinctive emphases of this approach to the application of salvation. Other distinctives include an emphasis on overcoming corruption, understood as a decay and dis-integration of the human nature, and an understanding of the restoration of the image of God through participation in the life of Christ. The latter doctrinal point pushes beyond the moral exemplarism discussed in chapter 4, which is impotent apart from the transformation made possible in the hypostatic union.[62] The most characteristic feature remains the essence/energies distinction, which leads us to an analysis of Gregory Palamas.

Gregory Palamas

Gregory Palamas was a Byzantine monk and theologian. Much of his life was marked by theological controversy concerning the divine energies. It was in this context that Palamas developed his understanding of the essence/energies distinction. Energies are often understood to refer to divine actions, but the term "energies" suggests that the divine actions are a durable aspect of God's ontology. Sometimes the energies are taken to externally manifest what internally is the essence.[63] However, Gregory often associates energies with divine power (*dynamis*) and with inherent essential properties of God, such that the distinction is more complex.[64] Functionally, the close link between the energies and essence helps Palamas explain how 2 Peter 1:4 can speak of participation in the divine nature, even though humans never have the divine nature proper to themselves, as if they have all divine attributes by nature.[65] Since grace is the chief divine energy, this ensures that for Palamas what transforms the Christian is nothing other than God. Because it is uncreated

60. For an extended discussion, see Blackwell, *Christosis*, 180–90.
61. P. Schreiner, *Transfiguration*, 19.
62. For example, see this emphasis in Meyendorff, *Byzantine Theology*, 163–65.
63. The latter interpretation is found in Kotiranta, "Palamite Idea of Perichoresis," 64.
64. Pino, *Essence and Energies*, 61, 66.
65. Pino, *Essence and Energies*, 67. Palamas, "Natural and Theological Science" §93.

and divine, grace is God and so can glorify us, for only God can do this. But since the energies are not the essence, they are not the fullness of God.[66] Thus, divine grace in us does not absorb us into the Godhead. As Palamas writes, "The Holy Spirit transcends the deifying life which is in Him and proceeds from Him, for it is his own natural energy, which is akin to Him, even if not exactly so."[67] The Spirit thus transforms the Christian with deifying grace, an energy proper to the Spirit, but the Spirit remains distinct from the transformed creature. Furthermore, Palamas says that all creation participates in God, having derived existence from him (Acts 17:28), but deification is participation that involves the willing self.[68]

Palamism is helpful because it resists any account of salvation rooted in something other than divine agency. After all, God claims salvation for himself, saying, "I—I am the LORD. Besides me, there is no Savior" (Isa. 43:11). The essence/energies distinction also ensures that no creature becomes consubstantial with the Father. Yet the distinction was a point of major concern in Palamas's own day as opponents worried that it resulted in two deities or that it ruptured divine simplicity, and critique has continued today. Several strategies can be used to respond to this concern. Palamas himself compares the essence/energies distinction with the distinction between persons in the Trinity, which does not undermine simplicity.[69] In fact, the very idea of the simple divine essence demands a distinction between essence and energies since participation in God through theosis means having part of God, but a simple essence cannot have parts and so cannot be participated in.[70] These points are well taken, though something short of a conceptual resolution of the problem. I understand Palamas to have something more of an apophatic understanding of divine simplicity.

Later Orthodox theologians vary in their interpretation of the essence/energies distinction in Palamas. Some think Palamas is affirming a real distinction between essence and energies.[71] Yet many Byzantine supporters offered different theories. Neilos Kabasilas said that the distinction was a difference, not a division—a helpful distinction yet vague. John VI Kantakouzenos, influenced by Palamas and Thomas Aquinas, offered an interpretation of the distinction that was something like the virtual distinction, where the human

---

66. See Williams, *Ground of Union*, 120–21.
67. Palamas, *Triads* 3.1.9.
68. Palamas, "Natural and Theological Science" §78.
69. Palamas, "Natural and Theological Science" §113.
70. Palamas, "Natural and Theological Science" §110.
71. This would undermine simplicity because it would affirm that there were two ontologically divisible and distinct realities in God: essence and energies.

mind conceives of a difference in what is one in God, but that conception has a basis in God. The less sharp the distinction is between essence and energies, the more difficult it is to understand how participation in the energies is not participation in the essence. The stronger the distinction, the more difficult it is to explain simplicity. In the end, perhaps this is why Manuel II Palaiologos simply asserts that the way essence and energies are different is incomprehensible.[72]

Union with Christ

Protestants tend to speak of the salvific consequences of the hypostatic union using the language of union with Christ. The Christian's union with the Savior is a fundamental feature of the *ordo salutis*, the order of salvation, which schematizes the benefits of salvation that are secured by the Son and applied by the Spirit. Language of union is especially clear in the Johannine and Pauline literature of the New Testament. I will begin by briefly exploring Jesus's Farewell Discourse.

Jesus's Farewell Discourse

In John's Gospel, Jesus has a final lengthy conversation with his disciples spanning John 13:31–17:26. This conversation is known as the Farewell Discourse, with the word "discourse" reflecting the fact that Jesus does most of the talking, primarily teaching his disciples about his departure and the coming of the Spirit. Throughout this discourse, Jesus explains his intimate spiritual connection with Christians in various ways. Anyone who wants to have access to the Father must go through Christ (14:6). Perhaps drawing on Old Testament imagery of Israel as a vine (e.g., Ps. 80:8–16; Isa. 27:2–6; Jer. 2:21; Ezek. 15:2–6),[73] Jesus describes himself as the vine and the disciples as the vine branches. "Remain in me, and I in you," Jesus says, or we cannot bear fruit (John 15:4). Thus, Jesus describes himself as the source of life and likely also as the most important part of the vine of Israel. The one who does not remain in Jesus is pruned and burned (15:6). Throughout the discourse we see regular language of the Son or Spirit being in the church (14:17, 20; 15:4–5), culminating in Jesus's prayer "so that they may be one as we are one" (17:11; cf. 17:21, 23, 26). Commenting on the text, Matthew Poole clarifies that this

---

72. These different perspectives are found, along with many others, in an excellent essay: Demetracopoulos, "Palamas Transformed," 286, 292–305, 339.

73. Keener, *Gospel of John*, 2:991–92.

oneness is "in some proportion to that union," which is between the Father and the Son, "though not in an equality."[74] Note that the union of Christ and Christians involves shared glory (17:10, 22) and love (14:21; 15:9–10; 17:26) with the result of knowing Christ (14:19), his teachings (14:26; 15:13–15), and his Father (14:7; 17:25–26). The Farewell Discourse also centers the coming of the Spirit, who will remain "with you and will be in you" (John 14:17). Such a pattern of speaking at so pivotal a point in John's Gospel demands a theological explanation, which Protestants, and the Reformed in particular, have given through the doctrine of union with Christ.

Union with Christ

In Reformed theology (as also in some other branches of Protestant thought), the significance of the hypostatic union for our salvation has been explained using the terminology of union with Christ.[75] This union is often said to render a double gift, the *duplex gratia* of justification and sanctification.[76] The concept itself is largely drawn from the Johannine passages just discussed and from several prominent features in Paul's epistles. Paul regularly[77] uses the phrase "in Christ" to describe both God's saving activity toward creation and the believer's condition toward God. "If anyone is *in Christ*, he is a new creation" (2 Cor. 5:17), but also "*in Christ*, God was reconciling the world to himself" (5:19). Clearly, the phrase signifies the mediatorship of the God-man, who is at once one of the divine three who are saving the world and also a human whose perfect hypostatic unity with God is a basis for all human salvific transformation. This transformation should be understood to be plural, as is often evident in what are called the *syn-* compounds, Greek verbs to which Paul has attached the prefix *syn-*, meaning "with." Seventeen examples of such words in Paul often relate to

---

74. Poole, *Commentary on the Holy Bible*, 369. I offer a detailed explanation of the difference between the union of Father and Son and the union between the church and God in Butner, *Trinitarian Dogmatics*, 145–50.

75. In older literature it was more common to see the terminology of "mystical union." The adjective has been dropped in most more recent literature.

76. There is some dispute as to whether justification is the legal basis for union or whether union grounds justification. On the former, see Horton, *Covenant and Salvation*, 147–48. For the latter, see M. Johnson, *One with Christ*, 91.

77. The frequency of Paul's usage depends somewhat on how one counts. Strictly counting instances where *en Christō* occurs as sequential words, Constantine Campbell counts seventy-three instances of this language. James Dunn includes instances where words may be included in the phrase *en . . . Christō*, reaching eighty-three instances. Campbell treats the latter as a separate category. There are many other categories that could be counted. For example, "in the Lord" occurs forty-seven times in Paul's letters. See Campbell, *Paul and Union*, 67; Dunn, *Theology of Paul*, 396–97.

"accompaniment," "association," or "participation."[78] Thus, in Romans 6, a key passage on Christian life following Paul's treatment of original sin and recapitulation in Romans 5, Paul writes that we "were buried with him by baptism into death" (6:4), we are "crucified with him" (6:6), "we died with Christ" and "we will also live with him" (6:8). Note that Paul uses these *syn-* compounds in the first-person plural—this is a corporate participation in Christ.

Reformed theologians have developed a four-stage understanding of union with Christ, beginning with election. Christians were chosen "in him [Christ], before the foundation of the world" (Eph. 1:4), a fact that grounds union in the eternal purposes of God and not anthropologically in human faith, which might lead to the erroneous conclusion that faith is somehow meritorious.[79] *Sola gratia* must prevail. To speak more precisely, we can distinguish between various kinds of causation in union. So, John Calvin will speak of salvation, including union, as having the eternal love of the Father as the efficient cause, Christ as the material cause, faith as the instrumental cause, and God's glory as the final cause. Calvin sees this pattern taught in Scripture (John 3:16; Rom. 3:23–24).[80] Other Reformed theologians offer clarifications, labeling Christ the only meritorious cause[81] or identifying the entire Trinity as the efficient cause and distinguishing between the active instrumental cause of the word of the gospel and the passive instrumental cause of faith.[82] The point is that union begins with the efficient cause of the eternal love of the Trinity, which prompts the sending of the Son into flesh. The loving eternal plan of God to save the church in Christ, often called the covenant of redemption by Reformed theologians, is thus the cause of the incarnation.

The incarnation is the second stage of union. Insofar as union is a joining of Christians to the humanity of Christ, not to the divine nature,[83] the assumption of a human nature by the Son is a precondition to the unfolding of union in redemption history. Union is therefore called "vital" by theologians like Archibald Alexander Hodge because "our spiritual life is sustained and determined in its nature and movement by the life of Christ."[84] More recently, union has been called "quasi-physical" because it depends on some connection

---

78. Campbell, *Paul and Union*, 228–36.

79. Berkhof, *Systematic Theology*, 447.

80. Calvin, *Institutes* 3.14.7. The practice of explaining union and salvation by appeal to Aristotle's categories of causation was common among the Reformers and Reformed Scholastics. Fesko, *Beyond Calvin*, 36–37.

81. Turretin, *Institutes* 16.2.6.

82. Wollebius, *Compendium Theologiae Christianae* 30.1 prop. 3–4.

83. The point is made clearly in M. Johnson, *One with Christ*, 50.

84. A. A. Hodge, *Outlines of Theology*, 483.

between the assumed human nature of Christ and our own.[85] The application of the benefits of salvation depends on the hypostatic union, which preserves the distinction between Creator and creature. Since the natures do not mix, our union with Christ's humanity is not a dissolution of our humanity into the divine nature, nor do we become demigods who are partly human, partly divine. For this reason, Paul can speak of salvation as "bear[ing] the image of the man of heaven" (1 Cor. 15:49), as being "clothed with Christ" (Gal. 3:27), and ultimately in the trinitarian language of being "alive to God in Christ Jesus" (Rom. 6:11), where implicitly it is the Spirit who makes us alive (see Rom. 8:2, 6, 10–11). Of course, the incarnation also serves as the basis for "instrumental" meanings of Paul's language of "in Christ," which point to the Father working through, in, and by the Son (Rom. 8:2, 39; 1 Cor. 1:4, 30; 2 Cor. 5:19; Gal. 3:26; Eph. 1:3; 2:6, 7, 10; 3:21; 4:32; Phil. 3:14; 4:7, 19; 1 Thess. 5:18).[86] It is necessary not only for two natures to exist in harmony but for a hypostatic union so that the one divine and human person of Christ can atone for sin, making union possible. This atoning work will be discussed in chapter 8.

This brings us to the application of the benefits of atonement, or subjective union with Christ in the experience of the Christian.[87] This union is called subjective not because it lacks any reality, for the ontological change to human nature as the Spirit conforms it to Christ is very real. Rather, this aspect of union is subjective because it is experienced and passively received through faith. The mediation of the Spirit is a necessary component of this union since there is no direct access to the divine essence[88] and since Christ's human nature is ascended. The Spirit also produces faith (1 Cor. 12:3; Eph. 2:8–9). As Louis Berkhof explains, subjective union requires a "reciprocal action": "The initial act is that of Christ, who unites believers to himself by regenerating them and thus producing faith in them. On the other hand, the believer also unites himself to Christ by a conscious act of faith, and continues this union, under the influence of the Holy Spirit, by the constant exercise of faith, John 14:23; 15:4, 5; Gal. 2:20; Eph. 3:17."[89] Subjectively, the fact that faith is a gift of the Spirit helps prevent the sanctification given through union from

85. Schweitzer, *Mysticism of Paul*, 110.

86. For a thorough discussion of these passages, see Campbell, *Paul and Union*, 127–41.

87. "The most common referent to union with Christ in Scripture is the union that follows both our election in Christ and the union of God and humanity in the incarnation. It is the union that occurs when these prior unions come to fruition and are subjectively realized and experienced by those who are savingly united to Christ through faith by the power of the Spirit." M. Johnson, *One with Christ*, 38.

88. Horton, *Covenant and Salvation*, 140–41.

89. Berkhof, *Systematic Theology*, 450.

laying a new burden on the Christian, for sanctification is not given because we have earned it or due to our effort to believe, for our motion to Christ in faith begins with the Spirit, who also preserves its inertia.[90]

Eventually, the union of the Christian with Christ reaches its termination in glorification, where Christians come to share by grace in the glory of God in the new creation as they are raised from the dead at the general resurrection. Yet the eschatological realization of perfect union with Christ is inseparable from the sovereign plan to save that originated with the covenant of redemption.[91] Further, as I explain throughout this book, the New Testament has a realized eschatology. This means that the kingdom is already breaking into the old creation, first through the incarnation of Christ and then through his sending of the Holy Spirit. This dimension of eschatology is sometimes inadequately emphasized in Reformed treatments of union, though Paul himself often uses union terminology as part of an exhortation to do the good.[92] The connection between the New Testament's ethic and union as a transformation making greater fulfillment of that ethic possible helps relieve the pressure of works righteousness.

Girolamo Zanchi

Girolamo Zanchi is today a lesser-known Reformer, but he was a man of considerable theological ability. His theology of union centers not only Christ but the Holy Spirit. He understood a threefold union that is incarnational, mystical by grace, and eschatological at the consummation.[93] In other words, union is possible due to the incarnation, mystical for Christians in the current life but fully realized in the eschaton. All three aspects are by the power of the Holy Spirit, who brings about the virginal conception and our spiritual union by faith (where faith is also by the working of the Spirit) and who will be active in new ways in the eschaton.[94] Each of these varieties of union is advanced through preaching and the Eucharist, but these are the means of promoting faith, with faith being the main instrument for the growth of union.[95] Zanchi

90. See the helpful discussion in Billings, *Union with Christ*, 46–53.

91. This perspective was important in Albert Schweitzer's understanding of "Christ mysticism," and though many contours of his thought must now be revised, this dimension remains plausible. Schweitzer, *Mysticism of Paul*, 105–13.

92. Dunn, *Theology of Paul*, 398. Think, for example, of Paul's language of our body as a temple in its implications for sexual ethics in 1 Cor. 6 or of his appeal to the church as a body in Christ to discuss church unity in 1 Cor. 12.

93. Zanchi, *Christian Religion* 12.5.

94. Zanchi, *Christian Religion* 12.6–8.

95. Fesko hypothesizes (reasonably) that Zanchi is rejecting a Catholic understanding of the sacraments as working *ex opere operato*. Fesko, *Beyond Calvin*, 215–17.

also emphasizes the role of grace in union: "So neither can we be joined and united unto him, unless he first join and unite himself to us."[96] This divine initiative begins in regeneration, which is technically distinct from union.[97] Those who are regenerated are joined to Christ by the Holy Spirit. If the Holy Spirit can join two natures in Christ, it can join together distinct humans into a mystical union.[98] Similarly, the omnipresence of the Holy Spirit means that spatial distance does not undermine the possibility of union.[99]

Dogmatic Summary

The hypostatic union grounds the doctrine of salvation as the precondition for Christ's atoning work on the cross and as the basis for the transformation of Christians from a state of original pollution and corruption into one of a renewed humanity. Since Christ's work on the cross is the subject of chapter 8, this chapter has focused on how the hypostatic union undergirds the transformation of the saved Christian by considering three theological understandings of such transformation: baptism in the Holy Spirit, theosis, and union with Christ. Though these perspectives are not necessarily mutually exclusive,[100] they do tend to focus on different aspects of the Christian's connection to the incarnate Son. Such emphases are further expanded by the tendencies of each perspective to be deployed within theological systems that are considerably different. The concluding task of this chapter, then, is to offer a dogmatic synthesis of what has been discussed above in hopes of presenting a foundational understanding that might find relatively broad support.

The doctrine of the hypostatic union brings human and divine nature into harmony in a single hypostasis yet without mixing the natures. This unity amid distinction allows Christians to be united to Christ without receiving the divine nature, preserving the Creator/creature distinction. Yet Scripture is clear that the Christian is *in Christ*, as branches in a vine (John 15:1–8),

---

96. Zanchi, *Christian Religion* 12.4. This emphasis on grace and faith is important for Protestants. Roman Catholic and Protestant theologians of the day had broadly similar views of the mechanics of union, but they differed on the cause. "The differences lie in the manner in which this union occurs: through the waters of baptism and the infusion of grace and virtues for Rome or by the work of the Spirit through faith alone for the Reformers such as Zanchi." Fesko, *Beyond Calvin*, 218.

97. Fesko, *Beyond Calvin*, 219.

98. Zanchi, *Christian Religion* 12.18.

99. Zanchi, *Christian Religion* 12.10.

100. For example, though he focuses on union, Michael Horton sees similarities between union and theosis while insisting on the necessary mediating role of the Holy Spirit in union. Horton, *Covenant and Salvation*, 140–41, 276, 279–82.

as members of his body (Rom. 12:4–5; 1 Cor. 12:12–27; Eph. 1:22–23; Col. 1:24), as those "made . . . alive together with Christ" (Eph. 2:5 ESV). Notice that these metaphors are all linked with the work of the Spirit. Those who remain in the vine produce fruit (John 15:5), a metaphor also applied to life in the Spirit, which bears fruit (Gal. 5:22–25). We are Christ's body through baptism of the Spirit (1 Cor. 12:13) and for the purpose of manifesting gifts from the Spirit (Rom. 12:6; 1 Cor. 12:4–11). If we are alive together in Christ, "the Spirit is the one who gives life" (John 6:63). There is good reason, then, to emphasize Christ's role as Spirit-giver and to suspect that the significance of his baptism was its empowerment and uplifting of the humanity of Christ, recapitulating humanity in the second Adam.[101] However, it would be a mistake to stop at this pneumatological step or to overemphasize it, as some Spirit Christologies do.

The assumption of a complete human nature by the Son enables the full transformation of the Christian, as is evident in Nazianzus's rule: "That which he has not assumed he has not healed; but that which is united to his Godhead is also saved."[102] The clear continuance of two distinct natures after the incarnation ensures that the Spirit's work in uniting the Christian to the Son does not result in Christians becoming God. This is certain.[103] A safer explanation of this union therefore focuses on Christians sharing the same sort of human nature that Christ possesses, eventually to the point of bearing the "spiritual body" of "the man of heaven" (1 Cor. 15:44, 48). However, this sharing might not go far enough to adequately capture the language of Christians becoming "partakers of the divine nature" (2 Pet. 1:4 NASB), so it could be that the Christian participates in the divine energies. This is less certain to me, given that it would require pushing the doctrine of God in a considerably more apophatic direction to preserve such doctrines as simplicity.[104] Somewhat counterintuitively, "partakers of the divine nature" does not mean possessing the divine essence and becoming equal with God or one with God. This is evident in two ways.

101. This link between Spirit Christology and recapitulation is drawn out more in Pinnock, *Flame of Love*, 93–98. Interestingly, Pinnock also makes use of language of divinization (94) and union (93). Pinnock's account perhaps underemphasizes the substitutionary satisfaction of Christ.

102. Gregory of Nazianzus, *To Cledonius*, 218.

103. A full theological argument for this point would derive from a robust doctrine of God and of creation, which must wait for a project on the doctrine of God. For now, it will have to suffice to point to the Fourth Lateran Council, which appeals to the doctrine of analogy (something quite important in my development of dogmatics) for the purpose of clarifying that the unity of Christians with God in John 17 is one of grace, while the unity of Father, Son, and Spirit in the same chapter is one of nature. See Denzinger, "Definition of the Fourth Lateran Council," in *Sources of Catholic Dogma*, §2.

104. Unlike some critics, I do not see the essence/energies distinction as any threat to the doctrine of the Trinity, a fact I have defended in Butner, "Communion with God."

First, similar phrasing in contemporary Greek and Jewish literature suggests that the phrase, which can also be translated "sharing in the divine nature" or "participating in the divine nature," refers to possessing some attribute(s) like God, not to full reception of the divine essence.[105] Second, the text was written before later Christians developed clear distinctions between terms like "nature," "hypostasis," "energy," "person," and "essence."

Finally, it is clear that our participation in Christ is thoroughly trinitarian. We are united to Christ as a result of the historical redemptive work of God, where the Father sends the Son (1 John 4:14), and the Son sends the Spirit from the Father (John 15:26), while the Spirit reminds the church of the Son's teaching until he returns (John 16:13), eventually handing the kingdom over to the Father (1 Cor. 15:24).[106] Since Christians are united to the person of the Son, they are also drawn into the personal relationships of the Son, through adoption with the Father and through indwelling with the Spirit. Yet this ought not be construed in purely individualistic terms, though those certainly apply. Rather, our communion with God is fostered in the community of churches that partake of the fellowship of the Trinity.[107] As Orthodox theologian Constantine Scouteris puts it, "The Church is intimately connected with the Person who joined humanity and divinity," for the incarnation is the starting point of the church, and the incarnate Son's gift of the Spirit is the means of entry into fellowship with the Trinity.[108] Yet entry into fellowship with the all-holy Trinity is impossible for fallen humans without atonement, so we turn now to the doctrine of dyothelitism, laying a final christological foundation for the final chapters on Christ's work in saving us.

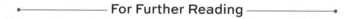

For Further Reading

Campbell, Constantine R. *Paul and Union with Christ: An Exegetical and Theological Study*. Zondervan, 2012.

> *Paul and Union with Christ* is a detailed exegetical analysis of the concept of union in Paul. Campbell works extensively in the Greek to develop a detailed understanding

105. See the discussions in Davids, *2 Peter*, 174–75; Bauckham, *2 Peter*, 179–81. Note Bauckham's misunderstanding of the doctrine of deification, which he understands to be "participation in the very life and being of God" (181), not in the divine energies.

106. Here we see the strength of Aimee Semple McPherson's thought.

107. Noble, *Holy Trinity*, 220–21. Writing from a perfectionist background, Noble emphasizes that Paul's prayer in 1 Thess. 5:23 for the Thessalonian church to be wholly sanctified pertains to a community, not to individuals.

108. Scouteris, *Ecclesial Being*, 29, 33–35.

of the multifaceted meaning of union for Paul. This will be a more difficult read for those who do not read Greek. But for those with proficiency in original languages, this will be a rewarding read.

Johnson, Marcus Peter. *One with Christ: An Evangelical Theology of Salvation.* Crossway, 2013.

> Johnson helpfully connects the doctrine of union to the incarnation, the steps of the *ordo salutis*, the doctrine of the church, and the sacraments. Drawing on Reformers and Scripture, his survey helps integrate a theology of union into a broad segment of systematic theology.

Pino, Tikhon. *Essence and Energies: Being and Naming God in St Gregory Palamas.* Routledge, 2023.

> Though more technical in nature than many books recommended at the end of each chapter, Pino's is well worth reading to understand Gregory Palamas's essence/ energies distinction. Pino draws on a wider scope of sources than most other treatments of Palamas, and the result is tremendously clarifying.

Sánchez M., Leopoldo A. *T&T Clark Introduction to Spirit Christology.* Bloomsbury T&T Clark, 2022.

Yong, Amos. *The Spirit Poured Out on All Flesh: Pentecostalism and the Possibility of Global Theology.* Baker Academic, 2005.

> Sánchez provides a helpful recent theological analysis of the sorts of Spirit Christology that are represented by Aimee Semple McPherson in this chapter. His work is a survey text. Amos Yong is an example of a recent theologian who has developed a Spirit Christology himself. His work is particularly fruitful in Christology and ecclesiology. Taken together, these two texts are a helpful survey of pneumatological Christology.

CHAPTER SEVEN

Dyothelitism

Now that we have covered the implications of the hypostatic unity of Christ for salvation, it is time to address the important subject of the wills of Christ. In the seventh century two important dogmatic concerns resulted in a conflict between dyothelites, who affirmed that the incarnate Son had two wills (one human and one divine), and monothelites, who taught that Jesus had only one divine will. Closely related was a debate between dyoenergists, who claimed that the incarnate Son had two operations, energies, or activities, one proper to each nature, and the monoenergists, who claimed that the incarnate Son possessed a single operation, energy, or activity. We will turn to the specific arguments of the dyothelites shortly, given that this group was vindicated first in the West at the Lateran Synod of 649 and then throughout Christendom at the Third Council of Constantinople (680–81). An initial sense of the issues at stake can be better provided from the later vantage point of Reformed Scholasticism in the thinking of Francis Turretin, who when discussing the hypostatic union is careful to explain that the union of natures in Christ is not like the "union of souls and the consent of wills" in which the natures are merely like two wills agreeing with each other, nor is the union of natures "the mystical union and grace of believers with Christ." The concern of monothelites in the sixth century and of some modern philosophers, as we shall see, is that positing a distinct will in the human nature of Christ risks the hypostatic unity of the Son. Perhaps if a human will exists beside the divine will in Christ, we will again face a *homo assumptus* theology that treats the humanity of Christ as a distinct being, supposedly united to the Son only at a moment of consent. It is therefore vital to explain willing in Christ such that there is greater unity between the human and divine than is found in any other human who consents to God's will. On the other hand, Turretin is careful to deny that the unity of natures is "the physical and essential union of two things to constitute one third nature" or like "the substantial or essential union of the persons of the Trinity in one essence."[1] Dyothelites were concerned, among other things, that denying a duality of wills in Christ resulted in a natural union of the sort rejected in chapters 3 and 5 of this book. Clearly, to explain the doctrine of the hypostatic union in detail we must tread carefully regarding the wills of Christ to develop a doctrine that allows for a distinction of nature joined in a hypostatic unity.

The doctrine of dyothelitism is closely connected to the doctrines of salvation, accomplished and applied. In terms of the application of the benefits of salvation in what is known as the *ordo salutis*, dyothelites recognized that Nazianzus's rule applied to the will of Christ. If the Son did not assume a human will in the incarnation, there is no redeemed human will with which the Christian can be conformed.[2] However, if the unity of Christ ends up being based in the two wills, or if the presence of two wills seems to divide the natures too sharply, then the humanity of Christ might not be related to God in a manner any different from the glorified humanity of any Christian at the final resurrection. Careful exposition of the distinction and unity of wills is therefore necessary. Later orthodox accounts of theosis also drew heavily on dyoenergism, understanding the essence/energies distinction to be rooted in the basic insights of the Third Council of Constantinople.[3] Turning to Christ's work in accomplishing salvation, we will see that dyothelitism is foundational for a proper dogmatic account of the crucifixion, death, resurrection, ascension, and second coming of Christ. Therefore, this chapter will explain the doctrines of dyothelitism and dyoenergism, drawing first on the late patristic sources that developed these doctrines, moving to consider the two medieval theories of Thomas Aquinas and John Duns Scotus, and addressing recent debates in analytic theology regarding the two wills and, especially, two minds of Christ. After this dogmatic account, I will consider two potential problem verses (Matt. 24:36; 26:39), exploring how dyoenergism and dyothelitism can provide a theological interpretation of these passages

---

1. Turretin, *Institutes* 2.13.6.3.
2. Dyothelite theology fits the thought of Gregory of Nazianzus well in this regard.
3. The Synodal *Tomos* of 1351, which formally endorsed the theology of Gregory Palamas, claimed his theology was based on Constantinople III (680–81), arguing that the earlier council distinguished between essence and energy, adding that a denial of an uncreated energy would result in monoenergism, where Christ had only a created energy. Synodal *Tomos* of 1351, §§6, 12, 30–31.

that preserves both the genuine humanity of Christ and the hypostatic unity of the incarnate Son. With this final chapter on the unity of Christ's nature complete, I will then turn to three concluding chapters focused on the victorious atoning work of Christ Jesus.

The Dogmatic Basis for Dyothelitism

Dyoenergism and dyothelitism were first clearly articulated in response to **monoenergism** and **monothelitism**. These latter positions were put forward as compromise positions in an effort to bring about unity between monophysites and Chalcedonian Christians. It was thought that affirming two natures but one energy or one will might result in some consensus, and for a time it seemed the formula might work. However, these views soon met with sharp resistance, first being condemned in Rome under Martin I, then condemned in the East thanks especially to the influence of Maximus the Confessor.

Seventh-Century Debates and the Third Council of Constantinople (680–81)

It is important to understand the reasoning behind the claim that Christ has two wills and two energies. In the seventh-century debates, dyothelite theologians developed arguments that combined biblical exegesis, philosophy, and the exposition of Christian doctrines like salvation and the Trinity.

In the philosophy of the day, the claim that Christ had a complete human nature entailed the claim that he had a human will and human operations (*energeia*). Consider the thought of Maximus the Confessor, who drew on earlier philosophy[4] to divide operations into two basic categories: internal/primary operations and **external**/secondary **operations**. **Internal operations** are a being's existence through an accomplished or completed ongoing act.[5] Moving beyond the terminology of Maximus, we might say that if essence identifies what something is and hypostasis identifies who someone is, internal operations speak of how something is by a certain distinguishing act. External

---

4. Tollefsen particularly notes the influence of John Philoponus. See Tollefsen, *Maximus*, 150–51.

5. Tollefsen, *Maximus*, 151. Maximus writes that Christ has the full essence of man because it has the "natural constitutive power" (*systatikē dynamis*), which "one would not be mistaken in calling a 'natural energy,' properly and primarily characteristic of the nature in question, since it is the most generic motion constitutive of a species, and contains every property that naturally belongs to the essence, apart from which there is only nonbeing." Maximus the Confessor, *Ambigua to Thomas* §5.

operations extend from internal operations to produce a result external to essence. Maximus gives the example of fire producing heat as an external operation.[6] Here is a more complete example to explain these concepts: I, Glenn (hypostasis), am a human being (essence) who—because I exist, am alive, and am conscious (three internal operations)—can write this example (external operation).

With these concepts in mind, it is not surprising that a denial of a human operation was taken to deny the Chalcedonian claim that Christ exists *in* two natures. Thus, Pope Martin I argued at the Lateran Synod of 649 against monothelitism that "every nature is only acknowledged to exist, as subsistent in true existence, in virtue of the natural and essential power that pertains to it and which also defines its nature."[7] Since rational natures have as essential powers or primary operations acts like willing, the will must be one of the fundamental natural powers and willing must be a fundamental internal operation of rational natures like human nature and divine nature.[8] Thus, like Martin, Stephen of Dora argued that Chalcedon's language of Jesus being consubstantial to us in humanity and consubstantial to the Father in divinity required that Jesus "was in no way incomplete in the essential will and operation of either his Godhead or his manhood, but that he possessed without diminution his natural wills and operations, equal in number to his natures."[9] Similar arguments were made by Maximus the Confessor, Sophronius of Jerusalem, and others.[10]

The claim that Jesus must have a human will and human internal operations because he is divine and human was not merely based on philosophy. Dyothelite theologians gave a close reading of Scripture in which they identified acts of the human Christ that would require a human will. For example, Jesus willed to hide but was "unable" (see Mark 7:24), yet the divine will is omnipotent and never unable to attain what it wills.[11] Similarly, the Son is obedient (Phil. 2:8); this is proper to servants but improper to God.[12] Most notably, the Son is tempted by Satan in the wilderness for forty days (Matt.

6. Tollefsen, *Maximus*, 152.

7. *Acts of the Lateran Synod*, 124.

8. Bathrellos, *Byzantine Christ*, 119.

9. *Acts of the Lateran Synod*, 147.

10. Maximus the Confessor, *Dispute at Bizya* §3. Sophronius of Jerusalem was the first to object to monoenergism. For a brief summary of his objections, including that each nature requires its own operation, see L. Davis, *First Seven Ecumenical Councils*, 264–66.

11. This passage is cited by Martin I in *Acts of the Lateran Synod*, 122. Maximus the Confessor, *Disputations with Pyrrhus* §§130–31, 134, 136.

12. These examples are given by Maximus the Confessor, *Disputations with Pyrrhus* §§130–31, 134, 136. See also Agatho, "Letter of Pope Agatho," 333.

4:1–11; Mark 1:12–13; Luke 4:1–13), and Hebrews insists that Jesus "has been tempted in every way as we are" (4:15), but James is clear that "God cannot be tempted by evil" (1:13 NASB). Various problematic responses may be given to this dilemma. Arians could wrongly suggest that this means Jesus is not divine, a position clearly rejected in this book. Kenoticism might mistakenly argue that the Son abandoned impeccability in the incarnation such that he could now be tempted. However, dyothelitism provides the most theologically satisfying answer in positing that Jesus's divine will cannot be tempted, but his human will can be. The philosophical meaning of "nature" entailed that if Christ had a human nature, he must have had human operations, including a human will, and Scripture appeared to back this up, but other interpretations were possible.

Monothelites argued that though Christ was one hypostasis in two natures, the unity of the two natures resulted in one theandric operation, a term derived from Pseudo-Dionysius the Areopagite and taken to imply a single operation and will.[13] Dyothelites argued against this, claiming on the basis of the philosophical assumption of the day that each nature had its own operation and that speaking of a single will or operation risked the distinction of natures.[14] In the West, Maximus of Aquileia could argue, "Everyone who explicitly denies the difference between the natural wills and operations of the one and the same Christ also denies the difference between his natures, from which and in which he exists."[15] We might suppose that a type of nature can exist without an internal operation or a will. If we supposed that the one will and one operation was proper to the divine nature and that the human nature had no will, then we would have to conclude that the entire divine nature was passible, including, for example, being hungry (e.g., Mark 11:12) when God does not eat (Ps. 50:13) or need anything (Acts 17:23–24).[16] On the other hand, a group of Greek monks argued that if we claimed that the incarnate Son had only the operations of the human nature, we might conclude that the divine nature was "without mind or soul or motion, like the lifeless idols," here citing Psalm 113:2–6.[17] Here again, the different human and divine actions of the human and divine natures demand operations proper to each nature.

13. For further information on the monoenergist and monothelite positions on this point, see Daley, *God Visible*, 216–17.

14. See Hovorun, *Will, Action, and Freedom*, 109–11. Hovorun surveys the leading scholars of the concept of *energeia* at the start of the controversy (David, Elias, and Stephan of Alexandria) to show consensus on the link between operations and nature.

15. *Acts of the Lateran Synod*, 128–29. Several decades later, Pope Agatho would link affirmation of one will and one operation with one nature. Agatho, "Letter of Pope Agatho," 332, 335.

16. On the Byzantine version of this argument, see Bathrellos, *Byzantine Christ*, 132.

17. *Acts of the Lateran Synod*, 153.

Could we perhaps argue that each of Christ's natures has an operation that is distinct in the nature but mixed in the hypostasis? An initial risk of divine and human operations blended into one is that this confuses the God-world relation so that the human nature becomes cocreator in the ongoing continuous creation of the sort described in passages like Job 34:14–15 and Hebrews 1:3, but humanity and human operations cannot be a part of the ongoing sustaining of the world.[18] Pope Martin I also argued directly against interpreting the theandric action of Jesus Christ as a synthesis of divine and human operations. If we claim that there is a composite operation in the hypostasis of the Son, then the Son's internal operation would be different from that of the Father and Spirit, who are simple in essence and natural operation, not composite.[19] This would seem to entail that the Son is no longer a member of the Trinity. Similarly, Maximus the Confessor argues that attributing operation to hypostasis would require that we also attribute hypostatic operations to the Father and Spirit, but this would clearly undermine the inseparable operations of the divine persons.[20] Since the doctrine of inseparable operations is clearly taught in Scripture (see especially John 5:17–19),[21] this is further reason to reject attributing operations to hypostasis instead of nature.[22] The division between the persons of the Trinity would be particularly acute if each divine person had a deliberating will such that they could disagree with one another.[23] Attributing operation to both hypostasis and nature also blurs the conceptual difference between these terms, rendering them less clearly meaningful. Monothelitism unravels the traditional doctrine of the Trinity if it attributes operations to hypostasis.

Denying two wills and operations in Christ is contrary to the normal meaning of "nature," risks blurring the distinction of natures in Christ, jeopardizes the God/world distinction, and undermines the Trinity. It also does not make sense of biblical patterns of texts suggesting that Christ does things like being tempted that are not possible for God. Instead, it is clear that the Son wills certain things in a human way, as when he desires to drink (Matt. 27:33–34), yet he desires other things in a divine way, as when he gives life to whom he wills (John 5:21). Therefore, the Third Council of Constantinople (680–81) affirmed that in Christ are "two natural wills and two natural operations

---

18. Maximus the Confessor, *Dispute at Bizya* §3.

19. *Acts of the Lateran Synod*, 148.

20. Maximus the Confessor, *Dispute at Bizya* §§3–4.

21. I make this case much more extensively in Butner, *Trinitarian Dogmatics*, 184–89.

22. For the fullest dogmatic case that I have made against attributing operation to hypostasis, see Butner, *Son Who Learned Obedience*.

23. Bathrellos, *Byzantine Christ*, 130, 132.

indivisibly, inconvertibly, inseparably, inconfusedly" while reaffirming and expanding the principle of Leo the Great that was endorsed at Chalcedon, that "each nature wills and does the things proper to it and that indivisibly and inconfusedly."[24] This is an expansion and clarification of language from Leo the Great's *Tome*, which was endorsed at Chalcedon: Each nature "does the acts which belong to it, in communion with the other."[25]

Two final concerns should be briefly addressed. First, many worry that a distinction in will risks the genuine unity of the hypostasis of the Son.[26] Would there be a problem of the human and divine wills disagreeing? Maximus of Aquileia argued that dissension between the wills of Christ can occur only if he is sinful, but otherwise the human will would naturally agree with the divine.[27] Recall from the discussion of impeccability in chapter 3 that Christ cannot sin, which leads us to conclude that the two natures could not be in fundamental disagreement. Maximus the Confessor explains why a human natural will would not disagree with the divine will. The natural will pursues a natural purpose for each created thing, and these purposes and wills are set by God. The natural will must agree with God's will or else God would be contradicting himself, which could not happen.[28] As Torstein Tollefsen explains, Maximus affirms that Christ acts "naturally, monadically, and uniformly," meaning "naturally, as one single agent, and in a uniform, not split up way."[29] Because it is sin that leads human beings to act contrary to the purposes of God, a human nature that does not sin would not act in contradiction to God.

The dyothelites thus resolve the possibility for fundamental disagreement between the two wills of Christ by denying the possibility of Christ sinning, but it seems to me that this does not entirely resolve the problem of two wills, for someone might object that the two wills might still disagree on some decision not marked by sinfulness and peripheral to Christ's messianic purpose. Is it not possible that the divine and human wills of Christ disagree on matters that would not count as sin? Such decisions might include anything from what

24. "Definition of Faith," 345–46.
25. Leo the Great, *Tome* §4. This quote was the most important piece of tradition for the conclusions of the Lateran Synod of 649, being cited by numerous figures against monothelitism, including Martin I, Sergius of Cyprus, and Victor of Carthage. See *Acts of the Lateran Synod*, 103, 150, 158, 185, 223.
26. Historically, this problem was central to Sergius, Patriarch of Constantinople, who was the most significant early advocate of monoenergism and monothelitism. See L. Davis, *First Seven Ecumenical Councils*, 266. We will address the similar concerns of some contemporary evangelicals in a section below.
27. *Acts of the Lateran Synod*, 363.
28. Maximus the Confessor, *Disputations with Pyrrhus* §17.
29. Tollefsen, *Maximus*, 217.

to say in a given sermon Christ gave to what he would eat for breakfast.[30] I see no basis for asserting confidently exactly how the wills would work in unity in such a situation, since I do not see anything in Scripture that definitively resolves this question. However, at least two possible answers might resolve the problem. The first is that the Son might direct the human nature and will of the Son as an instrument, such that they would agree in all situations.[31] This possibility will be addressed in the next section since this basic position was adopted by Thomas Aquinas.

A second solution comes from contemporary Spirit Christology and suggests that the human will of Christ is guided by the Holy Spirit to ensure that it conforms to the divine will of the Son.[32] Leopoldo Sánchez argues, for example, that "the Spirit guides the Son according to the Father's will, and the Son wills the Spirit to guide him, thus making his will one with the Father's."[33] Certainly we see evidence in the Gospels that the Spirit led Jesus to go to certain places (e.g., Luke 4:1, 14) that would fit this proposal. If the Son was open to guidance of the Spirit in a perfect manner, this could also ensure that all actions between the human and divine natures were harmonious.

Two Medieval Theories of the Son's Incarnate Action

The Byzantine debate over dyothelitism left ambiguity regarding how the two wills of Christ worked together. In particular, the debate was characterized by uncertainty regarding whether natures acted and willed enhypostatically in the person of the Son or whether persons willed and acted through the natures proper to those persons. Controversially, Leo's *Tome* affirmed that natures acted, a point of some controversy, leading some to reinterpret Leo to mean that "Christ performs his actions by each of the two natures in communion with the other."[34] This language was sometimes used by the

---

30. One could easily argue that vocation, including the incarnate Son's messianic vocation, is proper to a natural will because it is fundamental to the given purpose of a created thing. It does not seem obvious to me that the natural will would make decisions on which meal to eat or what words to say based on God-given purpose in the natural will. This could be the case, but it seems a stretch to suggest it is necessarily the case, suggesting to me that more theological argument is needed.

31. Maximus the Confessor can speak of the divine nature "moving willingly the assumed nature," so this might be the solution that he would most fully endorse. See Maximus the Confessor, *Ambigua to Thomas* 5.8.

32. Pneumatological Christology and dyothelitism are natural partners. Aaron Riches argues that "the role of the Spirit is decisive" for dyothelitism, opening up "the field of Christological speculation to the pneumatological infrastructure of Jesus' incarnate being." Riches, *Ecce Homo*, 149.

33. Sánchez, *Introduction to Spirit Christology*, 44.

34. See Bathrellos, *Byzantine Christ*, 176–78.

early dyoenergist Sophronius of Jerusalem, and it was incorporated into the definition of the Third Council of Constantinople (680–81), which taught that "each *nature wills and does* the things proper to it."[35] On the other hand, Maximus the Confessor and the decree of the Lateran Synod of 649 treated the person of Christ as the subject of willing and acting instead of the natures as the subject of acting. Inconsistently, Sophronius of Jerusalem sometimes did the same.[36] Though the definition of the Third Council of Constantinople bears the most weight as an ecumenical council, to my knowledge, the dogmatic significance of these two options was not fully explored in the debates surrounding monothelitism.

Thirteenth- and fourteenth-century medieval Scholastics devoted considerable theological attention to dyothelitism, but with different concerns in mind. Rather than focusing on the existence of two wills in Christ, which was universally assumed by the Middle Ages, Scholastic theologians explored in detail questions about the contrariety of wills in Christ, particularly as prompted by Christ's prayer in Gethsemane to the Father that the cup pass from him, though "not as I will, but as you will" (Matt. 26:39). We will turn to the exegesis of this passage in the next section. In this context, Thomas Aquinas and John Duns Scotus developed two distinct theologies of the Son's incarnate human actions, both drawing on one strand of earlier thought. For Aquinas, the supposit of the Son was the source of action, using the humanity of Christ as an instrument. In distinction, John Duns Scotus treated natures as the proximate cause of the actions. These theories include both risks and benefits that I will consider in this section, drawing also on the contemporary commentary tradition on both figures. The goal is to offer two possibilities for understanding the theandric action of Christ.

Thomas Aquinas understood the human will of Christ to be a rational instrument that was "always moved in accordance with the bidding of the divine will."[37] As Thomas Joseph White explains, the humanity of Christ is an instrument of the divinity, but neither is it "an inanimate instrument (like a violin or a saw), nor is it a rational instrument that is substantially separate from the person who employs it (like the thoughtful diplomat who is an instrument of the king). Rather, the human nature of the Word is a rational instrument that

---

35. "Definition of Faith," 345–46.

36. See Bathrellos, *Byzantine Christ*, 182–83. Besides the official statements of the Lateran Synod, many participants in the deliberations at this council used similar language. For example, Stephen of Dora argued that "it was by willing and performing what is divine and what is human by means of these [natures] that [Jesus] was known to be truly both God and man." Note that the Son is the subject of the acts and the natures are the means. *Acts of the Lateran Synod*, 147.

37. Aquinas, *Summa Theologica* III, Q. 18, A. 1. On the concept of a "rational instrument," see C. Barnes, *Christ's Two Wills*, 172–73.

is 'conjoined' hypostatically to the person of the Word and is expressive of that person."[38] White's explanation should be carefully considered. Different kinds of natures are moved in different ways—an inanimate nature, like a saw, is moved through the exertion of physical force, but a rational instrument is moved by the will. In White's example, a diplomat submits in will to the king and is moved to obey the king's instructions. Christ's humanity is rational, so moved in will, but unlike the diplomat and king, Christ's humanity and deity are "a united instrument"[39] that are one hypostasis, so the divine person of the Son moves his human will as an instrument that is proper to himself.

Aquinas's account is strong in its explanation of the unity of natures and wills, but it does have some risks. Language of the humanity being an instrument of deity has long been a concern of monothelite and non-Chalcedonian theologians.[40] For example, Theodore of Pharan and Cyris of Phasis, early monothelites, argued that if the humanity of Christ is a mere instrument, then it is proper to speak of only one energy.[41] Returning once again to the idea of a noncontrastive transcendence, it is possible to argue that the divine and human wills cause the theandric acts of Christ in different ways: the divine will as a cause that moves the human will and the human will as a genuine cause that serves as instrument. There is considerable parallel here with the concept of concurrence. A second risk is that positing actions to the person of the Son may imply a rejection of inseparable operations, a doctrine affirmed by both Maximus the Confessor and Thomas Aquinas, who speak of natures moved by persons, but at risk of being undermined in such account. With this concern in mind, we can turn to the next theory.

John Duns Scotus emphasized the inseparable operations of the Trinity to argue that all three trinitarian persons are involved in some way in causing the acts of the incarnate Son. After all, it is the incarnate Son who says that "the Son is not able to do anything on his own" (John 5:19). Scotus worries that if the human nature of Christ is merely an instrument of the divinity, as Thomas supposes, it might suggest that the human acts of Christ are not unique to the Son but proper to Father, Son, and Spirit, for the doctrine of inseparable operations implies that there can be no unique act of the Son, yet clearly acts like dying or being born of Mary are unique to the Son, not the Father or Spirit.[42] Therefore, Scotus develops a distinct theory in which human nature is the proximate subject of the human acts of the Son, and the

38. White, *Incarnate Lord*, 113.
39. Aquinas, *Summa Theologica* III, Q. 62, A. 5.
40. For example, see Ishak, *Council of Chalcedon*, 375.
41. L. Davis, *First Seven Ecumenical Councils*, 261–63.
42. Cross, *Metaphysics of the Incarnation*, 218–19; C. Barnes, *Christ's Two Wills*, 303–5.

person of the Son is the remote subject of those acts.[43] Scotus then explains the unity of the acts of the natures in the singular person of the Son by appeal to the communication of idioms. As Richard Cross explains, Scotus distinguishes between "*causal* and *predicative* aspects of agency. In virtue of the communication of properties, we can predicate human agency of the Word, without this entailing that the Word is the causal originator of the agency ascribed to him."[44] In other words, the hypostatic union enables us to say that the Word suffered on the cross (for example) without requiring that the Son's suffering was caused by his divine hypostasis or nature. Similarly, the Son is said to will because the acting will of the human nature exists in the hypostasis of the Son, but properly speaking the human nature would be the source of the action itself.[45]

We find in Scotus, in Leo the Great, and in the definition from Constantinople III theories that posit natures as the primary subjects of actions. Like the hypostasis-as-subject theory, this theory faces theological risks. The Oriental Orthodox theologian Shenouda Ishak worries that "if each nature performs only those things which are its own, they have not come to a union but only to a sort of partnership."[46] This might seem to be a variety of Nestorianism. This concern was already addressed in the seventh century, and I have covered some arguments above that help explain the unity of two willing natures into a single hypostasis, but one helpful point can be added here. Two willing natures would not be Nestorian if those wills always worked together, the divine and human contributing in their own proper way. Nestorianism posited discrete and subsequent acts between the human and divine natures, with one nature acting independently and then the other acting independently, while dyothelitism posits concurrent action. Further, dyothelitism accepts the hypostatic union, the communication of idioms, and the perichoresis of natures in a way that was not present in Nestorius.[47]

Another risk is less frequently recognized. Some contemporary Eastern Orthodox theologians, including especially John Zizioulas, have emphasized that since all reality comes from the person of the Father, including the Son and Spirit, then reality is at its most fundamental level *personal*. Behind this account of a personal cosmos is the belief that the acts of eternal generation

43. C. Barnes, *Christ's Two Wills*, 318.

44. Cross, *Metaphysics of the Incarnation*, 219–20.

45. Scotus writes, "How therefore is [the Word] said to will? I say that, just as the Son of God is coloured, so he is said to will because his soul is said to will, and because the nature subsists in the Word, [the Word] is therefore denominated in this way." John Duns Scotus, *Reportatio Parisiensis* 3.17.1–2n4, translated in Cross, *Metaphysics of the Incarnation*, 222.

46. Ishak, *Council of Chalcedon*, 376.

47. I have written on this more extensively in Butner, "Need for Nicene Dogmatics."

and eternal spiration are from the person, not from the divine nature.[48] Yet the compatibility criterion for divine personhood could imply that if acts like eternal generation are from the person, then incarnate acts were from the person, too, such that it is not proper to speak of natures acting or willing but of persons acting and willing through natures.

In my understanding, both formulas are somewhat speculative, and both aim at certain orthodox affirmations. Speaking of the person of the Son willing through the human will as a rational instrument more clearly indicates the unity of a two-willed person, but it can be taken to deny inseparable operations. Those who explain dyothelitism in this manner should be careful to ensure that the full doctrine of inseparable operations is affirmed, and they should also be careful to explain their theology in a manner that allows for the genuine human freedom of Christ. Speaking of the natures as the proximate cause of the Son's human acts and the person as the remote cause more clearly fits the trinitarian compatibility criterion given the doctrine of inseparable operations, and it has the added benefit of the backing of language from the definition of an ecumenical council. It is the manner of speaking that I tend to use. Yet those who prefer this language must be careful to ensure that other dimensions of their Christology emphasize the unity of subject of the incarnate Son, satisfying the singularity criterion of personhood. In the end, we must be careful not to separate persons and natures too sharply. No person or hypostasis exists without a nature, and no natures exist anhypostatically, for all are enhypostatic. Thus, if the human will of Christ is a rational instrument, it is an instrument of the person of the Son who also is the divine nature. If the human nature of Christ is the proximate cause of the human actions of the incarnate Son, we must remember that this nature exists only enhypostatically in the Son.

Contemporary Evangelical Objections to Dyothelitism

Some recent North American evangelical theology has raised pointed criticism against dyothelitism or against Christ having two minds, advocating a christological model where Christ has a single will or even a single mind. In part, this may be due to a diminished respect for tradition, including lesser regard for the Third Council of Constantinople.[49] While I tend to hold the

48. Zizioulas, *Being as Communion*, 40–41. Note especially, "the ontological 'principle' or 'cause' of the being and life of God does not consist in the one substance of God but in the *hypostasis*, that is, *the person of the Father*" (p. 40).

49. Jordan Wessling raises the most powerful objection to uncritical adherence to the creeds. Given all the other moral and theological failures of the church—here Wessling notes the

ecumenical councils in much higher esteem, it is important that the dispute not be reduced to a debate over the value of tradition. Important dogmatic matters are at stake, and many who object to dyothelitism raise substantive concerns, particularly in philosophical discussions. For that reason, we must briefly attend to these recent philosophical debates, considering objections to the conciliar model and offering a response. Therefore, I will present two representative objections to the conciliar model in detail, offering some response to each, before concluding with my argument for the continued viability of the conciliar model.

The first critique comes from William Lane Craig and J. P. Moreland, who advocate what they call a "reformulation (or rehabilitation!) of Apollinarius's insight" by correcting two problems they see in Apollinaris's theology: (1) His theology was accused of affirming an incomplete human nature because it denied a human mind, and (2) it resulted in incomplete salvation. Craig and Moreland argue that "in assuming a hominid body the Logos brought to Christ's animal nature just those properties that would serve to make it a complete human nature," for the combination of the mind of the Son, who was archetype of humanity, and the hominid body meant that the Son had all properties necessary to count as having a human nature.[50] Yet the authors argue that Christ is only one hypostasis because there is not a complete human nature apart from the Son. Though Christ had only one mind, Moreland and Craig argue that "the divine aspects of Jesus' personality were largely subliminal during his state of incarnation" such that he could still be tempted (e.g., Matt. 4:1–11) or grow in wisdom (Luke 2:52).[51] They admit that a singular mind or consciousness does not allow for two wills, but they do not consider this a problem "since dyothelitism, despite its conciliar support, finds no warrant in Scripture."[52]

Moreland and Craig are concerned about the incoherence of claiming two centers of consciousness in Christ. For example, they consider the philosophy of Thomas V. Morris, who presents a "two minds" view of Christ wherein "the divine mind of God the Son contained, but was not contained by, his earthly mind, or range of consciousness."[53] Rejecting a kenotic Christology, Morris

---

crusades, the Great Schism, medieval theological decline leading to the need for Reformation, and antisemitism—why believe God wouldn't allow an ecumenical council to err? Wessling, "Christology and Conciliar Authority," 164. Note also the bestselling and widely used textbook by Wayne Grudem, which affirms dyothelitism while dismissing the theology from figures like Maximus and Agatho, as I have discussed above, as ideas "from two rather obscure figures from church history." Grudem, *Systematic Theology*, 312, 697–98.

50. Moreland and Craig, *Philosophical Foundations*, 606.
51. Moreland and Craig, *Philosophical Foundations*, 607–8.
52. Moreland and Craig, *Philosophical Foundations*, 608.
53. T. Morris, *Logic of God Incarnate*, 103.

argues, as I did in chapter 1, that the incarnation is not a loss of deity but the addition of a more limited consciousness.[54] In response, Moreland and Craig reply that "it is very difficult to see why two self-conscious minds would not constitute two persons."[55] Here, I must agree and disagree with their concern. In my description of the united personhood of the incarnate Son in chapter 5, I was careful never to equate personhood with consciousness, for reasons that will soon become clear. I did, however, clearly argue for the hypostatic unity of the incarnate Son in terms of a singularity criterion that treated the Son as one subject. The reality of two distinct self-conscious minds does appear to suggest two subjects and hence two persons.[56] Perhaps this problem can be avoided with the divine preconscious model (or kryptic model) of Andrew Ter Ern Loke. The divine mind might be "preconscious," one component of the subconsciousness of Christ, meaning that divine knowledge is "accessible to consciousness by directing attention to [it]."[57] As a result of a change at the incarnation, the divine "mind came to include a consciousness and a preconscious." There was no unconscious part of the Son's mind, for then the Son would give up his omniscience, since the unconscious part of the mind cannot be accessed.[58] Loke's model is preferable to the ideas of Moreland and Craig because it preserves two distinct minds more clearly, as I have argued is necessary according to Nazianzus's rule. Surely, we cannot expect to be sanctified by having a divine mind like Christ's; there must be a distinct human mind that is different from the divine mind.[59]

I want to address the most important problem with many of the theories examined so far: They fail to recognize the considerable differences between the divine mind and human minds. The doctrine of analogy demands that we clarify through careful affirmation and negation how the word "mind" differs when speaking of God in comparison to when the word is used speaking of

---

54. T. Morris, *Logic of God Incarnate*, 104. Note that Morris makes comparisons between this model and the relation between the conscious and unconscious mind, treating the divine mind as unconscious to the human mind.

55. Moreland and Craig, *Philosophical Foundations*, 609.

56. This intuition or appearance is not insurmountable. As Richard Cross explains, there is no "knock-down argument sufficient to show that every centre of consciousness is a person in the required sense—that is, an ontologically independent subject of properties." Cross, *Metaphysics of the Incarnation*, 227.

57. Loke, *Kryptic Model of the Incarnation*, 66. Loke's model has a benefit over Moreland and Craig's in that it consciously rejects monothelitism whereas they consciously endorse it.

58. Loke, *Kryptic Model of the Incarnation*, 69.

59. Moreland and Craig treat the divine and human mind as identical in quality. Therefore, the human who bears the image of God is a person in the same way that the eternal Son is a person, a claim Moreland and Craig say is rooted in the doctrine of the image of God. Moreland and Craig, *Philosophical Foundations*, 606.

human beings. Consider the definition of consciousness provided by Moreland and Craig: "Consciousness is what you are aware of when you engage
in first-person introspection."[60] Further subcharacteristics of consciousness
include (1) phenomenal consciousness, which is a "raw feel" incorporating
such things as "tasting a lemon" and "hearing the note C"; (2) epistemic
authority, where a person is "in a position to know what is happening in my
own mental life with greater epistemic certainty than other people have in
knowing what is in my conscious life"; and (3) access consciousness, which
involves a mental state that can be used for "guiding speech, . . . directing
and controlling action and body movements, or . . . reasoning."[61] Careful
consideration reveals that none of these three dimensions of consciousness
obviously apply to the divine mind.[62] Human phenomenal consciousness involves sensory input through bodily organs such as tastebuds (for lemons) and
eardrums (for the note C), but God has no body with such sensory organs.
Words like "hearing" must have an analogical meaning when used of God
(e.g., Ps. 66:17–20), suggesting that divine phenomenal consciousness is different from human, if it is even appropriate to use such terminology. Similarly,
the divine omniscience of the three divine persons would seem to entail that
they all have equal epistemic authority regarding their shared knowledge.
This seems to be suggested at times in Scripture (1 Cor. 2:10) and across the
tradition.[63] Finally, "access consciousness" refers to mental states that guide
speech, action or body movements, and reason. Traditionally, each of these
acts is considered to apply differently to God, whose speech is creative (e.g.,
Gen. 1:3), whose action is not embodied, and whose reason is not discursive,
temporal, or finite like human knowledge. Surely, whatever it is for God to
have access consciousness must be different from what it means for humans
to have access consciousness, if the concept even applies.

This analysis of the term "consciousness" when applied to God leads me to
have serious reservations about Moreland and Craig's Christology and about

60. Moreland and Craig, *Philosophical Foundations*, 213.
61. Moreland and Craig, *Philosophical Foundations*, 214–16.
62. I have similar concerns about other attempts to explain singular consciousness in the
Son. For example, pace Sturch, *Word and the Christ*, 128–34, I cannot accept the argument
that the divine consciousness of the Son would count as a human consciousness if it also had
human experiences because it would then be a "center with human experiences" while also a
"center of divine experiences." Whatever it is to be a center of divine experiences must surely be
different from being a center with human experiences, so we have no reason to assume a divine
center with human experiences would be the same as a human center with human experiences.
Sturch himself admits that "experiences" may not be "the right word to use of God," but why
think our sense of having a center would apply to divine consciousness?
63. For example, Charles Hodge remarks that since what the Father knows the Son also
knows, it "implies a common consciousness." C. Hodge, *Systematic Theology*, 1:461.

Morris's two-minds Christology. When Moreland and Craig argue that the Logos is the "rational soul" and the "self-conscious ego of both natures,"[64] they treat divine and human consciousness as univocal, such that Jesus is fully human because he has a divine consciousness that satisfies the requirements of the human nature to be conscious. But divine consciousness is so different from human consciousness (Isa. 55:8; Rom. 11:34) that it would not satisfy the criteria for a full human nature. Similarly, though Thomas Morris admits that we cannot know what it is like to be the God-man,[65] claims that "the divine mind of God the Son contained . . . his earthly mind, or range of consciousness" may treat the divine and human minds as too comparable.[66] Here, I think Andrew Ter Ern Loke faces similar challenges when he argues that in Christ "the two minds shared one consciousness."[67] The divine and human minds are too divergent for this to be feasible. Loke's distinction between preconscious and unconscious is helpful—kenosis was not a change reducing the divine mind to an unconscious state but rather an addition of a human mind and consciousness. But I am concerned with language that the human consciousness of Christ can access the divine preconscious, finding it preferable and more fitting with the gratuitous quality of all human knowledge of God to say that the Spirit illuminates the Son, granting his human mind **ectypal knowledge** of the divine mind, that the Father's words and thoughts are given to the Son to express humanly, or that the divine nature of the Son elevates the human mind of Christ to greater knowledge. We are not dealing with two comparable consciousnesses, much less two selfs; a claim of two minds is not Nestorian. Rather, through the incarnation the Son, who eternally shared the one mind of God, took on a human mind, including a new mode of knowing and experiencing: human consciousness. But the same subject, the Son, knows divinely and humanly in a noncompetitive manner.

A second recent evangelical critique of dyothelitism comes from Garrett DeWeese, who makes three arguments against dyothelitism and a Christ with two minds. First, he argues that the idea of having two minds is prima facie implausible.[68] I hope that my analogical account of two minds shows that we are not dealing with something as obviously implausible as DeWeese suggests, so I will focus on his second and third arguments. Second, DeWeese

64. Moreland and Craig, *Philosophical Foundations*, 607.
65. T. Morris, *Logic of God Incarnate*, 104.
66. T. Morris, *Logic of God Incarnate*, 103.
67. Loke, *Kryptic Model of the Incarnation*, 73.
68. DeWeese, "One Person, Two Natures," 131–32. In my estimation, DeWeese rightly takes aim at Thomas Morris's comparison of the two minds to a person with schizophrenia or dreaming. On these, see T. Morris, *Logic of God Incarnate*, 104–6.

worries that the human will would basically be eclipsed since it could never disagree with the divine will and is "vanishingly small" in comparison with an omnipotent will. "Christ's human mind/will/consciousness becomes no more than a theoretical entity with no observable consequences in the life of Christ."[69] Here, I will make three responses. If the finitude of a human will makes that will inconsequential in light of the divine will, then the universal providence of the divine will renders all human willing inconsequential. Among other things, the moral significance of sin suggests that this is an incorrect conclusion, and a robust account of concurrent human and divine action should resolve this concern, though that doctrine is better reserved for a volume on patrology. Second, the doctrine of analogy again clarifies here: If the human mind, will, and consciousness are fundamentally different from the divine mind, will, and consciousness, then Christ's assumption of these in the incarnation is the addition of a new way of being—kenosis into a new, finite set of powers. The very frailty of these powers makes Christ susceptible to suffering, temptation, corruption, and death, all of which are salvifically significant.

DeWeese's third argument is to point to divergent consciousness, where each mind has quite different content. The human nature is conscious of being tempted in the wilderness; the divine nature is conscious of creating the world. Neither nature has consciousness of the other's acts. How is this one self-person?[70] The puzzle is real, but it is a subset of the larger christological puzzle, for acts of knowing are one subset of the larger set of human and divine acts of Jesus Christ. For example, the human nature was born of Mary, grew in wisdom, and died on the cross. The divine nature created the world and exists immutably and impassibly. This paradox prompts the same question that DeWeese's point about divergent consciousness prompts: How is this one person? Either the theological answers I have put forward here and in chapter 5 work, in which case DeWeese's question has no force, or else they fail, in which case DeWeese's argument stands against the entire hypostatic union, not just dyothelitism. I leave it to the reader to decide whether my account of the unity of Christ's plural natures and wills is sufficient. However, I turn now from considering these substantive philosophical concerns to consider two final problem texts for the account of the person of Christ I have put forward in this book. After these texts, we can turn to consider the culminating work of Christ in the cross, resurrection, ascension, and second coming in our final three chapters.

69. DeWeese, "One Person, Two Natures," 133.
70. DeWeese, "One Person, Two Natures," 134.

Considering Problem Texts

I have argued that Christ has two wills and two minds but that the divine will and mind of Christ are shared entirely with the Father and Holy Spirit. Two passages of Scripture pose the most pointed challenge to this theological proposal.[71] In Matthew 24:36 (and the parallel in Mark 13:32), Jesus is speaking about the eschatological return of the Son of Man, but he claims, "Now concerning that day and hour no one knows—neither the angels of heaven nor the Son—except the Father alone." This passage is easily taken to imply a kenoticist restriction of omniscience in the incarnate Son, for the Son does not know something. A second challenging passage appears two chapters later in the garden of Gethsemane when Jesus prays to the Father, "My Father, if it is possible, let this cup pass from me. Yet not as I will, but as you will" (Matt. 26:39; see also the paralells in Mark 14:36; Luke 22:42). In this situation, it appears that the Son has a will that is in conflict with, or at least contrary to, the divine will. If wills are strictly a property of nature, as dyothelitism posits, then this might imply too sharp a division within Christ, with his human and divine wills in conflict. Alternatively, the passage is sometimes taken to be evidence that wills are proper to hypostasis, perhaps suggesting that monothelitism is the orthodox position on Christ's wills.[72]

Some early manuscripts of Matthew leave out "nor the Son" in 24:36, which opens up the possibility that this saying was a later addition, which would resolve the theological issue. However, the general consensus of modern commentators is that it is more probable that concerned scribes removed the phrase, and, in any case, there is not such a variance found in the manuscript tradition for Mark 13:32, leaving the resolution of this puzzle to theology and exegesis.[73] Some features of the text complicate any kenoticist reading. For example, as Daniel Treier notes, the context of Christ's denial that the Son knows the day of his return is a considerable disclosure of knowledge about the eschaton, and Jesus speaks with a divine authority of words that

---

71. As a result, some theologians seem to read them as if they show that Father, Son, and Spirit have different minds and wills, as if both mind and will are proper to person. See, for example, Frame, *Systematic Theology*, 476.

72. These arguments are found in Ovey, *Your Will Be Done*, 108–12. Ovey makes much of the fact that "your will" is in the singular. I have dealt more extensively with Ovey's specific arguments about dyothelitism and Gethsemane in Butner, *Son Who Learned Obedience*, 87–94.

73. See, for example, Hagner, *Matthew*, 709; L. Morris, *Matthew*, 613. Though some have argued that the absence of "nor the Son" is original to Matthew, suggesting the phrase was later added from Mark, Ehrman has argued that the absence of "nor the Son" (*oude ho huios*) would not make grammatical sense, given the common "*oude . . . oude*" phrasing found in the passage—*oude* the angels, *oude* the Son know that hour. Further, the earliest manuscripts appear to be in agreement that the phrase was original. Ehrman, *Orthodox Corruption*, 91–92.

will never pass away (Matt. 24:35). This leads Treier to suggest that partitive exegesis explains the passage—in his humanity, Christ is ignorant of the day and hour, but he knows all omnisciently in the divine mind.[74] Yet how can the humanity not know what the deity knows? This puzzle has resulted in Catholic theology having a long tradition of teaching that in this passage Christ is merely refusing to share hidden knowledge with his disciples, perhaps in a manner similar to his refusal in Acts 1:7. But on this interpretation Christ does know the hour of his return.[75] As Hilary of Poitiers argues, the Father, too, speaks as if he does not know (Gen. 18:20–21; 22:12), but surely we take this as a figure of speech. So, too, is Jesus's saying that the Son does not know the hour—the point is to keep us ready for his sudden return (Matt. 24:44, 46).[76] I share Francis Turretin's skepticism of this interpretation, for it seems to ignore the real limitations of Christ's knowledge in his human mind, which grows in wisdom (Luke 2:52), and it stretches the plausibility of the language of Matthew 26:39 and Mark 13:32.[77]

Turning to the garden of Gethsemane, we can receive some help from the long dyothelite tradition of interpreting this passage. Paul Blowers explains, "The real struggle in Gethsemane for Maximus was not, then, between Christ's human and divine wills (as his deified will was 'naturally' disposed to obedience) but *within* his human volition itself, in the complexity of its relation to his deep-seated desires and aversions."[78] Several decades later, Pope Agatho could argue that "it could never be possible for [the Son's] immutable [divine] nature to will anything different from what the Father willed."[79] There is no plurality of divine wills here. Medieval theologians from the time of Peter Lombard distinguished between the will of reason and the will of sensuality in humans.[80] The former reflects the choices made rationally, while the latter reflects bodily desires. It became common to suggest that Jesus was tempted in his will of sensuality but that the human will of reason never disagreed with his Father. The temptation of the will of sensuality is reflected in Christ being "sorrowful," "troubled," and "deeply grieved" (Matt. 26:37–38), suggesting a profound emotional background to the prayer. According to Odo Rigaldus, both the sensual desire not to die and the rational desire to die for the atonement were morally good.[81]

74. Treier, *Lord Jesus Christ*, 205.
75. For example, see Robert of Melun, *Sentences* §49.
76. Hilary of Poitiers, *On the Trinity* 9.58–67.
77. Turretin, *Institutes* 2.13.2–5.
78. Blowers, *Maximus the Confessor*, 163. Maximus is clear that the human and divine wills are in "perfect harmony and concurrence." Maximus the Confessor, *Opusculum* 6, 173.
79. Agatho, "Letter of Pope Agatho," 334.
80. Lombard, *Sentences* 3.17.2.
81. C. Barnes, *Christ's Two Wills*, 61.

Later medieval commentators will even add that the natural component of the rational will, which is something like the instinctive reasonable desire for the good, could ethically will self-preservation and the avoidance of evil, including death.[82] Considered canonically, we also have evidence that the Son laid down his life voluntarily (John 10:18) and that his very purpose for coming was to willingly give his life (Matt. 20:28; Mark 10:45), which suggests that there was no ultimate contrariety between the divine and human wills in Christ. Rather, the two wills willed what was proper to them, the divine will immutably willing the atonement, and the human will also rationally willing the atonement while simultaneously overcoming the sensual fear of suffering and death—a morally good fear!—through a reasoned commitment to the need for the cross. Positing two wills in Christ at Gethsemane does not divide the person of Christ but rather displays the profound unity of the natures even in his darkest trials. Further, as we shall see in the next chapter, dyothelitism becomes foundational for the doctrine of the atonement.

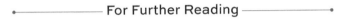

For Further Reading

Barnes, Corey L. *Christ's Two Wills in Scholastic Thought: The Christology of Aquinas and Its Historical Contexts*. Pontifical Institute of Medieval Studies, 2012.

> Barnes's text offers a close reading of major figures in twelfth- through fourteenth-century Scholastic theological treatments of the two wills of Christ. Though challenging, this text offers the most detailed analysis of the contrariety and/or unity of Christ's wills of any that I am aware, while also considering Christ's causal agency and the implications of dyothelitism for medieval theories of the atonement.

Bathrellos, Demetrios. *The Byzantine Christ: Person, Nature, and Will in the Christology of Saint Maximus the Confessor*. Oxford University Press, 2004.

> This work is foundational for any contemporary historical analysis of the dyothelitism of Maximus the Confessor. Besides providing valuable historical context, Bathrellos offers a detailed analysis of Maximus's theology of the will.

---

82. C. Barnes, *Christ's Two Wills*, 155.

CHAPTER EIGHT

Satisfaction

M uch of my discussion of Christ's work thus far has emphasized his role in reversing original sin. Thus, the incarnate
Christ recapitulates humanity so that, by union with Christ,
we can live a renewed life in the Spirit, guided in our moral lives by the
teaching and example of our Savior. The work of the Son of God is more
extensive than a reversal of original sin, because those born into original
pollution soon produce actual sins of their own, for which they are guilty
and culpable. In fact, much of the focus of the Bible is on actual sins. For
example, there is a widespread Pauline tendency to speak of plural or singular actual sins, not just sin (singular) as a power.[1] Certainly, one focus
of the Torah is on laws proscribing actual sins and provisions for atoning
for those actual sins. In the New Testament, the Mosaic covenant's provisions for sacrifices are shown to point typologically to Christ, where sins
are dealt with—yet further theological clarification is needed to explain
the manner of dealing itself.

This chapter will explore Christ's atoning work on the cross. Like the
Gospels, *Christological Dogmatics* will conclude with a lengthy treatment of
the work of Christ on and following the cross. This structure is not so much a
deviation from the structure of alternating chapters on the person and work
of Christ as it is a recognition that the entirety of the final dimension of the
work of Christ is too long for a single chapter. Chapter 8 will focus on satisfaction, beginning with the incarnate Son's role as priest and sacrifice before
moving to focus on the theology of Anselm of Canterbury. After introducing

---

1. Gathercole, *Defending Substitution*, 48–50.

Anselm's thought and the development of satisfaction theory among Protestants, I will answer common objections to satisfaction. The chapter will conclude by connecting the atonement to the doctrine of the Trinity and the hypostatic union, culminating in a dogmatic summation.

Jesus the Priest and Sacrifice

The New Testament depicts Jesus as both priest and sacrifice, so understanding both concepts provides an important foundation for understanding satisfaction. The Old Testament included various sorts of sacrifices, some atoning and others gift offerings. Atoning sacrifices resolved the consequences and reality of human sin as well as impurity.[2] Priestly literature focused on four consequences for human sin: (1) death; (2) being "cut off," which could reference premature death and perhaps eternal judgment; (3) "bearing sin," an often-indeterminate punishment; and (4) "suffering guilt's consequences," which often involved subjective feelings of guilt.[3] Atoning sacrifices and the act of offering atonement were closely associated with offering a payment or ransom to God, though atonement also included dimensions of cleansing from impurity.[4] A parallel is found in a debate in twentieth-century New Testament scholarship, where some argued whether Christ's sacrifice[5] only offered **expiation** (cleansing the consequences of sin) or whether it also served as **propitiation** (making God look favorably on sinners through payment). The expiatory role of sacrifice is clear, but it seems to me that propitiation is also likely intended.[6] Sacrifice is ultimately rooted in grace, both because God provides the sacrifice (paradigmatically in Gen. 22:8, 12–14)[7] and because accepting atonement to avert punishment requires the offended party to accept such a sacrifice.[8]

2. The global practice often relates to humanity as creatures, reaching out in recognition to the gods, or offering gifts, or seeking communion. These can be distinguished from a theory of sacrifice rooted in human beings as guilty sinners. Warfield, "Christ Our Sacrifice," 410–14.

3. Sklar, *Sin, Impurity, Sacrifice, Atonement*, 13–41.

4. Sklar, *Sin, Impurity, Sacrifice, Atonement*, 184–85.

5. The debate hinges on the proper understanding of *hilasmos* and *hilastērion* in such passages as 1 John 2:2 and Rom. 3:25.

6. The debate is quite technical, so I am avoiding extensive analysis of related arguments. The reader is advised to consult major texts in the debate, including important early works such as L. Morris, *Apostolic Preaching*; Dodd, *Romans*.

7. Young, *Construing the Cross*, 36. Young also points to Lev. 17:11, since it is by God's appointment that the animal and blood serve for atonement.

8. "If pardon for sin is granted when the Lord's law has been broken, it is because the offended party (the Lord) has agreed to allow for an [atonement] in place of the deserved penalty." Sklar, *Sin, Impurity, Sacrifice, Atonement*, 83.

Jesus is a high priest because it is not just his blood but his entire person that ascends into the holy of holies.[9] Interestingly, Second Temple Judaism began to see the origins of the priesthood in Isaac, who, having nearly been the sacrifice himself, allegedly taught Levi from firsthand experience how to perform the rite.[10] Christ could in some sense be seen as a fulfillment of this extrabiblical expectation of the unity of priest and sacrifice. The high priest represented Israel through the twelve precious stones on the ephod (Exod. 28:9–12; 39:6–7), while Israel as a whole represented all of humanity before the Lord (Exod. 19:6). Therefore, Jesus's priestly role is also a recapitulation of Israel's priestly role. Through Jesus, the nations will be blessed by Abraham's descendant (Gen. 12:3) as all the nations will be saved by the lamb seated on the throne (Rev. 7:9–10). Yet it is also clear that Jesus has a superior priesthood, being a priest "according to the order of Melchizedek" (Heb. 5:10; 7:11; cf. Ps. 110:4) because he has a permanent priesthood unstoppable by death (Heb. 7:24) and unmarked by sin and weakness, unlike all other priests (7:26–28). The Aaronic priesthood was marked from the start by sin and failure, beginning with the lighting of the sacrificial pyre in Leviticus 9, which was immediately followed by Nadab and Abihu using "unauthorized fire" (Lev. 10:1), which resulted in punishment.[11] In contrast, Christ's perfect priesthood continues in heaven, where we see Jesus wearing the high priestly garments in Revelation 1:13.[12] Given the clear depiction of Jesus as sacrifice and priest, theological accounts of atonement must explore how Jesus's service as priest and sacrifice absolves us from the guilt and consequences of our sins.

The Satisfaction Theory of Atonement

Precision of language is important in most doctrines, and no less so in the doctrine of the atonement. It is helpful to distinguish between a cluster of related terms.[13] "Substitution" involves one person or party fulfilling an obligation or bearing a duty or consequence proper to another. Joshua McNall helpfully

9. Outram, *On Sacrifices* 2.7.2.
10. Anderson, *That I May Dwell Among Them*, 168–73.
11. "Immediately after the sacrificial pyre was sanctified by fire, it was profaned." Anderson, *That I May Dwell Among Them*, 105.
12. See Winkle, "You Are What You Wear," 342–44. The *podērēs* of Rev. 1:13 is typically identified as a high priestly garment in the LXX, Philo, and elsewhere. *Podērēs* and *zōnē* (belt) are only found in close proximity in Exod. 28:4–29:9 and Ezek. 9, with the former referencing especially high priests and the latter a priestly figure. Josephus says the sash of the high priest in his day was uniquely golden.
13. In this, I follow the example of Gathercole, *Defending Substitution*, 15–23.

defines "penalty": "the suffering in person, rights, or property brought about by judicial decision on the grounds of crime or public offense."[14] **"Penal substitutionary atonement"** thus refers to any atonement theory where Christ receives a penalty due to Christians in our place, while explanations of what the punishment is vary considerably.[15] Substitution can also include the idea of "satisfaction," which references a payment or offering on behalf of another to remit or cancel debt and/or guilt. Closely related but conceptually distinct is the concept of "propitiation," which refers to Christ's act of making the Father favorable toward Christians.

Substitution in Scripture

Various parts of the biblical canon center the idea of substitutionary death. Perhaps most famously, Isaiah's prophecies of the suffering servant have often been taken by Christians to point to the substitutionary death of Christ, though these interpretations are also often contested.[16] The suffering servant songs depict God's "servant" (Isa. 52:13) "despised and rejected" (53:3), one who "bore our sicknesses" and "carried our pains" (53:4), ultimately "pierced because of our rebellion" (53:5) and "punished . . . for the iniquity of us all" (53:6). Ultimately, this servant is considered a "guilt offering" (53:10). The servant has been considered to be a messianic figure or the people of Israel.[17] However, Isaiah 42:6 and 49:5–6 depict the servant bringing Israel and Jacob back to God, suggesting that at least some aspects of the "servant" do not refer to the nation of Israel as a whole. The exalted description of the servant as one free from violence and deceit (53:9) is also a description that does not easily fit with Isaiah's earlier descriptions of the nation of Israel, or any

14. McNall, *Mosaic of Atonement*, 104.

15. McNall names nine different punishments in penal substitutionary theories: "death on a cross," "bearing the divine or covenantal curses," "experiencing divine wrath or judgment," "experiencing the divine abandonment (or withdrawal) that we deserved," "being forsaken unto death," "being God-forsaken," "descending into hell," "being pierced for our transgressions," and "giving his life as a sacrifice for human sin." McNall, *Mosaic of Atonement*, 104.

16. For example, Morna Hooker argues that Isa. 53 *can* be used to interpret the atonement in a sort of "reader response" method, but most New Testament citations of Isa. 53 do not actually focus on the substitutionary atonement aspects of the passage. She considers Mark 15:28; Luke 22:37; John 12:38; Acts 8:32; Rom. 10:16; 15:21; 1 Pet. 2:22–25. Hooker, "Use of Isaiah 53," 89–93. Against this perspective, one can point to various substitutionary motifs, notably in Matt. 20:28 and Mark 10:45, that imply that Jesus understood his role as substitutionary in nature. Stuhlmacher, "Isaiah 53," 150–53. If Stuhlmacher is right, the Christian messianic interpretation of Isa. 53 may go back to Jesus himself.

17. Note the similarities between the description of the servant and the man in Lamentations 3:1, suggesting a connection between those suffering exile and Isaiah's suffering servant. Heffelfinger, *Isaiah 40–66*, 222–23.

nation for that matter.[18] Perhaps the best interpretation imitates medieval approaches that recognize various layers of meaning, referencing in some ways Israel's priestly role to the world but more fully indicating the future messianic role of Jesus.

Turning to consider this messianic role, we can learn more about Jesus as a substitute. If we view Isaiah as an integrated whole, there are clear connections between what early chapters say about the king and what Isaiah 52–53 says of the suffering servant. The title "servant" (52:13; 53:11) is most frequently applied to David in Isaiah, and both the suffering servant and king bring justice (9:7; 42:1–4), light (9:2; 42:6–7), and sight to the blind (32:3; 42:7). Further, both king and suffering servant are associated with botanical imagery (11:10; 53:2) and God's promises to David (9:7; 55:3).[19] Such parallels validate the Christian interpretation of the suffering servant as Jesus the king, though it could validate other interpretations.[20] Viewing the suffering servant as Messiah is not unprecedented but certainly not universal. While Jewish interpretation of Isaiah 53 did occasionally posit a messiah who vicariously suffered—there was some point of contact when Christians proclaimed Isaiah 53 to Jews—this was only one possible interpretation, and it was not central to much of Second Temple Judaism.[21]

In the New Testament, penal dimensions of Christ's substitution on our behalf are implied in the mere fact that Christ died by crucifixion, a hideous means of execution that the Romans viewed as being "*damnatio ad bestias,* . . . condemned to the death of a beast."[22] The New Testament consistently views Christ's death as the plan of the triune God. This is certainly true indirectly. As Jesus remarked to Pilate, "You would have no authority over me at all . . . if it hadn't been given you from above" (John 19:11). The divine plan is more directly evident where Scripture claims the Father sent or "gave" his only Son to die (John 3:16), the Son came to give his life as a ransom (Matt. 20:28; Mark 10:45; Gal. 2:20), and the Spirit, who guided Jesus's steps (e.g., Matt. 4:1), set his face toward the cross from the start. The gracious nature of

18. Kaiser, "'Servant of the Lord,'" 89–91.

19. Treat, *Crucified King*, 70.

20. Treat himself acknowledges dissimilarities between the Davidic king and the suffering servant. Treat, *Crucified King*, 74.

21. For evidence of this substitutionary and messianic interpretation, see Hengel and Bailey, "Effective History of Isaiah 53." The authors note that Zech. 13:7 might originally have referenced God striking the shepherd—a kingly or messianic reference?—and further that this could draw from Isaiah's theology. The LXX of Dan. 3:40 also links atonement with the sacrifice of the three young men in the fiery furnace. Messianic sacrifice and atonement are also evident in small ways in 1QIsaᵃ, T. Benj. 3:8, with disputes about dating complicating matters.

22. Rutledge, *Crucifixion*, 89.

this substitution is clear, but so also should be the fact that the divine persons were in some respect responsible for the cross.

More generally, substitutionary language is evident throughout the New Testament. In 1 Corinthians 15:3–4, which Paul introduces as "the gospel [he] preached" (15:1), Paul states that Christ died "for our sins," a phrase which may draw on the Septuagint of Isaiah 53, where the same wording is found repeatedly (Isa. 53:4, 5, 6, 12).[23] Substitution is found in language of dying "for many" (Matt. 20:28; 26:28; Mark 10:45; 14:24) or "for you" (Luke 22:19).[24] Such an emphasis on the cross being for the people of God led to a long-standing emphasis on substitution in Christian history.[25] The most famous historical summary of substitutionary atonement is found in Anselm of Canterbury's work *Why God Became Man*.

Anselm's Satisfaction Theory

Anselm's influential and contested satisfaction theory interprets the cross in terms of Jesus offering a price, a satisfaction, to release Christians from their debt of sin. The word "theory" indicates a degree of separation between the text of Scripture and Anselm's dogmatic account of how the cross works, since Anselm is reasoning from Scripture and not merely exegeting it. However, the word "theory" can be problematic insofar as it implies that the theology I will soon discuss lacks a firm basis. The alternative language of "models" of atonement is sometimes used, but such can equally suggest that "no normative dogmatic core grounds the Christian teaching about salvation," as Khaled Anatolios warns.[26] It would be a mistake to assume that Anselm's satisfaction theory lacked a solid foundation. Rather, Anselm's account of satisfaction (like similar theories from other eras) is founded in several firm truths. First, no one but Christ could bring about salvation (e.g., John 14:6; Acts 4:12; 1 Tim. 2:5). Second, this salvation is particularly linked with the death of Christ by crucifixion, which is a central component of gospel proclamation (1 Cor. 2:1; cf. paradigmatic preaching in Acts 2:22–24).[27] In short,

---

23. Gathercole, *Defending Substitution*, 65.

24. For a slightly longer treatment, see Demarest, *Cross and Salvation*, 173–74.

25. Given such biblical patterns, it is no surprise that the earliest Christians spoke of substitution. Language of a "sweet exchange" was found as early as the Epistle of Diognetius and was present across numerous patristic sources. See Boersma, *Violence, Hospitality, and the Cross*, 159–63.

26. Anatolios, *Deification Through the Cross*, 8.

27. Of course, this is not to say that Anselm's particular account of satisfaction is above reproach. For example, his claim that a number of humans will be saved to replace the fallen angels seems unfounded in Scripture. See Anselm of Canterbury, *Why God Became Man* 1.16–17. Further references to *Why God Became Man* in this section will be given in the text.

satisfaction theory grows from the conviction that Christ alone could save and that his saving work focuses on the cross. The task at hand, then, is to understand why this is the case; satisfaction theory aims to explain Christian witness to the necessity of Christ's atoning death.

In order to understand why a God-man alone could bring about salvation, we need to understand Anselm's concept of sin. When someone follows the will of God, they are maintaining the order and beauty of the universe itself (1.15). Failure to follow God's will treats God with dishonor, and the balance of the God-given order of the universe demands restitution or recompense to correct the injustice.[28] Without recompense, there is not justice, for what was due has not been given. Therefore, humans must repay God for the debts they have incurred. The question becomes how such repayment might be possible.

Early chapters in Anselm's *Why God Became Man* deftly eliminate alternative routes to salvation other than repayment through the cross. God would not forgive sin without satisfaction, because to do so would be unjust (1.12–13). (Many have objected to this point, so I will consider objections extensively below.) God also would not leave his creation to death, for God does not fail, and he intended fellowship with a living creation (2.5). God would not allow someone other than himself to redeem humanity from death, for this would result in humans being indebted to someone other than God (1.5). Humans cannot offer recompense themselves, because anything they could give would already belong to God (1.20). Yet since humans have sinned, recompense must be given by a human being (2.6). Christ alone is the basis for satisfaction because he alone is both God and man, such that God alone will save, but humans, who alone have the debt, will repay. Christ alone offers such a combination of deity and humanity.

Anselm is aware that "the wages of sin is death" (Rom. 6:23), so he knows that the sinless Savior need not die (2.10). Yet Christ voluntarily submitted to death, and herein lies the basis for the satisfaction:

> No member of the human race except Christ ever gave to God, by dying, anything which that person was not at some time going to lose as a matter of necessity. Nor did anyone ever pay a debt to God which he did not owe. But Christ of his own accord gave to his Father what he was never going to lose as a matter of necessity, and he paid, on behalf of sinners, a debt which he did not

28. Anselm considers several arguments for this point. For example, when Adam fell, he took from God the divine plan for creation, and he gave control of himself to the devil. Proper restitution should therefore restore the divine plan and restore humanity to God from the devil. Thus, the work of satisfaction discussed in this chapter links with Christ's victorious work discussed in the next. Anselm of Canterbury, *Why God Became Man* 1.22–23.

owe. . . . He gave his life, so precious; no, his very self; he gave his person—think
of it—in all its greatness, in an act of his own, supremely great, volition. (2.18)

Because the death of Christ was voluntary, it must be seen as a gift to the
Father. Because it was the God-man who died, the gift was one of infinite
value. Sometimes gifts are obligatory. For example, in some cultural contexts
when a person receives a gift from another, it results in a social expectation
of reciprocation.[29] This is not the case with the Son's gift to the Father. The
Son's gift is not something owed in return for the Father's actions or attitude
toward the Son. Using technical jargon, we might name the Son's gift on the
cross a **supererogatory gift**—a gift well above what is required. As such, we see
a certain gratuity to Christ's atoning death in that it was an offering far beyond
what he was obligated to give. We can also see grace in the joint agreement
of the Father, Son, and Holy Spirit in the covenant of redemption to create
a world that would be redeemed through the death of the Son on the cross.

I must touch on a potential misunderstanding: Anselm argued that it would
be wrong for God to allow his creation to remain bound to death but also
that it was improper for God to forgive without recompense, through either
direct repayment by the offending party or satisfaction by another. Since God
cannot do what is wrong or improper, there is a certain sense in which it is
necessary for God to act to save and hence necessary for Jesus to die on the
cross.[30] Such necessity might seem to undermine the gratuity of the cross.
However, Anselm is careful to explain that we are dealing with a **consequent
necessity**[31]—that is, with a necessity that is conditional on a prior contingent
fact (2.17). In this case, the antecedent fact is that God eternally chose to create a world that would need to be redeemed, choosing a plan for the fullness
of time that culminated in the cross (Eph. 1:10). Therefore, Scripture can
rightly speak of the Son voluntarily dying (Matt. 26:53–54; John 10:17–18),
while acknowledging that any power over Christ was given from above (John
19:11). Moreover, if Jesus had been commanded to die by the Father, then
his death would have been for his own righteousness—one is obligated to do
what God commands. If that were the case, there would be no supererogatory
gift. But the plan to create and redeem a people was eternally the voluntary
plan of Father, Son, and Spirit, who work and plan all things together. The

29. For a helpful discussion on this phenomenon in the context of the theology of econom-
ics, see K. Tanner, *Economy of Grace*, 47–62.

30. For a helpful treatment of Anselm on necessity, see Hunter, *If Adam Had Not Sinned*,
39–59.

31. The terminology used across the tradition has included "subsequent necessity," "conditional necessity," and "consequent necessity." I will use "consequent necessity" because its
connotation is of a logical sequence more than a temporal sequence.

plan was also carried out as Christ's human will accepted suffering on the cross (Matt. 26:32, 42; Mark 14:35; Luke 22:42), such that the human and divine wills are in harmony. Yet since immutability is a divine perfection, it is a consequence of the divine plan to create humans who would need saving that the Son must necessarily be incarnate—God's plan does not change.[32]

Satisfaction Theory in Protestant Theology

Shortly after Anselm's day, theologians like Thomas Aquinas began to put more emphasis on the punitive dimensions of the cross, with a tendency to emphasize Jesus bearing our punishment more than his repaying our debt. Of course, Jesus paying our debt (e.g., 1 Cor. 6:20; 7:23) and bearing our punishment (e.g., Isa. 53:5–6) are both themes in Scripture. The emphasis on punishment was slightly more pronounced among the Reformers, yet Protestants continued to affirm satisfaction and to clarify its meaning. At times, the concepts of satisfaction and penal substitution were blurred.

Reformed theologians often made a careful distinction between an exact payment of what was owed and the satisfaction offered on the cross. Turretin explains that an exact payment is not possible, since we already owe all to God; Christ pays a satisfaction, which is a nonidentical payment by a different agent. One who accepts satisfaction—such acceptance is not obligatory—is being just, merciful, and forgiving.[33] Theologians like Turretin viewed satisfaction as a nonidentical payment, but when they analyzed how Christ bore our punishment, the question of exact punishment was more disputed, with some insisting Christ took our exact punishment (*solutio eiusdem*) and others claiming it was only a similar punishment (*solutio tantidem*).[34] If our punishment was to make payment, then the satisfaction of Christ would clearly be a nonidentical payment and punishment, but if punishment also involved suffering, then things were more disputed. As we will see in chapter 9, some see Christ as bearing even the punishment of hell to ensure exact punishment.

Satisfaction was not universally possible. Zacharias Ursinus helpfully clarifies the conditions under which satisfaction is acceptable: "1. He who is punished is innocent. 2. If he be of the same nature with those for whom he makes satisfaction. 3. If he, of his own accord, offer himself as a satisfaction.

---

32. See Hunter, *If Adam Had Not Sinned*, 52–53.

33. Turretin, *Institutes* 14.10.8. Note the continuity with the prior discussion of Old Testament sacrifices.

34. For a brief discussion of this debate focused on John Owen and Hugo Grotius, see Boersma, *Violence, Hospitality, and the Cross*, 169–70. Boersma worries that too strict an equivalence results in a commercialism that loses sight of God's "consistently gracious hospitality" (177).

4. If he himself be able to endure and come forth from this punishment. . . .
5. If he look to, and obtain the end which Christ had in view, viz: the glory of God and salvation of man."[35] In other words, not just anyone can offer a satisfaction. There must be some basis for the repayment, much like the kinsman-redeemer's familial ties in Old Testament examples of redemption (Lev. 25:23–28, 47–54). Some Reformed theologians particularly emphasized the federal headship of Christ as a parallel to their understanding of the federal headship of Adam.[36] Thus, the basis for satisfaction could be shared nature or covenantal unity.

Lutheran theology maintained a similar emphasis, though Protestant liberalism, with its rejection of vicarious atonement, was particularly felt in Lutheranism beginning in the nineteenth century. Nevertheless, early in this century one theological text could summarize atonement as involving vicarious suffering and purchase of salvation as a possibility for all, describing this view as "properly . . . termed the Lutheran view of the atonement."[37] Lutherans are here in agreement with the Reformed with respect to satisfaction and substitution, disagreeing on the extent of the purchase. The Reformed tended to accept limited atonement, where Christ died for the elect, while Lutherans tended to accept the universality of the offer of salvation, where anyone could hypothetically receive atonement. Such differences are not universal and are better reserved for discussions of predestination in patrology. Some Lutheran theology distinguished between (1) satisfaction that paid our debts and expiated our sins and (2) Christ's merit, which brought salvation and justification.[38] It is this latter point that introduces one of the major contributions of Protestant soteriology: clarification of the doctrine of justification.

The reason that satisfaction is such an important supplement to penal substitution is that it lays the groundwork for the doctrine of justification. In justification, the merit of Christ is imputed to humans, and this merit is precisely the reward earned by the supererogatory gift of his sacrifice on the cross. Christ has given what should earn a reward, but what reward can he receive from his Father since he is already one with his Father (John 10:30)? Christ's reward is imputed to us instead.[39] Sometimes, Anselm's theory of satisfaction is criticized because it appears to view the resurrection as superfluous. Yet

---

35. Ursinus, *Commentary*, 88.
36. For example, see Murray, *Imputation of Adam's Sin*.
37. Schmucker, *Popular Theology*, 140.
38. Schmid, *Doctrinal Theology*, 383.
39. The doctrine of justification could be fully explored under the heading of satisfaction and Christ's role as meritorious cause, but for efficiency's sake, I will save further discussion for a planned future treatment of pneumatology, since the Spirit bestows faith, which is the instrumental cause of justification.

satisfaction theories reveal that Jesus was "crowned with glory and honor *because he suffered death*" (Heb. 2:9; see also Phil. 2:8–9). The glory of Christ's bodily resurrection and the glory of his restored status as the second Adam are glories that we share because of the supererogatory gift of the cross, which earned a reward for the church, first imputed in justification and then imparted in glorification at the final resurrection.

Objections to Satisfaction Theory

When we consider the doctrine of the atonement, we move into some of the most contested theological territory in Christology. Anselm's satisfaction theory, for example, has been heavily criticized, especially by modern theologians. It is therefore important to respond to several of the leading objections, considering both their merit and the reasons why they ultimately fail. Doing so will sharpen our theological understanding of the cross.

Is Anselm's Theory of Justice Merely Feudalism?

One of the most common objections against Anselmian satisfaction is that it is a mere by-product of his feudal culture. Thus, Mark Baker and Joel Green argue that Anselm "used a framework and imagery taken, not from the Bible, but from the feudalistic system of his day." In the end, Anselm allegedly "allowed medieval concepts of honor to define how God ought to act."[40] Joerg Rieger is even more forceful in his conclusion: "Without an understanding of the logic of the Norman Empire and the importance of the notion of honor in this particular context, God appears either as a sadist or a masochist as God either takes pleasure in killing another or in killing part of Godself."[41] JoAnne Marie Terrell adds that Anselm's theory "consented to the class arrangements of feudalism," indicating a further moral concern arising from Anselm.[42] I will address the moral concerns arising from the

---

40. Baker and Green, *Recovering the Scandal of the Cross*, 133, 156.

41. Rieger, *Christ and Empire*, 135. Rieger says that, apart from the logic of empire, we are faced with the insuperable question of why God did not simply forgive, a question addressed in the next objection. Rieger also notes the ties between Anselm's ministry, his thought, and empire, also broaching the question of ethics. Thus, Rieger's work directly touches on all the major objections addressed in this section.

42. See Terrell, *Power in the Blood?*, 107. Terrell links this perspective with Luther siding with the powerful during the German Peasant Revolt of 1525, and she sees this general trend continue into Jim Crow laws in the United States and ongoing injustice. "The church is historically guilty of inflicting and perpetuating abuse, allying with oppressors and imposing the hermeneutics of sacrifice on subjugated peoples in order to justify the abusive policies of the state and of its own

atonement below, but first we must consider the extent to which Anselm's theology was culturally bound to a feudal context.

Though Anselm was undoubtedly influenced by his cultural milieu (as we all are), there are many cultures today that emphasize honor and shame that would share many features of Anselm's understanding of sin.[43] It is therefore mistaken to assume that honor-based understandings of the cross are limited only to medieval Europe. However, the most important concern in reducing his theology to a crass spiritualization of feudalism is that such a reduction ignores the significant biblical roots of Anselm's thought. These are often missed since his writing intends to avoid explicitly rooting arguments in Scripture so that they can be more widely accepted. Given that Anselm was a monk who would have been steeped in the Scriptures, it is certain that his thought has been shaped by the Bible.[44] Scripture calls on the Christian to give honor to the Father (1 Tim. 1:17; 6:16; Rev. 4:9, 11; 5:12, 13),[45] who gives honor to the Son (Heb. 2:9; 2 Pet. 1:17). The basic pattern of "honor[ing] . . . those you owe honor" (Rom. 13:7) is also biblical.[46] The idea of our sins creating a debt is frequently found in Scripture, notably even in the Lord's Prayer (Matt. 6:12). Combining these notions, there is clear basis for believing that humans are obligated to honor God and that failing to do so results in a debt. Furthermore, Scripture clearly teaches that we are unable to pay God anything, since he owns all (1 Chron. 29:14; Job 35:7; 41:11; Rom. 11:35–36). Even if we had a payment to offer, we are too unholy to bring the offering to the Father; this is reserved for the Son in the ascension.[47] The basic elements of Anselm's theory of justice are thus all in place in individual passages of Scripture. It seems to me that this vision also fits the Old Testament narrative of a God who graciously gives creation to Adam and Eve, a promise to Abraham, and

magisterium" (107). Abuses past and present must be owned and remedied by guilty Christians, but it is unclear that satisfaction theory is a major or necessary contributor to such concerns.

43. For example, many Asian cultures emphasize honor and shame in a way that mirrors Anselm's thought. Connections between Asian conceptions of the consequences of sin and Anselm's theology are made by S. Chan, *Grassroots Asian Theology*, 66–67; Park, *Wounded Heart of God*, 112–14.

44. Slotemaker, *Anselm of Canterbury*, 8. Slotemaker points out that Anselm would have recited the entirety of the Psalms once a week.

45. Khaled Anatolios notes that the medieval eucharistic liturgy included a doxology to give honor and glory to God, drawing on parallels between glorifying and honoring God in Scripture. Anatolios, *Deification Through the Cross*, 272. See also D. Brown, "Anselm on Atonement," 294–95.

46. In fact, categories of honor and shame may be more widespread in Scripture than is often recognized. See, for example, Lau, *Defending Shame*.

47. The point is made nicely in Alexander, *Face to Face with God*, 83–84. Where high priests served to bring the sacrifice into the holy of holies, they did so as a shadow of Christ, bringing a typological offering into a shadow of the heavenly dwelling of God.

a covenant to Moses and Israel; who sets terms within this creation, promised land, and covenant that are God-honoring; and who takes action to correct the failings of Adam, Abraham, Moses, and Israel after they fail to respond within the context of this gift as expected. The final, determinative act of satisfaction occurs on the cross of Christ.

Why Could God Not Simply Forgive?

Granting that there are biblical foundations for Anselm's notion of justice, one still might object that God should have simply forgiven our sins without atonement. For example, Derek Kubilus points to Jesus's Sermon on the Mount, where our Messiah commands us to love our enemies, being perfect like our heavenly Father (Matt. 5:43–48). Kubilus asks, "How could Jesus tell us to love our enemies in imitation of God, if God doesn't also love God's enemies?"[48] In Kubilus's eyes, Anselm's focus on justice unnecessarily constrains God's love.[49] Further, if the cross was about Jesus absorbing God's wrath, then the "gospel of the forgiveness of sins is a lie," for sin has not been forgiven but only wrongly transferred to "an innocent party."[50] Much earlier, the Socinians had similar concerns. Faustus Socinus, for example, argued that God as absolute Lord could forgive without requiring satisfaction, while he simultaneously critiqued the logic of satisfaction altogether.[51] The assumption that satisfaction is necessary is a crucial dimension of Anselm's argument. If this step of the argument fails, so does Anselm's entire understanding of atonement.

Anselm provides several reasons why God would not simply forgive. If God forgave without any recompense, then the sinner and saint would unjustly have similar standing. In fact, the sinner, who broke the law without consequence, would be in a condition of greater freedom than the one who followed the law. This is because the sinner would not be constrained by any law, where the righteous would be. This would put the sinner on an equal standing to God, for both would not be under any law. Anselm even directly addresses Kubilus's argument, claiming that God's teaching to forgive those who sin against us (Matt. 18:21–22; Eph. 4:32) is due to the fact that vengeance belongs to the Lord alone (Deut. 32:35; Ps. 94:1; Rom. 12:19).[52] Later theologians added their own reasons why God could not forgive without satisfaction. For example,

48. Kubilus, *Holy Hell*, 57–58.
49. Kubilus, *Holy Hell*, 54–55.
50. Kubilus, *Holy Hell*, 59.
51. For a summary of Socinus's arguments, see Gomes, "*De Jesu Christo Servatore*."
52. Anselm of Canterbury, *Why God Became Man* 1.12.

Wilhelmus à Brakel argues that forgiveness without satisfaction would not fit with the truthfulness of God, who said that he will not clear the guilty (Exod. 34:7; cf. Nah. 1:2) and who promised a curse for those who break the law (Deut. 27:26; cf. Gen. 2:17).[53]

Such arguments add weight to satisfaction theories of atonement, but they are not in themselves complete. Consider this possible response to à Brakel's argument: Yes, God's truthfulness demands that he not lie when he says he will not clear the guilty, but why did he make such a claim in the first place? The fundamental issue is one of justice and the question of how justice relates to divine love, and so we must develop a brief understanding of these divine attributes. God is not merely a creditor who can cancel a debt or three persons who are holding a grudge; rather, God is the perfect judge of the universe (e.g., Pss. 7:11; 50:6; Isa. 33:22), and as judge he must be impartial and just. As Fleming Rutledge explains, Anselm is showing that "a society of impunity is intolerable. If sin is not exposed, named, and renounced, then there has been no justice and God is dishonored."[54] Yet God is also love (1 John 4:8). Does this emphasis on justice merely detract from a theology of divine love? God's simplicity undermines such a contrast, for if God is his attributes, then divine justice is divine love.[55] How, then, do we explain why a loving God still demands satisfaction?

One approach would be to clarify Anselm's concept of justice, something that is frustratingly underdeveloped in his book on the atonement, *Why God Became Man*. Bernard van Vreeswijk appeals to Anselm's other works to clarify the monk's thoughts on divine justice. First, we might consider Anselm's *Proslogion*, which understands God as that than which nothing greater can be thought. On this account, divine justice would require that he act in a manner that could not be superior.[56] Anselm argues that a God who is merciful is greater than a God who is not, but a God who is just is also greater than one who is not. Thus, we can conclude that God must be both merciful and just, something provided more clearly in satisfaction than in merely forgiving sins.[57] Similarly, Anselm's *On Truth* explains that God's justice is identical

---

53. À Brakel, *Christian's Reasonable Service*, 1:471.

54. Rutledge, *Crucifixion*, 152–53.

55. See Vidu, *Atonement, Law, and Justice*, 236–38.

56. Van Vreeswijk, "Divine Justice," 420–21. See Anselm of Canterbury, *Proslogion* §§9–11.

57. Anselm of Canterbury, *Proslogion* §10. Regarding the "necessity" of *Why God Became Man*, Fleming Rutledge clarifies: "Anselm is not speaking of necessity in the way we might think. Nothing is 'necessary' for God in the sense of logical steps that he is bound by some external force to follow. Rather, it is *ontological* necessity—it arises out of God's own gracious nature, which he cannot deny." Rutledge, *Crucifixion*, 156.

with his nature.[58] Here, Anselm explains that justice involves (1) knowing and (2) willing rectitude / the good (3) for the sake of rectitude / the good.[59] In God, "will and rectitude do not differ," so God's willing the good is merely God being what he is.[60] In his treatment of satisfaction, Anselm does not consider God's justice as acting to maximize his greatness,[61] but we can make the connection explicit. God's justice is God's love since it would not be true to God's maximal nature to show only mercy but not justice. Such a divide between the two attributes cannot exist.[62]

While simplicity appeals to the divine nature to provide ontological reasons for why God could not simply forgive, readers might benefit from explanations that focus more on the human perspective, showing the need for satisfaction by linking God's justice, love, and divine forgiveness. Eleonore Stump offers a helpful explanation of the need for satisfaction. Drawing on Thomas Aquinas's definition of love, which is desiring the good of the other and desiring union with the other,[63] Stump argues that one could hypothetically forgive without retribution but that in some circumstances punishment might still be demanded. For example, it might be for the good of the sinner that retribution occurs. If the sinner is truly repentant, then they would likely desire that justice be done. If they were unrepentant, seeing the outflow of justice might help them move to repentance.[64] As Richard Watson explained centuries earlier, God's benevolence was the basis for atonement because "opposition to the will of God . . . must be the source of misery to the offender."[65] Nor can sins merely be forgiven, because when creatures act contrary to God's law, they act contrary to their own benefit, since God's law is good. If God forgave without punishment, it might entice creatures to further sin, which would be harmful to them.[66] Satisfaction meets the demands of justice in a

---

58. Van Vreeswijk, "Divine Justice," 423.

59. This is my summary of Anselm of Canterbury, *On Truth* §12. Anselm emphasizes knowing the good less in his definition, "Justice is rectitude of will preserved for its own sake," but he treats knowing as a prerequisite of being good.

60. Anselm of Canterbury, *On Truth* §12.

61. Van Vreeswijk points to *Why God Became Man* 1.12, 1.13, 1.15, and 2.4 as places where Anselm comes close to this definition. Van Vreeswijk suggests that failure to fully incorporate this insight may be due to a hurried release of the work after the incomplete manuscript was published without his consent. Van Vreeswijk, "Divine Justice," 424–27.

62. A similar perspective to van Vreeswijk's is found in Hunter, *If Adam Had Not Sinned*, 49–52.

63. Stump contrasts Aquinas and Anselm here, taking a rather sharp stance against Anselm, who purportedly emphasizes justice, against Aquinas, who emphasizes love. See Stump, *Atonement*, 70–80. I am not convinced that we can draw quite so sharp of a contrast.

64. Stump, *Atonement*, 90–91.

65. Watson, *Theological Institutes*, 8.

66. Watson, *Theological Institutes*, 12–13.

loving way, by showing the seriousness of sin—this is sometimes distinguished as the **governmental theory** of atonement—and by enticing the repentance of the sinner who can be moved by the love of God displayed on the cross.

God's loving justice in satisfaction is still properly called forgiveness in three ways, as illustrated again by appeal to Watson's theology.[67] First, God graciously sent his Son, and the Son voluntarily came to die, meaning that God initiated reconciliation. Second, God graciously accepts "the mediation of a third person." Third, when the sinner accepts this satisfaction, they are reconciled.[68] God is thus forgiving insofar as he graciously initiates reconciliation, willingly accepts a substitute payment, and truly imputes righteousness to the believer who by faith receives Christ. Further, as Joseph Pohle notes, Paul himself seems to combine payment and grace in Romans 3:24—"They are justified freely by his grace through the redemption that is in Christ Jesus."[69] The tension between grace and just payment is a biblical one. We can thus see that the death of Christ is a result of God's love *and* God's justice, which are one in the perfectly simple God.

Does Satisfaction Atonement Foster Injustice?

I have offered theological responses to those who see satisfaction as a feudal remnant hiding the purportedly deeper love of a God who forgives without atonement. Analysis shows satisfaction theory can weather these intellectual challenges. Yet many of the concerns regarding satisfaction theory have more to do with the ethical implications of the view of justice offered by Anselm and his heirs. I will briefly survey some of the primary objections before turning to offer brief responses to these objections.[70]

Painting with a broad brush, ethical concerns about satisfaction atonement tend to address the potential social harms these systems can produce. In the world of criminal justice, there is often concern that focus on retributive justice on the cross leads to overly harsh prison sentencing.[71] There is some evidence of

---

67. Watson's focus in this argument is technically reconciliation, but the ideas apply equally well to forgiveness.

68. Watson, *Theological Institutes*, 50.

69. Pohle, *Soteriology*, 38.

70. The focus of this book is dogmatic theology, not moral theology, though the two disciplines are inescapably connected. Yet the focus of the work means that my treatment of these ethical objections will be more cursory.

71. Marshall, *Beyond Retribution*, 44–45, 59–60; Gilliard, *Rethinking Incarceration*, 137–68. Gilliard distinguishes between Anselmian satisfaction theory and penal substitution, arguing that the latter is the main problem. Yet there is a clear link between the two theories, with biblical warrant for seeing the cross as both punishment and repayment by satisfaction. Further analysis is necessary.

such a correlation.[72] Modern theologians, especially feminist theologians, have raised concerns about theologies that treat a divine Father as the cause of the Son's death on the cross for God's creaturely children. Rita Nakashima Brock puts the concern as follows: "Such doctrines of salvation reflect by analogy, I believe, images of the neglect of children or, even worse, child abuse, making it acceptable as divine behavior—cosmic child abuse, as it were. The father allows, or even inflicts, the death of his only perfect son. The emphasis is on the goodness and power of the father and the unworthiness and powerlessness of his children, so that the father's punishment is just, and children are to blame."[73]

Granting the real concerns about cases where teaching satisfaction and penal substitutionary atonement fail to produce orthopraxis and orthopathy, it is important to recognize that failures can exist under other atonement theories as well. Eliminating ideas about satisfaction and substitution and replacing them with ideas deemed morally superior would not guarantee the elimination of sin and evil in Christian contexts. Consider the example of postapartheid South Africa, where centuries of racial discrimination and segregation, often violently enforced, came to an end. Desmond Tutu warns that the concepts of reconciliation and peace can be used "to justify evil." In the name of reconciliation, one might demand forgiveness before injustice has been resolved. Tutu appeals to the logic of the cross: "Christ is our peace, who bought at a great price His own death on the Cross. That is what real reconciliation has cost."[74] The costly nature of satisfaction can lead to the orthopraxy of Christians doing the serious work required for genuine reconciliation. Most aspects of atonement can be misinterpreted, leading to problems. For example, governmental theory's display of the seriousness of sin could lead to similar disciplinary harshness in church, state, or family settings. **Christus Victor** atonement, which focuses on Christ's triumph over sin, Satan, and death, can move in problematic directions due to the militaristic elements of the model. Genuine caution is needed.

Given the fact that some ethical risk exists on all sides for doctrines of the atonement, it is better to put theological safeguards in place against misapplications than to reject atonement theories on the grounds of ethical worries alone, particularly since satisfaction and substitution are so firmly attested in the Bible. A full response to each concern is beyond the scope of this work, but several initial premises are helpful. First, as Scripture recurringly reminds

---

72. Gilliard points to C. S. Lewis explicitly arguing for punitive theories of criminal justice. Gilliard, *Rethinking Incarceration*, 157–58.

73. Brock, *Journeys by Heart*, 56. Brock believes substitutionary views often develop a picture of the loving, forgiving father that are not accurate to reality.

74. Tutu, "Spirituality," 164.

us, Christ's atoning death was "once for all" (Rom. 6:10; Heb. 7:27; 9:12; 10:10),[75] one of many features leading to the affirmation that Christ alone (*solus Christus*) is our satisfaction. On this basis, the death of Christ must be understood as different from an earthly penal system, from a marriage, or from any other analogue. Of course, this is only a partial resolution to the problem since the cross certainly remains paradigmatic for Christians (Matt. 10:38; 16:24–25; Mark 8:34; Luke 9:23; 14:27). The point is not to remove Christ from ethics but to problematize a simple correlation that would say, "Christ suffers, so I must suffer" or "The cross reveals the need for harsh punishment."[76] Second, only God is a perfectly good and just judge (Mark 10:18), so, if nothing else, the partiality, ignorance, and immorality of other judges warrant a lessening of punitive measures to protect the wrongfully accused.[77] Similarly, authorities in the family, church, or state ought not equate themselves too sharply with God. Third, the doctrine of inseparable operations further separates the cross from other examples of authority, discipline, or power. The doctrine of inseparable operations entails that through their shared divine nature the Father, Son, and Spirit providentially coordinate the events leading to the crucifixion, while the Son in his human nature suffers and dies on the cross. Thus, the Son is in control of his own suffering in ways that no human who suffers can be.[78] Combined, these brief treatments begin to provide the needed safeguards. Mentioning inseparable operations also points to the important work of integrating the atonement with the doctrines of the Trinity and hypostatic union, a task to which we now turn.

God's Wrath, the Cross, and the Trinity

A theologian might pursue various paths to connect the doctrines of the Trinity and atonement. Fred Sanders proposes "two basic options" for

75. These verses all use the word *ephapax*—once for all—to describe Christ's death. Elsewhere it is emphasized that Christ suffered once (*hapax*) for our sins (1 Pet. 3:18), appeared once (Heb. 9:26), and was offered once to bear our sins (Heb. 9:28).

76. J. Denny Weaver argues that defense of this sort "leaves us with a view of Jesus that is not useful for ethics." Weaver, "Narrative *Christus Victor*," 14.

77. Such human limitations have been an important focal point in the argument to restrict the death penalty, even among conservative ethical commentators. See Feinberg and Feinberg, *Ethics for a Brave New World*, 241–42, 249–50. Feinberg and Feinberg note the racial and socioeconomic imbalances of capital punishment. Though they defend the death penalty, they argue for "demands for proof of guilt" that are "much more stringent than current judicial procedures," which would effectively reduce instances of the death penalty. (Note that there is more to the moral basis for emphasizing restitution over retribution than the limitations of human judges.)

78. For a full version of this argument, see K. Johnson, "Penal Substitution."

correlating Trinity and atonement: "placing the Trinity within the atonement" and "placing the atonement within the Trinity."[79] The former schema often manifests in the epistemological maxim that we know the Trinity through the missions of the Son and Spirit. In its problematic forms, the latter schema can often internalize atonement into the Trinity such that the cross is something that happens in the inner life of the Trinity, perhaps even rupturing the Trinity in some sense.[80] This modern phenomenon is to be distinguished from the ancient heresy of patripassianism, which lacked an adequate distinction between the Father and Son, thereby confusing the persons and teaching that the Father is the Son and so suffered and died on the cross. The modern theology I am addressing is a particular variant of penal substitution that sees the wrath of God as so prominent that "Jesus suffers dying in forsakenness" as an "event between God and God," to use Moltmann's terminology.[81] In such theologies, appeal is often made to Paul's teaching that God "made him to be sin who knew no sin" (2 Cor. 5:21 NRSV) and "Christ redeemed us from the curse of the law by becoming a curse for us" (Gal. 3:13).[82] Such texts could be taken to mean that Christ was punished and cursed on the cross in such a way that he became sin of the sort that could not be in the presence of the infinitely holy Father. Exegetically, it is possible to translate 2 Corinthians 5:21 in a less startling manner: Christ was a "sin offering."[83] This would fit with the broad theology of Christ as sacrifice discussed at the beginning of the chapter. More theological analysis is necessary to resolve the issue.

One of the most interesting modern examples of theology incorporating atonement into the Trinity is the Japanese theologian Kazoh Kitamori, who draws on Jeremiah 31:20 to describe God being in pain and so acting in mercy.[84] Kitamori argues that "the pain of God reflects his will to love the object of his wrath."[85] When God loves what he is wrathful toward, the result is pain

---

79. Sanders, *Fountain of Salvation*, 57.

80. The most well-known example is Moltmann, *Crucified God*.

81. Moltmann, *Crucified God*, 243–44.

82. E.g., Moltmann, *Crucified God*, 242. The pattern is widespread.

83. It may be that Paul has Isa. 53:10 in the back of his mind in 2 Cor. 5:21. The former passage more clearly references a sin offering. See Martin, *2 Corinthians*, 317. The point is made with patristic reference in McCall, *Forsaken*, 23–24.

84. Where many modern interpretations translate Jer. 31:20 to say that God's heart yearns for Ephraim, the King James Version better captures Kitamori's understanding when it depicts God saying, "My bowels are troubled for him; I will surely have mercy upon him, saith the Lord." Jeremiah 31:20 is translated in the Japanese Literary Version as "For his sake, my insides are in pain." Of course, the sense is imperfectly conveyed here since I am providing the JLV translated back into English by How Chuang Chua. See Chuang Chua, *Death of Christ*, 100–101.

85. Kitamori, *Pain of God*, 21.

as the Son bears the wrath in history in our stead.[86] "The cross is in no sense an external act of God, but an act within himself,"[87] says Kitamori, and he treats it as even more basic to the Trinity than ideas like eternal generation and consubstantiality, which are in his mind too abstract and detached from the cross.[88] Like many theologians who adopt such internalizations of the Trinity within atonement, Kitamori develops his theology in the context of events of painful suffering that he witnessed, ultimately concluding that a God who has pain offers the sufferer more consolation.[89] Through the cross, the Christian sufferer's pain witnesses to God and results in a mysticism whereby we recognize our sin but also the ever more prevailing love of God that heals us through the medium of pain.[90] This, then, is how Kitamori interprets substitutionary atonement: "The Lord was unable to resolve our death without putting himself to death. God himself was broken, was wounded, and suffered, because he embraced those who should not be embraced. By embracing our reality, God grants us absolute peace. *But the peace has been completely taken away from the Lord who grants us absolute peace.* 'My God, My God, why hast thou forsaken me?'"[91]

Like many other theologians who see the cross as something happening within the Trinity, Kitamori here appeals to Jesus using the words of Psalm 22:1 on the cross (Matt. 27:46; Mark 15:33–34). Some argue that Jesus would assume the listener (or the reader of Mark's Gospel) would bring the entire psalm to mind.[92] After all, the psalm ends on a positive note: "You answered me! I will proclaim your name to my brothers and sisters; I will praise you in the assembly" (Ps. 22:21b–22), moving on to extol the Lord until verse 31. In support of this thesis, the passion narrative in Mark is filled with references to Psalm 22, often using the exact wording of the Septuagint. Examples include casting lots for Jesus's clothing (Mark 15:24; Ps. 22:19 [21:19 LXX]), the phrasing "save yourself" (Mark 15:30; Ps. 21:21 LXX), "He saved others" (Mark 15:31; Ps. 21:9 LXX), and they "reviled him" (Mark 15:32 ESV; Ps. 21:7 LXX).[93] It seems likely that Mark had the entirety of Psalm 22 in mind.

86. Kitamori, *Pain of God*, 34.
87. Kitamori, *Pain of God*, 45.
88. "God the Father who simply begets his Son lacks something decisive: the *pain* of God." Kitamori, *Pain of God*, 47. Elsewhere, Kitamori argues that using Nicaea's ontological language is a risk because it seems to preclude the suffering of God. See Kitamori, "Pain in Christology," 85.
89. Chuang Chua details these helpfully, describing Kitamori's firsthand experience of several tragic deaths, including a child being killed by the train Kitamori rode to seminary. Chuang Chua, *Death of Christ*, 83–86.
90. Kitamori, *Pain of God*, 60, 76, 83.
91. Kitamori, *Pain of God*, 22.
92. For example, McCall, *Forsaken*, 41.
93. Shively, "Israel's Scriptures in Mark," 257.

Moreover, Jesus had already predicted his death and resurrection three times (Mark 8:31; 9:30–31; 10:33–34), showing that he knew not to give up hope on the cross. Looking more extensively at the canon, it is noteworthy that Jesus's final words in Luke and John are hopeful, not the despair of a Son whose relationship with his eternal Father has been broken.[94] Claims like Moltmann's that the cross results in "the death of [the Father's] Fatherhood" while the Son suffers "abandonment" and is "Godforsaken" move well beyond what the text of the Bible indicates.[95] Kitamori's theology is more subtle, so further theological and pastoral consideration is needed.

Kitamori sees the theology of the pain of God as the means of resolving our human pain by the divine pain overcoming God's wrath.[96] I am not convinced by his use of Psalm 22, but I must grant that language describing God that could be interpreted as pain is found in Scripture (e.g., Gen. 6:6). Historically, many have interpreted such statements as anthropopathisms—statements depicting God in a human manner so we can understand but not literal reflections of the mental states of God—if it is even appropriate to use language like "mental states" to speak of an infinite, eternal, omniscient being like God.[97] At the level of systematic theology, it is unclear how pain and suffering easily fit with a simple, perfect, and eternal God, though that full argument lies well outside the context of atonement. More closely related to atonement, however, is the fact that Kitamori's theology implies that God needed the cross to resolve his pain. "The cross is in no sense an external act of God, but an act within himself," such that the pain of God is "necessary to his essence." If this pain of the cross overcomes God's wrath, resolving divine pain, then the cross was necessary for God to overcome his pain. This might indicate that the cross is not a matter of grace but of necessity for God—the pain of God is "necessary to his essence," says Kitamori.[98]

---

94. "Father, into your hands I commit my spirit" (Luke 23:46 NIV), and "It is finished" (John 19:30).

95. Moltmann, *Crucified God*, 243.

96. I worry that I overstate the matter here. Chuang Chua interprets Kitamori: "For Kitamori, the pain of God is not a synthesis that resolves completely the contradiction between divine love and divine wrath. Rather, the divine pain is altogether a different, and unresolved, 'third thing' or 'tertium' that is generated by the chemistry between divine love and divine pain." Chuang Chua, *Death of Christ*, 97. Yet the English translation of Kitamori uses the language of "resolving" and "overcoming." Kitamori, *Pain of God*, 20, 109. I decided to rely on the translator more than Chuang Chua the interpreter, though I am unable to fully adjudicate the debate since I do not read Japanese.

97. Kitamori is not alone in his claim that love requires suffering. See Fiddes, *Creative Suffering of God*. Yet there are many recent defenses of impassibility. See, for example, Baines et al., *Confessing the Impassible God*.

98. Kitamori, *Pain of God*, 45.

One might rescue Kitamori's theology by appealing to the Scholastic idea of consequent necessity to suggest that God's pain is only necessary because of his choice to create a world in which his wrath toward the objects of his love must be resolved by the cross.[99] Still, the result is different from Anselmian atonement in that the consequent necessity is not a result of God being bound to act according to his maximally just and loving character. Rather, it would be a consequent necessity that God needed the cross to resolve his pain. The necessity would be consequent and yet still seemingly one that undermined the cross as divine gift, construing it instead as a divine/human exchange, where each is healed in different ways. Alternatively, one might take Kitamori to mean that God is eternally in pain, which raises the question of how this theology actually offers hope in the face of suffering.[100]

With the subject of hope we come to the pastoral heart of the theology of the cross. It is important to note that Jesus's cry, "My God, my God, why have you forsaken me?" (Matt. 27:46; Mark 15:33–34 NIV)—often called the cry of dereliction—is arguably part of the genre of lament. As Emmanuel Katongole explains, lament is "a way to name what is going on, to stand, to hope, and to engage God in the midst of ruins."[101] Katongole points to the sudden expression of hope found in Lamentations 3:21–25, where "the man who has seen affliction under the rod of God's wrath" (Lam. 3:1) suddenly proclaims reason to hope due to the Lord's love and mercy. One might also point to a similar hope in Psalm 22. The very act of crying out to God implies the hope that there may be an answer, so it is possible to interpret Jesus to be modeling hope-amid-distress on the cross, subtle though it may be in Matthew's or Mark's narration. Such hope offers an orthopathic response to suffering without denying the right to express to God whatever emotions or doubts one may be feeling. Expressing what one is feeling and narrating the suffering can be an important therapeutic tool that resolves pain and even embodied trauma.[102] To summarize, I do not see sufficient exegetical, dogmatic,

---

99. This would still differ from Anselm because the consequent necessity he claimed does not pertain to the divine essence.

100. I do not mean to disparage any spiritual benefit that Kitamori received from these insights, and he attests to the benefits being strong. Rather, I suspect that the benefit is contrary to the logic of his thought and not entailed by it.

101. Katongole, *Born from Lament*, 45.

102. As theologian and licensed counselor Jennifer Baldwin explains, the presence or absence of trauma after a crisis event may depend in large part on the social response and presence or absence of social support that an individual encounters. Baldwin advocates a trauma-sensitive theology that prioritizes bodily experience, accepts trauma narratives, affirms "human psychological multiplicity," and has faith in trauma survivors' resilience. Communities that allow lament allow space to accept trauma narratives and offer social support, while the expressing of emotion itself can reduce the embodied stress of suffering. Although I find great insight in

or pastoral basis for affirming a real pain in God, nor do I see reason to affirm that the relationship between the Father and Son was one of hostility or one in which the loving relationship of the Father and Son was broken.

How then do we relate substitutionary atonement and satisfaction to the Trinity?

Sometimes Anselmian atonement theologies are criticized for making God the object of atonement rather than the primary agent of salvation.[103] When considering God from the relational perspective of the Trinity, this is no problem, for the Son is the subject of atonement and the Father the object insofar as satisfaction brings humanity into the eternal Father-Son relationship. But considering the inseparable operations of the Godhead, such a conception might lead us to wrongly conclude that Christ's humanity alone is the agent of redemption. Far better to conceive of humanity's role in the mission of Christ as Adonis Vidu suggests, where the inseparable operations of God in redemption history refract like light through a prism such that the atonement is a joint trinitarian action, yet the distinct created terms of God's work such as Christ's body pierced for us or the Spirit's indwelling of us are a by-product of the triune God's engagement with us in and through creation.[104]

Does the doctrine of inseparable operations mean that the historical unfolding of the atonement is detached from the eternal reality of God? Is anything in God analogous to what happens on the cross? Perhaps the most helpful case study of this concerns justice, a central focus of the cross. Does justice pertain to the Trinity *ad intra*? Nicholas Wolterstorff helpfully explains that there is no "meting out justice" or "rendering judgment" in the Trinity, since the divine persons do not sin and are not in conflict.[105] There is no justice in the Trinity in this respect. If justice refers to "treat[ing] each other with due respect for their worth," then of course there would be justice in the Trinity.[106] Justice is understood as rendering to each one what is due, and each person of the Trinity is due and so receives honor, glory, and love from each other person. On this account, God simply is the eternal triune act of offering mutual love, honor, and glory between Father, Son, and Holy Spirit. Perhaps when God breathed on Adam (Gen. 2:7), the Holy Spirit filled Adam with a created human spirit[107] such that Adam (and shortly thereafter Eve)

Baldwin's pastoral theology, her dogmatic theology embraces divine change in a way that I fear undermines the pastoral point. Baldwin, *Trauma-Sensitive Theology*, 7, 26. See also Switzer, *Minister as Crisis Counselor*, 146.

103. See Aulén, *Christus Victor*.
104. Vidu, *Same God*, 236.
105. Wolterstorff, "Justice in the Trinity?," 177.
106. Wolterstorff, "Justice in the Trinity?," 185.
107. The same word is used for breath and Spirit. This is a venerable interpretation.

joined in loving, honoring, and glorifying God, as was proper. After the fall, this original righteousness was lost, and atonement was needed. God could not simply ignore that honor was not given, for to fail to give this honor, glory, and love would be to fail to live in harmony with the very nature of the triune God. Satisfaction can thus be understood as the en-humaned Son offering what was owed to the Father and thereby bringing humanity back into the communion of the Trinity (John 17). To put this another way, God the Son acted according to the maximal divine nature such that humans could again be partakers of that nature (2 Pet. 1:4). This, then, is a sound trinitarian interpretation of the atonement, but it is also an entryway into the question of how the hypostatic union clarifies the satisfaction offered on the cross.

The Hypostatic Union and the Cross

The joint work of the human and divine natures of Christ in atonement has also been an important point of debate in Christian history. Several key points will be briefly mentioned here. First, from the Second Council of Constantinople, we have the affirmation that "one of the Trinity" was "crucified in the flesh."[108] This affirmation preserves the unity of the person of the Son and ensures that it is only God who saves, as is taught in Scripture (Ps. 3:8; Isa. 43:11). Yet this statement leaves unresolved the question of how the divine persons relate to one another in the act of substitutionary atonement. Here, church history has been marked by several lesser-known theological conflicts. In the Byzantine era, we see a debate between Soterichos Panteugenos and Nicholas of Methone regarding how the two natures relate to the sacrifice of Christ. Panteugenos worried that if the Son were said to offer the sacrifice as a human but receive it as one member of the Trinity that you would have opposed actions in Christ (offering and receiving), resulting in Nestorianism. Nicholas countered that the ongoing distinction of natures in the hypostatic union is precisely what allowed the Son to perform the human act of offering and the divine of receiving.[109] The Synodal Tome of 1157 resolved the issue: "When Christ sacrificed himself willingly, He offered himself as a man and He received the sacrifice as God, together with the Father and the Holy Spirit."[110] To my mind, both sides of the debate are rooted in a legitimate

---

108. Canon 9 in Denzinger, *Sources of Catholic Dogma*, 88.

109. Meyendorff, *Byzantine Theology*, 40. Sadly, it is difficult to find lengthy treatments of the debate.

110. Translation quoted in Spingou, "Platonising Dialogue," 124. For a slightly fuller text (in French), see Grumel, *Des Actes du Patriarcat*, 498. The official acts of the council are too brief to provide an adequate theological analysis of the dispute.

concern, even if Panteugenos's was likely the more imbalanced position. We must preserve the unity of Christ so that the Son in his deity is involved in the satisfaction offered to the Father. Otherwise, a merely human offering would be insufficient. The dyothelite account of theandric agency developed in the previous chapter demands such action be rooted in the operations of both natures as well. The Synodal Tome of 1157 does not adequately protect these theological needs. I have attempted to offer more precision in speaking of satisfaction involving the humanity of Christ being drawn into the relational and reciprocal honoring of the persons of the Trinity. In this way Christians incorporated into Christ by the Spirit have communion with the Father. At the same time, Panteugenos is mistaken to believe that the Father could receive the sacrifice without the Son, for such would undermine inseparable operations and, ultimately, the unity of the Trinity. As the synod noted, it was not merely the Father who did not receive the honor due him but also the Son and Spirit.[111]

Similar disputes are found centuries later between Lutheran and Reformed theologians, especially during the era of Protestant Scholasticism. For example, Abraham Calov insists that "Christ is the *hilasmos* [atonement] according to both natures, that is, divine and human." Citing biblical evidence that Jesus offers flesh (John 6:51; cf. Rom. 8:3; 1 Pet. 2:24) and that it was also the "author of life" who was killed (Acts 3:15 NIV), Calov expresses concern about some Reformed theologians who attribute the sacrifice to Christ's humanity alone.[112] Yet some among the Reformed could rightly worry about the need to distinguish between the divine and human natures, a distinction sometimes insufficient in Lutheran theology.[113] The satisfaction offered on the cross must be seen as an offering of both natures, but the sort of offering made must be distinguished to ensure the distinction of natures.

Perhaps the issue may be further clarified by distinguishing between the passive and active obedience of Christ. "Active obedience" refers to Christ's perfect fulfillment of the law (Matt. 5:17), while "passive obedience" refers to Christ's voluntary death on the cross. Abraham Calov would distinguish the two in terms of active obedience atoning for guilt by the power of a sinless life, while passive obedience atones for punishment.[114] This should be supplemented by noting that passive obedience is also the basis for satisfaction,

111. Grumel, *Des Actes du Patriarcat*, 498.
112. Calov, *Propitiation* 2.2.2.
113. I will consider this debate between Reformed and Lutheran theologians on the work of Christ in atonement more heavily in chapter 10 in terms of the ongoing ministry of Christ after the ascension.
114. Calov, *Propitiation* 2.6.1.

which is conceptually distinct from punishment.[115] Regardless, Christ's active obedience is a result of the cooperative work of the human and divine natures and wills, each contributing what is proper to it to result in the sinless life of Christ. In terms of passive obedience only the human nature suffered death, both physical death and, as we shall see in the next chapter, a form of the tragic spiritual death that is the separation of soul from body. The divine nature is not limited by a soul or body in a manner that would allow it to undergo such death. Yet because this death was the death of a divine *person*, we can still properly speak of the death of God according to the communication of idioms.

If we consider specifically what the Son offered the Father on the cross, we must continue to analyze the cross according to the principles already discussed in earlier chapters. Recall, first, that kenosis refers to the Son humbly taking an inferior nature into his divine hypostasis without change. Second, we must remember the principles of dyoenergism—every incarnate act was an act of both natures in the one hypostasis. Given this, we can say that the Son made a twofold offering to the Father. In his deity, the begotten Son offered the Father the same mutual love and glory as had been offered eternally in the mutual relation between the two persons. I think we can go slightly further: The cross was an instrument of death, but it was also an instrument of shame.[116] On the cross, the divine nature did not die or feel pain, but in the person of the Son, deity was subjected to the ridicule of the crowds and authorities (e.g., Matt. 27:29; Mark 14:65; 15:17, 29–30; Luke 22:63; 23:11), though it is not as if this changed the divine nature in any way. This was a form of kenosis and recapitulation, as the divine Son accepted far less honor and glory than was due in the process of drawing humanity into the glory he had eternally given to the Father, thereby offering more glory and honor to God than any human could possibly deliver. On this account, we see two things offered to the Father by the divine person of the Son: (1) the glory he had eternally given to (and reciprocally received from) the Father and (2) self-humbling on the cross. The person of the Son is subjected to humiliation due to his humanity, a kenosis not of change but of immutable addition.[117] But since natures do not exist enhypostatically,

115. Satisfaction plays a more prominent role in my theology than in Calov's.

116. As Rutledge notes, excessive shame in punishment was prohibited between Israelites (Deut. 25:3), so the cross was quite a harsh punishment for God's Son to bear. Rutledge, *Crucifixion*, 79.

117. This shame should not be seen as an inhering property, as if the subsistent relation which is the person of the Son is changed in what it is—such would make the Trinity mutable. Rather, the shaming of the Son is best understood as a created, historical act toward the created,

it is truly the person of the Son accepting shame to the glory of the Father. We also see something offered from the Son in his humanity to the entire Trinity: human life. This is the christological balance of Philippians 2:8 ("He humbled himself by becoming obedient . . . on a cross"); this is the Son humbly accepting shame while honoring his Father ("to the point of death"); this is the humanity offering passive obedience to the entire Trinity. Yet the death is the death of a divine person, so God responds with exaltation (Phil. 2:9). With these christological reflections in hand, we can turn now to a dogmatic summary of satisfaction.

Dogmatic Summary

"Satisfaction" refers to the gracious acceptance of a substitutionary payment to atone for sin, resolving the sinner's indebtedness and thereby preventing the resulting consequences of eternal punishment and spiritual death. Christ alone could make satisfaction, for only a God-man could represent humanity while also offering something supererogatory in restitution. As such, Jesus is the supreme high priest and once-and-for-all sacrifice. The satisfaction offered on the cross is both necessary and gratuitous. By the logic of consequent necessity, once God chose to create a world that would fall into sin, he was necessarily also committed to redemption. However, the initial choice to create a world that would need redemption was a free, gratuitous choice. The cross is also gratuitous in three additional senses: (1) The sacrificed Son is given by God alone, (2) acceptance of a satisfaction is graciously accepted instead of strict legalism requiring payment by human sinners themselves, and (3) the merit of Christ earned on the cross is sufficient for justification such that Christians need to add no good works to be justified.

   Satisfaction should be understood within a trinitarian and christological framework. The Son has eternally honored and glorified the Father and Spirit, just as he has been honored and glorified, so when the Son takes on humanity, he brings a human nature into this reciprocal honoring, recapitulating Adam's role including through his death on the cross. Trinitarian theology does not permit speaking of the cross in such a way that the relationship between Father and Son is ruptured, nor does it allow us to contrast wrathful, loving, and/or just parts of the deity, since the triune God is perfectly simple. God is entirely loving and entirely just in requiring and accepting satisfaction. Christologically, the sacrifice of Christ must be seen as the joint work

---

historical human nature existing in the person of the Son, who is, as the bearer of this human nature, also the same eternal, begotten, consubstantial Son of the Father.

of both the human and divine operations in Christ. For example, in terms of substitution, the humanity of Christ suffers pain and death, but the deity through kenosis accepts ridicule that is contrary to what is owed to God.

Within the above dogmatic parameters, there is still room for debate on a number of points. Given some of the ambiguities of the doctrine of original sin, satisfaction likely involves the reversal of original guilt in addition to the removal of the effects of actual sin, but there is room for some disagreement. It is also likely that the cross offers not only expiation but propitiation, provided that one interprets propitiation to indicate not a change in God but only a perceived change from a human perspective. Those who hesitate to speak of propitiation to preserve divine immutability do so understandably. Further, there is room to disagree on whether the punishment suffered by Christ was exactly the same as or similar to what was owed to humans, provided that one does not explain the exact nature of the punishment in a way that undermines the Trinity. Finally, some theologians rightly highlight Christ's payment in personal form, from Son to Father, while others emphasize natural operations, from Christ's humanity to his deity shared with the Father and Spirit. There is some basis for speaking in both manners.

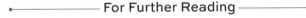

For Further Reading

Anderson, Gary A. *That I May Dwell Among Them: Incarnation and Atonement in the Tabernacle Narrative*. Eerdmans, 2023.

> Anderson offers a close reading of the tabernacle narratives in Exodus and Leviticus, illuminating the literary, historical, and theological contexts of important sacrificial and liturgical practices. The results are not obvious to most untrained modern readers. For example, Anderson fruitfully reveals the significance of repeated phrasing in groups of seven, something I had entirely missed in the text.

Kitamori, Kazoh. *Theology of the Pain of God*. 5th ed. Wipf & Stock, 2005.

> Though I have been critical of Kitamori's theology, his work has had such impact across the globe that it is important to read. Kitamori's theology of the pain of God is one of the more creative accounts of the cross, and it makes for a better dialogue partner than many other works on passibility.

McCall, Thomas H. *Forsaken: The Trinity and the Cross, and Why It Matters*. IVP Academic, 2012.

> McCall considers a number of important aspects of trinitarian theology and the atonement. McCall's robust yet accessible treatment of the cry of dereliction is particularly relevant for this chapter. I have had great success using this book with undergraduate students and in study with laity.

Vidu, Adonis. *Atonement, Law, and Justice: The Cross in Historical and Cultural Contexts*. Baker Academic, 2014.

Vidu's book helpfully surveys the Christian theology of atonement while focusing on what various historical theologians thought about justice. This focus allows Vidu to provide more detailed analysis of the assumptions behind various accounts of atonement.

CHAPTER NINE

Christus Victor

I n order to rightly understand the amazing scope of Christ's saving work, it is necessary to understand the full extent of human sin that demands a savior. Several chapters of *Christological Dogmatics* have already interpreted sin as more than merely wrong acts committed by individuals. Certainly, actual sin is an important target of Christ's saving work—we have seen how it is a central problem overcome in satisfaction. Yet the doctrine of sin must also consider original sin, remembering that original corruption is cleansed through union with Christ. Similarly, a doctrine of sin cannot remain individualistic, instead recognizing a theology of social sin that is fought by the inbreaking of the kingdom in Jesus's person, proclamation, and church. Yet these three dimensions of sin are still incomplete. I have yet to explore how individuals in sin are both guilty of wrong action and themselves victims. The complexity of sin in the individual is particularly clear in extreme situations of evil. For example, Emmanuel Katongole shows how child soldiers are both sinners committing atrocities and victims forced into military service.[1] Victimization occurs in the form of harm done to us by individuals, a theme prevalent in cries for deliverance in the Psalms (e.g., Ps. 59). A close reading of Scripture also reveals that human beings are victims of the power of sin apart from any particular harmful acts from other human persons.

Though its interpretation is hotly contested, Romans 7 remains the best place in Scripture to illustrate sin as a power. Paul famously says, "I do not understand what I am doing, because I do not practice what I want to do,

---

1. Katongole, *Born from Lament*, 10, 92. Katongole speaks of "the double identity of the children who are caught between innocence and guilt, between being victims and perpetrators" (69).

but I do what I hate. . . . For I do not do the good that I want to do, but I practice the evil that I do not want to do" (7:15, 19). In Romans 7 sin acts (7:5, 8, 9, 11, 13, 17, 20). Importantly, the same verb is used throughout Romans 7 to describe sin bringing about evil and the "I" bringing about evil (see 7:8, 13, 15).[2] I worded the last sentence awkwardly on purpose, for there is no agreement about who is referenced when Paul says "I." Some suggest this is merely an autobiographical reference to Paul's prior life as a persecutor and murderer of Christians, not a description of the power of sin in humanity.[3] However, interpreting this passage in light of Romans 3 and 5, which center the universality of sin and original sin, respectively, it is difficult to perceive of this struggle as one merely proper to Paul. The main exegetical question about this passage is then whether the "I" who cannot help but sin refers to the Christian prior to conversion or whether it refers to an ongoing condition after conversion.[4] It may also echo the "I" of the Psalms, given the similar context of a speaker threatened by enemies and needing deliverance.[5] Resolution of this debate can be delayed for an analysis of the doctrine of sanctification. For present purposes, it is sufficient to show that in Romans, sin is a power that controls human beings before and perhaps after conversion.

Christ's saving work must be explained such that it is seen to overcome our victimization to sin. More than that, Christ's saving work must be seen to defeat all three enemies of the Christian: sin, death (1 Cor. 15:26), and the devil (1 Pet. 5:8). Though we might try to explain these victories as consequences of the payment made on the cross, this conceptuality would reduce the condition of sin to a condition of guilt, neglecting the places where Scripture describes sin as a power that reigned in death (Rom. 5:21). In fact, Paul's descriptions of Christ's saving work have two important components: Through Christ, God "erased the certificate of debt, with its obligations, that was against us and opposed to us, and has taken it away by nailing it to the cross" (Col. 2:14)—this is satisfaction. He also "disarmed the rulers

2. Noting this, Jewett writes, "A kind of co-sponsorship of evil is evidently in view, in which human action is at the same time performed by sin as an alien power, so that no evasion of responsibility is possible." Jewett, *Romans*, 462.

3. Jewett, *Romans*, 462–64. Jewett argues that Paul elsewhere assumes that the Christian ethic can be fulfilled, and he draws on prior work from Krister Stendahl and E. P. Sanders, who argue that Paul was not wresting with a general situation of guilt and sin arising from inability to fulfill the law. Yet, as Thomas Schreiner shows, there was Second Temple precedent for the claim that the law could not be fulfilled and that powers of good or evil warred in each person. See T. Schreiner, *Romans*, 371.

4. For a defense of "I" referencing the Christian before conversion, see Moo, *Romans*, 454–56. For a defense of this passage applying to all Christians, see L. Morris, *Romans*, 285–89.

5. See Gaventa, "Shape of the 'I.'"

and authorities and disgraced them publicly; he [the Father] triumphed over them in him [Christ]" (2:15). A proper account of atonement must therefore supplement satisfaction with an account of this victory. For this reason, this chapter will introduce atonement in terms of Christ's victory, beginning with a modern treatment known as Christus Victor, moving to consider Christ's victory through exorcism, then analyzing the contested doctrine of Christ's descent to the dead, and finally offering a biblical and dogmatic account of Christ's resurrection as victory.

Christus Victor Atonement

The terminology of "Christus Victor," if not necessarily the concept itself, comes from the twentieth-century Swedish theologian Gustaf Aulén, who was concerned that Anselmian atonement was discontinuous, meaning that God was the agent of salvation until the offering is made "to God by Christ as man and on man's behalf." In contrast, Aulén argued that Christus Victor was continuous in depicting the work of reconciliation as "from first to last a work of God himself."[6] In my estimation, Aulén fails to recognize the role of dyoenergism in satisfaction atonement—the work of salvation is wrought by Christ in his deity throughout, yet the humanity of the Son is also brought into eternal mutual glorification of Father, Son, and Spirit through the incarnation, such that the work is also a work of the human nature.[7] Nevertheless, Aulén does well to remind us that there is more to Christ's work than his providing satisfaction and being a moral example.

Aulén is correct to highlight an important piece of the biblical testimony to salvation. Colin Gunton points to the Gospel of John as a source of such testimony of the cross as victory: "John's gospel depicts the progress of Jesus to the cross as a movement of victorious conquest, certainly if it is right to interpret 19:30 ('It is finished') in the light of 16:33 ('Be of good cheer, I have overcome the world') as a cry of triumph."[8] The victory is continued in the

6. Aulén, *Christus Victor*, 21–22.

7. Aulén considers the possibility that in Anselm's theology it might be "God himself who restores his own honor," noting that if "this interpretation . . . is right, there is evidently insufficient ground for the sharp distinction that we have made between Anselm's theory and the classic [Christus Victor] idea of the atonement." Aulén, *Christus Victor*, 101. He contextualizes Anselm's atonement theology within the Catholic system of penance, not within medieval feudalism, but argues that this renders the incarnation a matter of dogma to affirm rather than a clear component of atonement. In Aulén's mind, God is only "partly the agent being the author of the plan" (105). This misses the clear dyoenergist dimensions of Anselm's thought, where the deity of Christ is operative not only in planning but in executing the work of satisfaction. See Aulén, *Christus Victor*, 98–105.

8. Gunton, *Actuality of Atonement*, 56.

lives of Christians (Rom. 8:37; 1 John 5:4), and the victory on the cross antici-pates the final eschatological victory of Jesus, the rider on the white horse who will "strike the nations" and "rule them" while "trampl[ing] the winepress of the fierce anger of God" (Rev. 19:15). Fleming Rutledge explains Christus Victor in the broader context of apocalyptic literature and theology, which focuses on God intervening in history to bring about a discontinuous change in history and a universal defeat of forces hostile to God.[9] This theology is not only a central theme of certain books like Revelation and Daniel; it is also an important aspect of Jesus's preaching.

Dogmatically, Christus Victor atonement recognizes that reconciliation requires more than the elimination of guilt. As Aulén notes, "Since the fellow-ship has been broken by the hostile power of evil, the reconciliation implies the destruction and subjugation of that power which separates God and the world."[10] Guilt must be removed, but full salvation also requires securing the safety of the people of God such that they are no longer vulnerable to attack from their enemies. As Aulén explains, Paul's theology of sin is closely linked with his theology of death, such that Paul understands both sin and death to be powers controlling humanity and to be linked with another system, "a great complex of demonic forces, 'principalities and powers' [Eph. 6:12], which Christ has overcome in the great conflict."[11] As noted in chapter 4, such powers and principalities have recently been associated with empires in theologies of social sin, a link with some biblical precedent (e.g., Dan. 10:12–21). Christ's saving work must therefore be seen to defeat all three enemies of the Christian—sin, death (1 Cor. 15:26), and the devil (1 Pet. 5:8)—with some additional attention paid to earthly powers opposed to God.

Jesus and Evil Spirits

Demons are supernatural entities that are subject to Satan,[12] doing his bid-ding particularly through the possession of individuals who are afflicted with various forms of suffering as a result. New Testament depictions of demons sometimes present them as parasitic, seemingly needing a host.[13]

---

9. Rutledge, *Crucifixion*, 353–66.

10. Aulén, *Faith of the Christian Church*, 225.

11. Aulén, *Christus Victor*, 83.

12. Foerster notes that one of the striking things about New Testament accounts of demons is how, unlike in other first-century literature, demons are always subject to Satan. Foerster, "δαίμων," 18.

13. This is evident, for example, when the legion of demons beg Jesus to be cast into swine (Matt. 8:28–34; Mark 5:1–27; Luke 8:27–39) or in the story about exorcised demons returning

Yet, though faith in Christ and obedience to the law help an exorcism to endure, the Gospels do not interpret demon possession to be a consequence of particular sins. As Greg Boyd explains, "Jesus expressed intense anger toward those who were immoral, such as the self-righteous Pharisees, but he never suggested that they were demonized. Toward the demonized, however, he never expressed anger; rather, he exhibited only compassion."[14] To be possessed is to be afflicted, and defeat of demons is a direct defeat of Satan, the one whom the demons serve.

As C. S. Lewis once wrote, it is a mistake to either underemphasize or over-emphasize the demonic.[15] Underemphasis has been common in much modern theology, given increasing materialism and naturalism and the tendency to psychologize both radical evil and good as projections of the human ideals onto mythical figures.[16] The eighteenth-century Swedish theologian Emanuel Swedenborg overemphasizes Jesus's victory over evil spirits. According to Swedenborg, the Lord fully "conquered death or hell by combats," where "combats" refers to overcoming temptation.[17] Swedenborg reads Old Testament narratives about God's historical redemption and victory for Israel as allegorical prophecies about the Lord's victory over "hells," seemingly losing the historical referents altogether.[18] He denies satisfaction, interpreting Isaiah 53's references to the suffering servant bearing iniquities to actually mean "endur[ing] grievous temptations"[19] and references to taking away sins to mean "tak[ing] all power from the Devil, that is from hell."[20] Swedenborg rejects the doctrine of the Trinity and the hypostatic union, instead referring to the cross as a place where the divine Father is fully united to the human son through the ultimate decisive victory on the cross.[21] Swedenborg says that the Lord's human is the one who accomplishes salvation by enduring temptation on the cross, being glorified and becoming divine.[22]

Though the full details of Swedenborg's position are unimportant for present purposes, this limited treatment of his theology does show us a model of Christus Victor taken in a problematic direction. Where Aulén nearly

---

to the "house" from which they had been cast (Matt. 12:24–25; Luke 11:24–26). See Boyd, *God at War*, 195.

14. Boyd, *God at War*, 199.
15. Lewis, *Screwtape Letters*, ix.
16. Braaten, "Powers in Conflict," 97.
17. Swedenborg, *Concerning the Lord* §12.
18. See Swedenborg, *Concerning the Lord* §§13–14.
19. Swedenborg, *Concerning the Lord* §15.
20. Swedenborg, *Concerning the Lord* §17.
21. "The divine Lord (which is called the Father) . . . and the Divine human (which is called the Son) . . . are not two, but one." Swedenborg, *Concerning the Lord* §34.
22. Swedenborg, *Concerning the Lord* §35.

eliminates the work of the human nature of Christ, Swedenborg eliminates the work of the divine, making human merit the basis of the human son's adoption and glorification to deity. Yet close attention to the Bible's depictions of Jesus's battle with demons shows that this work is best understood through the doctrine of the Trinity and through dyoenergism. Christ's victory over evil is a consequence of his life in the Spirit and in relation to his Father.[23] The Son thus casts out demons through the Spirit (Matt. 12:28), and those who claim he exorcises by Satan's power miss that he truly binds the strong man through the Holy Spirit (Mark 3:22–30).[24] Jesus, sent by the Father, has a ministry empowered by truth, while Jesus's opponents are children of the devil and his lies (John 8:32–59). The exorcisms of Jesus thus testify to the identity of the divine Son as one who works together with the Father and Spirit in all divine works. But Jesus's exorcisms are also jointly the work of his human and divine natures, for he casts out demons by touch (Luke 13:10–13) and through speaking (e.g., Mark 1:23–26)—modeling that his human followers will also have power over evil spirits (Matt. 10:1; Mark 6:7; Luke 9:1).

Jesus's exorcisms have several important dogmatic roles. First, they challenge any reductionistic materialism that considers evil only in terms of human actions or any reductionistic psychologism that has no place for concepts of spiritual warfare.[25] Second, Jesus's exorcisms confirm for the Christian the existence of demons, which requires that we understand fallen humans not only as guilty sinners but also as victims of evil. Third, exorcisms are among the signs that the kingdom of heaven is at hand, and each exorcism anticipated the casting out of Satan, the "ruler of this world" (John 12:31).[26] Fourth, the phenomenon of exorcism suggests that the sanctification of the Christian includes a spiritual dimension that simply cannot be addressed by moral training, psychology, or medicine, as important as these things are.[27] Fifth and finally, exorcism reveals an important aspect of Christus Victor atonement,

23. Noble, *Holy Trinity*, 186.

24. The sin of blaspheming against the Holy Spirit (Mark 3:29) seems to be equating the Holy Spirit, by which Jesus exorcises, with an unclean spirit.

25. Keeping in mind the principle that both the neglect of and the overemphasis of the demonic are mistaken, it must also be said that a denial of the validity of many dimensions of psychology is also problematic.

26. Page notes that the same verb is used here as in many exorcisms. Page, "Satan, Sin, and Evil," 237.

27. Greg Boyd addresses naturalistic interpretations of demon possession, considering the case of the child who would convulse, foam at the mouth, and become rigid when seized by the demon (Matt. 17:14–21; Mark 9:14–30; Luke 9:37–45). Boyd notes that liberal interpretations of this child as an epileptic do not account for why he cried out when he saw Jesus (Luke 9:42) or when the demon left (Mark 9:26), how non-epileptics sometimes manifest similar symptoms today during exorcisms, or how the Son of God would misdiagnose the boy in this way. Boyd, *God at War*, 198.

extending the Son's spiritual warfare into his life and ministry, further helping us integrate the person and saving work of Christ. The cross and resurrection are of supreme importance, but the Son's saving work began in the incarnation, continued through his ministry, and triumphed through the cross and resurrection. In cultures that are more aware of spiritual warfare, Christus Victor therefore tends to play a more important role in theology.[28]

The Doctrine of the Descent

One of the most contested stages of Jesus's work and victory concerns his death. Through much of the Christian tradition, Jesus was understood to have descended to the realm of the dead, with this realm understood alternately as "the grave," Sheol, or hell. By this descent, Jesus was understood to have defeated the power of death itself, "harrowing hell" by freeing spirits who had been in captivity there. In more modern times, theologians and biblical exegetes have been more skeptical of the biblical basis and theological importance of this doctrine. This section will begin by considering the many contested passages of Scripture that might refer to the descent before developing a tentative theology of descent.

Is the Descent in Scripture?

If the descent is clearly taught in Scripture, we must make theological sense of it. If it is not found in Scripture, there is clear reason to question the doctrine. Thus, we must begin with close exegesis of several important passages of Scripture. One of the most important passages discussed in debates about the descent is 1 Peter 3:19. Paul Achtemeier has described 1 Peter 3:19 as "the most problematic [verse], in this letter, if not in the NT canon as a whole."[29] The verse reads, "in which [*en hō*] he [Christ] also went and made proclamation to the spirits in prison." Three primary disputes arise from the passage. First, how ought the phrase "in which [*en hō*]" be translated? Does it have the preceding word, *pneumati* ("by the Spirit/spirit"), as the antecedent? If so, would this refer to Christ preaching while a disembodied spirit,[30] or preaching through the mediation of the Holy Spirit, or preaching in a spiritual realm?[31] Or, is it better to translate the phrase temporally, meaning "during

28. This point is made with respect to African theology in Bediako, *Jesus and the Gospel in Africa*, 22.

29. Achtemeier, *1 Peter*, 252.

30. Hamm, "*Descendit*," 110.

31. Grudem, "Christ Preaching," 20–22.

which time"?[32] Such a translation might suggest that the proclamation occurred during the time between the burial and resurrection, or perhaps after being raised. In my estimation this textual ambiguity, substantial as it may be, is actually the smallest of the three interpretation problems in this verse.

The second dispute concerns the manner of proclamation made by Christ. Some have interpreted the proclamation in 1 Peter 3:19 in conjunction with the reference in 4:6 to the gospel being preached to those who are dead.[33] If so, such preaching has been thought to offer a second chance at salvation for the dead or even to result in universal salvation.[34] Others argue that this proclamation is one of victory, since the word "evangelize" (*euangelizō*) is not used here.[35] On such a reading, Christ's proclamation in 3:19 does not offer a new chance at salvation. Perhaps, given the context of 1 Peter 3:18–22, which compares baptism and the flood in Noah's day, Peter is setting up a contrast between the proclamation of judgment to those at the time of Noah and the preaching of the gospel today.[36] However, the verb "proclaim" (*kēryssō*) can be used for preaching the gospel, so the appeal to terminological difference is inconclusive in my mind.[37] This brings us to the third point of dispute: Who were the "spirits in prison" that received the proclamation of Christ?

There are three leading theories regarding the spirits in prison. First, the spirits may refer to dead human beings. If this is the case, 1 Peter 3:19 may refer to Christ descending to evangelize to the dead or perhaps to proclaim his victory to the faithful Israelites who had been waiting in Abraham's bosom (see Luke 16:19–31).[38] The latter possibility does not explain why the spirits would be described as "in prison."[39] Neither possibility makes sense of the fact that the term "spirits" typically refers to evil spirits or demons, not to dead human

---

32. Bass, *Battle for the Keys*, 89; Emerson, *"He Descended,"* 60. Bass and Emerson both note that this is how Peter uses the phrase four other times in 1:6; 2:12; 3:16; 4:4.

33. First Peter 4:6 is also the subject of some dispute, given that "the dead" in this passage may refer to those who are spiritually dead or to those who had faith when alive but are now dead. See Jobes, *1 Peter*, 267–68; McKnight, *1 Peter*, 227. For an interesting variant on the latter, see Michaels, *1 Peter*, 237. Michaels argues that "the dead" here may refer to those who died before Christ came. Since Peter basically considers the prophets to have proclaimed the gospel of Christ before his coming (see 1 Pet. 1:10–12), those who believed the prophets would now be dead.

34. The most influential recent proposal that preaching to the dead offers a second chance at salvation is found in D'Costa, "Descent into Hell," 146–71.

35. Emerson, *"He Descended,"* 62–63.

36. See Van Wierengen, "Descent into the Netherworld," 14–15.

37. As Justin Bass argues, this is actually the most prevalent usage of *kēryssō* in the New Testament. Bass, *Battle for the Keys*, 93.

38. This interpretation is particularly prevalent among the Eastern Orthodox. For example, see Alfeyev, *Christ the Conqueror of Hell*, 18–19.

39. Erickson, *Christian Theology*, 793.

beings.[40] A second theory proposes that the spirits in prison are those who were alive at the time of the flood when they heard proclamation from Noah as empowered by the Spirit of Christ, but are now dead. This theory runs into problems as well, given that it seems to ignore the temporal sequence found in 1 Peter 3:18–22.[41] However, Peter's discussion of the spirits (3:19) occurs in the context of his statement that Christ died for the unrighteous (3:18), which could suggest that dead human beings are the spirits in mind, even though this is not the most common usage of the term "spirits."[42] The third theory argues that 1 Peter had the mysterious "sons of God" found in Genesis 6:1–4 in mind, given the Noahic context. Given that various Second Temple texts like 1 Enoch view the offspring of these sons of God and human women as evil spirits or fallen angels, and that such texts often depict figures descending to proclaim God's victory to these spirits, 1 Peter 3:19 may also have something like this in mind.[43] This fits the context of Christ's triumph over evil spirits in 1 Peter 3:22, and compares well with 2 Peter 2:4, so Christ proclaiming victory to the cursed "sons of God" or to a wider group of captive evil spirits is another viable explanation. However, the fact that such Second Temple works tended to use terms like "angels" or "watchers" to reference these spirits may slightly tip the balance in favor of interpreting the spirits as dead humans.[44] Fortunately, though some contemporary interpreters place much weight on 1 Peter 3:18–22 as the basis for accepting or rejecting the doctrine of the descent, the passage itself is not the best foundation for the doctrine of the descent.[45]

40. See the discussions in Achtemeier, *1 Peter*, 254. Grudem objects with many alleged counterexamples from Scripture, but his examples all treat the spirit as a part of composite persons, not as representing the entirety of persons. Grudem objects that we do not have enough Greek data to make such a conclusion, and he considers a distinction between such partial referents and the term "spirit" used "absolutely" or substantively to be arbitrary. I would disagree. In English, for example, we might speak of "hearts" as a clear part of human persons, but we do not describe a group of humans as "hearts." See Grudem, "Christ Preaching," 6–7.

41. See Bass, *Battle for the Keys*, 87; Sarot, "Christ's Descent into Hell," 189. Michaels adds, "Peter's careful and explicit distinction between 'long ago' and 'now' in vv. 20–21 makes it highly implausible that an even more significant 'then/now' distinction in v.19 would have been left to the reader's ingenuity and imagination." Michaels, *1 Peter*, 210–11. The *men* . . . *de* contrast in 4:6 and the flesh versus spirit contrast suggest a sequential order—Christ was first put to death in the flesh, *and then* made alive in spirit to preach to the spirits in prison. Hamm, "*Descendit*," 110.

42. This point is helpfully made in Rutledge, *Crucifixion*, 455.

43. See Achtemeier, *1 Peter*, 256. Achtemeier lists 1 En. 6–16; 18:12–19:2; 106:14–15; 2 En. 7:1–3; Wis. 14:6; Jub. 5:6; 2 Bar. 56:1. He also notes that *phylakē* is often used of prisons for evil spirits or Satan, for example in Rev. 18:2.

44. See Michaels, *1 Peter*, 207–8. Michaels adds that the New Testament depicts fallen angels as being active, not imprisoned.

45. Here I agree with Justin Bass, who writes, "I do not believe that the doctrine of the *Descensus* in any way stands or falls on these two passages from Peter. . . . The doctrine of the

Ephesians 4:8–9 provides better evidence for Christ's descent into Sheol. Here, Paul cites Psalm 68, "When he ascended on high, he took the captives captive; he gave gifts to people," before saying as an aside, "but what does 'he ascended' mean except that he also descended to the lower parts of the earth [*katebe eis ta katōtera merē tēs gēs*]?" Some interpret the last phrase as an appositive, "he also descended to the lower parts, that is the earth,"[46] making the verse a reference to the incarnation.[47] However, a better translation is a partitive genitive, "he descended to the lower parts of the earth."[48] The Greek phrase is used in the Septuagint in Psalms 62:9 (63:9 ET) and 138:15 to describe the grave,[49] and the widespread cosmology of the day shows that the lower part of the earth would be assumed to be Sheol or Hades.[50] Furthermore, the construction *katabaino* (to go down) + *eis* (to/into) + a term for the underworld is a common construction, further suggesting that Paul may be speaking of a descent to Sheol here.[51]

W. Hall Harris has argued that interpreting Ephesians 4:9 as a reference to a descent to Sheol renders the verse irrelevant to the progression

---

Descensus arose independently of 1 Peter 3:18–22; 4:6 as early as Ignatius as a result of such texts as Matthew 12:40; 27:52–53; Acts 2:27, 31; and Ephesians 4:10." Bass, *Battle for the Keys*, 85.

46. In favor of this view is Paul's tendency to use such appositive genitives in Ephesians. W. Hall Harris III notes that thirteen or fourteen are present apart from 4:9, concluding, "Of course, the presence of other appositive genitives, no matter how frequent, cannot prove that *tēs gēs* in 4:9 should be understood in the same way. Nevertheless, there are sufficient instances of the appositive genitive in Ephesians to warrant the observation that its use constitutes a mark of the author's style. As such, it would represent, in a passage like Ephesians 4:9, a plausible explanation for the use of the genitive, if other contextual factors are in agreement." W. Harris, "Ascent and Descent of Christ," 204.

47. This is particularly prevalent among evangelicals who have rejected the doctrine of the descent. For one example, see Erickson, *Christian Theology*, 792.

48. If Paul intended to reference the incarnation, why not simply use "the earth" (*tēs gēs*) like Paul does in other passages contrasting heaven and earth (see Eph. 1:10; 3:15; Col. 1:16, 20; 3:2)? Bass, *Battle for the Keys*, 80.

49. Hoehner, *Ephesians*, 536. Ephesians 4:9 uses a comparative ("lower") rather than superlative ("lowest"), which leads Hoehner to conclude that Hades cannot be in mind. However, he is inconsistent when he cites Ps. 63:9 (62:9 LXX), which uses the superlative ("lowest parts of the earth") to refer to the grave, suggesting Paul has the grave in mind here. If a shift from the superlative to a comparative does not prevent Eph. 4:9 from referencing the grave, I see no reason why it would not reference Hades or Sheol, especially given that the two are often seen as synonymous.

50. See Bales, "Descent of Christ," 86–90. Bales shows that the underworld is consistently understood as being beneath the earth in Old Testament, New Testament, and broader Greco-Roman conceptions. Some object that Ephesians reflects a two-tiered view of the cosmos, since the evil spirits are in the heavens (Eph. 6:12). See W. Harris, "Ascent and Descent," 213. Bales counters that Ephesians assumes a place of the dead from which people are raised (1:20) or arise (5:14), suggesting an underworld. Bales, "Descent of Christ," 99. Harris also would need to assume that Paul did not write Ephesians, for the broader Pauline cosmology is certainly three-tiered. See Emerson, *"He Descended,"* 45.

51. Bales, "Descent of Christ," 95–96. See Num. 16:30, 33; Ps. 138:8; Isa. 14:11.

of the argument, which has focused on unity and gifts.[52] Instead, Harris proposes that the passage references Christ's return through the Holy Spirit at Pentecost. Christ first ascended, then descended as the Spirit providing gifts. Harris argues that his theory makes sense of Paul's change in his citation of Psalm 68:18 from "You received [*elabes*, 67:19 LXX] gifts from people," as it occurs in the Old Testament, to "He gave [*edōken*] gifts to people," as cited in Ephesians. Harris proposes that Ephesians draws on the oral tradition behind the Targum of the Psalms, a later Jewish commentary that reads Psalm 68 as a narrative of Moses's ascent to Sinai and descent to give the gift of the law (here, the targum uses the same word as Ephesians—*edōken*).[53]

Harris's proposal is unconvincing for several reasons. First, this translation does not make as good sense of the phrase "lower parts of the earth." Second, Harris situates Ephesians in a stream of rabbinic commentary stretching from oral tradition, through Ephesians, to the targums.[54] It is more plausible, to my mind, to read Psalm 68 as a psalm of victory, which Paul cites in Ephesians 4:8 to link the gift of the church's unity and offices to the victory of Christ through death (see Eph. 1:20–21), which later Christians developed into a more expansive theology of the descent. In other words, Christ's death included a descent to the underworld that set captives free such that these former captives could ascend through Christ to the Father's presence. (Something like this may be in mind in Matt. 27:52–53, where the dead exit the grave when Christ dies, though the author does not seem to think they are still present on earth at the time of his writing.) A third factor against interpreting Ephesians 4 as a discussion of Pentecost is that the link between death and gifts in Ephesians explains the purpose of the aside in 4:9. Harris is correct that the statement is parenthetical to the argument of chapter 4, but it is a parenthetical gesture to Paul's earlier discussion of unity as rooted in the death of Christ (see 2:13–16) and to his claim that Christ is head of the church precisely because of this victorious resurrection from death and ascension (1:20–22). Paul here extends his discussion of unity (4:3) and the body of Christ (4:12) from the death (a descent to Sheol) into the gifts given after the ascension. Fourth and finally, suggesting that Christ descended as

52. W. Harris, "Ascent and Descent," 205.
53. W. Harris, "Ascent and Descent," 208–11. Harris argues that this tradition is older and may be seen in the second-century-BC *Exagōge* of Ezekiel and in Philo.
54. Pace Emerson, *"He Descended,"* 44, I read Harris as allowing for the possibility that Ephesians draws on oral tradition that developed into the Targum rather than requiring that the audience of Ephesians be familiar with the "Aramaic gloss of the NT." Nevertheless, Emerson is right to argue that this is not the best context for interpreting Ephesians.

the Holy Spirit at Pentecost seems to conflate the divine persons without clear exegetical warrant. This modalism can be rejected based on the cumulative evidence of Scripture and tradition.

The Descent in Canonical Context

While Ephesians 4:9 provides a starting point for the doctrine of the descent of Christ, three supplemental dimensions of the canon are necessary to fully affirm a descent. The first is the widespread assumption in the Bible's first-century context that the dead went to the underworld, Sheol. Though the Old Testament is quite reserved in its discussion of the afterlife, the possibility of séances suggests a continued personal existence for the dead (see, for example, 1 Sam. 28:3–25).[55] The dead are depicted as continuing in their rank and calling,[56] but they live a diminished existence characterized by weakness (Isa. 14:10) or sleep (Nah. 3:18), and they are generally unaware of the world of the living (Job 14:21; Eccles. 9:5). Given this assumption, readers of the New Testament would have assumed that Christ descended to Sheol like others who died.

It is sometimes objected that Jesus's promise to the thief, "Today you will be with me in paradise" (Luke 23:43), is proof that Christ was actually in the Father's heavenly presence on Holy Saturday, rather than in Sheol.[57] However, "paradise" may also refer to a compartment of the underworld reserved for the righteous.[58] When interpreting Luke 23:43 in light of the canon, it makes more sense to think that Jesus is using "paradise" to refer to the underworld because Jesus tells Mary Magdalene at the resurrection, "Do not cling to me, . . . since I have not yet ascended to the Father" (John 20:17).[59] Apparently, Jesus was not in heaven in his humanity on Holy Saturday (his omnipresent divinity always remained present in heaven and through all the earth). Given that there are oblique references elsewhere to Christ being present in the abyss (Rom. 10:7) and Hades (Acts 2:27, citing

---

55. Van Wierengen, "Descent into the Netherworld," 22, 25. While the only example of a séance in the Old Testament occurs in 1 Sam. 28, the regular prohibitions of these practices suggest a more widespread possibility. See Lev. 19:31; 20:6, 27; Deut. 18:10–11.

56. Eichrodt, *Theology of the Old Testament*, 211. For example, prophets still wear their mantles (1 Sam. 28:14) and kings still sit on their thrones (Isa. 14:9).

57. See Ursinus, *Commentary*, 229. More recently, see Grudem, "He Did Not Descend," 112.

58. Emerson, "He Descended," 33; Bass, *Battle for the Keys*, 50–52. For broader information on Sheol containing chambers, see Ratzinger, *Eschatology*, 120–23.

59. Bird, *What Christians Ought to Believe*, 144.

Ps. 16:8–11), it seems that the New Testament assumes Jesus descends to the underworld.

Second, Old Testament prophecy gives reason to think that Jesus descended to the dead. Such prophecy was foundational for the acceptance of the descent by early Christians. From the time of the writing of the New Testament, Old Testament texts promising to ransom the faithful out of the grasp of Sheol (Hosea 13:14; cited in 1 Cor. 15:15) were read as prophecies pointing to Christ's victorious descent, while promises to deliver the psalmists from death (Ps. 16:8–11; cited in Acts 2:25–28) were seen as typologically pointing to Christ. In fact, it is noteworthy that many of the passages already discussed or soon to be explored in this section involve a New Testament text citing an Old Testament passage (e.g., Rom. 10:6–8/Deut. 30:11–14; Eph. 4:8–10/Ps. 68:18; Acts 2:27/Ps. 16:8–11; Matt. 12:39–41/Jon. 2). Clearly, where the Old Testament has language of descending, the New Testament finds warrant for applying this language to Christ. This provides canonical warrant for a search for further prophetic affirmations of a descent. By the second and third centuries, Christians found such prophecies across the Old Testament.

One strand of prophecy focused on Christ's dominion over Sheol and Hades. Within the New Testament corpus, Revelation 1:18 claims that Christ holds the keys to death and Hades. Justin Bass has argued that in the context of ancient narratives of victorious descents to Hades, frequent language of gates to the underworld (e.g., Job 38:17), and typical use of "the keys" representing an earned dominion over a region, first-century readers would see this verse as evidence of Christ's descent to Hades and victorious liberation of captives.[60] This is certainly true in subsequent centuries. By the second century, Christians began to connect God's promise in Isaiah 45:1–2 made to his Messiah that God will open the doors and gates[61] to passages like Psalm 107:10, 14, 16, where God takes people from out of the darkness, developing a Christus Victor atonement theory of Christ descending to darkness, breaking the doors of Hades, and liberating those in darkness.[62] Later texts even saw Isaiah's prophecy about a great light dawning on those "living in the land of darkness" (Isa. 9:2) to be a reference to Christ's descent to Sheol.[63] Similarly,

---

60. See Bass, *Battle for the Keys*.

61. The LXX uses the language of breaking the doors to pieces.

62. For a helpful summary of prophecy and the descent in early Christian theology, see Huidekoper, *Christ's Mission to the Underworld*, 33–38.

63. This is the interpretation taken by the Gospel of Nicodemus 13.2. The same apocryphal gospel (16.8) also cites Ps. 107:16, which is David's speaking of God breaking the gates of iron and bronze.

the exodus began to be interpreted typologically as a sign of the descent.[64] Thus, Melito of Sardis writes, Christ, having been slain as the paschal lamb, "redeemed us from slavery to the cosmos as from the land of Egypt and loosed us from slavery to the devil as from the hand of Pharaoh."[65] Origen traced the word "Passover" to "crossing (a boundary)" and therefore saw the Passover as a sign of Jesus helping those captive to death "leap over" the walls of Hades and escape into God's presence.[66] Such prophecies and others show a biblical expectation of a triumph over death and Sheol.

The third dimension of the canon justifying acceptance of a descent is the biblical depiction of Christ's work in defeating death. Consider, for example, the Gospel of Matthew. When pushed for a sign by the Pharisees, Jesus promises the sign of Jonah: "As Jonah was in the belly of the huge fish three days and three nights, so the Son of Man will be in the heart of the earth three days and three nights" (Matt. 12:40).[67] The idea of an underwater prison representing the underworld is common,[68] and Jonah himself describes it in familiar terms of the underworld: Sheol (Jon. 2:2), the heart of the seas (2:3), and a place where "the earth's gates shut behind [him] forever" (2:6).[69] (In fact, in Rom. 10:7, Paul can interpret "cross[ing] the sea" in Deut. 30:11–14 as "go[ing] down into the abyss," applying it to Christ.)[70] We have reason to believe that Matthew saw Jesus as the one who descended to the heart of the earth into Sheol, breaking the gates open and setting the dead free. When Peter first recognizes Jesus as the Messiah, Jesus promises to build his church on this "rock"—the debate between Catholics identifying the rock as Peter's

---

64. A summary and textual analysis are found in Rouwhorst, "Descent of Christ," 59–62.

65. Melito of Sardis, *Homily on the Passover*, 67.

66. Rouwhorst, "Descent of Christ," 62.

67. See also Luke 11:29–30. Comparing Luke 11 to Matt. 12, R. T. France notes, "References to the book of Jonah in extant Jewish literature show that it was not his preaching that was their main interest, but his experience in and deliverance from the sea monster, so that an unadorned reference to 'the sign of Jonah' would be more likely to be understood in that light." France, *Gospel of Matthew*, 490.

68. In the Bible, see passages like Ps. 88:4–12; Lam. 3:52–58; and Ezek. 26:19–21 that link concepts of water, darkness, confinement, death, and the pit. In fact, the underworld is often described as "the pit" in English translations of the Bible, but the several Hebrew terms used can also be translated as "well" or "cistern," the latter of which was sometimes used as a prison (e.g., see Jer. 38).

69. Notice also the echoes of Jonah's naming his location as the "heart of the seas" (Jon. 2:3) with Matthew's "heart of the earth" (Matt. 12:40).

70. "In fact, the 'sea' and the 'abyss' were somewhat interchangeable concepts in the OT and in Judaism; and some Aramaic paraphrases of . . . Deut. 30:13 used the language of the abyss. Therefore, Paul could very easily change the horizontal imagery of the crossing of the sea in Deut. 30:13 to the conceptually similar vertical imagery of descent into the underworld." Moo, *Romans*, 655–56.

apostolic office and Protestants identifying it as his faith need not detain us here. What is significant for our purposes is that Jesus adds, "and the gates of Hades will not prevail against [the church]" (Matt. 16:18 NRSV), a statement unique to Matthew's Gospel.[71] Only here is Peter called "Simon son of Jonah" (16:17), perhaps alluding to the earlier sign of Jonah.[72] Then, when Jesus dies, Matthew says that "the tombs were also opened and many bodies of the saints who had fallen asleep were raised. And they came out of the tombs after his resurrection, entered the holy city, and appeared to many" (Matt. 27:52–53). Matthew is going out of his way to say that the dead were raised before the resurrection (even if they only emerged after) and may suggest that this defeat of death is linked to a descent, as foretold in Matthew 12:40. These three canonical elements combine to provide stronger warrant for the doctrine of the descent.

The Dogmatic Function of the Descent

Theologians have deployed the doctrine of the descent for many purposes, but the ambiguity of several key passages believed to address the descent renders some of these deployments of the doctrine dubious at best. For this reason, recent centuries have seen an ongoing dispute regarding the validity of the descent, with some proposing that the doctrine should be removed from the Apostles' Creed, since it was a later addition and the purpose of its inclusion was unclear. From time to time Christians have opposed the doctrine of the descent altogether. Early in the Reformation, "Walter Deleonus, pastor of the London congregation of German refugees, fought for its omission as 'a plant that the Lord hath not planted.'"[73] Recently, Randall Otto has argued that including "such a mysterious article in the [Apostles'] creed, which is supposed to be a summary of the basic and vital tenets of the faith, seems very unwise."[74] While some details of the descent must remain unclear given what God has chosen to reveal in Scripture, it retains several clear dogmatic functions that warrant its inclusion in a basic presentation of the faith.

The descent ensures the full humanity of Jesus Christ. If Jesus descended into Sheol, he would have done so in his humanity. Occasionally medieval theologians like Peter Abelard and Durandus of Saint-Pourçain would argue

71. Redaction criticism would therefore suggest that we are dealing with a theme important to Matthew's Gospel.
72. Bass, *Battle for the Keys*, 68.
73. Hamm, "*Descendit*," 103.
74. Otto, "*Descendit in Inferna*," 150.

that an omnipresent divine person like the Son could not descend by changing location once disembodied because bodies are required to move location.[75] However, we ought not to view Sheol (or heaven, for that matter) as a space of the same sort as earthly space. For this reason, most theologians have argued that Jesus descended in his human soul, a fact which requires that Christ have a human soul, against the heresy of Apollinarianism, which denied that Christ had any soul.[76] At a more basic level, the descent of Christ ensures that Jesus died a true and full human death, against such groups as the docetists, who claimed that Christ only appeared human and, presumably, also only appeared to die.[77] The mere affirmation that Jesus died and was buried may combat docetism, but it does not point to Jesus having a human soul. The descent of Christ's human spirit into Sheol also challenges modern naturalistic swoon theories, which suggest that Christ merely passed out on the cross and later awoke in the tomb.[78]

The descent also serves to distinguish between revivification and resurrection. Other humans had experienced revivification before Christ (see 1 Kings 17:17–24; 2 Kings 4:18–37; Mark 5:35–43; Luke 7:11–15; 8:49–56; John 11:17–44), and modern medicine allows us to revive those who were briefly pronounced dead by medical standards. Only Christ has experienced genuine resurrection as the "firstfruits" of what is to come (1 Cor. 15:23). In the descent Christ was victorious over death, and so Sheol can hold him no longer.[79] Christ now holds the keys of death and Hades (Rev. 1:18), having entered into a state of human death and overcome it. The risen Jesus is finally clearly recognized as Lord. Justin Bass explains that the fact that Jesus has the keys means that "the believers of the seven churches in Revelation can rest assured that no god or goddess or demon or Roman emperor holds their destiny in his or her hands, but only the Lord Jesus Christ (Rev 1:18; 3:7; 9:1; 20:1)."[80] Holding these keys is also a sign of the lordship of Christ. While descent narratives were common in the ancient Near East, Jesus's account stands out in that he entered having died, not as one alive, and he then resurrected.[81] Every knee under the earth

---

75. Laufer, *Hell's Destruction*, 47–48, 50.

76. For example, see Cyril of Alexandria, *To Theodosius* §22.

77. See Laufer, *Hell's Destruction*, 181. Some historians have suggested that the descent clause was initially included in the Apostles' Creed for the purpose of combating the docetists or the Apollinarians. J. N. D. Kelly compellingly rejects these arguments on the basis that we never see authors appeal to the descent to openly combat docetism and because the descent was already present in Syrian contexts long before we first see the clause included in any creeds. See Kelly, *Early Christian Creeds*, 382–83.

78. This point is helpfully made in Laufer, *Hell's Destruction*, 181.

79. Laufer, *Hell's Destruction*, 182.

80. Bass, *Battle for the Keys*, 44.

81. Bass, *Battle for the Keys*, 62–64.

must now bow and confess him as Lord (Phil. 2:10–11), and the captives to Satan have been taken captive by Christ (Eph. 4:8). I will return to the theology of death, but first I must explore the doctrine of the resurrection in Scripture.

The Resurrection in Scripture

The resurrection is central to the Gospel narratives and to the theology of salvation, but it has been the subject of heated debate in biblical studies in the past several centuries. For this reason, it is important to begin with some discussion of the resurrection as a historical event that balances continuity and discontinuity in the human life of the Son. With this foundation in place, we will be able to turn to consider how the resurrection establishes victory.

The Resurrection as Historical Event

In modern times, one of the most contentious aspects of the doctrine of the resurrection concerns whether the resurrection was actually a historical event at all. With the emergence of historical critical methodology, notably historical Jesus studies, and with a rise in materialism and naturalism, it is no surprise that progressive theologies have sought to find a way to make sense of the resurrection narratives that did not rely on the supernatural. Critics have challenged the authorship of the Gospels, the accuracy of biblical narrative, and the possibility of miracles, including the resurrection. Biblical scholars sometimes reach conclusions similar to Bart Ehrman: "Your grounds for thinking [Jesus rose] are theological or personal, not historical (since they defy historical probabilities)."[82] In the mind of Choan-Seng Song, the empty tomb "has no historical significance as far as our faith in the risen Christ is concerned," for the resurrection points us to the need for all tombs to be empty.[83] In light of modern critique, it is not surprising to find numerous defenses of the historicity of the resurrection. Particularly among historical fundamentalists, a loss of a literal resurrection was rightly seen to be catastrophic. Thus, J. Gresham Machen can note that the basic proclamation of the first Christians was a proclamation of the bodily resurrection of Christ.[84] R. A. Torrey confidently adds, "While the literal bodily resurrection of Jesus Christ is the corner-stone of Christian doctrine, it is also the Gibraltar of Christian evidence, and the Waterloo of infidelity and rationalism."[85] Certainly, the

82. Ehrman, *Jesus*, 229.
83. Song, *Third-Eye Theology*, 188–89.
84. Machen, *Christianity and Liberalism*, 23–24.
85. Torrey, "Bodily Resurrection of Jesus," 299.

fundamentalists (and many who defended the resurrection but do not easily fit within that category) were in the spirit of Paul, who wrote, "If Christ has not been raised, then our proclamation is in vain, and so is your faith" (1 Cor. 15:14). With such high stakes, analysis of the historicity of the resurrection has been something of a modern preoccupation. A full survey of all relevant arguments will be impossible, but a brief survey of relevant arguments should convey the state of the question.

Skeptics toward the resurrection often critique the quality of the testimony about the resurrection, so many defenses focus on the quality and nature of early Christian testimony to the event. Wolfhart Pannenberg is an important representative of focus on the early nature of apostolic testimony. Pannenberg points to 1 Corinthians 15:3–8, which most scholars take to be an early Christian creedal affirmation—Pannenberg places the confession within eight years of Jesus's crucifixion.[86] Thus, we have early testimony to resurrection, and Pannenberg believes that a resurrection is more likely to explain this early testimony than this testimony is able to explain belief in the resurrection. While early testimony is preferable to late testimony in historical analysis, all other things being equal, it is also the case that many key events in the formation of the early church could have already occurred before this confession was crafted, and false stories can spread quickly.[87] Some seek to supplement the early nature of the testimony by examining the importance of some of those named in the confession. For example, James the brother of the Lord received an appearance (1 Cor. 15:7), which is noteworthy because James apparently had not been a follower of Christ until after his death (see Mark 3:20–25; 6:2–6; John 7:1–5; Acts 1:14; 15:1–21; 21:17–26; 1 Cor. 9:5; Gal. 1:19; 2:1–10). James's otherwise surprising conversion might make sense if he saw his brother risen from the grave.[88] Notably, tradition claims that James died for his faith, though the historical evidence is not strong enough to be conclusive.[89]

Many resurrection defenders not only appeal to early testimony but also defend the testimony as coming from eyewitnesses. While many critics of the resurrection point to variety within the Gospel accounts as evidence that the accounts are not reliable, others have argued that such variability would be

---

86. See Pannenberg, *Jesus*, 89–91. On the widespread acceptance of the early and confessional nature of 1 Cor. 15:3–8, see Theissen and Merz, *Historical Jesus*, 487–90. Identification of this passage as an early confession is based on language of receiving and passing on a tradition (1 Cor. 15:3), the use of verbs that are not characteristic of Paul, and the confessional structure of the verses.

87. See Lüdemann, *Resurrection of Jesus*, 175.

88. Licona, *Resurrection of Jesus*, 440–55.

89. Note that James the brother of Jesus is different from James the brother of John in Acts 12:2.

expected from eyewitness testimony.[90] Richard Bauckham has put forward the most interesting arguments that the Gospels offer eyewitness accounts of the life, death, and resurrection of Christ. Bauckham points to old arguments that second- and third-generation Christians like Papias named the authors of the Gospels as either eyewitnesses (Matthew and John) or as companions of eyewitnesses (Luke, companion of Paul, and Mark, Peter's scribe).[91] Bauckham adds newer arguments too. Names in the Gospels fit the early first century, not the late first century.[92] He adds that many of the specific names in the resurrection accounts serve no narrative purpose and are unlikely to be legendary additions; rather, they plausibly reflect once-known eyewitnesses, individuals who mattered to original audiences but whose identities have long since been forgotten.[93] Of course, there is heated debate about whether the Gospels were written early enough to preserve eyewitness accounts and whether early Christian testimony about authorship is reliable, but some recent studies like Bauckham's offer detailed support of early, eyewitness authorship.

N. T. Wright offers a defense of the resurrection that is less dependent on establishing early, eyewitness accounts. Wright argues, "When the early Christians spoke of Jesus being raised from the dead, the natural meaning of that statement, throughout the ancient world, was the claim that something had happened to Jesus which had happened to nobody else. A great many things happened to the dead, but resurrection did not. The pagan world assumed it was impossible; the Jewish world believed it would happen eventually, but knew perfectly well that it had not done so yet."[94] The Christian belief that Christ rose as the firstfruits (1 Cor. 15:20), being the "firstborn from the dead" (Col. 1:18), is a historical phenomenon that needs an explanation. More than that, a historical explanation is needed for why there was near-universal embrace of this new perspective on the afterlife across various first-generation Christian writings. Wright argues that Christians explain the resurrection in

---

90. Bryan, *Resurrection of the Messiah*, 167. Against this position, one might argue that there is too much overlap between the Synoptics to consider them independent eyewitness testimony rather than intentional retellings of a common tradition. See Theissen and Merz, *Historical Jesus*, 501.

91. Bauckham, *Jesus and the Eyewitnesses*, 12–38.

92. Bauckham, *Jesus and the Eyewitnesses*, 67–92.

93. Bauckham, *Jesus and the Eyewitnesses*, 39–55.

94. N. T. Wright, *Resurrection of the Son of God*, 83. Wright's claim has met some challenge. For example, Litwa points to postmortem bodily deification as a Greco-Roman parallel that might make sense of the resurrection belief, providing a historical backdrop other than an empty tomb and postcrucifixion appearances. Reading Litwa's claim, I am not sure that bodily deification as clearly involves revivification, and it remains uncertain whether Jesus's followers would be familiar with or adopt such concepts in their thinking of Christ. However, it does seem that Wright's claims are somewhat overstated. See Litwa, *Iesus Deus*, 149–51.

terms of postresurrection appearances and an empty tomb. One without the other would not yield resurrection belief.[95] Wright therefore proposes that the most plausible historical explanation is that the disciples saw the risen Christ and knew about the empty tomb. Many alternative historical theories have been put forward. Perhaps the disciples lied, inventing the story, but this theory does not explain how they arrived at the idea of a resurrection, nor does it account for the willingness of at least four disciples to die for this belief.[96] Further, since women did not count as legal witnesses, it is unlikely that the disciples would have invented a story that women first saw the risen Christ.[97] Some have suggested that the women and later the disciples experience mass hallucinations, but postmortem visions were common in antiquity, and Jesus's resurrection is not described in precisely these ways.[98] Yet we cannot be so certain about the psychological condition of the disciples after the crucifixion to know with certainty that hallucination is impossible; we can only say that mass hallucination would be extremely improbable, while skeptics could insist that the visions could have some yet unknown explanation.[99]

A responsible historical analysis of the resurrection needs to be far larger than what I can offer here. My intent in this section has only been to show that Christians who affirm the bodily resurrection do not do so against all reason, rather having historical evidence in favor of the resurrection, while I also acknowledge, as many scholars do, that we lack incontestable historical proof of the resurrection.[100] Faith is, after all, a gift of God and not a work of pure historical analysis. However, the historicity of the resurrection is of tremendous importance, and Christians can reasonably defend the resurrection's historicity if not universally prove it. As we shall see, the resurrection brings about victory over sin, death, the devil, and even empire, but if there is no historical, bodily resurrection, there is no victory. Before turning to that argument, I must first briefly consider two additional aspects of biblical theology and the resurrection.

95. N. T. Wright, *Resurrection of the Son of God*, 688–90. Because there was no expectation of an individual resurrection, an empty tomb would not lead to unanimous belief in Christ's resurrection. Appearances alone could be interpreted as something other than resurrection.

96. Allison, *Resurrection of Jesus*, 310. Perhaps the Gospels are entirely fabricated, hence no martyrdom of disciples, and no Jesus, hence no resurrection. Most historians affirm the historicity of Christ, and the early confession evident in 1 Cor. 15 suggests that at least the basic details of the resurrection are not inventions of later generations.

97. Bryan, *Resurrection of the Messiah*, 167.

98. Bryan, *Resurrection of the Messiah*, 163–64, 169–70. Bryan argues that chosen vocabulary was well known and would mislead if authors were intending to speak of a vision only.

99. See Allison, *Resurrection of Jesus*, 294–308.

100. See, e.g., Licona, *Resurrection*, 587; N. T. Wright, *Resurrection of the Son of God*, 706, 714.

Resurrected Bodies: Continuity and Discontinuity

The resurrection involves a transformation of the body of Christ from "a natural body" to "a spiritual body" (1 Cor. 15:44). The extent of the change is disputed. For example, there is an emphasis on the luminosity of those who are raised (Dan. 12:3; Matt. 13:43; 1 Cor. 15:41–42), though one might debate whether this is a literal or metaphorical luminosity. Either way, some real change of Jesus's body is expected. Perhaps the most extreme account of discontinuity is found in the teachings of certain later Origenists. Origen of Alexandria understood the resurrection to involve the resurrection of the form, not the matter, of the body. This form was the "seed" of the resurrected body in 1 Corinthians 15:38, and the form would materialize with a spiritual body much like that of the stars (which Origen thought to be alive).[101] Based on the belief that the sphere was the perfect geometric shape, some Origenists apparently believed we would be spherical at the resurrection, a claim explicitly condemned at the Second Council of Constantinople.[102] This surely goes too far. Others offer a less drastic account that still centers the ways that Jesus's postresurrection body is different from his preresurrection body. Murray Harris argues that, after the resurrection, Jesus's body's "essential state was one of invisibility and immateriality," noting that Jesus suddenly appears and vanishes (Luke 24:31–36), passes through closed doors (John 20:19, 26), and is typically described as "coming into visibility" (*ōphthē*—often translated as "appeared").[103] While a change in Christ's body is certainly evident, we must be cautious about overstating the extent of the change. After all, before the resurrection Jesus was able to walk on water (Matt. 14:25; Mark 6:48; John 6:19) and pass through hostile crowds (Luke 4:30), suggesting that his being able to overcome physical barriers or the typical function of the laws of physics may have more to do with his divine personhood than with the particulars of his embodied materiality. Yet there is clear change from perishability, dishonor, weakness, and "soulish" embodiedness (whatever Paul may mean by this)[104] to imperishability, glory, power, and spiritual embodiedness (1 Cor. 15:42–44).

Our bodies must be changed or else they will still be susceptible to decay and aging; yet our bodies must also have continuity or else we cannot say

---

101. Origen could point out that the matter of the body was constantly in flux, even during life. Origen did not, however, go so far as to deny the materiality or embodiedness of the resurrection. Scott, *Life of the Stars*, 151–57.

102. L. Davis, *First Seven Ecumenical Councils*, 247.

103. M. Harris, *Raised Immortal*, 53–54.

104. This might reference the difference between a spiritual and soulish man in 1 Cor. 2:14–15, where the spiritual man lives in relation to God. See S. Harris, *Refiguring Resurrection*, 181.

that resurrection has happened; instead, the creation of a new person has taken place.[105] Wolfhart Pannenberg has argued that the resurrection involves "historical continuity" of the body; surely this is suggested by the persistence of Christ's wounds after the resurrection (John 20:20, 27). Yet Pannenberg denies "substantial or structural continuity."[106] If by this Pannenberg means that the matter of Christ's body is discontinuous, this is not problematic— there is a process whereby atoms and molecules are constantly replaced in the body during normal life. However, the word "substance" can also refer to what something fundamentally is. If Pannenberg means to suggest that Christ has a new substance in this sense after the resurrection, then the risen Savior would no longer be consubstantial with humanity, a serious problem. Without having this consubstantiality and shared nature, as we have seen, union with Christ is impossible. There must in fact be substantial continuity in the sense that Christ still bears a human nature, albeit a glorified one, or else all is lost. Perhaps, in the end, we are rather limited in our ability to specify our resurrected state, even as it is important to insist that we will remain what we are to the extent that *we* are saved, while we will become something so different that we are *saved*.[107]

The Resurrection in Dogmatic Theology

As Christian doctrine, resurrection connects with other doctrines in systematic theology. A full elaboration of this fact could be explored in detail, but given this chapter's focus on soteriology, I will only briefly explore the connection between the resurrection and the broader doctrines of Christology and the Trinity.

Christology and Resurrection

At its most basic level, the doctrine of the resurrection is seen as a vindication of Jesus's christological status as Messiah. As Brandon Crowe explains, "It not only demonstrates the veracity of Jesus's prediction of his own resurrection (Luke 9:22; 18:33; cf. 24:6–7, 26, 46) but also proves that Jesus—and

105. Gregory of Nyssa, *On the Soul and Resurrection* 108–10.
106. Pannenberg, *Jesus*, 76.
107. Steven Harris cautions against undue speculation in our understanding of the resurrection, describing curiosity (following John Webster) as vicious, and, second, he notes that focusing on the risen Christ can help reduce some of the speculation of theologies of resurrection. I will attempt to adopt this approach in chapter 10. See S. Harris, *Refiguring Resurrection*, 168, 185–202.

his message—were 'in the right.'"[108] Therefore, Scripture frequently links the resurrection with the sonship and lordship of Christ (e.g., Acts 2:32–36), not because he was only adopted at the resurrection but because the full reality of his status as the eternal Lord and beloved begotten Son of the Father was only fully confirmed at the resurrection. Considered at an ontological level, the resurrection is the completion of the recapitulation begun in the incarnation—if flesh did not need to be redeemed, then flesh would not need to be assumed, to draw again on Nazianzus's rule.[109] More than this, the resurrection ensures the permanence of what was begun in the incarnation. As the Chalcedonian definition affirms, the natures are united in one hypostasis inseparably. This has tremendous significance for salvation. If death ended the hypostatic union of two natures, then the union of Christians with Christ would not be possible today. Given that Jesus was restored to his body, maintaining a full humanity, we can hope for the complete redemption of humanity. Jesus becomes an eternal priest in the order of Melchizedek, but this priesthood is also due to the resurrection. Since Jesus is not a Levite but of the tribe of Judah, he could not be an earthly priest (Heb. 8:4). Yet, because he suffered and was raised, he is able to be a priest in the order of Melchizedek because of his indestructible life (Heb. 5:8–10; 7:23–28).[110] Gustaf Aulén was concerned to show how Christus Victor atonement was continuous, with God acting for salvation from first to last. The resurrection helps preserve this continuity, with God's purpose to have communion with humanity evident since creation, enhanced through the assumption of humanity into the Son, extended through that humanity's glorification and honoring of the Father through satisfaction, and culminating in permanent communion through the resurrection and ascension.

Trinity and Resurrection

Robert Jenson argues that in the New Testament the resurrection becomes the event through which the person of the Father is identified. He is the God of the exodus but also the God who raised Jesus Christ (e.g., Exod. 20:2; Deut. 5:6; 2 Cor. 4:14; Phil. 3:20–21).[111] This relational emphasis in identifying the persons in the economy is a reflection of the eternal relations between the divine persons *ad intra*. Just as the eternal relation between the Father, Son, and Spirit does not break on the cross, so also the resurrection does not

---

108. Crowe, *Hope of Israel*, 109.
109. This point is also well noted by Irenaeus himself in *Against Heresies* 5.14.
110. Moffitt, *Rethinking the Atonement*, 79–82.
111. Jenson, *Systematic Theology*, 1:44.

(re)constitute the Trinity. Yet the eternal persons relate to one another through their actions in history in a manner that corresponds to their eternal relations. As such, it is no surprise that the resurrection is also an act performed by the Trinity that reveals the Trinity. Given the doctrine of inseparable operations, we must affirm that Father, Son, and Spirit were all involved in raising Christ. The Father's agency is clearly and regularly affirmed (e.g., Acts 2:24), and Jesus also lays down his life to take it back up again (John 10:17–18). Interestingly, there are occasional passages in Scripture naming the Spirit as the power in which Christ is raised (Rom. 1:4; 8:11). The promise of the gift of the Holy Spirit in Ezekiel 36 is followed by the account of resurrection through the Spirit/breath in Ezekiel 37.[112] The point is clearer with a dogmatic analysis. In baptism we are buried and raised with Christ (Rom. 6:4; Col. 2:12), but the baptism Christians receive is baptism in the Holy Spirit (Matt. 3:11; Mark 1:8; Luke 3:16; John 1:33). Baptism is by faith, with the immersion in water a sacramental sign of the indwelling of the Holy Spirit. Christ was raised by receiving in his human nature the Spirit of life anew, a reward for his self-offering on the cross. Similarly, Christians are indwelt with the power of the Spirit as a seal guaranteeing that same resurrection end (Eph. 1:13–14). Charles Nyamiti is therefore right when he says that "a theology of Christ's resurrection in which the role of the Spirit is not particularly emphasized is therefore necessarily incomplete."[113]

Victory in Descent and Resurrection

The descent has primarily a focused systematic significance of transforming death and enabling the defeat of sin through death. Broadly speaking, the resurrection of Jesus has tremendous significance across the span of systematic theology. Resurrection enters a new age with a changed relationship to the temple, law, Sabbath, and mission.[114] Given the focus of this chapter, I will particularly focus on the resurrection as a victory over death, sin, and the devil, adding in a brief additional treatment of corruption, a metaphysical concept that bridges the doctrines of sin and death. Further implications of the resurrection will be briefly discussed in chapter 10.

112. "Later Jewish texts frequently drew upon Ezekiel 37 in ways that related the restoration of Israel to resurrection (e.g., 2 Macc. 7:22–23; *4 Macc.* 18:17; *Pseudo-Ezekiel; Sib. Or.* 4:181–82; *Liv. Pro.* 3:12; *T. Ab.* 18:11; possibly *2 Bar.* 50:1–3)." Crowe, *Hope of Israel*, 24.
113. Nyamiti, *Christ as Our Ancestor*, 49. Nyamiti's point about the gift of the Spirit to the Son is helpful but must be clarified as applying only to the human nature of Christ. Obviously, the Son has always had the Spirit in his divine person.
114. Crowe, *Hope of Israel*, 116–25.

A Victorious Afterlife

The descent is an important component of Christus Victor atonement, for it shows the sweeping extent of Christ's victory as something that even extends into the afterlife. Our ultimate end is resurrection, but between death and the resurrection and new creation, death consists in an **intermediate state** alternately described in Scripture as Sheol, sleep, or being with the Lord (2 Sam. 22:6; Phil. 1:23; 1 Thess. 4:13). Christ has transformed this intermediate state through the descent, just as our final postmortem condition has been transformed through resurrection.

The Old Testament depicted Sheol as a negative condition characterized by solitude (Ps. 31:17–18; Isa. 47:5) and the absence of companionship (Ps. 88:10–12; Isa. 38:18), though some suggest the biblical emphasis on solitude in Sheol may have been intended more to prohibit séances than to describe the condition of the soul of a dead human in any detail.[115] Nevertheless, Sheol was not a place of joy but was rather characterized metaphorically as a trap entangling its victims (2 Sam. 22:6; Ps. 18:5), as a prison (Job 17:16), as a thing that swallows us (Prov. 1:12; Ps. 141:7). "In an interesting play on this metaphor, the Lord reverses the curse of the grave by 'swallow[ing] up death forever' (Isa. 25:8)."[116] After Christ's death and entry into Sheol, death itself is swallowed up and transformed such that Paul can confidently say, "To die is gain" (Phil. 1:21), for "to depart and be with Christ" is now "far better" (1:23).[117] Death itself has been transformed by Christ's entry into Sheol in his human soul. Thus, theologians from across the Christian tradition have confidently proclaimed the transformation of the afterlife through Christ.

More must be said on this decisive transformation of death through Christ's descent into Sheol. Alexander Schmemann makes a key point when he recognizes that "it is *this world*" and "it is *this life*" that "were given to man to be a sacrament of the divine presence." Creation is itself good (Gen. 1:10, 12, 18, 21, 25, 31), and our original goal was not disembodied life in God's presence but earthly life in a garden. But the "horror of death," Schmemann insists, is not the physical destruction of our natures nor the end of our historical existence in this world, as bad as those things are. Rather, the deepest evil of death is that "by being separation from the world and life, it is *separation from God*. The dead cannot glorify God."[118] Schmemann notes

---

115. For example, see Emerson, *"He Descended,"* 127.

116. "Grave," in Ryken, Wilhoit, and Longman, *Dictionary of Biblical Imagery*, 350.

117. For a discussion of Christ's transformation of death that is somewhat more limited, see Gathercole, *Defending Substitution*, 80–83.

118. Schmemann, *For the Life of the World*, 121.

how often the Psalms worry that the dead cannot praise God in Sheol (Pss. 6:5; 30:9; 88:11; 115:17; see also Isa. 38:18). It is striking, therefore, that one of the main images of those who have died in Christ in the book of Revelation is that they are singing God's praises in his heavenly presence (Rev. 7:9–17). The descent thus transforms the intermediate state of death from a condition in which one is separated from God to one of communion with Father, Son, and Holy Spirit.

Scripture is clear that the intermediate state has changed after Christ's death, but the means by which this change occurred is less clear. Fleming Rutledge puts it nicely when she writes, "What was going on in the life of God between Good Friday and Easter? We are not permitted to look into this mystery. Our responses to it will be more in the realm of poetry than of science."[119] The Old Testament is quite reserved in its descriptions of the afterlife in comparison with surrounding ANE cultures,[120] and the New Testament provides only minimal clarification. Reformation-era Protestant treatments of the descent are thus often wisely cautious,[121] with Protestant statements of faith often affirming the descent but leaving details unspecified.[122] As Georges Florovsky explains, through resurrection Christ has transformed death from a metaphysical catastrophe that divides soul and body contrary to God's purposes into an opportunity for the believer to be transformed as they are sown in perishable form in the grave and raised imperishable (1 Cor. 15:42).[123]

---

119. Rutledge, *Crucifixion*, 418.

120. See Van Wierengen, "Descent into the Netherworld," 24–25. Van Wierengen proposes that one reason for such hesitance is that many ANE depictions of the afterlife carried the social hierarchies of the present world into the next life, while Israelite religion was largely unwilling to do this.

121. For example, Ursinus, who denied any notion of a descent into Sheol, instead interpreting the doctrine as a reference to Christ's suffering on the cross, writes this of those holding to a more traditional understanding of a descent into Sheol: "Yet this view, or opinion, of Christ's descent into hell, has nothing of impiety in it, and has been approved of and held by many of the fathers. Hence it is not proper that we should contend strenuously with anyone in regard to it." Ursinus, *Commentary*, 230–31.

122. See Laufer, *Hell's Destruction*, 84–85, 93–94. Laufer details how Anglicans gradually minimized their confessional stances on the descent. The Forty-Two Articles (1552) affirmed the descent and preaching (Art. 3) but clarified that "Christ the Lord by his descent liberated none from their prisons and torments." In 1554, this clarifying line was removed, and by 1563, the (now) Thirty-Nine Articles removed any reference to Christ's preaching to the dead, simply affirming, "As Christ died for us, and was buried; so also it is to be believed that he went down into hell." This was a compromise position: Anglican Calvinists need not affirm preaching (which they rejected), while Anglo-Catholics could interpret the confession in terms of 1 Pet. 3:18–22. A similar degree of caution was found in the Lutheran Formula of Concord, which affirmed belief that Jesus defeated Satan and destroyed hell for believers, but we ought not to speculate on how nor dispute with one another over the doctrine (Art. 9).

123. Florovsky, *Creation and Redemption*, 104–10.

Yet here also the precise means by which the body is changed through death remains beyond us. Yes, we are changed by the power of God thanks to the victory of Christ, but beyond this, much will remain uncertain.

Though the means by which Christ is victorious over death is unclear, his victory over death, however it occurs, is clearly symbolized in baptism, for "all of us who were baptized into Christ Jesus were baptized into his death," being "buried with him by baptism into death" (Rom. 6:3, 4). While it is common to see baptism as a symbolic participation in the death of Christ, there seems to be a tendency to understand this death simply as Christ's bodily presence in the grave rather than referring to his spiritual presence in Sheol. However, hints of the descent are present in this symbolic dimension of baptism in several ways. First, if 1 Peter 3:18–22 refers to the descent, as I suspect that it does, we see a clear connection between Christ's descent (3:19), salvation by passing through water in Noah's ark (3:20), baptism (3:21), the resurrection as victory over death (3:21), and the subjection of powers to the ascended Christ (3:22). Admittedly, some think 1 Peter 3 references the preincarnate work of Christ, but a second notable connection between the descent and baptism may push against this interpretation. In any event, baptism is clearly linked with resurrection, so regardless of where one stands on the descent, the basic point regarding baptism remains. Baptism is at times associated with the defeat of the powers of sin and death and of evil spiritual beings (see Col. 2:12–15; Rom. 6:3–9; cf. Mark 10:38–39),[124] and this is the basic dogmatic claim of the descent—by entering into Sheol, Christ transformed death, disempowering the sin that leads to death and Satan, the ruler of this world. As Charles Hodge explains, to be "buried with Christ" (see Rom. 6:4) means that Christians "are as effectually shut out from the kingdom of Satan as those who are in the grave are shut out from the world."[125] In baptism, then, we find a reminder of our victory over death.

Victory over Sin and Corruptibility

Christ's death and resurrection also play an important role in accomplishing victory over sin and corruptibility. Salvation is spoken of in the past, present, and future tense in Scripture. We "have been raised with Christ" (Col. 3:1), unlike those "perishing" we "are being saved" (1 Cor. 1:18), and "the dead will be raised incorruptible" (1 Cor. 15:52). In the future, sin will

---

124. Mark 10:38–39 does not include a clear link with victory, but baptism is linked with Christ's death. Since the death of Christ serves to establish victory, it is not a stretch to posit an implied connection here.

125. C. Hodge, *Romans*, 194.

be entirely defeated when the faithful take on a glorified resurrected body, free from sin. While the bodily resurrection is an eschatological event, people tend to experience the power of sin and death in some particular evil, suffering, or sin in the present moment, and the present tense of the resurrection points to a current transformation in light of such present sin.[126] This current aspect of resurrection points to the new life we have received in the Holy Spirit, which offers a partial inauguration of the eschatological blessings we await. When Scripture speaks of Christians being raised in the past tense, it points to the objective victory over sin already attained through satisfaction, where Christ's resurrection confirms that the payment is accepted and the Messiah is vindicated in his righteousness. Combined, these three aspects of the resurrection provide a holistic understanding of how the resurrection relates to the defeat of sin.

Through resurrection, Jesus Christ defeats sin as a controlling power in our lives. However, sin is also something that we are victimized by, and the resurrection defeats sin in that respect too. Korean and diaspora Korean theologians, especially those of a progressive leaning, often speak of *han*, a concept referring to "the feelings and experiences of unjust suffering"[127] or "resentment plus bitterness."[128] This *han* can be something we are conscious of or something that remains in the unconscious, and it might be an individual or a group experience.[129] Interestingly, the concept can link the sinful act and the woundedness of the one sinned against, for the one who is victimized often hurts others. Further, the interconnectedness of humanity means that each person's *han* also affects everyone else.[130] The resurrection of Jesus promises a new creation free from *han*, and when the risen Christ sends the Spirit, he begins the healing necessary to overcome *han*. It also summons the church to mission. As Suh Nam-dong says, "If one does not hear the sighs of the *han* of the minjung [the people], one cannot hear the voice of Christ knocking on our doors."[131]

"So it is with the resurrection of the dead: Sown in corruption, raised in incorruption" (1 Cor. 15:42). The concept of corruption is not often central to modern Protestant understandings of the human predicament in a fallen world. Yet at times corruption was a central concern to Christian analysis of the atonement, notably in the patristic era. Corruption here has biological

---

126. Gebara, *Out of the Depths*, 127.
127. G. Kim, *Reimagining Spirit*, 25.
128. Park, *Wounded Heart of God*, 19.
129. Park, *Wounded Heart of God*, 31–41.
130. G. Kim, *Reimagining Spirit*, 119.
131. Nam-dong, "Towards a Theology of *Han*," 65.

and ontological connotations.[132] "Corruption" refers to the gradual decay of the body, which is reversed in the resurrection. Thus, Gregory of Nyssa explains that resurrection returns us to the original condition of Adam and Eve, where humans can no longer age, die, fatigue, or experience weakness.[133] The resurrection restores the "tabernacle" of our nature at a time when "all corruption which has entered in connection with evil will be abolished."[134] Augustine of Hippo centers the ontological dimensions of corruption when he writes that "corruption can consume the good only by consuming the being."[135] Augustine understands evil to be parasitic on the good, a diminishment of the good nature that God has created. Through this diminishment, human beings have wills and minds stained by concupiscence, which directs eros-love toward something other than God.[136] The resurrection promises "the hope of redemption" when "there will remain not a particle of this corrupt concupiscence; but our flesh, healed of that diseased plague, and wholly clad in immortality, shall live forevermore in eternal blessedness."[137]

For this reason, the resurrection also shows the possibility of embodied existence that overcomes even chronic pain and suffering, since uncorruptible resurrected flesh will no longer be subject to such pain.[138]

Victory over Satan

Scripture is clear that Jesus created all things in heaven and on earth, including all powers and authorities (Col. 1:15–16), which means that Satan was created by Jesus too. His rebellion against his creator never stood a chance of victory. Yet he was allowed to reign for a time as the prince of this world. With the resurrection of Christ, the defeat of Satan truly begins. While Satan's full defeat awaits the new creation, when he will be cast into the lake of fire to be tormented forever (Rev. 20:10), Satan is already defeated in several ways through the resurrection. He is defeated indirectly through the defeat of death, which gave the devil the ability to enslave us through

---

132. Both may be implied in Paul's terminology of flesh (*sarx*). In earlier Greek literature and at Qumran, the term referred to what was corruptible. The term also denotes the bodily side of humanity, though it can refer to the complete person. The former emphasis points to the biological aspects of corruption and the latter to the ontological aspects. See Schweizer, Meyer, and Baumgärtel, "σάρξ."

133. Gregory of Nyssa, *On the Soul and the Resurrection*, 113, 118.

134. Gregory of Nyssa, *On the Soul and the Resurrection*, 106.

135. Augustine of Hippo, *Enchiridion* §12.

136. For a helpful account of Augustine's understanding of concupiscence and sin nature, see Chambers, *Nature of Virtue and Sin*.

137. Augustine of Hippo, *On Marriage and Concupiscence* §35.

138. Kapic, *Embodied Hope*, 109.

the fear of death (Heb. 2:14–15),[139] and through the fulfillment of the law (Col. 2:13–15), so that Christians are no longer condemned as the serpent had enticed them to be (Gen. 3).[140] More directly, the resurrection defeats Satan since it is the completion of the Son's first-century work. Early ransom theories of the atonement thought Satan was tricked by thinking his role in killing Christ[141] would defeat the Messiah. On these theories, Satan held fallen humanity ransom through the power of death, but he lost his rights when he killed the innocent Son of God. We need not embrace the idea of God tricking Satan to acknowledge that every diabolic effort to stop the victory of Christ failed and that this failure was fully evident in the resurrection. All that remains is for Christ to return at the second coming, offering an eternal defeat of the devil.

Resurrection and Moral Theology

The resurrection also plays an important role in moral theology. Seen from a supernatural perspective, Jesus's death and resurrection are a central part of the divine plan for salvation. However, Jesus was fully human, and for this reason we must recognize that, like all humans, Jesus died for historical reasons as well.[142] Jesus's historical cause of death was not old age, a tragic accident, or disease. He "suffered under Pontius Pilate, was crucified, died, and was buried," as the Apostles' Creed reminds us. Jesus was killed by a representative of the Roman Empire and by the leaders of the Sanhedrin; no handwashing from Pilate (Matt. 27:24) can absolve him of the responsibility of killing an innocent and sinless man. Jesus's death is a product of the mishandling of justice by imperial powers. For this reason, some modern theologians have described Jesus as a victim. The word must be used carefully. It cannot suggest any powerlessness of Christ. As Jesus himself says, he could summon twelve legions of angels to protect him, if he so wished (Matt. 26:53).

---

139. Interestingly, Heb. 2 does not explicitly name resurrection as a central component of the defeat of Satan, but it does say that the cross served to "free those who were held in slavery [to the devil] all their lives by the fear of death" (2:15). Yet the most obvious way that the fear of death is taken away is through the resurrection, which prevents the finality of death. Something like the descent may also play a role, transforming death from a state of separation in Sheol to one of presence with the Lord.

140. "Paul obviously saw a close connection between the defeat of the evil powers, mentioned in [Col. 2] verse 15, and the fact that the guilty verdict we deserve and its accompanying punishment must have been annulled through the cross, mentioned in verse 14." Page, "Satan, Sin, and Evil," 238.

141. See especially Luke 22:3 and John 13:27, where Satan indwelled Judas.

142. See Ellacuría, *Ignacio Ellacuría*, 206.

The typical human victim cannot make such a claim. Furthermore, Pilate had authority only because it was given by God (John 19:11). Victimization cannot signify powerlessness in Christ, but it can point to the fact that he was an innocent man murdered (Acts 5:30; 7:51) by first-century authorities who were "lawless people" (Acts 2:23). Calling Jesus a victim also cannot replace the supernatural and spiritual goals of the crucifixion and resurrection. Yet neglecting the historical details of Jesus's death would also ignore the full account of Scripture. Once we recognize that Jesus was crucified by imperial powers as a victim, we are challenged to take the crucified people down from the cross, to draw on the imagery of Ignacio Ellacuría.[143] By this he means that since Jesus was tortured,[144] given a mock trial, and unjustly killed, Christians should be particularly concerned to advocate for those who are victims of torture, injustice, and the weapons of death deployed by empire. At a more basic level, the resurrection's emphasis on the importance of bodily life continues to develop the ethic of life that was discussed in the doctrine of the incarnation by showing the eschatological significance of bodies and the promise of an embodied creaturely life.

At its most important and fundamental level, the resurrection is God's victory over death, the devil, and sin, but it is also a challenge to empire and to the misuses of violence and political authority. The resurrection is what God does with a victim. Jon Sobrino helpfully notes that Isaiah 26:7–21, one of the earliest prophecies about resurrection, was given in the context of injustice.[145] Resurrection hope has thus always had political dimensions. The strongest weapon of empire is violence to the point of death, so when death has been defeated, evil earthly rulers have, in certain ways, been disarmed.[146] The power of the resurrection is therefore partly found in the reversal where a commoner can seem to have more confidence and power than a king (see Paul and Agrippa in Acts 26).[147] Jesus's resurrection vindicated his message, including his status as the Messiah. Since Jesus challenged the political and religious authorities of his day, his resurrection can also be seen as a vindication of that critique. "The resurrection, then, marks the *divine vindication* of

143. See Ellacuría, *Ignacio Ellacuría*, 195–224. While I find the concept of the crucified people helpful in moral theology, I cannot go as far as Ellacuría in how he incorporates them into the work of salvation.
144. He was flogged, beaten, mocked, crowned with thorns, and displayed naked for all to see, then ultimately killed in a painful and gruesome manner.
145. Sobrino, *Christ the Liberator*, 40.
146. I do not here mean to trivialize the continued evils wrought by political authorities. They can torture, impoverish, enslave, imprison, and kill individuals and their families. Yet such evils lose their finality through the resurrection.
147. Song, *Third-Eye Theology*, 254.

the *shape* and *way* of the kingdom that Jesus was."[148] The critique of these
powers continues in the narrative of the crucifixion and resurrection, where
Pilate is shown to not know truth (John 18:38) and to crucify a man he believed innocent because he was afraid (John 19:6). Resurrection thus reveals
that the systems of order in the world can be systems of unjust violence, and
it challenges such systems by revealing that they are contrary to the will and
power of God. While Christ is victor especially over sin, death, and the devil,
his victory over earthly powers cannot be ignored, for such a victory plays an
important role in setting the concerns of Christian social thought.

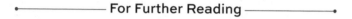

For Further Reading

Aulén, Gustaf. *Christus Victor: An Historical Study of the Three Main Types of the
Idea of the Atonement.* Translated by A. G. Hebert. SPCK, 1950.

> This classic text introduced the terminology of Christus Victor. It remains a
> foundational text in modern atonement theology, well worth reading though
> contested in various dimensions.

Emerson, Matthew Y. *"He Descended to the Dead": An Evangelical Theology of
Holy Saturday.* IVP Academic, 2019.

> Emerson offers a theological and biblical defense of Christ's descent, especially
> against the background of substantive evangelical critique of this doctrine. Emerson
> also considers the theological implications of the descent. This work is fairly
> accessible.

Wright, N. T. *The Resurrection of the Son of God.* Fortress, 2003.

> This lengthy book explores the theology of resurrection across the New Testament
> corpus, considers the Jewish and Hellenistic views of the afterlife, and concludes
> that the Christian perspective was unique and without serious precedent. From
> this, Wright argues that the combination of an empty tomb and postresurrection
> appearances serves as a plausible historical explanation for the new and near-
> universal Christian beliefs. An important read.

---

148. Collins Winn, *God's Reign*, 173.

Ascension and Second Coming

This chapter concludes the work of christological dogmatics by considering the remainder of the exaltation of Christ. The resurrection is only the first of four stages in the exaltation of Christ, with the ascension, session, and second coming completing his exaltation. The risen Christ did not linger on earth but instead returned to his Father, sending the Holy Spirit to be another advocate in his place (John 14). The church now awaits a second coming of the Son, known as the **parousia**, from a Greek term that refers to a coming, which has been used in theology as a technical term for the second coming of Christ. The ascension and second coming play important roles in biblical theology. By the ascension, the Son is vindicated, for not even David ascended to God's heavenly presence (Acts 2:34–36; 5:30–31).[1] The ascension also reminds us that we need not only satisfaction and a sacrifice but also a mediatorial high priest.[2] These dimensions of Christology are important, but one of the most fundamental and contentious issues in Christology as we turn to consider Christ's ministry after the resurrection is explaining how Christ continues to still be present to the church (Matt. 28:20) while also accounting for how Christ will return again in such a way that he has a fuller presence in the future.[3] Christ is truly absent yet is truly present in the church through the sacraments and as the omnipresent Son of God. Christ will also come again, and this second coming will truly result in our having a deeper knowledge and communion with him.

1. Davies, *He Ascended into Heaven*, 63.
2. Treier, *Lord Jesus Christ*, 289.
3. Berkouwer, *Return of Christ*, 142–51.

This chapter will survey the dogmatic components of the ascension and the second coming, including those aspects that are largely agreed on as important components of the teaching of the church and those that are the points of major dispute in the church. Recent theological treatments of the ascension and second coming agree on the importance of the biblical category of the Son of Man while also recognizing the significance of Christ's offices as prophet, priest, and king. Yet there has been significant debate regarding how the ascended God-man continues to be present: Does the human nature of Christ remain present in some fashion, or is the ascended Son present to us only in his deity? After exploring this question, I will briefly treat the session of Christ before turning to the second coming. Here, most theological debates are of lesser importance in my estimation, so I will develop an account of the dogmatic significance of the second coming in terms of hope, judgment, victory, new creation, and the Great Commission.

The Ascended Christ's Prophetic, Priestly, and Kingly Offices

The risen Christ ascends to his Father to fulfill his role as prophet, priest, and king. The ascension expands each dimension of the *munus triplex*, and it results in the sending of the Holy Spirit, an act that is closely linked with each of Christ's offices. Christ ascends as the Prophet who has special access to the mind of the Lord, as the Priest entering the true temple, and as the King set to be enthroned with his Father. Moses is the paradigmatic prophet of Israel, and one of his chief roles was to lead the people to the promised land. In the end, he could not complete this role due to his own imperfections (Deut. 32:51–52). Yet Jesus has gone to prepare a place for us (John 14:2) in the true promised land. Christ ascends in order to send his Holy Spirit, through which signs and the gift of prophecy are expanded to the larger body of Christ.[4] We can set aside here the nature and extent of such prophecy as best engaged in pneumatology; any provision of the gifts of prophecy and signs (1 Cor. 12:10) would be an expansion of the prophetic office. Interestingly, the ascension of Elijah in the Old Testament prefigures Christ's gift of the Spirit, for Elisha is able to receive a double portion of the Spirit Elijah possessed if he witnesses Elijah ascend (2 Kings 2:10). The disciples witness the ascension and receive the Spirit.[5]

---

4. "The ascent not only *authorized*, but *amplified* and *multiplies* his prophetic work. Because of the ascension, Christ sent the Spirit, continues to inspire his word, and fills and equips his church to perform his signs as his body on the earth. In all of these ways, Jesus birthed, builds, and grows his church as the ascended prophet." P. Schreiner, *Ascension of Christ*, 30.

5. P. Schreiner, *Ascension of Christ*, 28–29. Schreiner links Elisha witnessing the ascension to the emphasis in Acts 1:9–11 on the disciples seeing the ascension, noting the regular usage of verbs indicating seeing Christ ascend.

An important part of the priest's role is to intercede on behalf of the people. Just as the historical priests of Israel represented the people of God, which was symbolized in the high priestly breastplate bearing stones representing the tribes (Exod. 28:15–21), so Christ represents the church through his entry into the heavenly holy of holies. The priest was a member of the people of Israel, a nation of priests that represented all the nations before God (Exod. 19:6), and so Christ is able to represent not just Israel but all nations, as he is the recapitulation of Israel in its priestly role.[6] Sam Parkison links the gift of the Spirit to the ascended Christ's priestly role in the offering of the sacrifice. The sacrifice is incomplete until the priest enters the holy of holies (Lev. 16:11–15), and Christ our priest enters the heavenly holy of holies in the ascension. Parkison explains, "Christ purchased the gift of the Holy Spirit for his people with blood, and part of his priestly office is to retrieve that benefit for us in the ascension to thereafter send to us."[7]

The ascension is also closely linked with Jesus's kingly enthronement. For example, Luke situates the ascension in the context of the enthronement of the Davidic king. Jesus was announced as king (Luke 1:32–33), the kingdom is the immediate context of the ascension in Acts (1:3, 6), and enthronement psalms are used to interpret the ascension by Peter (Acts 2:22–36) and Paul (Acts 13:32–37).[8] As Patrick Schreiner explains, the Jewish king was "chosen by the Lord to rule with justice and righteousness, defeat Israel's enemies, promote the Torah, and bless the world."[9] Jesus rules from the heavenly throne, having defeated the enemies of sin, death, and the devil. Significantly, though, the ascension enables the sending of the Holy Spirit. By the sending of the Spirit, God's kingdom is expanded and enacted.[10]

The Manner of Christ's Presence After the Ascension

I have shown how the ascension is connected to Christ's titles as prophet, priest, and king, but we must remember that the ascended Christ is the same Son who was incarnate. Therefore, the doctrine of the ascension is still regulated

---

6. It is for good reason that Douglas Farrow describes Irenaeus as a theologian of the ascension. Farrow, *Ascension and Ecclesia*, 45. As discussed in chapter 2, Irenaeus also plays a central role in the history of the church's theology of recapitulation.

7. Parkison, *Unvarnished Jesus*, 163.

8. Jipp, "Enthroned-in-Heaven King," 43–46.

9. P. Schreiner, *Ascension of Christ*, 79–81. Schreiner explains that this role had only been an ideal until Christ.

10. "The first act of the enthroned king, in other words, is to send God's powerful *pneuma* as the means for the expansion of God's kingdom (cf. Acts 1:6–11)." Jipp, "Enthroned-in-Heaven King," 50.

by the metaphysics of the incarnation, as described through the affirmation of two natures united in one hypostasis, with each nature having its own will and operation. This christological metaphysic is evident in discussions from the earliest Christian creeds, some of which describe the ascension in the active voice, "He ascended," while others have the passive, "He was taken up." As J. G. Davies explains, "Later theologians were to see in these two usages an important theological distinction and to apply the first to the Godhead of Christ and the second to his humanity."[11] In the medieval period, Thomas Aquinas gives us his typical precision when he explains that Christ ascended to heaven through his human and divine natures.[12] The divine nature is the cause of the ascension, while the human nature is that which ascended—after all, the omnipresent divine nature cannot move from one location to another, and nothing is higher than it. Aquinas speculates that the glorified soul of Christ also contributed a secondary power to the elevation of his human body, preserving the principle that each nature "does the acts which belong to it, in communion with the other."[13] As both natures are active, though the humanity in a much lesser sense, both natures are also passively glorified, though the deity in a lesser sense. As Thomas Oden explains, the humanity was exalted by overcoming human infirmities, while the deity was exalted not by acquiring a new strength but by again manifesting that glory which had been veiled in the flesh.[14] Yet, though the ascension continues the hypostatic union, there has been serious debate about the condition of the humanity of Christ after the ascension, particularly in terms of the presence of Christ in the Eucharist.

Reformation-Era Eucharistic Debates and the Ascension

One of the more challenging aspects of the doctrine of the ascension concerns the manner of Christ's continued presence with his church. Christ's ascension suggests some form of absence, but statements affirming his absence are often balanced with promises of his continued presence (e.g., Matt. 28:6, 20). This tension produced its most contentious debates during the time of the Reformation, when arguments about Christ's ascension were one dimension of Protestant debates over the Eucharist. To simplify: The Reformed argued that a bodily ascension required a bodily absence, including from the Eucharist, prompting some Lutherans to argue that Christ's ascension

---

11. Davies, *He Ascended into Heaven*, 96.
12. See Aquinas, *Summa Theologica* III, Q. 57, A. 2–3.
13. Leo the Great, *Tome* §4.
14. Oden, *Word of Life*, 507.

is the basis for a new bodily presence in the Eucharist. The disagreement over the Eucharist played a major role in the split between the two groups.

One strand of Protestantism especially associated with the Reformed argues that Christ's ascension demands a real absence. Famously, Huldrych Zwingli argued directly against Luther that Christ's ascension demanded a real departure, citing, among other things, Jesus's promise to leave his disciples as evidence (see Matt. 26:11; John 16:28).[15] If Jesus was still bodily present, then he surely did not leave as Scripture attests. Therefore, Zwingli concludes that when Christ says, "This is my body" (Matt. 26:26; Mark 14:22; Luke 22:19; 1 Cor. 11:24), "is" means "signifies"—"This *signifies* my body."[16] The roots of the appeal to the ascension go far earlier, but appeal to the ascension as reason to deny Christ's bodily presence in the Eucharist probably made its way to the Reformers from origins among the followers of Jan Hus.[17] Taborite bishop Nicholas of Pelhřimov argued for Christ's spiritual presence in the Eucharist, while claiming that the body was in heaven due to the ascension.[18] Similarly, Brother Lukas, main representative of the *Unitas Fratrem* in the early 1500s, distinguished between Christ's "personal, true, essential and natural presence (*personalis, vera, substantialis et naturalis*)," which was in heaven due to the ascension, and "his presence in the church, which was [virtual], spiritual, and ministerial (*virtualis, spiritualis et ministerialis*); his spiritual presence in the soul; and his sacramental and spiritual presence in the elements."[19] This Hussite argument made its way to Johannes Oecolampadius, Heinrich Bullinger, and Zwingli, and through them became the dominant position in the Reformed tradition.[20]

Though Luther initially argued for the bodily presence of Christ in the Eucharist for other reasons, his debate with Zwingli led him to argue that the ascension could allow Jesus to have bodily presence in the Eucharist in a new way. Lutherans often followed suit, though there is some disagreement among Luther's successors.[21] For Luther, affirming the bodily presence of

---

15. Zwingli, *Lord's Supper*, 214.

16. Zwingli learned the interpretation of "is" meaning "signifies" from Cornelius Hoen, who wrote a letter in 1521 delivered to Oecolampadius, Luther, Bucer, and Zwingli. See Mathison, "Lord's Supper," 651.

17. Zwingli will also eventually appeal to Berengar of Tours, who argued from the ascension that the bread was not literally Christ's body. See Zwingli, *Lord's Supper*, 193–97; Wandel, *Eucharist in the Reformation*, 21.

18. A. Burnett, *Eucharistic Controversy*, 78.

19. A. Burnett, *Eucharistic Controversy*, 81.

20. A. Burnett, *Eucharistic Controversy*, 85–89. Zwingli learned the Hussite arguments through Oecolampadius. See Drake, *Flesh of the Word*, 42.

21. Note, however, the variety in early Lutheranism where Philip Melanchthon, for example, could agree that Christ's humanity was restricted to local presence in heaven, a position condemned by Chemnitz and Brenz. McGinnis, *Son of God Beyond the Flesh*, 81.

Christ is a necessary dimension of the **perspicuity of Scripture**, for Christ clearly said of the bread, "This is my body" (Matt. 26:26; Mark 14:22; Luke 22:19; 1 Cor. 11:24).[22] Initially, Luther was largely unwilling to speculate on how Christ's body was present. As Protestant theological debates unfolded, Luther drew on a medieval distinction to explain how Christ might be bodily present.[23] Something is locally or circumscriptively present where "the space and the object occupying it exactly correspond and fit into the same measurements," as with wine in a cask.[24] This was the Son's manner of bodily presence during the incarnation. Something has **definitive** or **uncircumscribed presence** when it is finitely present but neither tangible nor occupying a specific space. Traditionally angels and demons have been said to be present in this manner, explaining why demons in two men can also be cast into an entire herd of pigs (see Matt. 8:28–34). Like many medieval theologians, Luther suggested that this was the manner of Christ's bodily presence after the resurrection, explaining how Christ could walk through walls (John 20:19) or suddenly appear or disappear (e.g., Luke 24:31).[25] Luther adds that following the ascension Christ must have **complete presence**, which is basically omnipresence. Luther argues that this follows from the unity of the person of Christ. If he is present everywhere, and if he is human, then he is humanly present everywhere.[26] While there is some interpretative debate to be had regarding whether or not this distinction reflects Luther's understanding of Christ's postascension presence or merely one possible rebuttal to Zwingli,[27] it is at least clear that some Lutherans held clearly to the **ubiquity of Christ**.[28]

22. See the discussion in Wandel, *Eucharist in the Reformation*, 101–3. For an example of Luther appealing to the perspicuity and infallibility of Scripture here, see Luther, "Confession Concerning Christ's Supper," 267.

23. On this context, see Drake, *Flesh of the Word*, 97; Mathison, "Lord's Supper," 658.

24. Luther, "Confession Concerning Christ's Supper," 267.

25. Precedent for Luther's distinction is found in both William of Ockham and Thomas Aquinas, though the two used the concept in different ways. Sasse, *This Is My Body*, 157.

26. Luther, "Confession Concerning Christ's Supper," 268–69.

27. I'm thankful to David Luy for introducing me to this possibility. We might consider, for example, Luther's more apophatic perspective after introducing the distinction as one reason to think Luther only posits a possible interpretation. Speaking of the Son's humanity in its presence in the Trinity, Luther remarks: "But who can explain or even conceive how this occurs? We know indeed that it is so, that he is in God beyond all created things, and is one person with God. But how this happens, we do not know." Speaking then of his threefold distinction, Luther adds, "I do not wish to have denied by the foregoing that God may have and know still other modes whereby Christ's body can be in a given place. My only purpose was to show what crass fools our fanatics are when they concede only the first, circumscribed, mode of presence." Luther, "Confession Concerning Christ's Supper," 272.

28. For example, see Johannes Brenz, as discussed in Ehmer, "Johannes Brenz," 132–33.

Attempts to resolve the basic theological disagreement through exegesis were largely fruitless. Consider some examples: Francis Turretin argues that the real bodily absence of Christ is evident in the vocabulary used to describe the ascension, which implies a change in location. Christ was taken up (*analambanō* in Mark 16:19), carried up (*anapherō* in Luke 24:51), and parted from the disciples (*diistēmi* in Luke 24:51).[29] Martin Chemnitz responded to this sort of argument merely by agreeing that the local, bodily presence of Christ has indeed really been taken away while remaining present in other ways.[30] The Reformed also argue that Christ's body is locally present at the right hand of the Father (e.g., Acts 7:55–56; Rom. 8:34; Col. 3:1).[31] Lutherans sometimes counter that the Father does not have a literal right hand; rather, the phrase is a metaphor for God's power, which is omnipresent.[32] The Reformed counter that the ascension is depicted as an entry into a new place (e.g., 2 Cor. 12:2; Heb. 6:20),[33] as if this is what is signified by the metaphor of God's right hand. They also argue that Mary is told that the body of Christ is not here after the resurrection (Matt. 28:5).[34] Against this, Ephesians 1:10 and 4:10 teach, according to Luther, that Christ "in his human nature" is put over all things and is in all things, being omnipresent.[35] John Calvin responds to this sort of exegesis by arguing that the ascended Christ is truly bodily absent but fills all things in the sense of his spiritual presence by his Spirit.[36] And so the debates can continue to the point of exasperation, for the literal meaning of the text of Scripture does not intend to explain to us the manner of Christ's departure or the manner of his continued presence. Here, we must move beyond exegesis to questions of doctrinal significance, exploring how various interpretations of passages discussing the ascension fit with the larger dogmatic picture of Christ's humanity and divinity that Scripture demands.

A Dogmatic Analysis of Christ's Postascension Presence

At stake in the eucharistic debates is nothing less than the unity of Christ, his genuine humanity, and his full divinity. Lutherans often worry that the *extra Calvinisticum*, the Reformed claim that the Son's divine presence extends beyond or outside his human presence, undermines the unity of Christ

29. Turretin, *Institutes* 13.18.3.
30. Chemnitz, *Lord's Supper*, 211.
31. Zwingli, *Lord's Supper*, 216.
32. Mathison, "Lord's Supper," 658.
33. Turretin, *Institutes* 13.18.6.
34. Zwingli, *Lord's Supper*, 221.
35. Luther, *Sacrament of the Body and Blood*, 228.
36. Calvin, *Clear Explanation of Sound Doctrine*, 312.

by dividing the action of the natures in a purportedly Nestorian manner.[37] At times this worry can take the form of a critique of the very division of agency in the natures in the hypostatic union, as is the case in the modern Lutheran theologian Robert Jenson. Jenson argues that Leo the Great's insistence on each nature doing what is proper to it results in a theology that "cannot affirm the actuality of the human Christ in God's transcendence of space," a fact that ultimately divides the human Jesus from the divine Logos, a clearly "inadequate Christology."[38] For Jenson, then, the critique must go back to Leo's *Tome* itself and the bifurcation he believes that it establishes when it posits each nature as "the agent of what is proper to it."[39] Typically, though, Lutherans are more positive about the Chalcedonian formula, with some considering the ubiquity of Christ a natural outworking of its principles. This stream of Lutheran thought raises an important point that must be addressed: The ascension cannot be the basis for dissolving the unity of the person of Christ, so any explanation of the Eucharist or ascension must strive to ensure that hypostatic unity persists. If the ascended and enthroned Christ does not remain human in his priestly and kingly ministry, then our salvation is undermined—the enduring unity of Christ's person is a matter of fundamental importance.

The Reformed can appeal to the doctrines discussed earlier in this book to defend the claim that the unity of the person of Christ does not require ubiquity. To recognize this fact, we must begin with the ways in which the triune persons are one. They share consubstantiality, each having all necessary properties to count as God; their shared substance is simple, so three persons do not divide the divine nature into three things; the persons perichoretically interpenetrate one another, such that all aspects of the divine life are shared; and, finally, the persons work inseparably in all works toward creation. These four points establish the basis for the unity of the Trinity. Two of these four points are clearly not available when we consider the unity of the incarnation. First, the unity of the incarnation is not a unity of a single substance, for true humanity and true divinity are not the same. Second, the human and divine natures are not the same simple substance. Beyond this, however, we have seen that the unity of natures in Christ's person includes a unity of perichoresis

---

37. So, Luther: "We merge the two distinct natures into one single person, and say: God is man and man is God. We in turn raise a hue and cry against them for separating the person of Christ as though there were two persons." Luther, "Confession Concerning Christ's Supper," 266.

38. Jenson, *Systematic Theology*, 2:254–56.

39. Jenson, *Systematic Theology*, 1:130–33. Jenson remarks, "Chalcedon's more suspicious readers concluded that the decree's 'in one hypostasis' is not successfully a concept, so that the decree's repetition of 'one and the same' is verbiage. It is hard to say they are wrong, taking the text just as it stands." Jenson, *Systematic Theology*, 1:133.

and a unity of action. Though the forms of each variety of unity differ from their trinitarian variety, I have argued that they still constitute unity. These are forms of unity inclusive of distinction since perichoresis is the mutual interpenetration and coinherence of two distinct natures or hypostases and since inseparable operations and dyoenergism permit the ongoing distinction of persons and natures. For this reason, I do not see why a distinction between Christ's humanity and divinity necessitates a division of person.

The second major issue concerns the full humanity of Christ. The Reformed consistently argued that neither a truly human nature nor a true body could be omnipresent.[40] Bodies, by definition, must be locally present, and Christ's body was not locally present on earth after the ascension. While the Reformed position has been critiqued as rooted too heavily in **univocity** because it treats heaven as spatial, and thus God as spatial,[41] such objections miss the point. Following the ascension, heaven is the dwelling place of at least one human, and humans are spatially present. An affirmation of God's simultaneous radical transcendence and radical immanence is irrelevant. After all, both sides agreed on the omnipresence of Christ in his divinity, which brings us to our first dogmatic point of consensus: Christ remains omnipresent in his divinity after the incarnation. This fact has already been implied through my rejection of kenoticism in chapter 1, but here we can more clearly affirm it.[42] While the Reformed teach the **local presence** of the humanity of Christ after the ascension, they also balance this claim with the *extra Calvinisticum*, the idea that Christ's divinity is omnipresent, exceeding the limits of his humanity.[43] Thus, all creation continued to exist in and through the Word even

40. Thus Calvin argues that if the body of Christ were ubiquitous, "the body of Christ, if so constituted, was a phantasm, or fantastical." Calvin, *Institutes* 4.17.17. See also Zwingli's entreaty to "hold fast to the words: The body which is risen is necessarily in one place," at the right hand of God. Zwingli, *Lord's Supper*, 222.

41. Thus Brad Gregory: A "spatial dichotomizing of Jesus's divine and human natures" and pointing to Jesus at the right hand is "a logical corollary of metaphysical univocity. A 'spiritual' presence that is *contrasted* with a real presence presupposed an either-or dichotomy between a crypto-spatial God and the natural world that precludes divine immanence in its desire to preserve divine transcendence." Gregory, *Unintended Reformation*, 42–43.

42. Interestingly, we can also now more clearly understand why kenoticism emerged in the Lutheran Thomasius. If Christ's human nature and divine nature are understood as necessarily present in the same way to preserve the unity of the person of Christ, then it is no surprise that someone would eventually balance a postascension affirmation of the ubiquity of Christ with a postincarnation affirmation of kenoticism.

43. K. J. Drake offers a more expansive definition: "The following four propositions will constitute the extra Calvinisticum: (1) Jesus Christ, the God-man, maintained an existence *extra carnem* during his earthly ministry; (2) after the ascension and session the human body of Christ exists locally in heaven; (3) the presence of Christ to the Christian in the time between his first and second comings is according to his divinity, power, and the Holy Spirit; (4) the *communicatio*

after the incarnation (John 1:3; 1 Cor. 8:6; Col. 1:16). If Christ was, is, and will be fully divine, then his divine omnipresence must be affirmed after the ascension. Though affirmation of the continued omnipresence of the Son after the incarnation has more ancient roots, Reformation-era eucharistic debates brought this point more clearly into focus.[44]

A more contested question concerns the presence of Christ's humanity after the ascension. Generally, all sides of the debate agree that Christ is not locally present after the ascension, though the narrative of Acts may suggest occasional exceptions (e.g., Acts 23:11).[45] Therefore, all would agree with Zwingli that there is some sense in which Christ's body is truly absent following the ascension. All therefore also agree that Christ's continued presence is different from his incarnate presence during his life. Here we can add several other terms to Luther's notion of definitive presence and Brother Lukas's notion of virtual, spiritual, ministerial, and eucharistic presence. It is also possible to speak more ambiguously of eucharistic bodily presence in a supernatural mode,[46] or, following Augustus Strong, to suggest that though Christ's body is locally present in heaven, his soul might be omnipresent, since local presence is not a property of souls,[47] though Strong's position seems less plausible to me. Drawing on the Psalms' language of "lifting up" our souls in worship (see Pss. 25:1; 86:4; 143:8), many have argued that Christ is bodily present to us as we are brought by the Holy Spirit into heaven. Thus, Alexander Schmemann writes, "The Eucharist of Christ and Christ the Eucharist is the 'breakthrough' that brings us to the table in the Kingdom, raises us to heaven, and makes us partakers of the divine food."[48] Similarly, Douglas Farrow draws on an allegorical interpretation from the Venerable Bede to argue that just like Elisha is able to receive Elijah's mantle only if he sees him ascend in the chariot of fire (2 Kings 2:1–12), "only those who 'see' Jesus ascend are ready to receive the gift of the sacraments."[49] For Farrow, Christ's real presence in the Eucharist means that Christ is really here to us, and we are really in heaven with Christ.[50]

---

idiomatum within the hypostatic union terminates on the person of Christ, and therefore excludes a sharing of properties between the divine and human natures themselves. When these aspects are present, the full doctrine of the extra is achieved." Drake, *Flesh of the Word*, 16.

44. For example, see an extensive discussion by McGinnis on precedents for the *extra Calvinisticum* in Cyril of Alexandria. McGinnis, *Son of God Beyond the Flesh*, 15–46.

45. Chemnitz, *Lord's Supper*, 212. We cannot discount the possibility that any appearances are something more akin to visions, as is the case in Acts 9:10–11 and 18:9.

46. Dorner, *System of Christian Religion*, 319.

47. Strong, *Systematic Theology*, 709.

48. Schmemann, *For the Life of the World*, 50. Schmemann also allows for a form of bodily presence, though he eschews scholastic debates about the means of this presence.

49. Farrow, *Ascension Theology*, 65.

50. Farrow, *Ascension Theology*, 71.

Prudence demands some reservation in making dogmatic statements regarding the mode of Christ's human presence after the ascension. As Luther remarks, to say that Jesus ascended to heaven "is not the same as when you climb up a ladder into the house."[51] Or, to follow Chemnitz, we must admit that we do not know enough about the mode of existence in heaven to rule out the possibility that Christ is also substantially present in the Lord's Supper.[52] For this reason, at a dogmatic level I am content to argue that Christ certainly remains present to us in his divinity after the ascension and that his presence is as a united subject who is both fully human and fully divine. I am convinced that Christ is truly present in the Eucharist, though a full argument for this claim exceeds the scope of my current argument in a manner that would distract from the purpose at hand.[53] Further, Stephen Holmes raises a valid point when he contends that arguing for the ubiquity of Christ is trying to prove "far too much." Establishing the ubiquity of the humanity of Christ would suggest its equal presence in any given slice of pizza in comparison with the eucharistic elements; what would need to be established for real *bodily* presence is something like "an account of multiple particular local presences."[54] So, even granting room for debate regarding how the humanity of the ascended God-man is present at Communion, I see little sacramental basis for affirming the full ubiquity of Christ's humanity regardless of one's sacramental theology. Now is the time to consider what dogmatic insights the possibility of Christ's presence yields for Christology, not to explore the doctrine of the Eucharist in its entire dogmatic scope. Nevertheless, I do believe there is reason to hold that the ubiquity of Christ is less likely than the *extra Calvinisticum*, which brings us to our last dogmatic consideration.

Lutherans affirm the idea of the *genus maiestaticum*, referring to the fact that through the incarnation, "attributes which are proper to the divine nature have been given to Christ above and beyond its essential or natural properties."[55] It strikes me that there are two ways in which these divine attributes can be given to Christ's humanity. The first avenue would involve the communication of attributes by allowing the humanity to participate in the communicable attributes of God. Christians can, by grace through partaking in the divine nature (2 Pet. 1:4), become immortal, good, holy, and so forth. I see good reason to heartily endorse this proposal. As discussed in chapter

51. Luther, *Sacrament of the Body and Blood*, 228.
52. Chemnitz, *Lord's Supper*, 212–14.
53. At the very least, this argument would involve extensive exegetical analysis of passages like Matt. 26:17–30 and parr.; Luke 24:30–31; John 6:25–71; and 1 Cor. 10–11.
54. Holmes, "Reformed Varieties of the *Communicatio Idiomatum*," 75.
55. Chemnitz, *Two Natures in Christ*, 262.

6, we might understand this communication in terms of concepts like union or theosis. The second avenue, however, would involve the proper transmission of the divine attributes to the human nature of Christ, such that Christ bears these attributes in his humanity because the humanity has received the divine nature. It is difficult for me to see how this would avoid monophysitism. Divine simplicity would require that one cannot possess part of the divine nature without possessing all of the divine nature, so if genuine impartation of deity into humanity is intended in discussing the *genus maiestaticum*, then the humanity would receive the fullness of deity, being fully joined in nature with it. I reject such a claim based on my understanding of the hypostatic union, as discussed in chapter 5.

Christ's Session

The ascended Christ sits down at the right hand of his Father (e.g., Acts 7:55–56; Rom. 8:34; Col. 3:1). John Flavel explains that the right hand signifies that all honor and power are Christ's and that he is as near as possible to God.[56] The session at the right hand of the Father ought not be seen as a sign of the Son's subordination, as some recent commentators have suggested.[57] After all, Jesus claims to have "all authority . . . in heaven and on earth" (Matt. 28:18), and the Old Testament occasionally depicts God at the right hand of the king (Pss. 16:8; 110:5; 121:5; Isa. 41:13; 45:1). Surely, God is not subordinate to the king. In his session, Jesus plays several important roles for the church. Most obviously, he intercedes for us, representing us in the heavenly court.[58] Perhaps less well known is the significance of the ascension for our transformation. As Dumitru Stăniloae helpfully explains, "The ascension into heaven and the sitting at the right hand of the Father represent the complete . . . deification of his human body, his being filled to capacity with the divine infinity, and his complete rising to the state of unrestrictedly

56. Flavel, *Fountain of Life*, 515–16. The right hand is the "weapon hand, and the working hand," representing power. It also has a meaning similar to being "at one's elbow."

57. Grudem, "Biblical Evidence," 251. In fact, in many historical treatments of the session, conscious effort has been given to ensure that the session denotes the equality of the persons, not the subordination of the Son. See, for example, Levering, *Jesus and the Demise of Death*, 52–54.

58. Peter Toon helpfully explains that this intercession ought not be seen as pleading to persuade a hesitant Father, nor should the intercession be reduced to a sign of love or to the sacrificial office. Rather, "as glorified Man, Jesus adores, praises, worships, and offers thanksgiving to the Father. He asks that the Father will give the Holy Spirit to those who believe and bring them into eternal salvation. As glorified Man with a vicarious humanity, Jesus prays the prayers of all his people; all prayer, be it praise or petition, is 'through our Lord Jesus Christ.'" Toon, *Ascension of Our Lord*, 63–66.

transparent medium of God's infinite love in its work directed towards us."[59] The exaltation of Christ is also the exaltation of human nature, anticipating our own glorification at the eschaton as we are fully conformed to Christ.

The Second Coming of Christ

Though God is known as the eternal God (e.g., 1 Tim. 1:17; Heb. 13:8), Scripture also depicts God as the coming God. For example, Revelation describes God as "the one who is, who was, and who is to come" (1:4, 8). Where the reader might expect to read God described as he "who will be," instead God is he "who is to come." This gives an eschatological orientation to Christian thinking of the triune God,[60] and while all three persons will appear in new ways in the eschaton, special focus is given to the second coming of Christ, the Son of Man.

Jesus Christ is the Son of Man, a multifaceted term that I have already argued includes a reference to second-Adam Christology. However, commentators generally agree that the title also references the mysterious figure from Daniel 7:

> And suddenly one like a son of man
> was coming with the clouds of heaven.
> He approached the Ancient of Days
> and was escorted before him.
> He was given dominion
> and glory and a kingdom,
> so that those of every people,
> nation, and language
> should serve him.
> His dominion is an everlasting dominion
> that will not pass away,
> and his kingdom is one
> that will not be destroyed. (7:13–14)

There is considerable debate regarding whether this figure is a Davidic king, a historical figure like Judas Maccabeus, a symbol of the Israelite people as

---

59. Stăniloae, *Experience of God*, 3:149.

60. This eschatological thinking is important, and Jürgen Moltmann has done well to insist that "God's being in the world has to be thought eschatologically, and the future of time has to be understood theologically," but I do not see that this theological claim leads inexorably to a revised metaphysic where "the future is God's mode of being in history. . . . His eternity is not timeless simultaneity; it is the power of his future over every historical time." Moltmann, *Coming of God*, 23–24. It is possible to shape a theology of creation and history around eschatology without needing to shape a theology of the doctrine of God in a similar manner. Yet a theology of history is more constructive than dogmatic, so the full dispute on such matters need not be resolved here.

a whole, a celestial being, or a hypostatization of God.[61] Several arguments favor interpreting the son of man to be divine. First, the one like a son of man emerges in heaven among the clouds, symbolizing God's presence and dwelling, while in the preceding vision of beasts opposed to God (Dan. 7:2–8), the beasts arose from the sea, a place symbolizing chaos and disorder.[62] In many respects, this battle between creatures of chaos and a powerful hero mirrors ancient Near Eastern mythology with a similar plot. Likely, Daniel here alludes to such myth, renarrating it such that the true Lord is the Ancient of Days, and the true hero the one like a son of man.[63] Daniel was trained in the literature of the Babylonians, after all (Dan. 1:4).[64] Second, riding on the clouds likely mirrors similar imagery of God on a heavenly chariot (e.g., Pss. 68:4; 104:3; Isa. 19:1; Jer. 4:13; Nah. 1:3).[65] Third, there may be parallels between the narrative of Daniel 7, in which spiritual powers subordinate to God compete for and eventually are assigned dominion, and passages like Deuteronomy 32:8–9 and Psalm 82, where territories are divided among lesser gods, with the Lord ultimately having sovereign control over all.[66] This may suggest that the one like a son of man is filling a role traditionally filled in such narratives by a lesser deity. Fourth, as Michael Bird explains, "There is a fascinating textual variant in Daniel 7:13, where some Greek witnesses have the Son of Man coming not 'towards' (eōs) the Ancient of Days but 'as' (ōs) the Ancient of Days—either a scribal error or an acute theological judgment of the Son of Man as a second divine figure besides Yahweh."[67] This scribal tradition further connects the one like a son of man to the deity of the Ancient of Days. Finally, the placement of thrones (note the plural) in Daniel 7:9 may

61. For a brief and helpful summary of these perspectives, see Goldingay, *Daniel*, 365–70.

62. Widder notes that "fifty-eight of the eighty-seven occurrences of [cloud] appear in the context of God's presence" in the Old Testament. Widder, *Daniel*, 378–79.

63. For parallels, see Lester, *Daniel Evokes Isaiah*, 43–47. "Dan 7's rendering of the myth shows an important break from the chaos combat myth, in that the victory of the high god over the forces of chaos is represented as effortless, and as judicial rather than military" (47).

64. Setting aside debates about authorship of the book, Daniel, the protagonist and, at times, narrator, is depicted as trained by the Babylonians, so use of such mythology fits the depiction of Daniel.

65. Widder, *Daniel*, 379. Segal explores how this Old Testament imagery likely draws on Canaanite imagery of Baal as a rider-of-clouds, where Baal's depiction in this manner sometimes occurs in the context of a battle for control of the earth, much like the battle against the beasts in Daniel 7. Segal, *Dreams, Riddles, and Visions*, 135–36.

66. See Segal, *Dreams, Riddles, and Visions*, 145–50. This interpretation of Deut. 32 depends partly on accepting a textual variant of Deut. 32:9, that land is partitioned "in accordance with the number of the sons of God" instead of "sons of Israel." This would point to some sort of heavenly court within which lands were divided. Among other reasons, the "sons of God" textual tradition finds support in its preservation in many LXX manuscripts. See Harstad, *Deuteronomy*, 839.

67. Bird, *Jesus Among the Gods*, 197.

draw on imagery from Psalm 110:1, anticipating a Davidic heir to sit at the right hand of God, perhaps on a throne.[68] Yet sharing the divine throne blurs the line between divine and human sovereignty, to say the least. Such Davidic imagery also raises questions about the humanity of the one like a son of man.

Despite the arguments for the one like a son of man being a divine figure, elements of the text also point to a human, Davidic identity of the figure. Notably, David is promised an everlasting dominion (2 Sam. 7:13), and Psalm 8 depicts the Davidic son of man enjoying dominion over the beasts of the earth.[69] Daniel 6 emphasizes the rule of God, and John Goldingay is right to note that "as the one whom God commissions to exercise his kingly authority, the humanlike figure fulfills the role of the anointed one, whether or not he is an earthly Davidide."[70] Certainly, the language of "one like a son of man" (Dan. 7:13) could suggest a human ruling figure; given Israel's history, there would be an obvious impetus to think of the Davidic line. This vision thus depicts a likely divine figure of some sort who also bears similarity to the Davidic ruler, a human yet divine figure receiving authority. From this ambiguity, expressed in symbolic and mythic ways through a vision, one is prompted for a theological solution much akin to what has been developed earlier in this work. Christian theology is driven to read Daniel 7 through the lens of the theology of the divine Son incarnate of the line of David, descending to earth through kenosis and then elevated to authority as the reigning last Adam, receiving again the eternal authority possessed from the foundations of the earth.

What, then, does the arrival of the Son of Man in the clouds into the presence of the Ancient of Days signify? Commentators have been divided regarding whether Daniel 7 specifies one ascending into the presence of God or one coming from God toward earth. Certainly, on the first reading of the text of Daniel 7, it seems that one entering the presence of the Ancient of Days seems to speak of an ascension into God's presence. Yet most first-century texts interpreted the passage to speak of a figure coming to earth.[71] Since Jesus both departed the earth, ascending in the clouds (Acts 1:9), and promised to return in the clouds (Matt. 24:30; 26:64 and parr.), it is possible to affirm both senses for Christ.

---

68. Hamilton, *With the Clouds of Heaven*, 148–49.

69. Hamilton, *With the Clouds of Heaven*, 147. Hamilton argues that Jewish interpreters were unable to see the divinity of the Davidic ruler until after Christ's coming.

70. Goldingay, *Daniel*, 367.

71. Bühner remarks, "We have clear evidence that Jews in the first century CE did in fact understand it as a coming from the heavens down to earth. This can be seen in the book of Giants from Qumran (see 4Q530 frg. 2 II 16–20), in the Animal Apocalypse (see 1 En. 90:20), and most clearly in 4 Ezra 13. Indeed, except for the Parables of Enoch (1 En. 37–41), we lack clear evidence that any Jew in the Second Temple period understood it the way many modern scholars conclude from the Danielic text itself, that is, as a heavenly assent." Bühner, *Messianic High Christology*, 9.

Christological Exegesis and Inaugurated Eschatology

We turn now to consider the theological significance of Christ's second coming. Much modern discussion of eschatology focuses on the predictive dimensions of the doctrine. For example, when considering the thousand-year reign of Christ in Revelation 20:4–6, ought we to interpret this passage to reference a historical reign of a thousand years in the current creation with two resurrections on either end of this period?[72] Or ought we interpret the millennium as symbolic of the era of the church, with the "first resurrection" (Rev. 20:5) before this reign signifying our spiritual resurrection in Christ (e.g., Col. 3:1)?[73] I do not see anything of fundamental importance in such debates, provided that we affirm that Christ truly will come again as the victorious judge who brings about a new creation, so specific positions on these questions do not belong in a work of dogmatics.[74] Further, one must reject the teachings of Marcellus of Ancyra that the Son ceases to be a distinct person after the second coming.[75] Beyond such general details, however, much eschatology is secondary or tertiary in importance. In fact, we would do well to follow William Perkins in recognizing the strict biblical limitations on our knowledge of the details of the parousia. When Daniel asks for details about the vision he received regarding the end, "the words are shut up and sealed until the time of the end" (Dan. 12:9 ESV). When the disciples ask the risen Christ about the end, they are told, "It is not for you to know times or periods that the Father has set by his own authority" (Acts 1:7).[76] Rather than centering questions of timing and interpretation of prophetic symbols, it is better to focus on the identity and significance of the coming Christ, and to understand how Christ relates to the eschaton, we need to think about biblical prophecy.

Christians have long recognized that the divine authorship of Scripture allows for multiple levels of meaning.[77] Hugh of St. Victor, for example, affirmed three meanings in Scripture: the historical; the moral/tropological, through which the text guided Christian character; and the allegorical/anagogical, which

---

72. Erickson argues for this on the basis of the same verb being used to describe "living again" for both those before the millennium and those after (Rev. 20:4b–5a). Erickson, *Christian Theology*, 1216.

73. For example, see Pomazansky, *Orthodox Dogmatic Theology*, 342–43.

74. Recall that dogmatic theology as I define it seeks to navigate disputes especially necessary for the preservation of the gospel and that I am pursuing as ecumenical a dogmatic account as fidelity to Scripture permits.

75. Marcellus was initially a defender of Nicaea, but his understanding of the eschaton led to his condemnation by the pro-Nicenes.

76. Perkins, *Fruitful Dialogue*, 456–57.

77. As Craig Carter notes, the idea of predictive prophecy seems implausible in a secular naturalist framework, but a proper Christian metaphysic—Carter prefers Christian Platonism—allows for such a possibility. Carter, *Interpreting Scripture*, 145–46.

had a deeper meaning typically pointing to Christ.[78] Prophecy would have a historical meaning that provides an immediate comfort to the recipient. For example, Isaiah's prophecy of the coming child (Isa. 7–9) offers immediate hope to Ahaz (Isa. 7:3–12), who is threatened by two rival kings (2 Kings 16:5–19; Isa. 7:5). Before the prophetess's child, Maher-shalal-hash-baz, is old enough to know right from wrong (Isa. 8:1–4), those kings will be defeated. Yet certain features of the prophecy were not obviously fulfilled,[79] and the inclusion of prophetic texts in the canon suggested ongoing relevance for the people of God. This led to recognition of an allegorical sense. For example, ambiguity in the text of Isaiah 7, which could reference either a young woman or a virgin,[80] led to the recognition that the passage referred in a fuller sense to Christ. Similarly, Paul recognizes that Adam was a type of Christ (Rom. 5:14), who as second Adam was superior to and reversed the fall of the first Adam. Such fuller meaning does not undermine the reliability of prophecy. As Henry of Ghent would clarify, a prophet might have perfect knowledge for his situation but not exhaustively perfect knowledge. Prophets might also grasp the mystical sense of a prophecy (for example, the likelihood of judgment coming from sin) without fully understanding the literal fulfillment of the prophecy.[81]

With the coming of Christ, Christians recognized aspects of Scripture that were fulfilled in him—indeed, the risen Christ taught his disciples to read this way on the road to Emmaus (Luke 24:27). Eventually Christians could categorize dimensions of the prophecies of Christ in terms of what was fulfilled in Christ and in the early church as opposed to what was still awaited at the second coming.[82] Eventually, this led to a fourfold distinction in meanings, sometimes called the quadriga after a chariot drawn by four horses. This method retained the historical and moral senses but divided the allegorical and anagogical sense in two, with the allegorical sense pointing to Christ and the anagogical to eschatological hope. Each text will have a literal or historical reference, but not every text will have all four meanings, and we should be guided by the literal meaning of the canon when finding a spiritual

78. Hugh of St. Victor, *Sentences on Divinity*, 118.

79. The historical-critical perspective often suggests that theological beliefs were later fabrications due to the failings of messianic expectations. For example, one might think the entire idea of a second coming derives from certain unfulfilled messianic hopes instead of from the historical Jesus. See Robinson, *Jesus and His Coming*, 142–43. Ironically, where prophecies are too accurate, they are often also suspected of being fabrications "prophesied" after the fact. The common ground here is the naturalist denial of prophecy. A full historical analysis of the debate exceeds the scope of this book.

80. See chapter 1, under "The Virginal Conception," for more information.

81. Levy, *Medieval Biblical Interpretation*, 225.

82. For example, Quodvultdeus made such a catalog in the patristic era. See Daley, *Hope of the Early Church*, 153.

meaning in a text. As Henri de Lubac observes, "The doctrine of the four meanings of Scripture (history, allegory, tropology, anagoge) is fulfilled and finds its unity in traditional eschatology."[83] He understands these four aspects of the texts' meaning to unfold from one another. The historical sense finds its fullest meaning in allegory, typically fulfilled in Christ. For example, Jesus was the awaited child more truly than Maher-shalal-hash-baz. The moral sense, which calls us to be conformed to Christ, proceeds from the allegorical. Moral transformation is a bearing of fruit whose harvest is in the new creation, so the moral sense necessarily leads to the anagogical and eschatology.[84]

The fourfold sense has a basic structural similarity to what contemporary Bible scholars mean when they discuss inaugurated eschatology, where the inbreaking of the kingdom has begun but will be ongoing until the return of Christ. Here we must especially name two Old Testament hopes related to the kingdom. The people of Israel awaited the coming of a messiah and also the day of the Lord. While the Messiah was often expected to bring political liberation and economic prosperity, the outcome of the day of the Lord was much more ambiguous. It is both a day of judgment to be feared and avoided (Amos 5:18–20; Zeph. 1:14–16) and an opportunity for Israel's deliverance from enemies (Isa. 34:8; Jer. 30:7–11; 46:10–12). Inaugurated eschatology and christological hermeneutics point us toward a helpful approach to the second coming of Christ, which can be understood as the fulfillment of what has already been partly completed in Christ's first-century life, ministry, death, and resurrection. Therefore, I will conclude discussion of the second coming by focusing on hope, judgment, victory, new creation, and the Great Commission.

The Second Coming and Hope

Perhaps the most fundamental theological dimension of eschatology is hope, and the recent theologian most focused on hope is Jürgen Moltmann.[85] Though Christ's historical life and ministry have ended with the resurrection, Moltmann insists that there is still a future for Jesus Christ, signaling the historical dimensions of Christ's second coming. The Messiah has already come, but messianic hope remains. This return prompts hope, a virtue that resists the dual vices of presumption and despair.[86] These vices can occur at an individual or corporate

83. De Lubac, *Scripture in the Tradition*, 217.
84. De Lubac, *Scripture in the Tradition*, 218.
85. "From first to last, and not merely in the epilogue, Christianity is eschatology, is hope, forward looking and forward moving, and therefore also revolutionizing the present." Moltmann, *Theology of Hope*, 16.
86. Moltmann, *Theology of Hope*, 23.

level. Individually, presumption believes salvation is attainable by works, where despair seeks no deliverance from the "present evil age" (Gal. 1:4). At a corporate level, despair fails to seek justice in this world, while presumption trusts in a social program to bring what only Christ's return brings: a kingdom of perfect peace.[87] Against this presumption, Moltmann insists, "Those who hope in Christ can no longer put up with reality as it is, but begin to suffer under it, to contradict it. Peace with God means conflict with the world, for the goad of the promised future stabs inexorably into the flesh of every unfulfilled present."[88] Moltmann characterizes the coming of this new kingdom as *adventus*, something beyond the capabilities of human history, not *futurum*, something brought about by our efforts across time.[89] Again, grace must prevail in a christological dogmatic.

The Judged One Who Judges

The first coming of Christ included a clear call to repentance, for the kingdom was at hand (Matt. 3:2; 4:17; Mark 1:15). This inauguration of the kingdom heightened the threat of condemnation.[90] Yet the second coming is most closely associated with judgment, and here Christ the judge will both acquit and condemn (John 5:25–29), offering eternal life or "throw[ing] . . . into the outer darkness, where there will be weeping and gnashing of teeth" (Matt. 22:13). As Daniel Treier explains, the fact that Christ is the judge reflects "the unity of law and gospel."[91] Jesus is both lawgiver and priestly mediator, and the resulting verdict will center entirely on the Messiah fulfilling the demands that he himself has placed on humanity. For those who have believed, the awaited judgment will be a reaffirmation of the judgment that those justified through faith face no condemnation now (Rom. 8:1) and will be "blameless in the day of our Lord Jesus Christ" (1 Cor. 1:8).[92] In this role as judge, Christ takes on the

87. This focus on the social dimensions of utopia has brought about considerable discussion of the concept of utopia in modern theology. Most critique utopia, identifying it with human efforts to bring the kingdom. João Batista Libânio claims utopia can be explained etymologically in two ways: *ouk-topos* (no-place) and *eu-topos* (good-place). There are utopias in the Bible, such as the "land flowing with milk and honey" (Exod. 3:8, 17; 13:5; 33:3) or the promise that every man shall sit under his vine and under his fig tree (1 Kings 4:25; Mic. 4:4; Zech. 3:10). Given this, Libânio claims that utopian "good places" can begin to be spawned today through Christ. Libânio, "Hope, Utopia, Resurrection," 718–23.

88. Moltmann, *Theology of Hope*, 21.

89. Moltmann, *Coming of God*, 25–26.

90. "The first coming of Jesus sharpens the antagonism between death and life, divine and human, and therefore heightens the threat of judgment." S. Harris, *Refiguring Resurrection*, 221.

91. Treier, *Lord Jesus Christ*, 307.

92. Whether this juxtaposition means that justification is technically an eschatological act, as Anthony Thiselton suggests, must be considered in a later work of pneumatological dogmatics. See Thiselton, *Life After Death*, 176.

curious role of being the judge who was judged, the lamb on the throne (Rev. 5:6–14) who was judged and punished in our place and now is in a position to judge. Those theologies that downplay penal substitution can fail to account for the eschatological judgment, where having Christ accept our punishment is good news, for who could be more sure that our punishment has been fulfilled than one who has borne it in our place? Our hope in Christ's second coming as the deliverance of the Messiah and not as judgment from the day of the Lord thus relies on Christ as the lamb who was slain that we might be acquitted.

The Second Coming and Victory over Sin

Christ will return not only as the judge who will declare those who have believed to be innocent but also as the victor over his enemies. This fulfills the hope of the day of the Lord. On that day, the new figure of the "man of lawlessness" will rise against the Son of Man (2 Thess. 2:2–3), a figure often also linked with the antichrist, a term that can be used in the plural to reference many individuals (1 John 2:18). Similar imagery of a beast (Rev. 13) or an "abomination that causes desolation" (Matt. 24:15 NIV) has led to much speculation regarding who is signified by this prophecy. Theories range from seeing antichrist as a power or movement against God's people[93] to claiming that the antichrist is a historical figure indwelt by Satan from birth.[94] I have cautioned against overly confident identifications of such eschatological figures; the figure of the antichrist is capacious enough to enable Christians to view many sinful worldly institutions and figures with concern. Whoever or whatever the antichrist is, the ultimate point is that even this final opposition to the Lord is defeated in the parousia, with the beast and Satan the deceiver both cast into the lake of fire (Rev. 20:10). In the new creation with the second coming of Christ, all sin and evil are defeated, and Christ's victory becomes complete. Social sin is defeated through the instantiation of the kingdom of God, actual sins are forgiven through the final declaration of righteousness and are committed no more, and original sin is defeated through resurrection, glorification, and new creation.

The Second Coming and the New Creation

The resurrection can be seen as a new creation *ex nihilo*—out of nothing. God spoke creation into existence (Gen. 1:3), and the Son will speak at the

---

93. On this, see Berkouwer, *Return of Christ*, 261.

94. This was the view of Adso of Montier-en-Der, who also described the antichrist in this way: "The fullness of diabolical power and of the whole character of evil will dwell in him in bodily fashion; for in him will be hidden all the treasures of malice and iniquity." Adso of Montier-en-Der, "Antichrist," 90, 93.

second coming to bring about resurrection (John 5:25; 1 Thess. 4:16–17). Resurrection language is used to describe Isaac's new life created from Abraham's "already dead" body and from "the deadness of Sarah's womb" (Rom. 4:19). Abraham is justified for believing that the "God . . . who gives life to the dead and calls things into existence that do not exist" (4:17) would do what he promised because he was able to bring life from the deadness in Abraham and Sarah (4:20–22).[95] The paradigmatic example of faith is thus closely linked to resurrection and new creation. This link is one of several ways that *sola gratia* is preserved in the doctrines of the last things. As Philip Ziegler explains, "Nothing militates against synergism as fully and finally as the reality of the death of the sinner; and nothing affirms the divine monergism of salvation as fully and finally as its designation as 'new creation.'"[96]

Theologians have long speculated that when the new creation is completed, a new Sabbath rest will occur,[97] with Jesus, the "Lord . . . of the Sabbath" (Mark 2:28) who gives rest (Matt. 11:28). Peter Damian understands the Sabbath itself to be typologically designating Christ. Genesis 2:1–2 does not describe the Sabbath as bracketed by morning and evening like the other six days of creation, a fact that leads Damian to conclude that the Sabbath has no beginning or end. Appropriately, the Son, who is the Melchizedekian priest of peace (Salem) without beginning or end (Heb. 7:2–3), is the eternal Sabbath rest.[98] Damian explores how Christ is explicitly depicted as the temple (John 2:21) and how the temple and Sabbath are to be revered (Lev. 19:30).[99] Ultimately, God the Son rests within the created humanity of Jesus of Nazareth, in whom deity tabernacled (John 1:14). To read the Sabbath christologically according to inaugurated eschatology is to see that a literal Sabbath was given to the people of Israel for worshipful rest and to ensure justice.[100] This Sabbath was christologically extended into the ministry of Christ, who came to give rest (Matt. 11:28) and who secured this rest, having completed his own work (Heb. 4:8–10). Eschatologically, then, a final Sabbath rest will begin with his return to a new creation no longer marked by the toil seen in a fallen world (Gen. 3:17–19).

95. S. Harris, *Refiguring Resurrection*, 253.
96. Ziegler, *Militant Grace*, 12. Ziegler links this eschatological dimension of the theology of grace with other crucial Protestant principles such as imputation, alien righteousness, and salvation coming *ab extra* (from the outside). Ziegler, *Militant Grace*, 11–12.
97. The empty tomb was found on the day after the Sabbath (e.g., Matt. 28:1), which also led to considerable speculation about the significance of the eighth day taking an eschatological form.
98. Damian, *Letter 49* §5. In this letter, Damian reads the entire creation account as an allegory for Christian spiritual development. One need not go as far as Damian in such allegorical interpretation to accept the basic premise that Christ is the Sabbath.
99. "For he who is a sabbath is also a sanctuary." Damian, *Letter 49* §6.
100. For a brief treatment of Sabbath as an instrument of justice for the worker, see C. Wright, *Old Testament Ethics*, 159–60.

The Second Coming and Evangelism

Where the parousia promises a future Sabbath rest, it calls the church to the labor of evangelism. For example, Jesus's parables of the coming kingdom regularly instill an urgency in the audience. This is especially true in a fifth and final block of teachings found in the Gospel of Matthew, where the coming judgment is centered.[101] The audience is urged to not be like the bridesmaids who have not kept oil for their lamps at the unexpected coming of the bridegroom (Matt. 25:1–13). Instead, we should be like the blessed servant "whom the master finds doing his job when he comes" (24:46), and we should be like the faithful servants who invested the talents they received in anticipation of their master's return (25:14–30). In the end, the shepherd will separate the sheep and the goats based on their conduct toward him as he has been present in "the least of these" (25:40, 45).[102] Richard France summarizes well: "There appears to be a moment of decision—when the master returns, the bridegroom arrives, or the shepherd separates the flock. At that time, it will be too late to change sides, to go looking for oil, or to start trading. The door will be shut! And there will be some inside and outside!"[103]

Consider a similar parable in the Gospel of Luke. Here, a rich fool decides to build a bigger barn to store up his wealth, but that very night he dies (Luke 12:16–21). Again, this parable sets before the hearer or reader a sense of urgency, this time based not on the second coming but on the frailty of human life and the possibility of our death at any moment. The parable also has an important christological element, for Christ Jesus tells this parable in response to someone in the crowd asking him to tell his brother to divide an inheritance with him (12:13). Jesus refuses the role of judge that might resolve legal disputes (12:14), Peter Jones explains. Instead, "He spoke in God's name (v. 20). He functioned as a creator of scripture. He acted as definer of existence. He became a teacher and prophet and evangelist. He functioned as a proclaimer of crisis and conversion. . . . Most importantly, Jesus' own personal existence was not predicated upon possessions but upon God."[104]

---

101. France, "On Being Ready," 177–78. France argues that though the first parables in this sequence may reference judgment on Israel at its destruction by Rome, the later ones (many of which are unique to Matthew) focus on the parousia.

102. While some have interpreted this parable to be about receiving poor disciples who have gone forth to evangelize, I have defended the interpretation that it references judgment based on our treatment of those in need in Butner, *Jesus the Refugee*, 148–52. This reward for works need not entail that justification itself is based on merit, but rather remains one of many passages in Scripture that speak of possible varying rewards in the life to come for those who are justified.

103. France, "On Being Ready," 194.

104. P. Jones, *Studying the Parables of Jesus*, 153.

Here Jesus subtly issues a call parallel to that given more overtly to the rich young ruler: "Sell all you have and distribute it to the poor, and you will have treasure in heaven. Then come, follow me" (Luke 18:22).

The eschatological urgency placed before us given the return of Christ and impending judgment challenges us to hurry in our evangelism. As Kwame Bediako explains this commission, "Our task . . . is to demonstrate how the Scriptural witness to the life and ministry of Jesus Christ, illuminated by the Holy Spirit, is the clue to the yearnings and quests in the religious lives of people."[105] I have tried to offer a dogmatic theology that is academically rigorous but that also explains who the incarnate Son is and what he has done relevant to such fundamental yearnings and quests. What does a good life look like? How does the Creator of the universe reveal himself to us? Am I trapped in guilt before such a perfect God? How do we face death as victors over it? Can I pray to God with confidence? Such questions have comforting answers only if Christ is the incarnate God-man, two natures in one person, with each nature working and willing what is proper to it. These questions can be faced head-on with hope if that God-man has recapitulated our human nature, reversing the original sin of Adam, provided that we accept his satisfaction in faith, so that through union we might be bearers of a new humanity, able to follow the example of the righteous one and confident of our victory over sin, death, and the devil at Christ's imminent second coming. Such good news of the gospel can be proclaimed to simple shepherds and peasants, but we cannot forget that there are deep dogmatic roots beneath this proclamation. And so, at the end of this exploration of who Christ is and what he has done, there is nothing left to say but to reiterate the Great Commission that he gave to his disciples in Matthew 28:19–20: "Go, therefore, and make disciples of all nations, baptizing them in the name of the Father and of the Son and of the Holy Spirit, teaching them to observe everything I have commanded you. And remember, I am with you always, to the end of the age."

For Further Reading

Harris, Steven Edward. *Refiguring Resurrection: A Biblical and Systematic Eschatology*. Baylor University Press, 2023.

> Harris's treatment of eschatology draws especially on careful and insightful exegesis, twentieth-century European systematic theology, and medieval Scholasticism to develop a helpful and robust treatment of eschatology centered on the resurrection

105. Bediako, *Jesus and the Gospel in Africa*, 41.

and second coming of Christ. The centrality of Christology for his project makes this an excellent resource for thinking about the second coming.

Moltmann, Jürgen. *Theology of Hope.* Translated by James W. Leitch. Harper & Row, 1967.

Moltmann's *Theology of Hope* is one of the more influential texts in twentieth-century theology. Though his focus on history ultimately undermines the account of God and Christ I offer in my own dogmatic theology such that I have serious concerns about many parts of his work, I still consider his call to a return to eschatology an important read for any serious student of theology.

Schreiner, Patrick. *The Ascension of Christ: Recovering a Neglected Doctrine.* Lexham, 2020.

Schreiner offers a brief biblical theology of the ascension. This introductory survey of the ascension is surprisingly substantive in its treatment of figural precursors of the ascension and in its analysis of Christ's role as prophet, priest, and king.

Wandel, Lee Palmer. *The Eucharist in the Reformation: Incarnation and Liturgy.* Cambridge University Press, 2006.

While not strictly speaking a book about the ascension's connection to the Eucharist, Wandel's helpful volume provides an excellent survey of the eucharistic debates and practices at the time of the Reformation and gives extensive context for and significant detail about these debates.

Glossary

The following terms are particularly pertinent to Christology, and the definitions provided are given with christological implications and usage especially in mind.[1]

accident In Aristotelian thought, accidents are the properties of a being that are contingent and caused in some sense by substance. The doctrine of divine simplicity prohibits speaking of accidents in the divine substance or being.

ad extra A Latin phrase that literally means "toward the outside." In this context it typically refers to God's acts that terminate on creation. See also *ad intra*.

ad intra A Latin phrase that literally means "toward the inside." In this context it typically refers to God's acts that terminate within the Godhead, such as the divine processions. See also *ad extra*.

adoptionism An ancient heresy that states that Jesus was a human person adopted by God to become his Son at some point in history after that person's birth, usually identified as his baptism.

adventus An event coming in the future that could not be brought to pass based on the historical or causal capabilities of the present. In Christology, this is used specifically to refer to the second coming of Christ.

---

1. When crafting the glossary, I defined each term in my own words, then cross-referenced several theological dictionaries, making adjustments to my wording where necessary. Sources consulted: Morgan and Peterson, *Concise Dictionary of Theological Terms*; McKim, *Westminster Dictionary of Theological Terms*; Muller, *Dictionary of Latin and Greek Theological Terms*; Parente, Piolanti, and Garofalo, *Dictionary of Dogmatic Theology*; and Grenz, Guretzki, and Nordling, *Pocket Dictionary of Theological Terms*.

analogy The treatment of God as like or proportionate to creation yet fundamentally dissimilar. As a result of the doctrine of analogy, all human language of God must be qualified to identify properly the ways that the meaning of words differs when applied to God rather than to creation. *See also* univocity.

anhypostatic Having no (independent) existence; used in Christology, Jesus's human nature is anhypostatic, having no independent existence apart from the Son.

aphthartodocetism A christological heresy originating in the sixth century that denied the reality of Christ's human suffering due to the immutability and impassibility of Christ's divine nature.

Apollinarianism Named after Apollinaris of Laodicea, this christological heresy denies that Jesus has a human mind (*nous*), instead claiming that the divine Logos serves as the mind of Christ.

apophatic theology Theology that relies on the way of negation, understanding God by denying that which cannot be said of him.

articular noun In Greek, an articular noun has a definite article.

aseity God's attribute of needing and receiving nothing from creation, having his existence entirely determined by himself. The term is synonymous with "self-existence."

christological monotheism A perspective in debates on Christology in biblical studies that focuses on how Jesus Christ is incorporated into the singular deity of the Father. This approach tends to look at Christ's mediatorial status, his reception of worship, and/or his identity in key passages of Scripture.

Christotokos Bearer of Christ. Nestorius used the term as an alternative to *Theotokos* to describe Mary. See also *Theotokos*.

Christus Victor A broad category of atonement theologies that focus on the Son's victory over sin, death, and/or the devil.

circumscribed presence *See* local presence.

communication of idioms The practice of attributing the properties of Christ's divine and human natures to his singular person, even if this practice results in seemingly paradoxical claims, such as the divine Son dying or Mary's son being omnipresent. The communication of idioms was a key component of the doctrine of the hypostatic union.

complete presence When something is present everywhere simultaneously, yet without being circumscribed or limited in space. This is the divine manner of presence, but Lutherans sometimes ascribe this presence to the Son. *See also* definitive presence; local presence.

consequent necessity Something that necessarily must happen or must be true based on a prior contingent fact; it was a consequent necessity that the Son die on the cross given the prior commitment of the triune God to create a world that would fall and need atonement.

consubstantial Derived from the Latin translation of *homoousios*, the term refers to sharing substance, which entails sharing all attributes that are essential to a particular type of thing. When deployed in the doctrine of the Trinity, "consubstantiality" refers to the Father, Son, and Holy Spirit sharing the same single primary substance without division.

definitive presence When something is present, but not in a tangible manner or by occupying a specific place. Many theologians have argued that Christ's body had definitive presence after the resurrection, including perhaps in the elements of the Eucharist. *See also* complete presence; local presence.

divinization See *theosis*.

docetism A christological heresy that considers Jesus to have only appeared (from the Greek *dokeō*, "to seem") to be human while actually remaining immaterial.

duplex gratia The double grace of justification and sanctification given to the Christian through union with Christ.

dyoenergism A theology affirming that the incarnate Son had two energies or operations, one human and one divine, each proper to their own nature. *See also* energies.

dyothelitism A theology affirming that the incarnate Son had two wills, one human and one divine, each proper to their own nature.

economy Derived from the Greek word *oikonomia*, which refers to oversight of a household or management according to a plan, the divine economy refers to the work of the Father, Son, and Spirit in history. It includes creation, redemption, and the future eschatological renewal of all things.

ectypal knowledge Knowledge of God in a human mode that attempts to mirror the knowledge that God has of himself.

energies The operations produced by the power of a nature. In much Eastern Orthodox theology, *theosis* involves Christians participating in the divine energies, not the divine essence or persons. *See also* dyoenergism; theosis.

enhypostatic Having subsistence in another. In Christology, this term reflects the principle that the human nature of Christ only ever existed in the person of the Son.

epistemology The philosophy of how we know and learn.

euergetic deities In ancient Greco-Roman culture, euergetic deities were those whose divinity was gifted to them, often as a result of certain accomplishments.

expiation The act of removing sin and its consequences.

external operations Acts of a nature that produce an effect outside of that nature.

extra Calvinisticum The idea that Christ's divine nature exceeds his human nature, being present and active beyond the spatial, temporal, and agential limitations of Christ's humanity, limits that persist even after the ascension.

federal headship A condition where one individual represents others in a covenant. This headship is typically thought to belong to Adam, resulting in original sin, and to Christ, making possible satisfaction and justification. *See also* justification; originating original sin (*peccatum originale originans*); original sin as originated (*peccatum originale originatum*); satisfaction.

foursquare gospel A theological perspective that emphasizes Jesus as savior, baptizer, healer, and returning Son of Man.

functionalist Christology A Christology that discerns Christ's person and natures through inference from his actions.

genus A class of similar things.

genus majestaticum A category of the communication of idioms wherein the humanity of Christ receives certain divine attributes. This category is affirmed by Lutherans but rejected by the Reformed. *See also* communication of idioms.

Gnosticism A group of early Christian heresies that sought a secret knowledge for salvation while denying the goodness of creation and therefore the incarnation, the Old Testament depiction of God, and the general resurrection.

governmental theory That theology of the atonement that considers the cross in terms of what it publicly reveals about justice, sin, and God's governance of creation.

habitus **theory of the incarnation** A medieval theory of the incarnation that considered Christ's humanity to be an accident affixed to the divine nature, much like a monk wearing a cloak (habit).

Hamaitic curse A sinful interpretation of Genesis 9 that interprets Noah's curse of Ham's son Canaan to justify racial hierarchies and oppression.

historical Jesus *See* quest for the historical Jesus.

homo asumptus **theory of the incarnation** A medieval theology of the incarnation that understands the Son to have taken on a complete human. This view was rejected because it seemed too close to adoptionism.

hypostasis A Greek term that refers to that which makes a thing real. In Christology the term is used to reference a unique, singular, relational existence of a rational nature (or, in the case of Christ, of rational natures), though Christ's hypostasis is dissimilar from ours in certain ways.

iconoclast controversy The eighth-century Byzantine controversy regarding the elimination of cultic images of Christ, with iconoclasts favoring their removal and/or destruction.

impeccability Inability to sin.

imputation Counting to someone a status or identity that is not proper to them by nature or merit. In theology, original guilt claims that Adam's sin is imputed to all humanity, and Protestants view justification as an imputation of Christ's righteousness to the Christian.

inseparable operations A doctrine explaining that the Father, Son, and Holy Spirit work all divine acts *ad extra* inseparably. See also *ad extra*.

instrumental cause The means through which an efficient cause works to bring about an effect. In justification, faith is an instrumental cause.

intermediate state The state of the soul between death and the final resurrection.

internal operations Acts of a nature that produce an effect within that nature.

justification God's gracious declaration of sinners' innocence before the law through the imputation of Christ's righteousness to those who believe.

kenosis Self-emptying (as drawn from Philippians 2). In Christology, various theories interpret how Christ's kenosis relates to his divine nature, his assumed human nature, his resulting work, and our knowledge of his status.

kenoticism The claim particularly associated with Gottfried Thomasius that in kenosis the Son gave up certain nonessential divine properties for a time in order to be fully human.

kind *See* genus.

local presence When something is present in space and occupies a specific, circumscribable space, as the body of Christ does.

monoenergism A seventh-century heresy that claimed that though Christ had two natures, he only had one divine-human operation or energy. *See also* dyoenergism.

monothelitism A seventh-century heresy that claimed that though Christ had two natures, he only had one divine-human will. *See also* dyothelitism.

nature The character of a thing considered particularly in terms of its distinctive powers and resulting operations.

Nazianzus's rule A principle claiming that those human faculties that Jesus did not assume in the incarnation are not healed through union. The rule requires a complete human nature in the hypostatic union.

noncontrastive transcendence A theological perspective which does not treat immanence and transcendence as opposites. God can radically be both. In Christology, this serves as a basis for the possibility of the incarnation.

ontology The philosophical study of being.

ordo salutis The "order of salvation," referring to the stages of the application of redemption. *See also* justification.

original corruption A theory of original sin that claims Adam's sin resulted in an innate tendency toward sin in fallen humanity.

original guilt A theory of original sin that understands Adam's guilt to be imputed to every human being from conception.

originating original sin (*peccatum originale originans*) The sinful condition of all of humanity as a result of Adam's sin. *See also* original sin as originated (*peccatum originale originatum*).

original pollution *See* original corruption.

original righteousness A grace-given empowerment of Adam and Eve's human nature making it good.

original sin as originated (*peccatum originale originatum*) Adam's sin that brought about the subsequent sinfulness of all of humanity. *See also* originating original sin (*peccatum originale originans*).

orthodoxy Right belief.

orthopathy Right experience or spirituality.

orthopraxis Right action.

parousia The return of Christ and his full presence at the eschaton.

partitive exegesis An interpretive practice whereby the reader discerns whether a statement of Christ is said with reference to his humanity or deity.

Pelagianism A heresy originating in the fourth century that denied original sin and the need for grace for humans to do the good.

penal substitutionary atonement Any atonement theory where Christ receives in our place a penalty due to Christians.

perfectionism A perspective on sanctification claiming that the Holy Spirit can bring Christians to a state wherein they do not intentionally sin.

perichoresis A term referring to the mutual interpenetration and coinherence of the divine persons and of the two natures in Christ. This concept is often explained with reference to metaphors of motion and space and to unity of love, consciousness, and will.

perspicuity of Scripture The doctrine that says that Scripture is clear on matters necessary for salvation.

preexistence The real, not potential, existence of a being prior to a specific time, typically its manifestation in history.

propitiation An act causing someone to gain the favor of someone else. In the doctrine of the atonement, the cross is often thought to propitiate God, though this is debated due, among other reasons, to questions about how propitiation works with an immutable God.

prosopological exegesis An ancient method of interpreting texts that reads a passage as if it is a dialogue between multiple unnamed characters, identifying shifts in speaker based on small textual clues. The New Testament often reads Old Testament passages through prosopological exegesis, identifying speakers as one or more of the divine persons.

prosoponic union A term describing Nestorius's theory of the conjunction of humanity and divinity in Christ in a single *prosōpon*, where a *prosōpon* is understood to be an object of perception.

qeb'at A seventeenth-century christological perspective from Ethiopia that considered the Holy Spirit to be the means of uniting the two natures of Christ. This alternative to both miaphysitism and the hypostatic union was condemned as a heresy.

quest for the historical Jesus A modern biblical-studies methodology that seeks to identify the true Jesus behind the Gospel accounts, often due to a distrust of the reliability of these accounts.

realism In relation to original sin, realism refers to the theory that Adam's sin stained an actually existing human nature. When other humans participate in this real nature, they are shaped by Adam's sin within this nature.

recapitulation A theology that sees humanity fulfilled and restored in Christ, a new head for humanity, reversing the result of Adam, the first head. *See also* second-Adam Christology.

reduplicative A qualifying phrase that clarifies a statement using the communication of idioms, identifying which nature is performing the action or possessing the attribute ascribed to the person of the Son.

regulative principle The conviction that Christian worship should only do things explicitly commanded in the New Testament.

re-messianization A perspective that claims the political dimensions of the title messiah should be restored within modern Christology.

satisfaction A payment or offering on behalf of another to remit or cancel debt and/or guilt. When a creditor or judge accepts a satisfaction, the demands of justice are met, but in a manner that displays grace.

second-Adam Christology Depiction of Jesus as a new Adam, reversing the sin brought about by the first Adam. *See also* recapitulation.

seminal presence A theory of original sin that understands all humans to have been present within Adam in a form that would develop into a later complete form. Because these nascent forms were in Adam, they were stained by his sin.

Sheol The shadowy underworld where the deceased would go, especially in Old Testament descriptions of death.

simplicity The doctrine that God is not composed of parts. In its strongest form, simplicity denies material parts, a real distinction between the divine attributes, and a distinction between God's essence and God's existence.

social sin A term broadly used to refer to the corporate and institutional aspects of sin. In this book, social sin refers more narrowly to those aspects of sin that are shaped by social groups. *See also* structures of sin.

sola gratia Grace alone. In the Protestant understanding of salvation, this phrase excludes any merit or achievement by which Christians earn salvation, which is by grace alone, not through works.

Spirit Christology Any Christology that emphasizes the work of the Holy Spirit in the life and ministry of the incarnate Son.

structures of sin Those rules, laws, institutions, practices, distributions, or other nonpersonal aspects of society that are shaped by sin and, in turn, can cause humans to sin. *See also* social sin.

supererogatory gift A gift well above what is required; in the context of atonement, the supererogatory gift is the voluntary death of the sinless Son who did not need to die.

supposit A specific self-existing reality.

theandric action A term naming the united product of the distinct operations of Christ's divine and human natures working in cooperation with one another.

theosis An especially Eastern Orthodox means of understanding our union with Christ that emphasizes our participation in God, often especially the divine energies. *See also* energies.

Theotokos Literally "God bearer." This term was used to describe Mary as the mother of God. See also *Christotokos*; communication of idioms.

traducianism The theory that sexual reproduction causes a new soul within the resulting human fetus.

triple virginity of Mary The idea that Mary was a virgin when Christ was conceived in her, remained a virgin through birth, and remained perpetually virginal.

typology A method of reading the Bible that sees earlier persons, acts, or even places as symbolically prefiguring a deeper or later theological reality, especially Jesus Christ.

ubiquity of Christ The belief that Christ's human nature was rendered omnipresent as a result of its union with the divine nature, particularly discussed in debates about Christ's bodily presence in the Eucharist.

uncircumscribed presence. *See* definitive presence.

unctionists See *qeb'at*.

universalism The claim that all people will be saved.

univocity An alternative to the doctrine of analogy that treats words used of God as if they mean the same thing in the same way as when they are used of creation. *See also* analogy.

vice A developed innate tendency toward evil, often shaped in community through repeated malforming practices.

virtue A developed innate tendency toward good, often shaped in community through repeated ethical practices. In theology, grace is involved in causing virtue.

Dates for Historical Figures

Abelard, Peter (1079–1142)
à Brakel, Wilhelmus (1635–1711)
Agatho (577–681)
Akindynos, Gregory (1300–1348)
Alexander III (d. 1181)
Alexander of Hales (1185–1245)
Ames, William (1576–1633)
Anselm of Canterbury (1033/34–1109)
Apollinaris of Laodicea (d. 382)
Aquinas, Thomas (1225–74)
Arius of Alexandria (ca. 250–336)
Athanasius of Alexandria (ca. 296/98–373)
Augustine of Hippo (354–430)
Babai the Great (ca. 551–628)
Barlaam the Calabrian (ca. 1290–1348)
Bavinck, Herman (1854–1921)
Bullinger, Heinrich (1504–75)
Calov, Abraham (1612–86)
Calvin, John (1509–64)
Cassian, John (ca. 360–ca. 435)
Chemnitz, Martin (1522–86)
Cyril of Alexandria (ca. 376–444)

Cyris of Phasis (ca. 6th century–642)

Damian, Peter (ca. 1007–72/73)

Diodore of Tarsus (d. ca. 390)

Duns Scotus, John (ca. 1265/66–1308)

Durandus of Saint-Pourçain (ca. 1275–1332)

Eutyches (ca. 380–456)

Evagrius of Pontus (345–99)

Fisher, Edward (1627–55)

Flavel, John (ca. 1627–91)

Gregoras, Nikephoros (ca. 1295–1360)

Gregory of Nazianzus (ca. 329–90)

Gregory of Nyssa (ca. 335–94)

Gregory of Sinai (ca. 1260s–1346)

Henry of Ghent (ca. 1217–93)

Hilary of Poitiers (ca. 310–67)

Hodge, Charles (1797–1878)

Honorius I (d. 638)

Hugh of St. Victor (ca. 1096–1141)

Hus, Jan (ca. 1370–1415)

Irenaeus of Lyons (ca. 130–202)

Irving, Edward (1792–1834)

John VI Kantakouzenos (ca. 1292–1383)

John of Damascus (ca. 675/76–749)

Julian of Halicarnassus (d. after 527)

Kabasilas, Neilos (1300–1363)

Lawson, Robert Clarence (1883–1961)

Lee, Jarena (1783–1864)

Leontius of Byzantium (485–543)

Leo the Great (ca. 400–461)

Lombard, Peter (ca. 1096–1160)

Luther, Martin (1483–1546)

Machen, J. Gresham (1881–1937)

Marcellus of Ancyra (d. ca. 374)

Marcion (ca. 85–160)

Martin I (ca. 590/600–655)

Maximus of Aquileia (d. 388)

Maximus the Confessor (ca. 580–662)

McPherson, Aimee Semple (1890–1944)

Melito of Sardis (d. ca. 180)

Nestorius (ca. 386–451)

Nicholas of Methone (d. 1160/66)

Nicholas of Pelhřimov (ca. 1385–1459)

Oecolampadius, Johannes (1482–1531)

Origen of Alexandria (ca. 185–ca. 253)

Owen, John (1616–83)

Palaiologos, Manuel II (1350–1425)

Palamas, Gregory (ca. 1296–1357/59)

Palmer, Phoebe (1807–74)

Panteugenos, Soterichos (12th century)

Pelagius (ca. 354–418)

Perkins, William (1558–1602)

Philoxenus of Mabbug (d. 523)

Pohle, Joseph (1864–1939)

Rigaldus, Odo (d. 1275)

Robert of Melun (ca. 1100–1167)

Roscelin of Compiègne (ca. 1050–ca. 1121)

Severus of Antioch (d. 538)

Simon of Tournai (ca. 1130–1201)

Socinus, Faustus (1539–1604)

Sophronius of Jeruselam (ca. 560–638)

Sozon of Phillipi (5th century)

Stephen of Dora (7th century)

Strong, Augustus (1670–1733)

Swedenborg, Emanuel (1688–1772)

Tertullian of Carthage (ca. 155–ca. 220)

Theodore of Pharan (6th and 7th centuries)

Theodore the Studite (759–826)

Thomasius, Gottfried (1802–75)

Torrey, R. A. (1856–1928)
Turretin, Francis (1623–87)
Ursinus, Zacharias (1534–83)
Valentinus (ca. 100–ca. 180)
Venerable Bede (ca. 672/73–735)
Watson, Richard (1781–1833)
William of Ockham (ca. 1287–1347)
Yohannes IV (1837–89)
Zanchi, Girolamo (1516–90)
Zwingli, Huldrych (1484–1531)

Bibliography

à Brakel, Wilhelmus. *The Christian's Reasonable Service*. Vol. 1, *God, Man, and Christ*, translated by Bartel Elshout, edited by Joel R. Beeke. Reformation Heritage Books, 1992.

Achtemeier, Paul J. *1 Peter*. Fortress, 1996.

The Acts of the Council of Chalcedon. 3 vols. Translated by Richard Price and Michael Gaddis. Liverpool University Press, 2005.

The Acts of the Lateran Synod of 649. Translated by Richard Price. Liverpool University Press, 2014.

Adams, Marilyn McCord. *Christ and Horrors: The Coherence of Christology*. Cambridge University Press, 2006.

———. *What Sort of Human Nature? Medieval Philosophy and the Systematics of Christology*. Marquette University Press, 1999.

Adso of Montier-en-Der. "Letter on the Origin and Time of the Antichrist." In *Apocalyptic Spirituality: Treatises and Letters of Lactantius, Adso of Montier-en-Der, Joachim of Fiore, the Franciscan Spirituals, Savanarola*, translated by Bernard McGinn, 89–96. Paulist Press, 1979.

Agatho. "The Letter of Pope Agatho." In *The Nicene and Post-Nicene Fathers*, second series, edited by Philip Schaff and Henry Wace, 14:328–39. Reprint, Eerdmans, 1956.

Alexander, T. Desmond. *Face to Face with God: A Biblical Theology of Christ as Priest and Mediator*. IVP Academic, 2022.

Alfeyev, Hilarion. *Christ the Conqueror of Hell: The Descent into Hades from an Orthodox Perspective*. St. Vladimir's Seminary Press, 2009.

Allison, Dale C., Jr. *The Resurrection of Jesus: Apologetics, Criticism, History*. T&T Clark, 2021.

Ames, William. *The Marrow of Theology.* Translated by John Dykstra Eusden. Labyrinth, 1968.

Anatolios, Khaled. *Deification Through the Cross: An Eastern Christian Theology of Salvation.* Eerdmans, 2020.

Anderson, Gary A. *That I May Dwell Among Them: Incarnation and Atonement in the Tabernacle Narrative.* Eerdmans, 2023.

Anselm of Canterbury. *The Major Works.* Edited by Brian Davies and G. R. Evans. Oxford University Press, 1998.

———. *On the Incarnation of the Word.* In *The Major Works,* 233–59.

———. *On the Virgin Conception and Original Sin.* In *The Major Works,* 260–356.

———. *On Truth.* In *The Major Works,* 151–74.

———. *Proslogion.* In *The Major Works,* 82–104.

———. *Why God Became Man.* In *The Major Works,* 357–89.

Aquinas, Thomas. *On Evil.* Translated by Richard Regan. Edited by Brian Davies. Oxford University Press, 2003.

———. *Summa Theologica.* Translated by Fathers of the English Dominican Province. 5 vols. 1911. Reprint, Christian Classics, 1981.

Asproulis, Nikolaos. "Eucharistic Personhood: Deification in the Orthodox Tradition." In *With All the Fullness of God: Deification in Christian Tradition,* edited by Jared Ortiz, 29–57. Lexington, 2021.

Athanasius of Alexandria. *On the Incarnation.* Translated by a Religious of C.S.M.V. St. Vladimir's Seminary Press, 1977.

———. *Orationes contra Arianos IV.* In *Nicene and Post-Nicene Fathers,* second series, edited and translated by Philip Schaff and Henry Wace, 4:303–448. Reprint, Eerdmans, 1952.

Atkins, Peter. *Ascension Now: Implications of Christ's Ascension for Today's Church.* Liturgical Press, 2001.

Augustine of Hippo. *Enchiridion.* Translated by J. F. Shaw. In *Nicene and Post-Nicene Fathers,* first series, edited by Philip Schaff, 3:229–76. Reprint, Eerdmans, 1998.

———. *Faith and the Creed.* Translated by Michael G. Campbell. In *On Christian Belief,* edited by Boniface Ramsey, 155–74. New City, 2005.

———. "Of the Words of St. Matthew's Gospel, Chap. III.13, 'Then Jesus Cometh from Galilee to the Jordan unto John, to Be Baptized of Him,' Concerning the Trinity." In *Nicene and Post-Nicene Fathers,* first series, edited by Philip Schaff, 6:259–66. Reprint, Eerdmans, 1996.

———. *On Forgiveness of Sins, and Baptism.* Translated by Peter Holmes, Robert Ernest Wallis, and Benjamin B. Warfield. In *Nicene and Post-Nicene Fathers,* first series, edited by Philip Schaff, 5:15–79. Reprint, Eerdmans, 1997.

———. *On Marriage and Concupiscence.* Translated by Peter Holmes, Robert Ernest Wallis, and Benjamin B. Warfield. In *Nicene and Post-Nicene Fathers*, first series, edited by Philip Schaff, 5:258–309. Reprint, Eerdmans, 1997.

———. *On the Grace of Christ, and on Original Sin.* In *Nicene and Post-Nicene Fathers*, first series, edited by Philip Schaff, 5:213–55. Reprint, Eerdmans, 1997.

———. *On the Holy Trinity.* Translated by Arthur West Haddan. In *Nicene and Post-Nicene Fathers*, first series, edited by Philip Schaff, 3:1–228. Reprint, Eerdmans, 1956.

Aulén, Gustaf. *Christus Victor: An Historical Study of the Three Main Types of the Idea of the Atonement.* Translated by A. G. Hebert. SPCK, 1950.

———. *The Faith of the Christian Church.* 4th ed. Translated by Eric H. Wahlstrom and G. Everett Arden. Muhlenberg, 1948.

Avila, Charles. *Ownership: Early Christian Teaching.* Orbis Books, 1983.

Ayres, Lewis. *Nicaea and Its Legacy: An Approach to Fourth-Century Trinitarian Theology.* Oxford University Press, 2004.

Baines, Ronald S., Richard C. Barcellos, James P. Butler, Stefan T. Lindblad, and James M. Renihan, eds. *Confessing the Impassible God: The Biblical, Classical, and Confessional Doctrine of Divine Impassibility.* Reformed Baptist Academic Press, 2015.

Baker, Mark D., and Joel B. Green. *Recovering the Scandal of the Cross: Atonement in New Testament and Contemporary Contexts.* 2nd ed. InterVarsity, 2011.

Baldwin, Jennifer. *Trauma-Sensitive Theology: Thinking Theologically in the Era of Trauma.* Cascade Books, 2018.

Bales, William. "The Descent of Christ in Ephesians 4:9." *Catholic Biblical Quarterly* 72, no. 1 (2010): 84–100.

Barclay, John M. G. "Kenosis and the Drama of Salvation in Philippians 2." In *Kenosis: The Self-Emptying of Christ in Scripture and Theology*, edited by Paul T. Nimmo and Keith L. Johnson, 7–23. Eerdmans, 2022.

Barnes, Corey L. *Christ's Two Wills in Scholastic Thought: The Christology of Aquinas and Its Historical Contexts.* Pontifical Institute of Medieval Studies, 2012.

Barnes, Michel René. *The Power of God: Δύναμις in Gregory of Nyssa's Trinitarian Theology.* Catholic University of America Press, 2001.

Barnett, Paul. *The Second Epistle to the Corinthians.* Eerdmans, 1997.

Barth, Karl. *Church Dogmatics.* Edited by G. W. Bromiley and T. F. Torrance. Translated by G. W. Bromiley, G. T. Thomson, et al. 4 volumes in 13 parts. Edinburgh: T&T Clark, 1936–77.

Barth, Markus. *Ephesians: Introduction, Translation, and Commentary on Chapters 1–3.* Doubleday, 1974.

Bass, Justin W. *The Battle for the Keys: Revelation 1:18 and Christ's Descent into the Underworld.* Wipf & Stock, 2014.

Bates, Matthew W. *The Birth of the Trinity: Jesus, God, and Spirit in New Testament & Early Christian Interpretations of the Old Testament.* Oxford University Press, 2015.

Bathrellos, Demetrios. *The Byzantine Christ: Person, Nature, and Will in the Christology of Saint Maximus the Confessor.* Oxford University Press, 2004.

Bauckham, Richard. *The Climax of Prophecy: Studies on the Book of Revelation.* T&T Clark, 1993.

———. *Jesus and the Eyewitnesses: The Gospels as Eyewitness Testimony.* 2nd ed. Eerdmans, 2017.

———. *Jude, 2 Peter.* Word, 1983.

Baugus, Bruce P. *The Roots of Reformed Moral Theology.* Reformation Heritage Books, 2022.

Bavinck, Herman. *Reformed Dogmatics.* Vol. 3, *Sin and Salvation in Christ,* edited by John Bolt, translated by John Vriend. Baker Academic, 2006.

Bediako, Kwame. *Jesus and the Gospel in Africa: History and Experience.* Orbis Books, 2004.

Beeley, Christopher A. "The Early Christological Controversy: Apollinarius, Diodore, and Gregory Nazienzen." *Vigiliae Christianae* 65, no. 4 (2011): 376–407.

———. *The Unity of Christ: Continuity and Conflict in Patristic Tradition.* Yale University Press, 2012.

Bello, Rafael. *Sinless Flesh: A Critique of Karl Barth's Fallen Christ.* Lexham, 2020.

Berkhof, Louis. *Systematic Theology.* 4th ed. Eerdmans, 1941.

Berkouwer, G. C. *The Person of Christ.* Eerdmans, 1994.

———. *The Return of Christ.* Translated by James Van Oosterom. Edited by Marlin J. Van Elderen. Eerdmans, 1972.

———. *Sin.* Translated by Philip C. Holtrop. Eerdmans, 1971.

Billings, J. Todd. *Union with Christ: Reframing Theology and Ministry for the Church.* Baker Academic, 2011.

Bird, Michael F. *Jesus Among the Gods: Early Christology in the Greco-Roman World.* Baylor University Press, 2022.

———. *Jesus the Eternal Son: Answering Adoptionist Christology.* Eerdmans, 2017.

———. *What Christians Ought to Believe: An Introduction to Christian Doctrine Through the Apostles' Creed.* Zondervan, 2016.

Blackwell, Ben C. *Christosis: Pauline Soteriology in Light of Deification in Irenaeus and Cyril of Alexandria.* Mohr Siebeck, 2011.

Blocher, Henri. *Original Sin: Illuminating the Riddle.* InterVarsity, 1997.

Blowers, Paul M. *Maximus the Confessor: Jesus Christ and the Transfiguration of the World.* Oxford University Press, 2016.

Bockmuehl, Markus. *The Epistle to the Philippians*. A & C Black, 1998.

Boersma, Hans. *Violence, Hospitality, and the Cross: Reappropriating the Atonement Tradition*. Baker Academic, 2004.

Boff, Leonardo. *Jesus Christ Liberator: A Critical Christology for Our Time*. Translated by Patrick Hughes. Orbis Books, 1978.

Bonaventure. *Disputed Questions on the Mystery of the Trinity*. Translated by Zachary Hayes. Franciscan Institute of St. Bonaventure University, 1979.

Boslooper, Thomas. *The Virgin Birth*. Westminster, 1962.

Boyd, Gregory A. *God at War: The Bible and Spiritual Conflict*. InterVarsity, 1997.

Braaten, Carl E. "Powers in Conflict: Christ and the Devil." In *Sin, Death, & the Devil*, edited by Carl E. Braaten and Robert W. Jenson, 94–107. Eerdmans, 2000.

Brand, Chad Owen, ed. *Perspectives on Spirit Baptism*. B&H Academic, 2004.

Brock, Rita Nakashima. *Journeys by Heart: A Christology of Erotic Power*. Crossroad, 1993.

Brown, David. "Anselm on Atonement." In *The Cambridge Companion to Anselm*, edited by Brian Davies and Brien Leftow, 279–302. Cambridge University Press, 2004.

Brown, Raymond E. *The Birth of the Messiah: A Commentary on the Infancy Narratives in the Gospels of Matthew and Luke*. Updated ed. Doubleday, 1993.

———. *An Introduction to New Testament Christology*. Paulist Press, 1994.

———. *The Virginal Conception and Bodily Resurrection of Jesus*. Paulist Press, 1973.

Brunner, Emil. *The Christian Doctrine of God*. Vol. 1 of *Dogmatics*. Translated by Olive Wyon. Westminster, 1950.

Bryan, Christopher. *The Resurrection of the Messiah*. Oxford University Press, 2011.

Bühner, Ruben A. *Messianic High Christology: New Testament Variants of Second Temple Judaism*. Baylor University Press, 2021.

Bulgakov, Sergius. *The Comforter*. Translated by Boris Jakim. Eerdmans, 2004.

———. *The Lamb of God*. Translated by Boris Jakim. Eerdmans, 2008.

Burkett, Delbert. *The Son of Man Debate: A History and Evaluation*. Cambridge University Press, 2004.

Burnett, Amy Nelson. *Karlstadt and the Origins of the Eucharistic Controversy: A Study in the Circulation of Ideas*. Oxford University Press, 2011.

Burnett, Paul. *The Second Epistle to the Corinthians*. Eerdmans, 1997.

Butner, D. Glenn, Jr. "Communion with God: An Energetic Defense of Gregory Palamas." *Modern Theology* 32, no. 1 (2016): 20–44.

———. *Jesus the Refugee: Ancient Injustice and Modern Solidarity*. Fortress, 2023.

———. "The Need for Nicene Dogmatics: Eternal Functional Subordination's Dogmatic Inadequacy." In *On Classical Trinitarianism: Retrieving the Nicene Doctrine of the Triune God*, edited by Matthew Barrett, 706–29. IVP Academic, 2024.

———. "Probing the Exegetical Foundations of Consubstantiality: Worship, Mediatorial Figures, and the *Homoousion*." *Modern Theology* 37, no. 3 (2021): 679–702.

———. *The Son Who Learned Obedience: A Theological Case Against the Eternal Submission of the Son*. Pickwick, 2018.

———. *Trinitarian Dogmatics: Exploring the Grammar of the Christian Doctrine of God*. Baker Academic, 2022.

———. *Work Out Your Salvation: A Theology of Markets and Moral Formation*. Fortress, 2024.

Cahill, Lisa Sowle. *Global Justice, Christology, and Christian Ethics*. Cambridge University Press, 2013.

Calov, Abraham. *Disputation: Theological Dissertation on the Propitiation for Our Sins from 1 John 2:2*. In *Atonement in Lutheran Orthodoxy: Abraham Calov*, translated by Matthew Carver, 145–70. Synoptic Text Information Services, 2024.

Calvin, John. *The Clear Explanation of Sound Doctrine Concerning the True Partaking of the Flesh and Blood of Christ in the Holy Supper to Dissipate the Mists of Tileman Heshius*. In *Calvin: Theological Treatises*, edited and translated by J. K. S. Reid, 258–324. Westminster, 1954.

———. *Institutes of the Christian Religion*. Translated by Henry Beveridge. Hendrickson, 2008.

Campbell, Constantine R. *The Letter to the Ephesians*. Eerdmans, 2023.

———. *Paul and Union with Christ: An Exegetical and Theological Study*. Zondervan, 2012.

Canty, Aaron. *Light and Glory: The Transfiguration of Christ in Early Franciscan and Dominican Theology*. Catholic University of America Press, 2011.

Capes, David B. *The Divine Christ: Paul, the Lord Jesus, and the Scriptures of Israel*. Baker Academic, 2018.

Carter, Craig A. *Interpreting Scripture with the Great Tradition: Recovering the Genius of Premodern Exegesis*. Baker Academic, 2018.

Cassian, John. *The Conferences*. Translated by Boniface Ramsey. Newman, 1997.

Cavanaugh, William T., and James K. A. Smith, eds. *Evolution and the Fall*. Eerdmans, 2017.

Chambers, Katherine. *Augustine on the Nature of Virtue and Sin*. Cambridge University Press, 2024.

Chan, Lúcás. *Biblical Ethics in the 21st Century: Developments, Emerging Consensus, and Future Directions*. Paulist Press, 2013.

Chan, Simon. *Grassroots Asian Theology: Thinking Faith from the Ground Up.* InterVarsity, 2014.

Chemnitz, Martin. *The Lord's Supper.* Translated by J. A. O. Preus. Concordia, 1979.

———. *The Two Natures in Christ.* Translated by J. A. O. Preus. Concordia, 1971.

Childs, Brevard S. *Biblical Theology of the Old and New Testaments: Theological Reflection on the Christian Bible.* Fortress, 1992.

———. *The Book of Exodus: A Critical, Theological Commentary.* Westminster, 1974.

Chuang Chua, How. *Japanese Perspectives on the Death of Christ: A Study in Contextualized Christology.* Regnum, 2021.

Ciraulo, Jonathan M. "Divinization as Christification in Erich Przywara and John Zizioulas." *Modern Theology* 32, no. 4 (October 2016): 479–503.

Clark, John C., and Marcus Peter Johnson. *The Incarnation of God: The Mystery of the Gospel as the Foundation of Evangelical Theology.* Crossway, 2015.

Coakley, Sarah. "Does Kenosis Rest on a Mistake? Three Kenotic Models in Patristic Exegesis." In Evans, *Exploring Kenotic Christology,* 246–64.

———. *Powers and Submissions: Spirituality, Philosophy, and Gender.* Blackwell, 2002.

Cole, Graham A. *He Who Gives Life: The Doctrine of the Holy Spirit.* Crossway, 2007.

Collins Winn, Christian T. *Jesus, Jubilee, and the Politics of God's Reign.* Eerdmans, 2023.

Cone, James H. *God of the Oppressed.* Rev. ed. Orbis Books, 1997.

Cortés, Juan B., and Florence M. Gatti. "The Son of Man or the Son of Adam." *Biblica* 49, no. 4 (1968): 457–502.

Cosgrove, Charles H. *Appealing to Scripture in Moral Debate: Five Hermeneutical Rules.* Eerdmans, 2002.

Cox, Raymond L. "What Is the Foursquare Gospel?" In *The Foursquare Gospel,* edited by Raymond L. Cox, 3–12. Foursquare Publications, 1969.

Crisp, Oliver D. *Divinity and Humanity: The Incarnation Reconsidered.* Cambridge University Press, 2007.

———. *God Incarnate: Explorations in Christology.* T&T Clark, 2009.

———. "Sin." In *Christian Dogmatics: Reformed Theology for the Church Catholic,* edited by Michael Allen and Scott R. Swain, 194–215. Baker Academic, 2016.

Cross, Richard. *The Metaphysics of the Incarnation: Thomas Aquinas to Duns Scotus.* Oxford University Press, 2002.

Crowe, Brandon D. *The Hope of Israel: The Resurrection of Christ in the Acts of the Apostles.* Baker Academic, 2020.

———. *The Last Adam: A Theology of the Obedient Life of Jesus in the Gospels.* Baker Academic, 2017.

Crummey, Donald. "Orthodoxy and Imperial Reconstruction in Ethiopia, 1854–1878." *Journal of Theological Studies* 29, no. 2 (1978): 427–42.

Cullmann, Oscar. *The Christology of the New Testament.* Rev. ed. Translated by Shirley C. Guthrie and Charles A. M. Hall. Westminster, 1963.

Cyril of Alexandria. *Cyril's Letter to Acacius of Beroea.* In *St. Cyril of Alexandria: The Christological Controversy—Its History, Theology, and Texts,* edited and translated by John A. McGuckin, 336–42. St. Vladimir's Seminary Press, 2004.

———. *Cyril's Letter to Eulogius.* In *St. Cyril of Alexandria: The Christological Controversy—Its History, Theology, and Texts,* edited and translated by John A. McGuckin, 349–51. St. Vladimir's Seminary Press, 2004.

———. *Homily 51 on Luke.* In *Light on the Mountain: Greek Patristic and Byzantine Homilies on the Transfiguration of the Lord,* translated by Brian Daley, 99–104. St. Vladimir's Seminary Press, 2013.

———. *On Orthodoxy to Theodosius.* In *Saint Cyril of Alexandria: Three Christological Treatises,* edited by Daniel King, 35–82. Catholic University of America Press, 2014.

———. *On the Unity of Christ.* Translated by John Anthony McGuckin. St. Vladimir's Seminary Press, 1995.

———. *Scholia on the Incarnation of the Only Begotten.* In *St. Cyril of Alexandria: The Christological Controversy—Its History, Theology, and Texts,* edited and translated by John A. McGuckin, 294–335. St. Vladimir's Seminary Press, 2004.

———. *The Third Letter of Cyril to Nestorius.* In Hardy and Richardson, *Christology of the Later Fathers,* 349–54.

Dahan, Gilbert. "L'exégèse médiévale de Philippiens 2, 5–11." In *Philippiens 2, 5–11: La kénose du Christ,* edited by Matthieu Arnold, Gilbert Dahan, and Annie Noblesse-Rocher, 75–113. Cerf, 2013.

Daley, Brian E. *God Visible: Patristic Christology Reconsidered.* Oxford University Press, 2018.

———. *The Hope of the Early Church: A Handbook of Patristic Eschatology.* Baker, 1991.

Damian, Peter. *Letter 49.* In *Peter Damian: Letters 31–60,* translated by Owen J. Blum, 272–88. Catholic University of America Press, 1990.

Davids, Peter H. *The Letters of 2 Peter and Jude.* Eerdmans, 2006.

Davies, J. G. *He Ascended into Heaven: A Study in the History of Doctrine.* Association Press, 1958.

Davila, James R. "Of Methodology, Monotheism and Metatron: Introductory Reflections on Divine Mediators and the Origins of the Worship of Jesus." In *The Jewish*

Roots of Christological Monotheism: Papers from the St. Andrews Conference on the Historical Origins of the Worship of Jesus, edited by Carey C. Newman, James R. Davila, and Gladys S. Lewis, 3–18. Brill, 1999.

Davis, Carl Judson. *The Name and Way of the Lord: Old Testament Themes, New Testament Christology.* Sheffield Academic, 1996.

Davis, Leo Donald. *The First Seven Ecumenical Councils (325–787): Their History and Theology.* Liturgical Press, 1990.

Davis, Stephen T. "Is Kenosis Orthodox?" In Evans, *Exploring Kenotic Christology,* 112–38.

Dawson, Gerrit Scott. "Far as the Curse Is Found: The Significance of Christ's Assuming a *Fallen* Human Nature in the Torrance Theology." In *An Introduction to Torrance Theology: Discovering the Incarnate Savior,* edited by Gerrit Scott Dawson, 55–74. T&T Clark, 2007.

D'Costa, Gavin. "The Descent into Hell as a Solution for the Problem of the Fate of Unevangelized Non-Christians: Balthasar's Hell, the Limbo of the Fathers and Purgatory." *International Journal of Systematic Theology* 11, no. 2 (2009): 146–71.

"The Definition of Faith [from the Sixth Ecumenical Council]." In *Nicene and Post-Nicene Fathers,* second series, edited by Philip Schaff and Henry Wace, 14:344–47. Reprint, Eerdmans, 1956.

de Lubac, Henri. *Scripture in the Tradition.* Translated by Luke O'Neill. Crossroad, 1968.

Demarest, Bruce. *The Cross and Salvation: The Doctrine of Salvation.* Crossway, 1997.

Demetracopoulos, John A. "Palamas Transformed: Palamite Interpretations of the Distinctions Between God's 'Essence' and 'Energies' in Late Byzantium." In *Greeks, Latins, and Intellectual History, 1204–1500,* edited by Martin Hinterberger and Chris Schabel, 263–372. Peeters, 2011.

Denzinger, Henry. *The Sources of Catholic Dogma.* 13th ed. Translated by Roy J. Deferrari. Christ the King Library, 1955.

DeWeese, Garrett J. "One Person, Two Natures: Two Metaphysical Models of the Incarnation." In *Jesus in Trinitarian Perspective: An Intermediate Christology,* edited by Fred Sanders and Klaus Issler, 114–53. B&H Academic, 2007.

DeYoung, Rebecca Konyndyk. *Glittering Vices: A New Look at the Seven Deadly Sins and Their Remedies.* Brazos, 2009.

Dodd, C. H. *The Epistle of Paul to the Romans.* Hodder & Stoughton, 1932.

Dolezal, James E. "Neither Subtraction, nor Addition: The Word's Terminative Assumption of a Human Nature." *Nova et Vetera* 20, no. 1 (2022): 133–57.

Doran, Robert M. *The Trinity in History: A Theology of the Divine Missions.* Vol. 1, *Missions and Processions.* University of Toronto Press, 2012.

Dorner, I. A. *System of Christian Religion*. Vol. 1. Rev. ed. Translated by Alfred Cave. T&T Clark, 1888.

Douglas, Kelly Brown. *The Black Christ*. 25th anniv. ed. Orbis Books, 2019.

Dowling, Maurice. "Incarnation and Salvation in Leontius of Byzantium." In *Salvation According to the Fathers of the Church: The Proceedings of the Sixth International Patristic Conference*. Edited by D. Vincent Twomey and Dirk Krasmüller. Four Courts, 2010.

Draguet, René. *Julien d'Halicarnasse et sa Controverse avec Sévère d'Antioche sur l'Incorruptibilité du Corps du Christ*. Imprimerie P. Smeesters, 1924.

Drake, K. J. *The Flesh of the Word: The extra Calvinisticum from Zwingli to Early Orthodoxy*. Oxford University Press, 2021.

Duby, Steven J. *Jesus and the God of Classical Theism: Biblical Christology in Light of the Doctrine of God*. Baker Academic, 2022.

Dunn, James D. G. "Christ, Adam, and Preexistence." In *Where Christology Began: Essays on Philippians 2*, edited by Ralph P. Martin and Brian J. Dodd, 74–83. Westminster John Knox, 1998.

———. *Christology in the Making: A New Testament Inquiry into the Origins of the Doctrine of the Incarnation*. Westminster, 1980.

———. *Romans 1–8*. Thomas Nelson, 1988.

———. *The Theology of Paul the Apostle*. Eerdmans, 1998.

Durham, John I. *Exodus*. Word, 1987.

Ehmner, Hermann. "Johannes Brenz." In *The Reformation Theologians: An Introduction to Theology in the Early Modern Period*, edited by Carter Lindberg, 124–39. Blackwell, 2002.

Ehrman, Bart D. *How Jesus Became God: The Exaltation of a Jewish Preacher from Galilee*. HarperOne, 2014.

———. *Jesus: Apocalyptic Prophet of the New Millennium*. Oxford University Press, 1999.

———. *The Orthodox Corruption of Scripture: The Effect of Early Christological Controversies on the Text of the New Testament*. Oxford University Press, 1996.

Eichrodt, Walther. *Theology of the Old Testament*. Vol. 2. Translated by J. A. Baker. Westminster, 1967.

Ellacuría, Ignacio. *Ignacio Ellacuría: Essays on History, Liberation, and Salvation*. Edited by Michael E. Lee. Orbis Books, 2013.

Emerson, Matthew Y. *"He Descended to the Dead": An Evangelical Theology of Holy Saturday*. IVP Academic, 2019.

Erickson, Millard. *Christian Theology*. 2nd ed. Baker, 1998.

———. *The Word Became Flesh*. Baker, 1991.

Escobar, Samuel. *In Search of Christ in Latin America: From Colonial Image to Liberating Savior.* IVP Academic, 2019.

Evagrius of Pontus. *On the Eight Thoughts.* In *Evagrius of Pontus: The Greek Ascetic Corpus,* translated by Robert E. Sinkewicz, 66–90. Oxford University Press, 2003.

Evans, Christopher P. "Introduction." In *Victorene Christology: A Selection of Works of Hugh and Achard of St. Victor, and of Robert of Melun, and Excerpts Taken from the "Summa Sententiarum,"* edited by Christopher P. Evans, 21–82. Brepols, 2018.

Evans, C. Stephen, ed. *Exploring Kenotic Christology: The Self-Emptying of God.* Regent College, 2010.

———. "Kenotic Christology and the Nature of God." In Evans, *Exploring Kenotic Christology,* 190–217.

Evans, David Beecher. *Leontius of Byzantium: An Origenist Christology.* Dumbarton Oaks Center for Byzantine Studies, 1970.

Evans, James H., Jr. *We Have Been Believers: An African American Systematic Theology.* 2nd ed. Edited by Stephen G. Ray Jr. Fortress, 2012.

Everhart, D. T. "Communal Reconciliation: Corporate Responsibility and Opposition to Systemic Sin." *International Journal of Systematic Theology* 25, no. 1 (2023): 134–56.

Ezigbo, Victor I. "Jesus as God's Communicative and Hermeneutical Act: African Christians on the Person and Significance of Jesus Christ." In *Jesus Without Borders: Christology in the Majority World,* edited by Gene L. Green, Stephen Pardue, and K. K. Yeo, 37–58. Eerdmans, 2014.

Fairbairn, Donald. *Life in the Trinity: An Introduction to Theology with the Help of the Church Fathers.* IVP Academic, 2009.

Farkasfalvy, Denis. *A Biblical Path to the Triune God: Jesus, Paul, and the Revelation of the Trinity.* Edited by Thomas Esposito. Catholic University of America Press, 2021.

Farrow, Douglas B. *Ascension and Ecclesia: On the Significance of the Doctrine of the Ascension for Ecclesiology and Christian Cosmology.* Eerdmans, 1999.

———. *Ascension Theology.* T&T Clark, 2011.

Fee, Gordon D. "The New Testament and Kenosis Christology." In Evans, *Exploring Kenotic Christology,* 25–44.

Feinberg, John S., and Paul D. Feinberg. *Ethics for a Brave New World.* 2nd ed. Crossway, 2010.

Felder, Cain Hope. "Race, Racism, and the Biblical Narratives." In *Stony the Road We Trod: African American Biblical Interpretation,* edited by Cain Hope Felder, 127–45. Fortress, 1991.

Fesko, J. V. *Beyond Calvin: Union with Christ and Justification in Early Modern Reformed Theology (1517–1700).* Vandenhoeck & Ruprecht, 2012.

Fiddes, Paul S. *The Creative Suffering of God*. Clarendon, 1988.

Fisher, Edward. *The Marrow of Modern Divinity*. Philadelphia, n.d.

Fitzmyer, Joseph A. *Romans*. Doubleday, 1992.

Flavel, John. *The Fountain of Life: A Display of Christ in His Essential and Mediatorial Glory*. In *The Works of John Flavel*, 1:17–561. Banner of Truth, 1968.

Fletcher-Louis, Crispin. *Jesus Monotheism*. Vol. 1, *Christological Origins: The Emerging Consensus and Beyond*. Cascade Books, 2015.

Florovsky, Georges. *The Collected Works of Georges Florovsky*. Vol. 3, *Creation and Redemption*. Nordland, 1976.

Foerster, Werner. "δαίμων." In *Theological Dictionary of the New Testament*, edited by Gerhard Kittel, translated by Geoffrey W. Bromiley, 2:1–20. Eerdmans, 1965.

Frame, John M. *Systematic Theology: An Introduction to Christian Belief*. P&R, 2013.

France, R. T. *The Gospel of Matthew*. Eerdmans, 2007.

———. "On Being Ready." In *The Challenge of Jesus' Parables*, edited by Richard N. Longenecker, 177–95. Eerdmans, 2000.

Fredriksen, Paula. "How High Can Early High Christology Be?" In *Monotheism and Christology in Greco-Roman Antiquity*, edited by Matthew V. Novenson, 293–320. Brill, 2020.

Furnish, Victor Paul. *II Corinthians*. Doubleday, 1984.

Gabrielson, Timothy A. *Primeval History According to Paul: "In Adam" and "In Christ" in Romans*. PhD diss., Marquette University, 2016.

Gathercole, Simon. *Defending Substitution: An Essay on Atonement in Paul*. Baker Academic, 2015.

———. *The Preexistent Son: Recovering the Christologies of Matthew, Mark, and Luke*. Eerdmans, 2006.

Gaventa, Beverly Roberts. "The Shape of the 'I': The Psalter, the Gospel, and the Speaker in Romans 7." In *Apocalyptic Paul: Cosmos and Anthropos in Romans 5–8*, edited by Beverly Roberts Gaventa, 77–92. Baylor University Press, 2013.

Gebara, Ivone. *Out of the Depths: Women's Experience of Evil and Salvation*. Translated by Ann Patrick Ware. Fortress, 2002.

Gilliard, Dominique DuBois. *Rethinking Incarceration: Advocating for Justice That Restores*. InterVarsity, 2018.

Gilson, Étienne. *The Philosophy of St. Thomas Aquinas*. Translated by Edward Bullough. Books for Libraries, 1979.

Gleede, Benjamin. *The Development of the Term ἐνυπόστατος from Origen to John of Damascus*. Brill, 2012.

Goheen, Michael W. *Introducing Christian Mission Today: Scripture, History and Issues*. IVP Academic, 2014.

Goldenberg, David M. *Black and Slave: The Origins and History of the Curse of Ham*. De Gruyter, 2017.

Goldingay, John. *Daniel*. Rev. ed. Zondervan, 2019.

Gomes, Alan W. "*De Jesu Christo Servatore*: Faustus Socinus on the Satisfaction of Christ." *Westminster Theological Journal* 55 (1993): 209–31.

Gorman, Michael. *Aquinas on the Metaphysics of the Hypostatic Union*. Cambridge University Press, 2017.

Gorman, Michael J. *Inhabiting the Cruciform God: Kenosis, Justification, and Theosis in Paul's Narrative Soteriology*. Eerdmans, 2009.

The Gospel of Nicodemus. In *The Lost Books of the Bible: Being All the Gospels, Epistles, and Other Pieces Now Extant Attributed in the First Four Centuries to Jesus Christ, His Apostles and Their Companions*, 63–90. Testament, 1979.

Green, Joel B. "Adam, What Have You Done?" In *Evolution and the Fall*, edited by William T. Cavanaugh and James K. A. Smith, 98–116. Eerdmans, 2017.

Gregory, Brad S. *The Unintended Reformation: How a Religious Revolution Secularized Society*. Belknap Press of Harvard University Press, 2012.

Gregory of Cyprus. *Exposition of the Tomus of Faith Against Beccus*. Translated by Aristeides Papadakis. In *Crisis in Byzantium: The Filioque Controversy in the Patriarchate of Gregory II of Cyprus (1283–1289)*, rev. ed., edited by Aristeides Papadakis, 212–26. St. Vladimir's Seminary Press, 1997.

Gregory of Nazianzus. *The Second Letter to Cledonius Against Apollinaris (Epistle 102)*. In Hardy and Richardson, *Christology of the Later Fathers*, 225–29.

———. *The Theological Orations*. Translated by Charles Gordon Browne and James Edward Swallow. In Hardy and Richardson, *Christology of the Later Fathers*, 128–214.

———. *To Cledonius Against Apollinaris (Epistle 101)*. In Hardy and Richardson, *Christology of the Later Fathers*, 215–24.

Gregory of Nyssa. *On the Soul and the Resurrection*. Translated by Catharine P. Roth. St. Vladimir's Seminary Press, 1993.

Gregory of Sinai. "Discourse of Our Holy Father Gregory the Sinaite on the Holy Transfiguration of Our Lord Jesus Christ." In *Light on the Mountain: Greek Patristic and Byzantine Homilies on the Transfiguration of the Lord*, translated by Brian E. Daley, 327–49. St. Vladimir's Seminary Press, 2013.

Grenz, Stanley J. *Theology for the Community of God*. Eerdmans, 1994.

Grillmeier, Aloys. *Christ in Christian Tradition*. Vol. 1, *From the Apostolic Age to Chalcedon (451)*. Translated by John Bowden. John Knox, 1975.

Grindheim, Sigurd. *The Letter to the Hebrews*. Eerdmans, 2023.

Grudem, Wayne. "Biblical Evidence for the Eternal Submission of the Son to the Father." In *The New Evangelical Subordinationism? Perspectives on the Equality of God the Father and God the Son,* edited by Dennis W. Jowers and H. Wayne House, 223–61. Pickwick, 2012.

———. "Christ Preaching Through Noah: 1 Peter 3:19–20 in the Light of Dominant Themes in Jewish Literature." *Trinity Journal* 7 (1986): 3–31.

———. "He Did Not Descend into Hell: A Plea for Following Scripture Instead of the Apostles' Creed." *Journal of the Evangelical Theological Society* 34, no. 1 (1991): 103–13.

———. *Systematic Theology: An Introduction to Biblical Doctrine.* 2nd ed. Zondervan Academic, 2020.

Grumel, Venance, ed. *Les Regestes des Actes du Patriarcat de Constantinople.* Vol. 1, *Les Actes des Patriarches.* 2nd ed. Revised by Jean Darrouzès. Institut Français d'Études Byzantines, 1989.

Gunton, Colin E. *The Actuality of Atonement: A Study of Metaphor, Rationality, and the Christian Tradition.* T&T Clark, 1988.

Gustafson, James M. *Christ and the Moral Life.* Westminster John Knox, 2009.

Gutiérrez, Gustavo. *A Theology of Liberation: History, Politics and Salvation.* Translated and edited by Caridad Inda and John Eagleson. Orbis Books, 1971.

Haag, Herbert. *Is Original Sin in Scripture?* Translated by Dorothy Thompson. Sheed & Ward, 1969.

Habets, Myk. "Spirit Christology: The Future of Christology?" In *Third Article Theology: A Pneumatological Dogmatics,* edited by Myk Habets, 207–32. Fortress, 2016.

Haddad, Najeeb T. *Paul, Politics, and New Creation: Reconsidering Paul and Empire.* Lexington, 2021.

Hagner, Donald A. *Matthew 14–28.* Word, 1995.

Haight, Roger. "Sin and Grace." In *Systematic Theology: Roman Catholic Perspectives,* edited by Francis Schüssler Fiorenza and John P. Galvin, 2:75–142. Fortress, 1991.

Haile, Getatchew. "Materials on the Theology of Qǝbᶜat or Unction." In *Ethiopian Studies: Proceedings of the Sixth International Conference, Tel-Aviv, 14–17 April 1980,* edited by Gideon Goldenberg, 205–50. A. A. Balkema, 1986.

Hamilton, James M. *With the Clouds of Heaven: The Book of Daniel in Biblical Theology.* IVP Academic, 2014.

Hamm, Jeffery L. "*Descendit:* Delete or Declare? A Defense Against the Neo-Deletionists." *Westminster Theological Journal* 78 (2016): 93–116.

Hansen, G. Walter. *The Letter to the Philippians.* Eerdmans, 2009.

Hanson, R. P. C. *The Search for the Christian Doctrine of God: The Arian Controversy, 318–381.* Baker, 1988.

Hardy, Edward R., and Cyril C. Richardson, eds. *Christology of the Later Fathers.* Westminster John Knox, 1954.

Harrington, Daniel, and James Keenan. *Jesus and Virtue Ethics: Building Bridges Between New Testament Studies and Moral Theology.* Rowman & Littlefield, 2002.

Harris, Murray J. *Jesus as God: The New Testament Use of Theos in Reference to Jesus.* Baker, 1992.

———. *Raised Immortal: Resurrection & Immortality in the New Testament.* Eerdmans, 1983.

Harris, Steven Edward. *Refiguring Resurrection: A Biblical and Systematic Eschatology.* Baylor University Press, 2023.

Harris, W. Hall, III. "The Ascent and Descent of Christ in Ephesians 4:9–10." *Bibliotheca Sacra* 151 (April–June 1994): 198–214.

Harstad, Adolph L. *Deuteronomy.* Concordia, 2022.

Hawthorne, Gerald F. *Philippians.* Word, 1983.

Hays, Richard B. *The Moral Vision of the New Testament: A Contemporary Introduction to New Testament Ethics.* HarperOne, 1996.

Heffelfinger, Katie M. *Isaiah 40–66.* Cambridge University Press, 2024.

Heidgerken, Benjamin E. *Salvation Through Temptation: Maximus the Confessor and Thomas Aquinas on Christ's Victory over the Devil.* Catholic University of America Press, 2021.

Hellerman, Joseph H. *Philippians.* B&H, 2015.

Hengel, Martin. *Between Jesus and Paul: Studies in the Earliest History of Christianity.* Baylor University Press, 2013.

Hengel, Martin, with Daniel P. Bailey. "The Effective History of Isaiah 53 in the Pre-Christian Period." In *The Suffering Servant: Isaiah 53 in Jewish and Christian Sources,* edited by Bernd Janowski and Peter Stuhlmacher, translated by Daniel P. Bailey, 146–75. Eerdmans, 2004.

Hereth, Blake. "Mary, Did You Consent?" *Religious Studies* 58, no. 4 (2021): 677–700.

Hilary of Poitiers. *On the Trinity.* Translated by E. W. Watson and L. Pullan. Edited by W. Sanday. In *Nicene and Post-Nicene Fathers,* second series, edited by Philip Schaff and Henry Wace, 9:40–234. Reprint, Eerdmans, 1955.

Hill, Daniel Lee, and Ty Kieser. "Social Sin and the Sinless Savior: Delineating Supra-Personal Sin in Continuity with Conciliar Christology." *Modern Theology* 38, no. 3 (2022): 568–91.

Hill, Wesley. *Paul and the Trinity: Persons, Relations, and the Pauline Letters.* Eerdmans, 2015.

Hodge, Archibald Alexander. *Outlines of Theology.* Rev. ed. Eerdmans, 1949.

Hodge, Charles. *Commentary on the Epistle to the Romans.* Rev. ed. Eerdmans, 1965.

———. *Systematic Theology.* 3 vols. Eerdmans, 1982.

Hoehner, Harold W. *Ephesians: An Exegetical Commentary.* Baker Academic, 2002.

Hofer, Andrew. *Christ in the Life and Teaching of Gregory of Nazianzus.* Oxford University Press, 2013.

Holmes, Stephen R. "Reformed Varieties of the *Communicatio Idiomatum.*" In *The Person of Christ,* edited by Murray Rae and Stephen R. Holmes, 70–86. T&T Clark, 2005.

Hooker, Morna D. "Did the Use of Isaiah 53 to Interpret His Mission Begin with Jesus?" In *Jesus and the Suffering Servant: Isaiah 53 and Christian Origins,* edited by William H. Bellinger Jr. and William R. Farmer, 88–103. Trinity Press International, 1998.

Horton, Michael S. *Covenant and Salvation: Union with Christ.* Westminster John Knox, 2007.

Houck, Daniel W. *Aquinas, Original Sin, and the Challenge of Evolution.* Cambridge University Press, 2020.

Hovorun, Cyril. *Will, Action, and Freedom: Christological Controversies in the Seventh Century.* Brill, 2008.

Hugh of St. Victor. *Sentences on Divinity.* In *Trinity and Creation: A Selection of Works of Hugh, Richard, and Adam of St. Victor,* edited by Boyd Taylor Coolman and Dale M. Coulter, 113–78. New City, 2011.

Huidekoper, Frederic. *The Belief of the First Three Centuries Concerning Christ's Mission to the Underworld.* New York, 1876.

Hunter, Justus H. *If Adam Had Not Sinned: The Reason for the Incarnation from Anselm to Scotus.* Catholic University of America Press, 2020.

Hurst, L. D. "Christ, Adam, and Preexistence Revisited." In *Where Christology Began: Essays on Philippians 2,* edited by Ralph P. Martin and Brian J. Dodd, 84–95. Westminster John Knox, 1998.

Hurtado, Larry W. *Lord Jesus Christ: Devotion to Jesus in Earliest Christianity.* Eerdmans, 2003.

Irenaeus of Lyons. *Against Heresies.* In *The Ante-Nicene Fathers,* edited by Alexander Roberts and James Donaldson, 1:309–567. Reprint, Eerdmans, 1956.

Irons, Charles Lee. "A Lexical Defense of the Johannine 'Only-Begotten.'" In *Retrieving Eternal Generation,* edited by Fred Sanders and Scott R. Swain, 98–116. Zondervan, 2017.

Irving, Edward. *The Doctrine of the Incarnation Opened.* In *The Collected Writings of Edward Irving,* edited by G. Carlyle, 5:3–448. London, 1866.

Isasi-Díaz, Ada María. "Kin-dom of God: A Mujerista Proposal." In *In Our Own Voices: Latino/a Renditions of Theology,* edited by Benjamín Valentín, 171–89. Orbis Books, 2010.

Ishak, Shenouda M. *Christology and the Council of Chalcedon*. Outskirts, 2013.

Jamieson, R. B., and Tyler R. Wittman. *Biblical Reasoning: Christological and Trinitarian Rules for Exegesis*. Baker Academic, 2022.

Jenkins, Philip. *The Next Christendom: The Coming of Global Christianity*. 3rd ed. Oxford University Press, 2011.

Jenson, Robert W. *Systematic Theology*. 2 vols. Oxford University Press, 1997–99.

———. *The Triune Identity*. Fortress, 1982.

Jewett, Robert. *Romans*. Fortress, 2007.

Jipp, Joshua W. "Reprogramming Royal Psalms to Proclaim the Enthroned-in-Heaven King." In *Ascent into Heaven in Luke-Acts: New Explorations of Luke's Narrative Hinge*, edited by David K. Bryan and David W. Pao, 41–59. Fortress, 2016.

Jobes, Karen H. *1 Peter*. 2nd ed. Baker Academic, 2022.

John of Damascus. *On the Orthodox Faith*. In *St. John of Damascus: Writings*, translated by Frederic H. Chase Jr., 165–406. Catholic University of America Press, 1958.

———. "Oration on the Transfiguration of Our Lord and Savior Jesus Christ." In *Light on the Mountain: Greek Patristic and Byzantine Homilies on the Transfiguration of the Lord*, edited by Brian E. Daley, 205–31. St. Vladimir's Seminary Press, 2013.

———. *Three Treatises on the Divine Images*. Translated by Andrew Louth. St. Vladimir's Seminary Press, 2003.

Johnson, Elizabeth. "Redeeming the Name of Christ: Christology." In *Freeing Theology: The Essentials of Theology in Feminist Perspective*, edited by Catherine Mowry LaCugna, 115–38. HarperCollins, 1993.

Johnson, Keith E. "Penal Substitution as an Undivided Work of the Triune God." *Trinity Journal* 36, no. 1 (2015): 51–67.

Johnson, Marcus Peter. *One with Christ: An Evangelical Theology of Salvation*. Crossway, 2013.

Johnson, Sylvester A. *The Myth of Ham in Nineteenth-Century American Christianity*. Palgrave Macmillan, 2004.

Jones, Beth Felker. *Practicing Christian Doctrine: An Introduction to Thinking and Living Theologically*. Baker Academic, 2014.

Jones, Peter Rhea. *Studying the Parables of Jesus*. Smyth & Helwys, 1999.

Justin Martyr. *Dialogue with Trypho*. In *Writings of Saint Justin Martyr*, edited by Thomas B. Falls, 147–368. Catholic University of America Press, 1948.

Kähler, Martin. *The So-Called Historical Jesus and the Historic Biblical Christ*. Translated and edited by Carl E. Braaten. Fortress, 1964.

Kaiser, Walter C., Jr. "The Identity and Mission of the 'Servant of the Lord.'" In *The Gospel According to Isaiah 53: Encountering the Suffering Servant in Jewish and Christian Theology*, 87–107. Kregel, 2012.

Kamitsuka, Margaret D. *Abortion and the Christian Tradition: A Pro-Choice Theological Ethic.* Westminster John Knox, 2019.

Kapic, Kelly M. *Embodied Hope: A Theological Meditation on Pain and Suffering.* IVP Academic, 2017.

Käsemann, Ernst. *Commentary on Romans.* Translated and edited by Geoffrey W. Bromiley. Eerdmans, 1980.

Katongole, Emmanuel. *Born from Lament: The Theology and Politics of Hope in Africa.* Eerdmans, 2017.

Keck, Leander E. *Why Christ Matters: Toward a New Testament Christology.* Baylor University Press, 2015.

Keener, Craig S. *The Gospel of John: A Commentary.* 2 vols. Baker Academic, 2003.

Kelly, J. N. D. *Early Christian Creeds.* 3rd ed. Longman, 1972.

———. *Early Christian Doctrines.* Rev. ed. HarperCollins, 1978.

Kim, Dong-Kun. *The Future of Christology: Jesus Christ for a Global Age.* Lexington, 2019.

Kim, Grace Ji-Sun. *Reimagining Spirit: Wind, Breath, and Vibration.* Cascade Books, 2019.

Kim, Uriah. "Uriah the Hittite: A (Con)text of Struggle for Identity." *Semeia* 90/91 (2002): 69–85.

Kirk, J. R. Daniel. *A Man Attested by God: The Human Jesus of the Synoptic Gospels.* Eerdmans, 2016.

Kitamori, Kazoh. "The Problem of Pain in Christology." In *Christ and the Younger Churches: Theological Contributions from Asia, Africa, and Latin America*, edited by Georg F. Vicedom, 83–90. SPCK, 1972.

———. *Theology of the Pain of God.* 5th ed. Wipf & Stock, 2005.

Kitchen, Robert A. "Babai the Great." In *The Orthodox Christian World*, edited by Augustine Casiday, 237–43. Routledge, 2012.

Komline, Han-luen Kantzer. "Augustine, Kenosis, and the Person of Christ." In *Kenosis: The Self-Emptying of Christ in Scripture and Theology*, edited by Paul T. Nimmo and Keith L. Johnson, 97–121. Eerdmans, 2022.

———. *Augustine on the Will: A Theological Account.* Oxford University Press, 2020.

Kotiranta, Matti. "The Palamite Idea of Perichoresis of the Persons of the Trinity in the Light of Contemporary Neo-Palamite Analysis." *Acta Byzanta Fennica* 9 (1999): 59–69.

Krikorian, Mesrob K. *Christology of the Oriental Orthodox Churches: Christology in the Tradition of the Armenian Apostolic Church.* Peter Lang, 2010.

Kubilus, Derek Ryan. *Holy Hell: A Case Against Eternal Damnation.* Eerdmans, 2024.

Kuhn, Michael F. *God Is One: A Christian Defense of Divine Unity in the Muslim Golden Age.* Langham Academic, 2019.

Kurz, William S. *Reading Luke-Acts: Dynamics of Biblical Narrative.* Westminster John Knox, 1993.

Lau, Te-Li. *Defending Shame: Its Formative Power in Paul's Letters.* Baker Academic, 2020.

Laufer, Catherine Ella. *Hell's Destruction: An Exploration of Christ's Descent to the Dead.* Ashgate, 2013.

Law, David R. "Gottfried Thomasius (1802–75)." In *The Blackwell Companion to the Theologians,* edited by Ian S. Markham, 2:148–68. Blackwell, 2009.

Lawson, Robert C. "The Anthropology of Jesus Christ Our Kinsman." Edited and revised by William Howard Collier. Ohio Ministries, 2000.

Lee, Dorothy. *Transfiguration.* Continuum, 2004.

Lee, Hak Joon. *Christian Ethics: A New Covenant Model.* Eerdmans, 2021.

Lee, Jarena. "A Prayer for Sanctification." In *Conversations with God: Two Centuries of Prayers by African Americans,* edited by James Melvin Washington, 14–15. HarperCollins, 1994.

Leo the Great. *The Tome of Leo.* Translated by William Bright. In Hardy and Richardson, *Christology of the Later Fathers,* 359–70.

Leontius of Byzantium. *Complete Works.* Edited and translated by Brian E. Daley. Oxford University Press, 2017.

———. *Contra Aphthartodocetas.* In *Complete Works,* 337–410.

———. *Contra Nestorianos et Eutychianos.* In *Complete Works,* 125–268.

———. *Solutions to the Arguments Proposed by Severus (Epilyseis).* In *Complete Works,* 268–311.

Lester, G. Brooke. *Daniel Evokes Isaiah: Allusive Characterization of Foreign Rule in the Hebrew-Aramaic Book of Daniel.* T&T Clark, 2015.

Levering, Matthew. *Jesus and the Demise of Death: Resurrection, Afterlife, and the Fate of the Christian.* Baylor University Press, 2012.

Levy, Ian Christopher. *Introducing Medieval Biblical Interpretation: The Senses of Scripture in Premodern Exegesis.* Baker Academic, 2018.

Lewis, C. S. *The Screwtape Letters.* HarperSanFrancisco, 1996.

Libânio, João Batista. "Hope, Utopia, Resurrection." Translated by Dinah Livingstone. In *Mysterium Liberationis: Fundamental Concepts of Liberation Theology,* edited by Ignacio Ellacuría and Jon Sobrino, 716–27. Orbis Books, 1993.

Licona, Michael R. *The Resurrection of Jesus: A New Historiographical Approach*. IVP Academic, 2010.

Linden, Ian, and Jane Linden. *Church and Revolution in Rwanda*. Africana Publishing, 1977.

Litwa, M. David. "Behold Adam: A Reading of John 19:5." *Horizons in Biblical Theology* 32 (2010): 129–43.

———. *Iesus Deus: The Early Christian Depiction of Jesus as a Mediterranean God*. Fortress, 2014.

Loke, Andrew Ter Ern. *A Kryptic Model of the Incarnation*. Routledge, 2016.

Lombard, Peter. *The Sentences*. Book 3, *On the Incarnation of the Word*. Translated by Giulio Silano. Pontifical Institute of Medieval Studies, 2008.

Long, D. Stephen. *On Teaching and Learning Christian Ethics*. Georgetown University Press, 2024.

Longenecker, Richard N. *The Epistle to the Romans: A Commentary on the Greek Text*. Eerdmans, 2016.

Lossky, Vladimir. *Dogmatic Theology: Creation, God's Image in Man, and the Redeeming Work of the Trinity*. Edited by Olivier Clément and Michel Stavrou. Translated by Anthony P. Gythiel. St. Vladimir's Seminary Press, 2017.

Louth, Andrew. "Christology in the East from the Council of Chalcedon to John Damascene." In *The Oxford Handbook of Christology*, edited by Francesca Aran Murphy with Troy A. Stefano, 139–53. Oxford University Press, 2015.

Lüdemann, Gerd. *The Resurrection of Jesus: History, Experience, Theology*. Fortress, 1994.

———. *Virgin Birth? The Real Story of Mary and Her Son Jesus*. Translated by John Bowden. Trinity, 1998.

Luther, Martin. "Confession Concerning Christ's Supper—From Part I (1528)." In *Martin Luther's Basic Theological Writings*, 3rd ed., edited by Timothy F. Lull and William R. Russell, 262–79. Fortress, 2012.

———. *The Freedom of a Christian*. In *Martin Luther: Selections from His Writings*, edited by John Dillenberger, 42–85. Anchor, 1962.

———. *The Sacrament of the Body and Blood of Christ: Against the Fanatics (1526)*. In *Martin Luther's Basic Theological Writings*, 3rd ed., edited by Timothy F. Lull and William R. Russell, 224–39. Fortress, 2012.

Macchia, Frank D. *Jesus the Spirit Baptizer: Christology in Light of Pentecost*. Eerdmans, 2018.

Machen, J. Gresham. *Christianity and Liberalism*. New ed. Eerdmans, 2009.

———. *The Virgin Birth of Christ*. 1930. Reprint, Baker, 1967.

Macleod, Donald. *The Person of Christ*. InterVarsity, 1998.

Madueme, Hans, and Michael R. E. Reeves, eds. *Adam, the Fall, and Original Sin: Theological, Biblical, and Scientific Perspectives*. Baker Academic, 2014.

Malherbe, Abraham J. *Light from the Gentiles: Hellenistic Philosophy and Early Christianity; Collected Essays, 1959–2012*. Vol. 1. Edited by Carl R. Holladay, John T. Fitzgerald, Gregory E. Sterling, and James W. Thompson. Brill, 2014.

Mantzaridis, Georgios I. *The Deification of Man: St. Gregory Palamas and the Orthodox Tradition*. Translated by Liadain Sherrard. St. Vladimir's Seminary Press, 1984.

Marcus, Joel. "Son of Man as Son of Adam." *Revue Biblique* 110, no. 1 (2003): 38–61.

Marshall, Christopher D. *Beyond Retribution: A New Testament Vision for Justice, Crime, and Punishment*. Eerdmans, 2001.

Martin, Ralph P. *Philippians*. Eerdmans, 1976.

———. *2 Corinthians*. 2nd ed. Zondervan, 2014.

Martinez-Olivieri, Jules. *A Visible Witness: Christology, Liberation, and Participation*. Fortress, 2016.

Maslov, Boris. "The Limits of Platonism: Gregory of Nazianzus and the Invention of *theōsis*." *Greek, Roman, and Byzantine Studies* 52 (2012): 440–68.

Mathison, Keith A. "The Lord's Supper." In *Reformation Theology: A Systematic Summary*, edited by Matthew Barrett, 643–74. Crossway, 2017.

Mattison, William C., III. *Introducing Moral Theology: True Happiness and the Virtues*. Brazos, 2008.

Maximus the Confessor. *Ambigua to Thomas*. In *On Difficulties in the Church Fathers: The Ambigua*, edited and translated by Nicholas Constas, 1:1–60. Harvard University Press, 2014.

———. *Ambiguum 42*. In *On the Cosmic Mystery of Jesus Christ: Selected Writings from Saint Maximus the Confessor*, translated by Paul M. Blowers and Robert Louis Wilken, 79–96. St. Vladimir's Seminary Press, 2003.

———. *Disputations with Pyrrhus*. Translated by Joseph P. Farrell. St. Tikhon's Monastery Press, 2014.

———. *Dispute at Bizya*. In *Maximus the Confessor and His Companions: Documents from Exile*, edited by Pauline Allen and Bronwen Neil, 75–119. Oxford University Press, 2002.

———. *Opusculum 6*. In *On the Cosmic Mystery of Jesus Christ: Selected Writings from Saint Maximus the Confessor*, translated by Paul M. Blowers and Robert Louis Wilken, 173–76. St. Vladimir's Seminary Press, 2003.

Mayerson, Deborah. *On the Path to Genocide: Armenia and Rwanda Reexamined*. Berghahn, 2014.

Mburu, Elizabeth. *African Hermeneutics*. Hippobooks, 2019.

McCall, Thomas H. *Against God and Nature: The Doctrine of Sin*. Crossway, 2019.

———. *Forsaken: The Trinity and the Cross, and Why It Matters*. IVP Academic, 2012.

McClendon, James William, Jr. *Systematic Theology*. Vol. 2, *Doctrine*. Abingdon, 1994.

McCormack, Bruce Lindley. *The Humility of the Eternal Son: Reformed Kenoticism and the Repair of Chalcedon*. Cambridge University Press, 2021.

McDonnell, Kilian, and George T. Montague. *Christian Initiation and Baptism in the Holy Spirit: Evidence from the First Eight Centuries*. Liturgical Press, 1991.

McFarland, Ian. *In Adam's Fall: A Meditation on the Christian Doctrine of Original Sin*. Wiley-Blackwell, 2010.

McGinnis, Andrew M. *The Son of God Beyond the Flesh*. Bloomsbury, 2014.

McGrath, Alister E. *Christian Theology: An Introduction*. 3rd ed. Blackwell, 2001.

McGrath, James F. *The Only True God: Early Christian Monotheism in Its Jewish Context*. University of Illinois Press, 2009.

McGuckin, John A. *St. Cyril of Alexandria: The Christological Controversy—Its History, Theology, and Texts*. St. Vladimir's Seminary Press, 2004.

McKim, Donald K. *Westminster Dictionary of Theological Terms*. Westminster John Knox, 1996.

McKnight, Scot. *1 Peter*. Zondervan, 1996.

McNall, Joshua M. *The Mosaic of Atonement: An Integrated Approach to Christ's Work*. Zondervan, 2019.

McPherson, Aimee Semple. "The Baptism of the Holy Ghost." In *The Foursquare Gospel*, edited by Raymond L. Cox, 114–22. Foursquare Publications, 1969.

———. *Fire from on High*. Foursquare Publications, 1969.

———. "Jesus Christ the Baptizer." In *The Foursquare Gospel*, edited by Raymond L. Cox, 93–114. Foursquare Publications, 1969.

———. *This Is That*. Garland Publishing, 1985.

Meier, John P. *A Marginal Jew: Rethinking the Historical Jesus*. 5 vols. Doubleday, 1991–2016.

Melito of Sardis. *A Homily on the Passover*. In *The Christological Controversy*, edited and translated by Richard A. Norris Jr., 33–48. Fortress, 1980.

Metselaar, Marijke. *Defining Christ: The Church of the East and Nascent Islam*. Peeters, 2019.

Meyendorff, John. *Byzantine Theology: Historical Trends & Doctrinal Themes*. Fordham University Press, 1974.

Michaels, J. Ramsey. *1 Peter*. Word, 1988.

Miles, Margaret R. *The Word Made Flesh: A History of Christian Thought*. Blackwell, 2005.

Minns, Denis. *Irenaeus: An Introduction.* T&T Clark, 2010.

Moffitt, David M. *Rethinking the Atonement: New Perspectives on Jesus's Death, Resurrection, and Ascension.* Baker Academic, 2022.

Moltmann, Jürgen. *The Coming of God: Christian Eschatology.* Translated by Margaret Kohl. Fortress, 1996.

———. *The Crucified God: The Cross of Christ as the Foundation and Criticism of Christian Theology.* Fortress, 1993.

———. *Theology of Hope.* Translated by James W. Leitch. Harper & Row, 1967.

———. *The Trinity and the Kingdom.* Translated by Margaret Kohl. Harper & Row, 1981.

Moo, Douglas J. *The Epistle to the Romans.* Eerdmans, 1996.

Moreland, J. P., and William Lane Craig. *Philosophical Foundations for a Christian Worldview.* IVP Academic, 2003.

Morgan, Christopher W., and Robert A. Peterson. *A Concise Dictionary of Theological Terms.* B&H Academic, 2020.

Morgan, J. Nicole. *Fat and Faithful: Learning to Love Our Bodies, Our Neighbors, and Ourselves.* Fortress, 2018.

Morris, Leon. *The Apostolic Preaching of the Cross.* 3rd ed. Eerdmans, 1965.

———. *The Epistle to the Romans.* Eerdmans, 1988.

———. *The Gospel According to Matthew.* Eerdmans, 1992.

Morris, Thomas V. *The Logic of God Incarnate.* Wipf & Stock, 2001.

Mott, Stephen Charles. *Biblical Ethics and Social Change.* Oxford University Press, 1982.

Mujawiyera, Eugenie. *The Rwandan Tutsis: A Tutsi Woman's Account of the Hidden Causes of the Rwandan Tragedy.* Adonis & Abbey, 2006.

Muller, Richard A. *Dictionary of Latin and Greek Theological Terms Drawn Principally from Protestant Scholastic Theology.* Baker, 1985.

Murray, John. *The Imputation of Adam's Sin.* Presbyterian and Reformed, 1959.

———. *Redemption Accomplished and Applied.* Eerdmans, 1955.

Nam-dong, Suh. "Towards a Theology of *Han.*" In *Minjung Theology: People as the Subjects of History,* edited by Kim Yong Bock, 51–68. Commission on Theological Concerns, 1981.

Nestorius of Constantinople. "Second Letter to Cyril." In *The Cambridge Edition of Early Christian Writings,* vol. 3, *Christ: Through the Nestorian Controversy,* edited by Mark DelCogliano, 570–76. Cambridge University Press, 2022.

Nielsen, J. T. *Adam and Christ in the Theology of Irenaeus of Lyons: An Examination of the Function of the Adam-Christ Typology in the "Adversus Haereses" of Irenaeus, Against the Background of the Gnosticism of His Time.* Van Gorcum, 1968.

Nimmo, Paul T., and Keith L. Johnson, eds. *Kenosis: The Self-Emptying of Christ in Scripture and Theology.* Eerdmans, 2022.

Noble, T. A. *Holy Trinity: Holy People: The Theology of Christian Perfecting.* James Clarke, 2013.

Nyamiti, Charles. *Christ as Our Ancestor: Christology from an African Perspective.* Mambo, 1984.

———. *Jesus Christ, the Ancestor of Humankind: Methodological and Trinitarian Foundations.* Catholic University of Eastern Africa, 2005.

Oakes, Peter. "Re-Mapping the Universe: Paul and the Emperor in 1 Thessalonians and Philippians." *Journal for the Study of the New Testament* 27, no. 3 (2005): 301–22.

O'Collins, Gerald. *Christology: A Biblical, Historical, and Systematic Study of Jesus.* 2nd ed. Oxford University Press, 2009.

Oden, Thomas C. *The Word of Life.* HarperCollins, 1989.

Origen of Alexandria. *Dialogue with Heraclides.* In *Alexandrian Christology,* translated and edited by John Ernest Leonard Oulton and Henry Chadwick, 437–55. Westminster, 1954.

Orr, James. "The Virgin Birth of Christ." In *The Fundamentals: A Testimony to the Truth,* edited by R. A. Torrey, A. C. Dixon, et al., 2:247–60. Reprint, Baker Books, 2003.

Osborn, Eric. *Irenaeus of Lyons.* Cambridge University Press, 2004.

Otto, Randall E. "*Descendit in Inferna*: A Reformed Review of a Creedal Conundrum." *Westminster Theological Journal* 52 (1990): 143–50.

Outram, William. *Two Dissertations on Sacrifices.* Translated by John Allen. London, 1828.

Ovey, Michael. *Your Will Be Done: Exploring Eternal Subordination, Divine Monarchy and Divine Humility.* Latimer Trust, 2016.

Owen, John. *Communion with the Triune God.* Edited by Kelly M. Kapic and Justin Taylor. Crossway, 2007.

———. *A Declaration of the Glorious Mystery of the Person of Christ.* In *The Works of John Owen,* edited by William H. Goold and Charles W. Quick, 1:1–272. Philadelphia, 1871.

Padilla, C. René. *Mission Between the Times: Essays on the Kingdom.* Langham, 2010.

Page, Sydney H. T. "Satan, Sin, and Evil." In *Fallen: A Theology of Sin,* edited by Christopher W. Morgan and Robert A. Peterson, 219–42. Crossway, 2013.

Palamas, Gregory. *Dialogue Between an Orthodox and a Barlaamite.* Translated by Rein Ferwerda. Global Publications, 1999.

———. *Homily 34: On the Venerable Transfiguration of Our Lord and God and Savior, Jesus Christ.* In *Light on the Mountain: Greek Patristic and Byzantine*

Homilies on the Transfiguration of the Lord, translated by Brian E. Daley, 355–66. St. Vladimir's Seminary Press, 2013.

———. "Topics of Natural and Theological Science and on the Moral and Ascetic Life: One Hundred and Fifty Texts." In *The Philokalia*, compiled by St. Nikodimos of the Holy Mountain and St. Makarios of Corinth and translated by G. E. H. Palmer, Philip Sherrard, and Kallistos Ware, 4:346–417. Faber and Faber, 1995.

———. *The Triads*. Edited by John Meyendorff. Translated by Nicholas Gendle. Paulist Press, 1983.

Palmer, Phoebe. *The Way of Holiness (1843)*. In *Phoebe Palmer: Selected Writings*, edited by Thomas C. Oden, 165–84. Paulist Press, 1988.

Pannenberg, Wolfhart. *Jesus—God and Man*. Translated by Lewis L. Wilkins and Duane A. Priebe. Westminster, 1968.

Parente, Pietro, Antonio Piolanti, and Salvatore Garofalo. *Dictionary of Dogmatic Theology*. Translated by Emmanuel Doronzo. Bruce, 1951.

Park, Andrew Sung. *The Wounded Heart of God: The Asian Concept of Han and the Christian Doctrine of Sin*. Abingdon, 1993.

Parkison, Samuel G. *The Unvarnished Jesus: The Beauty of Christ & His Ugly Rivals*. Christian Focus, 2025.

Pawl, Timothy. *In Defense of Conciliar Christology: A Philosophical Essay*. Oxford University Press, 2016.

Peeler, Amy. *Hebrews*. Eerdmans, 2024.

———. *Women and the Gender of God*. Eerdmans, 2022.

Peppard, Michael. *The Son of God in the Roman World: Divine Sonship in Its Social and Political Context*. Oxford University Press, 2011.

Perkins, William. *A Fruitful Dialogue Concerning the End of the World*. In *The Works of William Perkins*, edited by Joel R. Beeke and Greg A. Salazar, 6:445–74. Reformation Heritage Books, 2018.

Perrin, Nicholas. *Jesus the Priest*. Baker Academic, 2018.

Petersen, David L. *The Prophetic Literature: An Introduction*. Westminster John Knox, 2002.

Petrella, Ivan. *The Future of Liberation Theology: An Argument and a Manifesto*. Ashgate, 2004.

Pinnock, Clark H. *Flame of Love: A Theology of the Holy Spirit*. InterVarsity, 1996.

Pino, Tikhon. *Essence and Energies: Being and Naming God in St Gregory Palamas*. Routledge, 2023.

Pohle, Joseph. *Soteriology: A Dogmatic Treatise on the Redemption*. Edited by Arthur Preuss. Herder, 1947.

Pomazansky, Michael. *Orthodox Dogmatic Theology*. St. Herman of Alaska Brother-hood, 2015.

Poole, Matthew. *A Commentary on the Holy Bible*. Vol. 3, *Matthew–Revelation*. Hendrickson, n.d.

Porter, Stanley E., and Bryan R. Dyer. *Origins of New Testament Christology: An Introduction to the Traditions and Titles Applied to Jesus*. Baker Academic, 2023.

Powell, Mark Allan. *Jesus as a Figure in History: How Modern Historians View the Man from Galilee*. Westminster John Knox, 1998.

Prestige, G. L. *God in Patristic Thought*. 2nd ed. SPCK, 1952.

Principe, Walter H. *Alexander of Hales' Theology of the Hypostatic Union*. Pontifica Institute of Mediaeval Studies, 1967.

Rahner, Karl. *Foundations of Christian Faith: An Introduction to the Idea of Christianity*. Seabury, 1978.

Ratzinger, Joseph Cardinal. *Behold the Pierced One: An Approach to a Spiritual Christology*. Ignatius, 1986.

———. *Eschatology: Death and Eternal Life*. 2nd ed. Catholic University of America Press, 1988.

Reichenbach, Bruce R. "Healing View." In *The Nature of the Atonement: Four Views*, edited by James Beilby and Paul R. Eddy, 117–42. IVP Academic, 2006.

Reynolds, Brian K. *Gateway to Heaven: Marian Doctrine and Devotion, Image and Typology in the Patristic and Medieval Periods*. Vol. 1, *Doctrine and Devotion*. New City, 2012.

Richard of St. Victor. *On the Trinity*. In *Trinity and Creation*, edited by Boyd Taylor Coolman and Dale M. Coulter, 195–382. New City, 2011.

Richards, Jay Wesley. "Can a Male Savior Save Women?" In *Unapologetic Apologetics: Meeting the Challenges of Theological Studies*, edited by William A. Dembski and Jay Wesley Richards, 156–78. InterVarsity, 2001.

Riches, Aaron. *Ecce Homo: On the Divine Unity of Christ*. Eerdmans, 2016.

Ridderbos, Herman N. *The Epistle of Paul to the Churches of Galatia*. Eerdmans, 1953.

Rieger, Joerg. *Christ and Empire: From Paul to Postcolonial Times*. Fortress, 2007.

Rivera, Mayra. *Poetics of the Flesh*. Duke University Press, 2015.

Robert of Melun. *Sentences*. In *Victorine Christology*, edited by Christopher P. Evans, 249–443. New City, 2019.

Roberts, Kyle. *A Complicated Pregnancy: Whether Mary Was a Virgin and Why It Matters*. Fortress, 2017.

Robinson, John A. T. *Jesus and His Coming*. 2nd ed. Westminster, 1979.

Rodríguez, Rafael. "The Embarrassing Truth About Jesus: The Criterion of Embarrassment and the Failure of Historical Authenticity." In *Jesus, Criteria, and the Demise of Authenticity*, edited by Chris Keith and Anthony Le Donne, 132–51. Bloomsbury T&T Clark, 2012.

Romanides, John S. *The Ancestral Sin*. Translated by George S. Gabriel. Zephyr, 1998.

Rommen, Edward. *Get Real: On Evangelism in the Late Modern World*. William Carey, 2010.

Rouwhorst, Gerard A. M. "The Descent of Christ into the Underworld in Early Christian Liturgy." In *The Apostles' Creed: "He Descended into Hell*," edited by Marcel Sarot and Archibald L. H. M. van Wierengen, 54–78. Brill, 2018.

Ruether, Rosemary Radford. *Sexism and God-Talk: Toward a Feminist Theology*. Beacon, 1993.

Russell, Norman. *The Doctrine of Deification in the Greek Patristic Tradition*. Oxford University Press, 2005.

Rutledge, Fleming. *The Crucifixion: Understanding the Death of Jesus Christ*. Eerdmans, 2015.

Ryken, Leland, James C. Wilhoit, and Tremper Longman III. *Dictionary of Biblical Imagery*. InterVarsity, 1998.

Samuel, V. C. *The Council of Chalcedon Re-Examined*. British Orthodox Press, 2001.

Sánchez M., Leopoldo A. *T&T Clark Introduction to Spirit Christology*. Bloomsbury T&T Clark, 2022.

Sanders, Fred. *Fountain of Salvation: Trinity & Soteriology*. Eerdmans, 2021.

———. *The Triune God*. Zondervan, 2016.

Sarot, Marcel. "The Scope of Redemption on Finding Meaning in Christ's Descent into Hell." In *The Apostles' Creed: "He Descended into Hell,"* edited by Marcel Sarot and Archibald L. H. M. van Wierengen, 185–206. Brill, 2018.

Sasse, Hermann. "κοσμός." In *Theological Dictionary of the New Testament*, edited by Gerhard Kittel, translated by Geoffrey W. Bromiley, 3:868–95. Eerdmans, 1965.

———. *This Is My Body: Luther's Contention for the Real Presence in the Sacrament of the Altar*. Augsburg, 1959.

Schaberg, Jane. *The Illegitimacy of Jesus: A Feminist Theological Interpretation of the Infancy Narratives*. Crossroad, 1990.

Schmemann, Alexander. *For the Life of the World: Sacraments and Orthodoxy*. St. Vladimir's Seminary Press, 2018.

Schmid, Heinrich. *The Doctrinal Theology of the Evangelical Lutheran Church, Exhibited, and Verified from the Original Sources*. 5th ed. Translated by Charles A. Hay and Henry E. Jacobs. Philadelphia, 1876.

Schmucker, S. S. *Elements of Popular Theology: With Special Reference to the Doctrines of the Reformation as Avowed Before the Diet at Augsburg.* 2nd ed. New York, 1834.

Schreiner, Patrick. *The Ascension of Christ: Recovering a Neglected Doctrine.* Lexham, 2020.

———. *The Transfiguration of Christ: An Exegetical and Theological Reading.* Baker Academic, 2024.

Schreiner, Thomas R. *Romans.* 2nd ed. Baker Academic, 2018.

Schwarz, Hans. "Gottfried Thomasius (1802–1875)." In *Nineteenth-Century Lutheran Theologians,* edited by Matthew L. Becker, 99–120. Vandenhoeck & Ruprecht, 2016.

Schweitzer, Albert. *The Mysticism of Paul the Apostle.* Translated by William Montgomery. Henry Holt, 1931.

———. *The Quest of the Historical Jesus.* Translated by W. Montgomery. Reprint, Dover, 2005.

Schweizer, Eduard, Rudolf Meyer, and Friedrich Baumgärtel. "σάρξ." In *Theological Dictionary of the New Testament,* edited by Gerhard Friedrich, translated by Geoffrey W. Bromiley, 7:98–151. Eerdmans, 1971.

Scott, Alan. *Origen and the Life of the Stars: A History of an Idea.* Clarendon, 1991.

Scott, Margaret. *The Eucharist and Social Justice.* Paulist Press, 2009.

Scouteris, Constantine B. *Ecclesial Being: Contributions to Theological Dialogue.* Edited by Christopher Veniamin. South Mount Thabor, 2005.

Segal, Michael. *Dreams, Riddles, and Visions: Contextual and Intertextual Approaches to the Book of Daniel.* De Gruyter, 2016.

Seitz, Christopher R. *The Elder Testament: Canon, Theology, Trinity.* Baylor University Press, 2018.

Semujanga, Josias. *Origins of Rwandan Genocide.* Humanity Books, 2003.

"The Session of 22 June." In *The Council of Ephesus of 431: Documents and Proceedings,* translated by Richard Price, 217–92. Liverpool University Press, 2020.

Severus of Antioch. *Ad Nephalium.* In *Severus of Antioch,* edited by Pauline Allen and C. T. R. Hayward, 59–66. Routledge, 2004.

Shively, Elizabeth Evans. "Israel's Scriptures in Mark." In *Israel's Scriptures in Early Christian Writings: The Use of the Old Testament in the New,* edited by Matthias Henze and David Lincicum, 236–62. Eerdmans, 2023.

Silva, Moisés, ed. *New International Dictionary of New Testament Theology and Exegesis.* Vol. 2. Zondervan, 2014.

Silva, Moisés. *Philippians.* 2nd ed. Baker Academic, 2005.

Simon of Tournai. *On the Incarnation of Christ: Institutiones in sacram paginam 7.1–67*. Edited and translated by Christopher P. Evans. Pontifical Institute of Medieval Studies, 2017.

Sklar, Jay. *Sin, Impurity, Sacrifice, Atonement: The Priestly Conceptions*. Sheffield Phoenix, 2015.

Slotemaker, John T. *Anselm of Canterbury and the Search for God*. Lexington, 2018.

Smith, Brandon D. *The Trinity in the Book of Revelation: Seeing Father, Son, and Holy Spirit in John's Apocalypse*. IVP Academic, 2022.

———. "What Christ Does, God Does: Surveying Recent Scholarship on Christological Monotheism." *Currents in Biblical Research* 17, no. 2 (2019): 184–208.

Smith, James K. A. "What Stands on the Fall? A Philosophical Exploration." In *Evolution and the Fall*, edited by William T. Cavanaugh and James K. A. Smith, 48–64. Eerdmans, 2017.

Soares-Prabhu, George M. *The Dharma of Jesus*. Edited by Francis Xavier D'Sa. Orbis Books, 2003.

Sobrino, Jon. "Central Position of the Reign of God in Liberation Theology." In *Systematic Theology: Perspectives from Liberation Theology*, edited by Jon Sobrino and Ignacio Ellacuría, 38–74. Orbis Books, 1996.

———. *Christology at the Crossroads: A Latin American Approach*. Translated by John Drury. Orbis Books, 1978.

———. *Christ the Liberator: A View from the Victims*. Translated by Paul Burns. Orbis Books, 2001.

———. *Spirituality of Liberation: Toward Political Holiness*. Translated by Robert R. Barr. Orbis Books, 1988.

Song, Choan-Seng. *Third-Eye Theology: Theology in Formation in Asian Settings*. Orbis Books, 1979.

Sparks, James T. *The Chronicler's Genealogies: Towards an Understanding of 1 Chronicles 1–9*. Society of Biblical Literature, 2008.

Spingou, Foteini. "A Platonising Dialogue from the Twelfth Century." In *Dialogues and Debates from Late Antiquity to Late Byzantium*, edited by Averil Cameron and Niels Gaul, 123–36. Routledge, 2017.

Stackpole, Robert A. *The Incarnation: Rediscovering Kenotic Christology*. 2nd ed. Chartwell, 2021.

Stăniloae, Dumitru. *The Experience of God: Orthodox Dogmatic Theology*. 6 vols. Holy Cross Orthodox Press, 1994–2013.

Stead, Christopher. *Divine Substance*. Oxford University Press, 1977.

Stensvold, Anne. *A History of Pregnancy in Christianity: From Original Sin to Contemporary Abortion Debates*. Routledge, 2015.

Stinton, Diane. "Africa, East and West." In *An Introduction to Third World Theologies*, edited by John Parratt, 105–36. Cambridge University Press, 2004.

Strom, Mark. *Reframing Paul: Conversations in Grace and Community*. InterVarsity, 2000.

Strong, Augustus Hopkins. *Systematic Theology: A Compendium and Commonplace-Book*. 3 vols. Griffith and Rowland, 1907.

Stuckenbruck, Loren T. *Angel Veneration and Christology: A Study in Early Judaism and in the Christology of the Apocalypse of John*. 1995. Reprint, Baylor University Press, 2017.

Stuhlmacher, Peter. "Isaiah 53 in the Gospels and Acts." In *The Suffering Servant: Isaiah 53 in Jewish and Christian Sources,* edited by Bernd Janowski and Peter Stuhlmacher, 147–62. Eerdmans, 2004.

———. "The Messianic Son of Man: Jesus' Claim to Deity." In *The Historical Jesus in Recent Research*, edited by James D. G. Dunn and Scot McKnight, 325–46. Eisenbrauns, 2005.

Stump, Eleonore. *Atonement*. Oxford University Press, 2018.

Sturch, Richard. *The Word and the Christ: An Essay in Analytic Christology*. Clarendon, 1991.

Suchocki, Marjorie. *The Fall to Violence: Original Sin in Relational Theology*. Continuum, 1994.

Swain, Scott. "John." In *The Trinity in the Canon: A Biblical, Theological, Historical, and Practical Proposal,* edited by Brandon D. Smith, 177–218. B&H Academic, 2023.

Swedenborg, Emanuel. *The Doctrine of the New Jerusalem Concerning the Lord*. In *The Four Doctrines of the New Jerusalem*, Rotch ed., 1–111. Houghton Mifflin, 1907.

Switzer, David K. *The Minister as Crisis Counselor*. Abingdon, 1974.

Synodal *Tomos* of 1351. In *Gregory Palamas: The Hesychast Controversy and the Debate with Islam,* translated and edited by Norman Russell, 323–76. Liverpool University Press, 2020.

Talbert, Charles H. *The Development of Christology During the First Hundred Years: And Other Essays on Early Christian Christology*. Brill, 2011.

Tanner, Kathryn. *Christ the Key*. Cambridge University Press, 2010.

———. *Economy of Grace*. Fortress, 2005.

———. *God and Creation in Christian Theology: Tyranny or Empowerment?* Fortress, 1988.

———. "Is God in Charge? Creation and Providence." In *Essentials of Christian Theology,* edited by William C. Placher, 116–31. Westminster John Knox, 2003.

———. *Jesus, Humanity, and the Trinity: A Brief Systematic Theology.* Fortress, 2001.

Tanner, Norman P., ed. *Decrees of the Ecumenical Councils.* 2 vols. Georgetown University Press, 1990.

The Teaching of the Twelve Apostles, Commonly Called Didache. In *Early Christian Fathers,* edited and translated by Cyril C. Richardson with Eugene R. Fairweather, Edward Rochie Hardy, and Massey Hamilton Shepherd, 171–79. Westminster, 1953.

Tennent, Timothy C. *Invitation to World Missions: A Trinitarian Missiology for the Twenty-First Century.* Kregel, 2010.

Terrell, JoAnne Marie. *Power in the Blood? The Cross in the African American Experience.* Orbis Books, 1998.

Tertullian. *On the Flesh of Christ.* Translated by Dr. Holmes. In *The Ante-Nicene Fathers,* edited by A. Cleveland Coxe, 3:521–42. Reprint, Eerdmans, 1957.

Theissen, Gerd, and Annette Merz. *The Historical Jesus: A Comprehensive Guide.* Translated by John Bowden. Fortress, 1998.

Theodore the Studite. *On the Holy Icons.* Translated by Catharine P. Roth. St. Vladimir's Seminary Press, 1981.

Thiselton, Anthony C. *Life After Death: A New Approach to the Last Things.* Eerdmans, 2012.

Thomas, Stephen. *Deification in the Eastern Orthodox Tradition: A Biblical Perspective.* Gorgias, 2007.

Thomasius, Gottfried. *Christ's Person and Work. Part II: The Person of the Mediator.* In *God and Incarnation in Mid-Nineteenth Century German Theology,* edited and translated by Claude Welch, 31–102. Oxford University Press, 1965.

Thompson, Thomas R. "Nineteenth-Century Kenotic Christology: The Waxing, Waning, and Weighing of a Quest for a Coherent Orthodoxy." In Evans, *Exploring Kenotic Christology,* 74–111.

Thomson, R. W. "An Armenian List of Heresies." *Journal of Theological Studies,* new series, 16, no. 2 (1965): 358–67.

Tibebe, Eshete, and Tadesse W. Giorgis. "The Ethiopian Orthodox Church: Theology, Doctrines, Traditions, and Practices." In *The Routledge Handbook of African Theology,* edited by Elias Kifon Bongmba, 265–79. Taylor & Francis, 2020.

Toews, John E. *The Story of Original Sin.* Pickwick, 2013.

Tollefsen, Torstein Theodor. *The Christian Metaphysics of St Maximus the Confessor: Creation, World-Order, and Redemption.* Brepols, 2023.

Toon, Peter. *The Ascension of Our Lord.* Thomas Nelson, 1984.

Torrance, Alan. *Persons in Communion: Trinitarian Description and Human Participation.* T&T Clark, 1996.

Torrance, Alexis. "Precedents for Palamas' Essence-Energies Theology in the Cappadocian Fathers." *Vigiliae Christianae* 63, no. 1 (2009): 47–70.

Torrance, Thomas F. *Atonement: The Person and Work of Christ.* IVP Academic, 2009.

———. *Incarnation: The Person and Life of Christ.* Edited by Robert T. Walker. IVP Academic, 2008.

Torrey, R. A. "The Certainty and Importance of the Bodily Resurrection of Jesus Christ from the Dead." In *The Fundamentals: A Testimony to the Truth,* edited by R. A. Torrey and A. C. Dixon, 2:298–322. Reprint, Baker Books, 2003.

Treat, Jeremy R. *The Crucified King: Atonement and Kingdom in Biblical and Systematic Theology.* Zondervan, 2014.

Treier, Daniel J. *Lord Jesus Christ.* Zondervan, 2023.

Turretin, Francis. *Institutes of Elenctic Theology.* 3 vols. Translated by George Musgrave Giger. Edited by James T. Dennison Jr. P&R, 1992.

Tutu, Desmond. "Spirituality: Christian and African." In *Resistance and Hope: South African Essays in Honour of Beyers Naudé,* edited by Charles Villa-Vicencio and John W. De Gruchy, 159–64. Eerdmans, 1985.

Twombly, Charles C. *Perichoresis and Personhood: God, Christ, and Salvation in John of Damascus.* Pickwick, 2015.

Ursinus, Zacharias. *The Commentary of Zacharias Ursinus on the Heidelberg Catechism.* Translated by G. W. Williard. P&R, 1992.

Van Kuiken, E. Jerome. *Christ's Humanity in Current and Ancient Controversy: Fallen or Not?* Bloomsbury, 2017.

———. "Sinless Savior in Fallen Flesh? Toward Clarifying and Closing the Debate." *Journal of the Evangelical Theological Society* 64, no. 2 (2021): 327–40.

Van Vreeswijk, Bernard J. D. "Interpreting Anselm's Thought About Divine Justice: Dealing with Loose Ends." *Scottish Journal of Theology* 69, no. 4 (2016): 417–31.

Van Wierengen, Archibald L. H. M. "Descent into the Netherworld: A Biblical Perspective." In *The Apostles' Creed: "He Descended into Hell,"* edited by Marcel Sarot and Archibald L. H. M. van Wierengen, 9–32. Brill, 2018.

Verhey, Allen. "The Gospels and Christian Ethics." In *The Cambridge Companion to Christian Ethics,* 2nd ed., edited by Robin Gill, 41–53. Cambridge University Press, 2012.

Vidu, Adonis. *Atonement, Law, and Justice: The Cross in Historical and Cultural Contexts.* Baker Academic, 2014.

———. *The Same God Who Works All Things: Inseparable Operations in Trinitarian Theology.* Eerdmans, 2021.

von Campenhausen, Hans. *The Virgin Birth in the Theology of the Ancient Church.* SCM, 1954. Reprint, Wipf & Stock, 2011.

von Rad, Gerhard. *Old Testament Theology*. 2 vols. Translated by D. M. G. Stalker. Harper & Row, 1962.

Wandel, Lee Palmer. *The Eucharist in the Reformation: Incarnation and Liturgy*. Cambridge University Press, 2006.

Ward, Samuel Ringgold. *Autobiography of a Fugitive Negro: His Anti-Slavery Labours in the United States, Canada, and England*. London, 1855.

Warfield, Benjamin Breckinridge. "Christ Our Sacrifice." In *Biblical Doctrines*, 401–38. Baker Books, 2003.

Watson, Richard. *Theological Institutes*. In *The Works of Richard Watson*. Vol. 11. 7th ed. London, 1858.

Wawrykow, Joseph. "Hypostatic Union." In *The Theology of Thomas Aquinas*, edited by Rik van Nieuwenhove and Joseph Wawrykow, 222–51. University of Notre Dame Press, 2005.

Weaver, J. Denny. "Narrative *Christus Victor*: The Answer to Anselmian Atonement Violence." In *Atonement and Violence: A Theological Conversation*, edited by John Sanders, 1–32. Abingdon, 2006.

Wedgeworth, Steven. "Abortion." In *Protestant Social Teaching: An Introduction*, edited by Onsi Aaron Kamel, Jake Meador, and Joseph Minich, 115–43. Davenant Press, 2022.

Weinandy, Thomas G. "Cyril and the Mystery of the Incarnation." In *The Theology of St. Cyril of Alexandria: A Critical Appreciation*, edited by Thomas G. Weinandy and Daniel A. Keating, 23–54. T&T Clark, 2003.

———. *In the Likeness of Sinful Flesh: An Essay on the Humanity of Christ*. T&T Clark, 1993.

Welch, Claude, ed. *God and Incarnation in Mid-Nineteenth Century German Theology: G. Thomasius, I. A. Dorner, A. E. Biedermann*. Oxford University Press, 1965.

Wells, Samuel. *Introducing Christian Ethics*. John Wiley & Sons, 2017.

Wellum, Stephen J. *God the Son Incarnate: The Doctrine of Christ*. Crossway, 2016.

Wenham, Gordan J. *Genesis 1–15*. Word, 1987.

Wesley, John. *The Doctrine of Original Sin, According to Scripture, Reason, and Experience*. In *The Works of John Wesley*, 3rd ed., 9:191–464. Hendrickson, 1991.

Wessling, Jordan. "Christology and Conciliar Authority: On the Viability of Monothelitism for Protestant Theology." In *Christology Ancient and Modern: Explorations in Constructive Dogmatics*, edited by Oliver D. Crisp and Fred Sanders, 151–70. Zondervan, 2013.

Westermann, Claus. *Elements of Old Testament Theology*. Translated by Douglas W. Stott. John Knox, 1982.

White, Thomas Joseph. "Divine Perfection and the Kenosis of the Son." In *Kenosis: The Self-Emptying of Christ in Scripture and Theology*, edited by Paul T. Nimmo and Keith L. Johnson, 137–56. Eerdmans, 2022.

———. *The Incarnate Lord: A Thomistic Study in Christology*. Catholic University of America Press, 2017.

Widder, Wendy. *Daniel: God's Kingdom Will Endure*. Zondervan, 2023.

Wiles, Maurice. *Working Papers in Doctrine*. SCM, 1976.

Wiley, Tatha. *Original Sin: Origins, Developments, Contemporary Meanings*. Paulist Press, 2002.

Williams, A. N. *The Ground of Union: Deification in Aquinas and Palamas*. Oxford University Press, 1999.

Winkle, Ross E. "'You Are What You Wear': The Dress and Identity of Jesus as High Priest in John's Apocalypse." In *Sacrifice, Cult, and Atonement in Early Judaism and Christianity: Constituents and Critique*, edited by Henrietta L. Wiley and Christian Eberhart, 327–46. SBL Press, 2017.

Winner, Lauren F. *The Dangers of Christian Practice: On Wayward Gifts, Characteristic Damage, and Sin*. Yale University Press, 2018.

Wollebius, Johannes. *Compendium Theologiae Christianae*. In *Reformed Dogmatics: Seventeenth-Century Reformed Theology Through the Writings of Wollebius, Voetius, and Turretin*, edited and translated by John W. Beardslee, 29–262. Baker, 1965.

Wolterstorff, Nicholas. "Is There Justice in the Trinity?" In *God's Life in Trinity*, edited by Miroslav Volf and Michael Welker, 177–87. Fortress, 2006.

Work, Telford. *Jesus—the End and the Beginning: Tracing the Christ-Shaped Nature of Everything*. Baker Academic, 2019.

Wright, Christopher J. H. *Old Testament Ethics for the People of God*. IVP Academic, 2004.

Wright, N. T. *Jesus and the Victory of God*. Fortress, 1996.

———. *The Resurrection of the Son of God*. Fortress, 2003.

Yong, Amos. *The Spirit Poured Out on All Flesh: Pentecostalism and the Possibility of Global Theology*. Baker Academic, 2005.

Young, Frances M. *Construing the Cross: Type, Sign, Symbol, Word, Action*. Cascade Books, 2015.

———. *God's Presence: A Contemporary Recapitulation of Early Christianity*. Cambridge University Press, 2013.

Young, Frances M., with Andrew Teal. *From Nicaea to Chalcedon: A Guide to the Literature and Its Background*. 2nd ed. SCM, 2010.

Zanchi, Girolamo. *The Whole Body of Christian Religion*. Translated by D. Ralph Winterton. John Redmayne, 1659. Available at https://quod.lib.umich.edu/e/eebo2/A97309.0001.001.

Ziegler, Philip G. *Militant Grace: The Apocalyptic Turn and the Future of Christian Theology*. Baker Academic, 2018.

Žižek, Slavoj. *The Plague of Fantasies*. Verso, 1997.

Zizioulas, John D. *Being as Communion: Studies in Personhood and the Church*. St. Vladimir's Seminary Press, 1985.

Zwingli, Huldrich. *On the Lord's Supper*. In *Zwingli and Bullinger*, edited by G. W. Bromiley, 185–238. Westminster, 1953.

Index of Names

Index of Scripture and Other Ancient Writings

Index of Subjects

abortion, 8, 36
accident, 32–33, 91, 129–30, 133n58
act, 13, 25. *See also* potency
actual sin, 53, 54, 57, 110–11, 194, 221, 223. *See also* sin
adoption, 70, 153, 154
adoptionism, 17, 29n90, 30–33, 143, 151
age of accountability, 58
analogy, doctrine of, 20–21, 80n35, 187, 190
anhypostatic, 129, 185
antichrist, 274
anti-Judaism, 120
aphthartodocetism, 75, 93–94
Apollinarianism, 30, 75, 88–92, 186, 238
apophatic theology, 21, 148, 164, 171
Arianism, 88, 124
ascension, 21, 38, 168, 205, 232, 233, 245, 255–66
assumption of humanity, 26, 20, 34, 129, 146.
    See also incarnation
atonement, 192, 225
  continuous, 225, 245
  discontinuous, 225
  ethical risks, 209–10
  lack of conciliar resolution about, 6
  models of, 43–44, 199
  as necessary, 24, 201–2, 206, 214, 215, 220
  and witness, 7
  See also penal substitutionary atonement; satisfaction

baptism, 77, 85, 97, 246, 249
  of Jesus, 30, 46, 50, 140, 151, 153–54
  and original sin, 58
  threefold, 154

beatific vision, 97
Brother Ancestor Christology, 69–71

Chalcedon, Council of, 6, 32, 73–74, 76, 123, 126–27, 135, 177, 180, 245, 262
Christ (title). *See* Messiah
Christ Jesus
  deity of, 75–87
  enthronement, 78–79, 108, 256–57 (*see also* session of Christ)
  exorcisms of, 228–29
  as image of God, 33, 38, 161
  as judged one who judges, 273–74
  as king, 83, 198, 256–57 (*see also* Christ Jesus: enthronement)
  ministry, 46, 103–4, 106–14, 117–18, 226–27, 273, 276
  miracles, 109, 179
  obedience, 37, 47, 192, 218–20
  person and work in theology, 43–44
  as priest (*see* priesthood)
  as prophet, 103–4, 256–57
  and race, 40–41
  as Spirit Baptizer, 152, 155–57, 171
  as suffering servant, 197–98
  as *theos*, 76
  as victim, 252–53
  visual representation of, 38–41
  wills of (*see* dyothelitism)
  as YHWH, 79
  See also Lord (title); Messiah; natures of Christ; priesthood; Son of God; Son of Man
christological monotheism, 77